# THE JEWISH LAW ANNUAL

## VOLUME NINETEEN

Volume 19 of the *Jewish Law Annual* is a festschrift in honor of Professor Neil S. Hecht. It contains ten articles in English and three in Hebrew. Several articles discuss judicial institutions, among them the decision rules–conduct rules dichotomy, the biblical "two witnesses" requirement and authorized departures from it, the *prosbul*, and the doctrine of normative transparency. Two articles discuss legal sources pertaining to the sanctity of life. One focuses on human dignity, the other addresses the imperative of preserving life in the context of terminal illness. Other articles are written from a broad range of perspectives. One is comparative, examining Persian and talmudic law on the status of promises and the role of the divine in their enforcement. Another is a historical survey documenting the composition and communal role of Jerusalem's "official" rabbinical court from 1841 to 1921. A multi-disciplinary article addresses the little-studied issue of shame punishment in Jewish legal culture, adducing historical, literary, and ethnographic sources in addition to responsa and semi-legal documents. And one article has a pedagogic focus, addressing the teaching of Jewish law in contemporary universities, and offering programmatic suggestions. The volume also features several topical articles. One explores tort remedies for negligent misrepresentation by investment advisors. Another considers a suggested direction for resolving the *agunah* problem, namely, inducing the recalcitrant husband to grant a divorce by awarding his wife compensatory tort damages; it rejects this remedy as infeasible. A third comments on the notion of conversion invoked by a recent English court decision on eligibility for admission to denominational schools, and how it compares to the concept of conversion arising from the biblical story of Ruth.

The Institute for Research in Jewish Law
Faculty of Law, The Hebrew University of Jerusalem

# THE JEWISH LAW ANNUAL

VOLUME NINETEEN

In honor of Neil S. Hecht

Edited by

Hanina Ben-Menahem

Berachyahu Lifshitz

THE INSTITUTE FOR RESEARCH IN JEWISH LAW
FACULTY OF LAW
THE HEBREW UNIVERSITY OF JERUSALEM

Routledge
Taylor & Francis Group
LONDON AND NEW YORK

First published 2011
by Routledge

2 Park Square, Milton Park, Abingdon, Oxfordshire OX14 4RN
52 Vanderbilt Avenue, New York, NY 10017

*Routledge is an imprint of the Taylor & Francis Group, an informa business*

First issued in paperback 2020



Typeset in Palatino by
RefineCatch Limited, Bungay, Suffolk



*British Library Cataloguing in Publication Data*
A catalogue record for this book is available from the British Library

*Library of Congress Cataloging in Publication Data*
A catalog record for this book has been requested

ISSN 0169–8354

ISBN13: 978-0-415-61958-5 (hbk)
ISBN13: 978-0-367-60209-3 (pbk)

For Neil Hecht

Man of vision and action

*The Jewish Law Annual* is published under the auspices of the
Institute for Research in Jewish Law,
Faculty of Law, the Hebrew University of Jerusalem



Editorial communications should be addressed to Prof. Berachyahu Lifshitz, Institute for Research in Jewish Law, Faculty of Law, The Hebrew University of Jerusalem, Mount Scopus, 91905 Jerusalem, Israel. All communications should be clearly marked "Attention: Editor, Jewish Law Annual." Contributors should consult the style sheet that appears at the end of the volume; it is also available from the editor upon request. Submissions are welcome from all. Neither the editor nor members of the Board of Editors are to be associated with the views expressed by contributors.

This book is part of a series. The publisher will accept continuation orders, which may be cancelled at any time, and which provide for automatic billing and shipping of each title in the series upon publication. Please write for details.

## CONTENTS

## FROM THE EDITORS

The publication of this volume coincides with the transition of the *Jewish Law Annual*'s editorial base to the Institute for Research in Jewish Law at the Hebrew University of Jerusalem. For over twenty-five years–since 1985–the *Annual* was published by the Institute of Jewish Law at Boston University's School of Law, headed by its founder, Professor Neil Hecht. This year Professor Hecht is retiring, after teaching for almost fifty years. The present volume is dedicated to him as a token of our gratitude and appreciation for his monumental contribution to the flourishing of Jewish law scholarship in the United States. Neil Hecht understood that for a discipline to thrive, it must have an intellectual 'home' to provide the infrastructure for the exchange of information and research, and serve both as a meeting place for researchers and an anchor for individual scholars. With this imperative in mind, he founded the Institute of Jewish Law some thirty years ago. From then on, Neil Hecht and the Institute have been initiators of or partners in almost every major endeavor in the field of Jewish law, from preparation of innovative teaching materials and translations to publication of scholarly monographs and anthologies, from assisting young scholars and new programs to organizing and providing financial support for symposia and conferences.

Working with Neil has been an honor and a pleasure. Neil will remain active on the *Jewish Law Annual*'s Editorial Board. We wish him many more years of productivity, learning, and continued sharing of his erudition and expertise.

Hanina Ben-Menahem　　　　Berachyahu Lifshitz

# ENGLISH SECTION

*The Jewish Law Annual*, Vol. XIX

# The *Prosbul* — A Legal Fiction?

Elisha Ancselovits*

It is often alleged that the "*prosbul*," a document developed by the Tannaim, is a legal fiction. Biblical law cancels all debts every seventh year (Deut. 15:1–2).[1] Many scholars argue that the *prosbul* was intended to circumvent the biblical prohibition against demanding repayment of such debts.[2] The *prosbul* allegedly transfers debts owing to private creditors to the courts, so that they can continue to collect the debts from borrowers. In this paper, I will argue that the Sages did not view the *prosbul* as a legal fiction, but viewed the non-cancellation of debts in the Sabbatical year as an adaptation of the original biblical concerns to changed conditions. In their view, during the period when the land of Israel was occupied by the Romans, Jewry's religious leadership openly changed the traditional law (or validated such a change) in order to better realize, in the contemporary reality, the original biblical intent of creating a mutually-supportive society.

* R. Elisha S. Ancselovits teaches at Maale Gilboa Yeshiva and the Pardes Institute for Jewish Studies.

1 One reading of the passage suggests that the debt was merely to be suspended for a year — possibly for the year that the farmer is not farming (the Sabbatical year). However, this possibility is irrelevant to our discussion, as the Sages understood the Torah to be canceling the debt completely.

2 Those who view the *prosbul* as a legal fiction include Z. Falk, *Introduction to the Jewish Law of the Second Commonwealth* (Leiden: 1972), 1:112; I. Klein, *Responsa and Halakhic Studies* (NY: 1975), 132; G. Plaut, "Can we speak of Reform halacha?" in Elliot L. Stevens (ed.), *Rabbinic Authority* (NY: 1982), 67; J. Neusner, *Uniting the Dual Torah: Sifra and the Problem of the Mishnah* (Cambridge: 1990), 122; N. Gillman, *Conservative Judaism: The New Century* (West Orange NJ: 1993), 23; P. Shiffman, "*Prosbul* and legal fiction," *S'vara: A Journal of Philosophy, Law and Judaism* 2 (1991), 64; and D. Henshke, "How does the *prosbul* work? The history of interpretation of Hillel's enactment" (Hebrew), 22 *Shenaton Hamishpat Haivri* (2003), 96–97.

## 1 First stage in the history of the *prosbul*

The *prosbul* referred to in the Tannaitic sources is a document that does not pertain specifically to the Sabbatical year (*shmita*).[3] This is not surprising, since a *prosbul* (προσβολαι in Greek) was a general means of documenting debts with the courts and public archives; such documentation granted a lender a permanent lien against the debtor's real estate, and permanent ownership of it should the debtor default.[4] The Tannaim recorded that the decision to accept the use of a *prosbul* among Jews was made at the end of the Second Temple period, and attributed its acceptance to Hillel the Elder's authorization: "Hillel established προσβολαι in order to rectify society (*tikun olam*)."[5]

This attribution of the *prosbul* to Hillel the Elder was particularly important, because adoption of the Greek rule allowed the permanent transfer of a defaulting debtor's estates, in violation of the biblical commandment to release land back to its original owners or their heirs every fifty years (Lev. 25:8–17, 25). Furthermore, the Greek procedure of registering liens at the courts in order to grant the lender semi-ownership and potentially permanent ownership of the borrower's land for debt failure inherently violated the biblical law that loans should be cancelled every seven years (Deut. 15:1–2). As the Mishnah notes explicitly, "A *prosbul* is not cancelled."[6] The Tannaim therefore found validation for this change in their tradition that it was the great sage Hillel the Elder who had decided to permit this permanent transfer of land in order to ensure that loans to the poor would remain available.

According to Tannaitic tradition, Hillel decided that the biblical mandate that Jews lend money to their fellow Jews (Deut. 15:9) was more vital than the biblical mandate that loans were to be cancelled by the Sabbatical year. Recourse to the *prosbul* would ensure that credit would be available to the poor:

3 See D. Bigman, "Halakhic problem or social enactment? The significance of the *prosbul*" (Hebrew), *Akdamut, A Journal of Jewish Thought* 20 (2008), 155–66. Llewelyn missed this point in his description of the Jewish *prosbul*, despite his review of Ptolemaic and Roman parallels; see S. Llewelyn, "The procedure of execution and the προσβολαι" in *New Documents Illustrating Early Christianity: A Review of Greek Inscriptions and Papyri* (North Ryde NSW: 1994), 7: 225–32.

4 See Llewelyn, ibid., 197–224.

5 mGitin 4:3.

6 mSheviit 10:3.

> The following is one of the matters that Hillel established: When he saw that the people were refraining from lending to each other and violating that which is written in the Torah, "Be careful, lest there be a base thought [i.e., the thought that you will not lend to the poor] in your heart" (Deut. 15:9), he instituted the προσβολ.[7]

According to the sources cited thus far, then, the Tannaitic basis for countenancing the possibility that an indebted borrower would permanently lose his land due to debt — despite the Deuteronomic command that debts be remitted in the Sabbatical year and the Levitical restoration of land in the Jubilee year — was an explicit assessment that the availability of credit was more important. The Tannaim employed no legal fiction — nor did they creatively misread the biblical law[8] — but rather, they adopted a straightforward policy that emphasized one of several biblical social concerns — ensuring that the poor could get loans.

Nor did the Tannaim use rhetoric disingenuously. They did not emphasize the specific biblical concern that loans not be withheld, yet ignore the other biblical concerns, namely, that people not lose their land over debts, and that they be relieved of their debts. The Tannaim were sensitive to the range of biblical social concerns pertaining to loans, and endorsed the biblical cancellation of loans only when appropriate.

The Tannaim did not rule that all loans could avoid cancellation; they permitted only *prosbul* loans to be impervious to cancellation, in contrast to loans contracted orally or documented loans that were not registered with the courts. That is, the Tannaim allowed for the non-cancellation of a loan only if it was mortgaged and the lien was deposited at the courts as a public lien:

> This is the content of the προσβολαι [document, which was submitted along with the loan contract]: "I submit to you named judges of a named locale each debt that is owed me so that I may collect it anytime I wish." The judges [themselves] or witnesses then sign [the προσβολαι document] at the bottom.[9]

7 mSheviit 10:3.

8 Contra S. Zeitlin, "Prosbol: A study in Tannaitic jurisprudence," *Jewish Quarterly Review*, ns 37 (1947), 360.

9 mSheviit 10:4. Henshke has shown that the correct version is "*kol hov*," and not "*shekol hov*," indicating that the lender submits the debt itself. See Henshke, n. 2 above, 85–92.

The Tannaim lived in a somewhat literate society, but it was a society that remained dependant on scribes.[10] Non-cancellation of debts was thus limited to cases in which the debt was significant enough to the lender to justify his spending money both on drawing up a document for each loan,[11] and on the costs of depositing the document in the public archives.[12]

Moreover, the *prosbul* could only prevent cancelation of a loan that would be collected from a defaulting borrower's assets, and not his future income. The Mishnah asserts: "Προσβολαι are written only against land,"[13] and the Tosefta concurs, "Προσβολαι can be written against a debtor who has land, but not against one who does not have land . . . unless the debtor's guarantors or debtors own land."[14] The borrower or his guarantors had to have sufficient assets, such as land, to ensure that the debt would be repaid. In other words, the only type of debt that could be protected from cancellation by the Sabbatical

10 Among the upper classes, literacy was apparently not uncommon during the Tannaitic period; see mNedarim 4:3. This does not necessarily mean, however, that those who could read could also write; see J. Monaghan, "Literary instruction and gender in colonial New England," *American Quarterly* 40 (1988), 18–41; S. Niditch, *Oral World and Written Word: Ancient Israelite Literature* (Louisville KY: 1996). Tannaitic evidence indicates that the upper classes used scribes; see, e.g., mBaba Metzia 5:11. Even those who did know how to write used scribes for contractual and formulaic material; see tGitin 2:8. Later, however, Torah scholars were indeed expected to know how to write; see bHulin 9a. On the phenomenon of limited literacy among Sassanian Babylonian Jewry, see Y. Elman, "Orality and the redaction of the Babylonian Talmud," *Oral Tradition* 14 (1999), 55–56. Among the lower classes, many Jews could not read well into the Geonic period ($8^{th}$–$11^{th}$ c.); see *Shaarei Teshuva*, sec. 24. On the factors necessary for widespread literacy, see W.V. Harris, *Ancient Literacy* (Cambridge MA: 1989), 12–13.

11 The phrase "each debt that is owed me" ("*kol hov sheyesh li*") was not a general descriptive statement, but rather a "blank" to be filled in with the sums of each loan, similar to the Tannaitic requirement that all names and nicknames be listed in a bill of divorce (*get*): "*Vekhol shum vehanikha deit lei.*"

12 See A.C. Johnson et al., *Ancient Roman Statutes: A Translation with Introduction, Commentary, Glossary, and Index* (Austin TX: 1961), 172.

13 mSheviit 10:6.

14 tSheviit 8:8–9.

year was debt that would be collected from the defaulting debtor's land, or the land of his guarantor.[15]

The Tannaim also ruled that pawn-broking loans are not cancelled by the Sabbatical year. The Sifre explicitly justifies the decision not to cancel mortgage and pawn loans on the basis of the fact that the lender merely collects property that he already holds or property of which he has already been publicly granted conditional ownership, in contrast to property in which he holds a right to collect future earnings:

> "That [debt] matter which you have with your brother" (Deut 15:3) [which can be read as "that which you will have with your brother"] — and not anything of your brother that is already in your hand. From here you may conclude that one who lends against a pawn does not remit [the loan].
>
> "That [debt] matter which you have with your brother, your hand shall remit" (ibid.) — and not someone who deposited his contracts at the court [and thus can recover his outlay by taking the land, rather than enslaving the debtor].[16]

Thus, the Tannaitic understanding of the Sabbatical remission rule did follow the biblical model of canceling loans when it came to personal loans to family and neighbors. The Tannaitic view is based on a conception of a society in which lending was not done for profit; people provided others with money with the understanding that they would generally be repaid, and that others would provide them with money in the future should they need it.[17] The Tannaitic model limited the biblical model to loans between people who truly had reciprocal relationships, as opposed to loans from pawnbrokers and publicly-documented loans from land speculators.

15 mSheviit 10:7 records an interesting debate regarding whether a borrower is also forced to relinquish a beehive given as collateral for a non-cancelled loan. Z. Safrai, *The Economy of Roman Palestine* (London: 1994), 103–4, notes that beehives were a significant supplementary source of food in Roman Palestine.

16 Sifre Deuteronomy, 113.

17 On reciprocal exchanges in traditional societies, see M. Mauss, *The Gift: The Form and Reason for Exchange in Archaic Societies*, trans. W.D. Halls (NY and London: 1990). Cf. Maimonides, *Code*, Laws concerning Mourning 6:6; *SA*, EH 60:1.

Accordingly, we find that the Jerusalem Talmud explains that because it is based on biblical values, the *prosbul* is biblically valid, despite the fact that it violates biblical law:

> "That [debt] matter which you have with your brother, your hand shall remit" (Deut 15:3) — and not someone who deposited his contracts at the court [and thus can recover his outlay by taking the land, rather than enslaving the debtor]. This is the source that indicates that the *prosbul* is biblical.
>
> But is the *prosbul* biblical? When Hillel established it, he [did so] on the basis of biblical law.[18]

In other words, Hillel's enactment was based on the biblical value of encouraging lending, as long as the creditor will not be able to enslave the debtor in the future, as opposed to merely impoverishing him.

R. Jose, a fourth-generation Amora in the land of Israel, later explained that the cancellation of debts in the seventh year is not absolute; it only applies biblically when the community in the land of Israel is economically independent and mutually supportive, such that it is also able to fulfill the biblical obligation to cease farming during the seventh year. Under non-ideal conditions, however, some loans can remain un-cancelled.[19] In arguing thus, R. Jose extended a more straightforward and apparently older Tannaitic argument regarding the applicability of the laws of *shmita* in contemporary times.[20] Although the Bible explicitly demands that farmers abandon their fields during the Sabbatical year (Exod. 23:10–11), the Sages permitted farmers to work their fields and distribute the produce to the poor, because the circumstances of the times necessitated a different response to the biblical mandate that God's mastery over the world be acknowledged,[21] and all citizens be periodically restored to a state of

18 jSheviit 10:2 (39c); cf. Sifre Deuteronomy 113 and mSheviit 10:6, quoted above.

19 jGitin 4:3 (45d): "When *shmita* is practiced as a biblical requirement in the land of Israel, monetary *shmita* is in effect as a biblical requirement both in and outside the land of Israel. When *shmita* is practiced as a Rabbinic requirement in the land of Israel, monetary *shmita* is in effect as a Rabbinic requirement both in and outside the land of Israel."

20 Mekhilta de-Rabbi Ishmael, Mishpatim, parsha 20: "*Shegidru hakhamim mipnei tikun olam.*"

21 Cf. Leviticus 25:23 and Nahmanides' commentary on Leviticus 25:2. See also the other Spanish commentators ad loc.: Rabbenu Bahya, Ibn Ezra, *Akeidat Yitzhak*, and Abarbanel, as well as the *Sefer Hahinukh*, §84.

equality.[22] When the social conditions necessary for the applicability of the biblical law of agricultural *shmita* are in effect, R. Jose argued, the biblical law of debt cancellation is also in effect. When, due to adverse economic conditions, the *shmita* laws cannot be implemented, debt cancellation similarly does not apply across the board. The connection between the *prosbul* and *shmita,* however, is related only to the social circumstances of the times. Inasmuch as the *prosbul* was not a *shmita*-specific document, it is clear that the non-cancellation of loans that had been registered with the courts was not based on a legal fiction that a registered loan was the equivalent of a fine or payment imposed by the courts.[23] The Mishnah and Sifre make it quite clear that when land has been mortgaged for a debt, the debt is not cancelled in the seventh year.

## 2 Second stage in the history of the *prosbul*

The fact that a *prosbul* was utilized only for liens against land limited the range of those who could acquire large commercial loans, since urban dwellers do not own land. Thus, possibly due to the worsening economic conditions preceding the Bar Kokhba revolt,[24] R. Akiva ruled that the *prosbul* is also valid against any real property, including one's garden or home: "R. Akiva says: Even a minimal amount of land is liable to *peia* [leaving the corners of the field for the poor], *bikurim* [first fruits, taken to the Temple], and the writing of a *prosbul*."[25]

Eventually, after the Bar Kokhba rebellion was quashed, the requirement that the borrower own real property in order to use a *prosbul* was lifted entirely. Nevertheless, the Tannaim still required that a loan to a landless borrower be a documented loan that was registered at the local court along with a *prosbul* document, and that the loan be significant enough for the lender to transfer a minimal amount of his own land to the borrower, who thereby forwent part of the loan:

22 This intent of the commandment is stated quite clearly in the continuation of Exodus 23:12; cf. the parallel source in Leviticus 25:5–7. Also consider that the Hakhel ceremony takes place after the end of the Sabbatical year; cf. Nehemiah 4:9–6:4. This explanation is cited in R. Samuel David Luzzatto (Shadal)'s commentary, R. Kalischer's *Sefer Habrit,* and R. Kook's introduction to *Shabat Haaretz.*

23 Contra Henshke, n. 2 above, 96–97.

24 J.D. Haas, *History of Palestine: The Last Two Thousand Years* (NY: 1934), 52.

25 mPeia 3:6.

"A *prosbul* is written only against land. If he [the borrower] does not have any, he [the lender] grants him [the borrower] a minimal amount of his [the lender's] land."[26]

These requirements still ensured both that the sum was significant enough to justify the lender's expenditure (on registering the loan, etc.) and that the borrower (or his guarantors) had enough wealth to make it worthwhile for the lender to lose money on these expenses. A poor borrower would receive no more than a non-documented "charity" loan or a pawn-broking loan.[27]

Later, Jews in the land of Israel discontinued their use of the public Roman προσβολαι in their interactions among themselves,[28] as they ceased to register their land claims in public Roman-supervised archives.[29] The late Tanna R. Judah the Prince thus explicitly noted that the implication of the traditional acceptance of προσβολαι was that the biblical law of canceling debts every seventh year inherently requires a simple society that is able to carry out the Jubilee return of land to its original owners.[30]

A generation later, the early Palestinian Amora R. Johanan elaborated on why registering the debt in a public archive is not the critical element in deciding whether a loan should or should not be cancelled by the Sabbatical year. He focused on the more important points that the loan be both documented and mortgaged (thus enabling the debt to be collected from the debtor's assets, as opposed to creating a continuous personal lien), and explained why the earlier Tannaitic position

26 mSheviit 10:6.

27 Based on the above, we can explain the Tosefta's position that the Sabbatical does not cancel a loan if the collateral is worth less than the loan. If the collateral is worth less than the debt, it must serve only as evidence of the loan. Since the desperate borrower can practically always exercise the (unethical) option of repudiating his debt to the lender by abandoning the collateral and denying the loan, the Rabbis did not have to grant the borrower the right not to repay the debt.

28 R. Shimon b. Gamaliel II in mKetubot 9:9.

29 See C. Hezser, *Jewish Literacy in Roman Palestine* (Tubingen: 2001), 156. Contra Hezser, it should be noted that the evidence in this paper from attributed Tannaitic statements regarding the προσβολαι suggests that Jews did use the public archives throughout the period of R. Akiva and R. Jose the Galilean, until the Bar Kokhba revolt.

30 jSheviit 10:2 (39c): "Rabbi [Judah the Prince] said . . . When the Jubilee year is observed, *shmita* is observed as a biblical law. Once the observance of the Jubilee year has ceased, *shmita* is observed as a Rabbinic law."

had been that any documented loan that was not registered at a public archive was cancellable.[31] Given that under earlier Tannaitic conditions, a documented loan that would not have been publicly archived was a loan between family members and friends, who would not wish to gain right to the borrower's property, he explained that such a loan (in his contemporary terms) would be a documented but unmortgaged loan: "'The seventh [year] cancels documented loans' (mSheviit 10:1). R. Johanan said: Explain it as referring to a document[ed loan] that is not mortgaged."[32] In short, he agreed with the post-Bar Kokhba Tannaim in taking the post-biblical law of debt non-cancellation to be based on an evaluation of how to apply biblical law appropriately in contemporary circumstances.

## 3 The *prosbul* in Sassanian Babylonia

Sassanian Babylonia resembled the Roman Empire in that "one copy of each contract involving long-term or high-value transactions had to be registered in a local archive."[33] Thus, Babylonian Jews accepted the ruling that a debt registered at the local public archive is not cancelled by the Sabbatical release. In fact, the leading first-generation Babylonian Amora Samuel explicitly expressed frustration over his inability to restore the biblical ideal of a society of mutual support by opposing the innovative *prosbul* attributed to Hillel. Samuel could do no more than reemphasize the Tannaitic rule of προσβολαι, which limited protection from cancellation to significant commercial debts and liens whose contracts were deposited in the public archives of the large cities Sura and Nehardea.[34] Similarly, he invalidated attempts by lenders to introduce loan clauses to the effect that a loan would not be subject to Sabbatical remission.[35]

31 On the use of private archives, see Hezser, n. 29 above, 157.
32 jSheviit 10:1 (39d).
33 G. Hermann, "Sassanians," in G.W. Bowersock et al. (eds.), *Late Antiquity: A Guide to the Postclassical World* (Cambridge MA: 1999), 684.
34 bGitin 36b.
35 bMakot 3b. This lending practice did not begin in Babylonia. Loan documents from the Second Temple period demonstrate that rich Jews in the villages of Palestine — that is, far from the public archives — added clauses to the effect that a loan was not to be subject to Sabbatical remission; see S. Schwartz, *Imperialism and Jewish Society, 200 BCE to 640 CE* (Princeton: 2001), 68–69.

Neither Samuel nor any other Tanna or Amora viewed this arrangement as a legal fiction.[36] Samuel accepted the Tannaitic understanding that loans should not be cancelled when no mutual relationship exists or is created between the lender and borrower. Samuel accepted the morality of the non-cancellation of loans if the lender gains no future reciprocity from having offered a loan: "R. Judah [said] in the name of Samuel: Orphans do not need a *prosbul*."[37] Money lent from a minor orphan's property by a guardian is automatically not cancelled, presumably because the sum is significant enough from the orphan's perspective, and it is the guardian, and not the orphan, who gains from the relationship.

Samuel's student, R. Anan, extended this last consideration further, giving up on Samuel's idealistic vision of a mutually-supportive society in favor of the less idealistic Tannaitic position. R. Anan reinterpreted Samuel's ruling invalidating a lender's non-cancellation clause to mean that although a lender cannot stipulate that Sabbatical remission does not apply to a loan, he can stipulate that the borrower will not seek remission of the loan or that the loan will not be cancelled despite the fact that loans are cancelled by the Sabbatical year.[38] In other words, in place of Samuel's attempt to retain the law of remission (and the ideal of reciprocal relations) for loans that were not recorded in the public archives, R. Anan merely demanded that the lender and borrower recognize the ideal of loan remission.

Much later, Rava or the editor of the following talmudic passage, repeated the Tannaitic argument that absolute remission of loans is more appropriate to an agrarian society (with its secondary characteristic of extended families) than to a commercial society. Furthermore, he restated this concept in a more generalized fashion, declaring all economic laws inherently context-dependent.

> Could it be possible that according to biblical law the Sabbatical [year] cancels [loans] and Hillel issued an enactment that it does not cancel [loans]?
>
> Abbaye said: [The latter pertains to] the Sabbatical in our times, as taught by Rabbi [Judah the Prince] . . .

36 Contra Henshke, n. 2 above, 84–85.

37 bGitin 37a.

38 bMakot 3b. There are different textual variants of the valid formulation. One is found in the printed Vilna edition and in Babylonischer Talmud — BSB Cod.hebr. 95, [S.l.] Frankreich, 1342 [BSB-Hss Cod.hebr. 95], fol. 358a. The second variant is found in Yad Harav Herzog — 1, fol. 115.

> Rava said: Expropriations by the court are valid (*hefker beit din haya hefker*) [i.e., legislation of an economic nature is within the rabbinical purview].[39]

The Babylonian Amora Abbaye argues that absolute cancellation of loans was no longer appropriate under the circumstances of contemporary Jewish society, which was no longer completely agrarian. The Talmud then proceeds to a more general argument in the name of Rava, asserting that the rabbinical authorities have the right and obligation to enact legislation appropriate for contemporary economic conditions.

In the end, we find later Amoraim in both Babylonia and the land of Israel holding a compromise position:

> The rabbis of the School of R. Ashi would hand over their [loan] documents [lit., words] to each other.
>
> R. Jonathan handed over his [loan] documents to R. Hiya b. Abba. He [then] asked him: Do I need anything else? He answered: You do not.[40]

On the one hand, documented loans could still be remitted by the Sabbatical release. On the other hand, the lender of a documented loan could avoid its remission by publicizing in front of a rabbi (including a rabbinical colleague) the amount loaned, a requirement that would embarrass a lender seeking to forestall cancellation of a small loan or any other type of loan that carried the social expectation that it would

39 bGitin 36a–b. For additional Tannaitic parallels to Abbaye's approach, found, to the best of my knowledge, only in the Babylonian Talmud, see bArakhin 29a. Rava's principle, "*Hefker beit din haya hefker*," applies to the right of eminent domain, taxation, regulation, currency, etc. There is a long-running debate regarding whether Rava's position explains Hillel's *prosbul* or Abbaye's claim that the Rabbis reconfigured the *shmita* laws. David Henshke has defended the latter reading of Rava's statement, arguing that if Abbaye and Rava were commenting on the same point, the *stama* would have first introduced their positions together, and only afterwards challenged Abbaye's position; see Henshke, n. 2 above, 74. This argument, however, ignores the fact that the *stama* is classically not a work meant to be read step-by-step. It was actually weaving together two unrelated statements to make a point both about Hillel's partial abrogation of the *shmita* laws and of the Rabbinic reconfiguration of them; the *stama*, as is not uncommon, introduced Rava's position on economic laws in a manner that both formulates Abbaye's stance more clearly and resolves the challenge to it — economic laws are always context-dependent and are to be legislated accordingly.

40 bGitin 37a.

be remitted in the Sabbatical year,[41] and induce such a lender to live up to the biblical ideal of forgiving loans to one's associates.

## 4 Conclusion

To summarize, we saw that Hillel, or the leadership of Roman-occupied Jewry, living in a stratified Hellenistic society, were understood by the Tannaim to have explicitly changed the law governing Sabbatical loan remission in order to maintain the best balance between the biblical mandates of fostering a mutually-supportive society and extending credit to those in need. We saw that a *prosbul* is not an example of the manipulative use of a legal fiction — "the sale of the debt to the court . . . [and] also a power of attorney . . . of a debt which has not yet matured"[42] — as no Tannaitic or Amoraic source suggests such an interpretation. More significantly, we found no evidence of a Tannaitic willingness to enact legislation out of social necessity, on the basis of an adduced biblical directive, which could be taken to imply that the rabbinical authorities have the right to issue legislation that conflicts with other Torah rules.[43] Rather, we saw that the Tannaim internalized a range of biblical directives and attempted to determine what the best balance of biblical concerns would be under the circumstances of their times. The biblical mandate that people be mutually supportive and periodically cancel their loans to each other is applied by the Tannaim to the changed conditions of an increasingly urban society whose members are no longer all known to each other and supportive of each other.

As a result, every application of the Tannaitic rule that the Sabbatical loan cancellation does not apply absolutely in their contemporary circumstances was limited in some way — limited to commercial and pawn-broking loans, to documented and mortgaged loans, or to documented loans regarding which one is willing, to gain protection from the Sabbatical loan remission, to appear before a

41 Obviously, in a society in which all lenders agree to act miserly, there is no longer any shame involved in doing so. Indeed, an innovative reading of the talmudic law by an 18th century halakhist contends that it is a *mitzva* to cancel some of the debts that one is owed despite the *prosbul* clause, just as it is a *mitzva* to actually burn some *hametz* despite the option of nullifying or selling it; see R. Jonathan Eibeschutz, *Urim Vetumim*, 67:1.

42 Shiffman, n. 2 above, 64.

43 As claimed by Shiffman, n. 2 above, 63.

rabbinical authority and publicly announce the amounts in question. In other words, the talmudic Sages did not conceive their culture as accepting the untrammeled revisability of laws in contradistinction to biblical society's "permanent" standards[44]; they did not think in terms of exclusionary values.

To generalize my findings, the tentative thesis that arises from this limited study is that Tannaim may very well not have viewed religious law as a formalistic deductive legal system[45] that requires intentional misreads of authoritative texts[46] or the introduction of legal fictions[47] in order to allow for change. Rather, they may very well have viewed it as a system of interpretive legislation in which sages are expected to openly discuss multiple religious texts/values[48] in order to apply those values to contemporary conditions so as to reach a wise balance of competing considerations. They may have understood that law cannot be deductive, since "law is an evaluation of reality in the direction of justice."[49]

Accordingly, if the Tannaitic approach to law is to be compared to another legal system, it does not resemble Roman law, as it does not

44 As argued in W. Dean, *The Religious Critic in American Culture* (Albany: 1994), 179.

45 Contra S.J.D. Cohen, *The Beginnings of Jewishness: Boundaries, Varieties, Uncertainties* (Berkeley: 1999), 306; M. Jaffee, *Mishnah's Theology of Tithing: A Study of Tractate Maaserot* (Chico CA: 1981), 2; J. Neusner, *The Evidence of the Mishnah* (Chicago: 1981), 27, 143; idem, *The Theology of the Halakhah* (Leiden and Boston: 2001), xiii; idem, *How Not to Study Judaism, Examples and Counter Examples: Parables, Rabbinic Narratives, Rabbis' Biographies, Rabbis' Disputes* (Lanham MD: 2004), 90–91; J. Wegner, *Chattel or Person? The Status of Women in the Mishnah* (Cambridge: 1988), 17–18.

46 Contra M. Halbertal, *People of the Book: Canon, Meaning, and Authority* (Cambridge MA: 1997), 47–49; idem, *Commentary Revolutions in the Making: Values as Interpretative Considerations in Midrashei Halakhah* (Hebrew), (Jerusalem: 1997), 172, 181, 185–86, 198–203; idem, "David Hartman and the philosophy of halakha" (Hebrew) in Avi Sagi and Zvi Zohar (eds.), *Renewing Jewish Commitment: The Work and Thought of David Hartman* (Hebrew), (Jerusalem: 2001), 1:47, 54; M. Fisch, "Canon, controverse et réforme; une réflexion sur l'autre voix du judaïsme talmudique," *Les Cahiers du judaïsme* 18 (2005), 61–75.

47 Contra L. Moscovitz, *Talmudic Reasoning: From Casuistics to Conceptualization* (Tübingen: 2002), 131 and n. 119.

48 Contra Moscovitz, ibid., 131.

49 W. Fikentscher, *Modes of Thought: A Study in the Anthropology of Law and Religion* (Tübingen: 2004), xxxv.

proffer legal conceptual explanations that differ from the true underlying "non-conceptual considerations, such as common sense [and] consequentialist concerns (e.g., ensuring equity)."[50] Rather, it resembles Greek law, in which change is accomplished through the concept of equity. Given that Tannaitic law is a religious legal system, however, it invokes equity by analogizing from its trusted sources[51] — biblical rules (verses) and considerations.[52]

50 Moscovitz, n. 47 above, 201.

51 I would argue that only one who does not understand the role of the traditional sage could argue that the reason that "the vast majority of citations of legal change ... are accompanied by a rationale for that change" is because "legal evolution was, for the rabbis, a matter of significant anxiety" given their "system of law that granted almost limitless power to a divinely sanctioned Torah and its revered oral accompaniment" (A.D. Panken, *The Rhetoric of Innovation: Self-Conscious Legal Change in Rabbinic Literature* [Lanham MD: 2005], 333, xvii–xviii). Rather, in my view, the so-called "rationales" are shorthand presentations of the issues in question by a sage to an educated community. Similarly, I would argue that only one who does not understand the role of the traditional sage could argue that Tannaitic "doubts about ... the authority of their tradition" led [the Sages] to "seek to prove ... that all the innovations and inventions of their tradition can already be found in the text of the Bible ... no matter how contrived the connection may be" (D. Stern, *Midrash and Theory: Ancient Jewish Exegesis and Contemporary Literary Studies — Rethinking Theory* [Evanston IL: 1997], 32). In my view, the Tannaim were engaged in serious substantive discussions, in the course of which they made uncontrived analogical use of biblical verses.

52 In so doing, it exemplified the fact that "law is originally analogical," since "we cannot perceive the 'essence' of a thing in an ... exact manner, but only in an analogical one"; see A. Kaufmann, "Preliminary remarks on a legal logic and ontology of relations," in Patrick Nerhot (ed.), *Law, Interpretation, and Reality: Essays in Epistemology, Hermeneutics, and Jurisprudence* (Dordrecht: 1990), 117, 120.

*The Jewish Law Annual*, Vol. XIX

# Shame Punishment in Jewish Legal Culture: Some Preliminary Observations

Hanina Ben-Menahem*



Two related questions can be asked about shame punishment. First, is there a special problem raised by shame punishment? That is, does shame punishment call for justification above and beyond the justifications invoked for other types of punishment? This is an ethical question, much discussed in contemporary legal writing, but rarely addressed in the rabbinical literature. The other question is that of consistency, namely, how is shame punishment related to other elements of the legal system? Is shame punishment compatible with human dignity and human rights? Or is shame punishment a manifestation of an internal tension that exists in a legal system as a result of contradictory values being endorsed simultaneously? It is the latter problem, in the context of Jewish law, that will be my focus. I will begin by remarking on four issues related to the consistency question.

* Hanina Ben-Menahem is on the Faculty of Law at the Hebrew University of Jerusalem, and is Gruss Visiting Professor of Talmudic Civil Law at Harvard Law School.

A slide show with photos, drawings, and other illustrative materials can be found on the page for this article on the *Jewish Law Annual* website (http://law.huji.ac.il/eng/pirsumim.asp?cat=2245&in=2244).

## I Four aspects of the consistency problem

### i "Neither shall ye walk in their statutes" (Lev. 18:3)

As we are about to see, in the post-talmudic period, the administration of shame punishment is in essence an emulation of the standard practice in the surrounding Gentile society. This emulation violates the biblical prohibition "neither shall ye walk in their statutes" (Lev. 18:3). Of course, it goes without saying that there were many outside influences on the development of Jewish law, but the "neither shall ye walk in their statutes" prohibition, according to the Talmud, applies specifically to the penal system, and strictly prohibits any punitive procedure that is carried out "as is done by the Gentile authorities" (bSanhedrin 52b). The undeniably Gentile source of some specific shame punishments thus raises the question of their compatibility with the normative halakhic attitude to punishment, and specifically, with the normative halakhic attitude to copying Gentile modes of punishment.

### ii Human dignity

The received view among scholars of Jewish law is that halakhic penal law is very sensitive to human dignity, and takes great care to avoid humiliation of the offender. So entrenched is this view that if an explicit talmudic instance to the contrary is cited — for example, the case of the woman suspected of adultery (*sota*)—it is considered puzzling. But perhaps Jewish penal law is not as sensitive to human dignity as it is reputed to be. For while it is true that the Talmud, in describing the procedure for executing convicted offenders, is highly sensitive to human dignity, we must remember that this discussion is merely theoretical, since the authority to impose capital punishment ended upon the destruction of the Temple in 70 CE. Indeed, the Talmud itself on occasion speaks of shaming offenders, though it does not set out the specifics of how such shaming is to be carried out. A Tannaitic Midrash states: "as long as he has not been flogged, you are to treat him with ignominy, but once he has been flogged, you are not to treat him with ignominy."[1] In post-talmudic times, references to procedures for

1 Midrash Tannaim (Hoffman edition), on Deuteronomy 25:3: "Forty stripes he may give him, he shall not exceed; lest, if he should exceed, and beat him above these with many stripes, then thy brother should be dishonored before thine eyes."

shaming offenders become more explicit and varied, and recourse to such punishments comes to be widespread, at least in Ashkenaz, that is, central and eastern Europe, which will be my focus here.

It seems, therefore, that there is a gap between the perception of Jewish penal law, and the reality. The ethos of Jewish law did not prevent actual shaming.

## iii Rationale for permitting infliction of shame punishment

For the most part, shame punishments are not mentioned in the canonical texts of Jewish law. There is, however, a general dispensation allowing the infliction of shame punishment. Maimonides (*Code*, Laws concerning the Sanhedrin, chapter 24), basing himself on the Talmud (bMoed Katan 16a) asserts that a Jewish court is authorized to shame and humiliate — to the extent deemed appropriate by the court — anyone who breaks the law.

> 5 So too the courts may, in all places and at all times, flog one whose reputation is bad, and about whom the people talk, ascribing to him sexual transgressions — provided the rumors about him are persistent, as has already been stated, and he has no avowed enemies who may be spreading evil rumors about him. Similarly, one of ill repute may be disdained, and she who bore him shamed in his presence.
>
> 8 So too, the judge may quarrel with he who deserves to be quarreled with, curse him, beat him, pull out his hair, and compel him to take an oath that he will not commit the offense again or that he has not committed it. . . .
>
> 9 Likewise his hands and feet are to be fettered, and he is to be incarcerated in prison, knocked down and dragged on the ground, as it is written: "[Let judgment be executed upon him with all diligence] whether by death, corporal punishment, confiscation of possessions, or imprisonment" (Ezra 7:26).

The examples of shame punishments Maimonides invokes here are taken from the Talmud (which itself adduces biblical precedents), and do not reflect any reality. In other words, they are just abstract examples of shaming. Though he authorizes recourse to shaming, Maimonides adds that the court should always remember that human dignity is a fundamental principle, and the utmost caution must be exercised in cases where infliction of humiliating punishment may be called for.

> 10 With regard to all these measures, the judge is to do that which he deems fit to be done, and act in accordance with the needs of the time. But whatever he does should be done for the sake of heaven. Let him not regard human dignity as insignificant, since it supersedes prohibitions enacted by the Sages. And this applies with even greater force to the dignity of the children of Abraham, Isaac, and Jacob, who adhere to the true Law. The judge must be careful not do anything that destroys their self-respect, but rather he must act solely to enhance God's honor. For whoever disgraces the Torah — his physical person is defiled by others, and whoever honors the Torah — his physical person is honored by others. And to honor the Torah means to act in accordance with its statutes and laws.[2]

I must point out, however, that this admonition is meant to ensure that humiliation is not inflicted on those who do not deserve it—that is, those who have not transgressed. It is not meant to restrict the shaming of those who **deserve** to be so treated.

Maimonides has thus provided us with the rationale for permitting the infliction of shame punishment. One is entitled to be treated with respect if one conducts himself honorably. Someone who strolls around naked — who treats himself without respect — is not entitled to be treated with respect by others, and if he is humiliated by others, it is of no legal consequence. Likewise, one who does not follow the ways of the Torah is humiliating himself, and is not entitled to be treated with respect. In law 10, Maimonides is taking an ethical principle found in mAvot — "R. Jose said: whoever honors the Torah — his physical person is honored by others, and whoever defiles the Torah — his physical person is defiled by others" — and reframing it as a legal principle.

According to Maimonides, the principle of human dignity has universal applicability and applies a fortiori to Jews. The obligation to treat one's fellow with respect is an obligation that arises from the said individual's conduct. That is, one acquires a right to be treated with respect if one conducts oneself properly. But one has no innate right to be treated with respect merely by virtue of being human. This idea can also be formulated in the following way: One has an innate **conditional** right to be treated with respect — a right one can forfeit through shameful conduct. Practically speaking, however, there is no difference between the two formulations.

2 Maimonides, *Code*, Laws concerning the Sanhedrin, ch. 24.

iv Inclusive notion of legality

The fact that some shame punishments are not listed in the canonical texts of Jewish law (which in itself calls for explanation) might lead one to think that these punishments are extra-legal. This raises a question that goes beyond the scope of our discussion here, namely, how to distinguish the "legal" from the "extra-legal." I would suggest that the important question is this: what procedures were used by communal officials to maintain social order? And from this perspective, the commonplace recourse to shaming and humiliation is more important than theoretical discussions of the procedures for execution, which were never implemented in practice. In any event, examination of the post-talmudic halakhic sources clearly reveals that the Talmud's theoretical strictures did little to deter the emergence of shame punishments in Jewish society.

## II Shame punishments in post-talmudic Jewish society

Given that the canonical Jewish legal texts — the Talmud and law codes — do not reflect actual practice with respect to shame punishment, to gain knowledge of specific shame punishments that were actually meted out, we have to look at external sources, such as historical documents, literary works, and extant realia. Due to the contingencies of Jewish life, these types of evidence are mainly available only for the last few centuries. I want to stress this point, because I do not want to give the impression that my focusing on the past three hundred years implies that there was no recourse to shame punishments earlier on. Indeed, the case of head-shaving attests to the fact that shame punishments were imposed as far back as the Geonic era.

Three types of shame punishment imposed in post-talmudic times attest to recourse to shaming and humiliation in Jewish legal culture: shaving the offender's head, "donkey's burial," and the pillory (*kune*). Let me present some documentary evidence as to the first two of these punishments.

### Shaving the offender's head

A Geniza document attests to the fact that the punishment of shaving the head was explicitly set out in early medieval legal regulations:

> 41 And it is forbidden for a woman to adorn her daughter and take her to the market, because she thereby endangers herself. And a woman

> who perfumes herself and frequents abodes of idolatry is to be flogged, and her hair shaved off. And it is forbidden for a woman to put earrings in her son's ears.
>
> 42 And if a man is suspected of [sexual relations with] a woman, and he married her, both are to be flogged and their hair shaved off. And it is forbidden for a man to say to a woman, "Get a divorce from your husband and I will marry you." And if he did so, he is to be flogged and his hair shaved off. And if she got a divorce from her husband and married [the inciter], she is to be separated from him, and they are both to be lashed and their hair shaved off, and their deeds are to be publicized.[3]

Shaving was not, it should be noted, the sole punishment mandated by the regulations in question, but was, rather, imposed along with other punishments: flogging and publicizing the miscreants' deeds.

A ruling from late medieval Germany similarly calls for the shaving of an offender; here again, it is not imposed on its own, but along with corporal punishment, exile, and public recounting of the misdeeds.

> Reuben beat his wife with a tree limb that had broken off . . . and she was pregnant. And he did not desist until she died. And witnesses saw that the beaten spot was red, and there was a wound there, though earlier it had been healthy. He is to be beaten without compassion, and his head shorn, and he is to be exiled from his locale for two or three years, as the dignitaries of his congregation see fit. And in every congregation he is to tell his story, as it is written, "and this is the case of the murderer" (Deut. 19:4).[4]

### "Donkey's burial"

In the Bible, "donkey's burial" was a divinely-imposed punishment of ignominious burial, whereby the body, rather than being duly buried, was dragged until it fell apart. Responsa by eminent halakhic authorities attest to the fact that the punishment of "donkey's burial" was invoked by rabbinical authorities as a punitive measure to be imposed by the court, alongside other measures, on miscreants. The first, by a thirteenth-century Italian halakhic authority, describes the case of an adulterer:

3 Jacob Mann, "*Sefer hamaasim livnei eretz yisrael*" [Halakhic rulings from the land of Israel from the Cairo Genizah] (Hebrew), *Tarbiz* 1:3 (1930), 12.

4 R. Menahem of Merseburg (Germany, 15th c.), *Nimukei R. Menahem of Merseburg* at the end of *Responsa Mahari Weil*.

And this evil person who controlled her so high-handedly — his haughty forearm should be broken, "and his right eye shall be utterly darkened" (Zech. 11:17), since he has committed so many adulterous acts with his fellow's wife. . . . God will astound with His blows [to the offender] and blows to his descendants, for he has astounded by acting very despicably among Israel, and he is accursed unto the Lord of Hosts, and he is to be separated from the congregation of Israel, "and the Lord shall separate him unto evil out of all the tribes of Israel" (Deut. 29:20) — him and all those who aid him and sustain this great guilt. And no son of Israel will be permitted to have dealings with him, to pray with him and associate with him, or to circumcise his sons or be present at their burial; but each of them is to have a donkey's burial—"dragged and thrown out" (Jer. 22:19) — so that they do not receive a proper Jewish burial until he removes this evil from his home, and abides by the law.[5]

Here too, as in the case of head-shaving, the shame punishment of "donkey's burial" is imposed together with other punishments, in this case ostracism, social and religious shunning.[6] It is important to note that the punishment of "donkey's burial" differs from corporal punishment and social shunning in that it is anticipatory: obviously, it cannot be carried out upon sentencing, as the defendant is still alive. Donkey's burial is, therefore, more in the nature of a threat than an immediately-imposed penalty.[7] But the very fact that this threat existed had very real societal impact, frightening people to keep them in line. Yet sentencing transgressors to "donkey's burial" was by no means mere rhetoric;[8] such sentences were actually carried out, as the case of Solomon Maimon attests.[9]

5 R. Isaiah di Trani the Elder (Italy, 12th–13th c.), *Responsa Rid*, #22. The punishments imposed by the Rid call to mind Church decrees mandating the shaming of those deemed enemies of the Church; see the highlighted sentences in the decree quoted in n. 12 below.

6 In this article, I provide only an overview of the institution of ignominious burial; a fuller treatment of the subject will be published elsewhere.

7 See *Responsa Maharshal* #28; *Responsal Raanah*, #51.

8 Although, as noted above, "donkey's burial" does not appear in the canonical halakhic sources, there is nonetheless some theoretical controversy about its legal status, see *Responsa Rashba*, 5, #236; *Responsa Hayim Bayad*, #109 (R. Hayim Palagi).

9 See Abraham Socher, *The Radical Enlightenment of Solomon Maimon: Judaism, Heresy, and Philosophy* (Stanford: 2006), 50, 182. Some historians, e.g., Levitats, have found this difficult to accept, and have defined "donkey's burial" as interment at the end of the cemetery, by the fence—the burial traditionally associated with suicides (I. Levitats, *Jewish Community in Russia 1772–1844* (NY: 1943), 198–217). There is considerable documentary

Another responsum, written in Poland several centuries later, also speaks of imposing the punishment of "donkey's burial." As in the preceding example, the offense in question is sexual in nature. And as in all the previous examples, it is imposed together with other punishments, in this case severe religious shunning.

> Hence whichever of the sides [to the agreement] breaks any aspect of what the three agreed-upon learned mediators decided, whether it is a major point or a minor point — the offender is to be punished with excommunication by the heavenly court and punished with excommunication by the earthly court. And he is to be separated from all the holy duties of Israel: he is not to serve as a communal prayer leader, or to [read from] the Torah scroll. And he is not to be counted for any religious function, nor is he even to be counted in the prayer quorum. And his bread is to be regarded as Gentile bread, and his wine as Gentile wine, and his burial will be a donkey's burial — until he regains his former status. And from this, others will learn a lesson, so that they do not continue to act despicably among Israel, and treat our sister, heaven forbid, like a harlot.[10]

The third type of shame punishment, being locked in the pillory (*kune; kuna*), will be discussed in detail below.

All three punishments are basically an emulation of practices in the surrounding culture and do not have a talmudic basis. "Donkey's burial" appears in the Bible and talmudic sources, but it is a divine punishment.[11] Only in the Middle Ages was this punishment, imposition of which had been a divine prerogative, arrogated by the rabbinical authorities, and imposed in practice. It would appear that this development is due to the influence of the surrounding culture.[12]

---

evidence of cases where burial societies refused to bury transgressors, or refused burial as a means for extorting money. Peretz Smolenskin's story "*Kevurat Hamor*" (Donkey's burial) is significant in this context, as it attests to the fact that the concept of ignominious burial was part of the cultural mindset at the time.

10 R. Moses Isserles (Poland, 1530–1572), *Responsa Rema*, #16 s.v. *veal shear*. The last sentence quoted is paraphrasing Genesis 34:31.

11 See 1 Kings, ch. 13; 14:5–20; 2 Kings 9:6–10, 33–37; Jeremiah ch. 22 and R. David Kimhe (Radak) on Jeremiah 22:19; jTerumot 8:3 (45c); bSanhedrin 46b-47a; bPesahim 56a; bSanhedrin 82a.

12 Ignominious burial was, however, a recognized institution in Christianity and Islam. A document of excommunication from the year 900 reads as follows:

> In the name of God, and by the power of the Holy Ghost, and the authority divinely granted to bishops by Peter, chief of the Apostles,

So too, shaving the head appears in the Bible, but not as a punishment imposed by the court. In the Bible it was carried out by non-Jews as an act of violence and aggression.[13] During the Geonic period, however, it did come to be imposed by Jewish courts, as the above-quoted sources attest, though there was no legal precedent for this.

All three of these shame punishments — shaving of the head, donkey's burial, and being locked in the *kune* — call into question the myth that Jewish law is careful to maintain human dignity in the penal context; and all raise the question of whether they are part of the halakhic system of punishment, since they do not appear in the canonical sources of Jewish law. In this article, however, my focus will be the *kune*.

## III *Kune* (pillory)

"*Kuna*" is a Polish word that appears in Polish dictionaries as "pillory" or "torturing device." It consists of a two-sided neck ring that opens at the front (the ends are clasped shut after the offender's neck has been inserted), and is attached to a chain affixed to a wall; or a plain metal ring affixed to the wall, to which an offender's neck and/or limbs were chained. In Poland, *kuna*s were commonly situated at the entrance to churches or chapels. The imposing brick St Mary's Basilica (Kosciol Mariacki), off the Grand Square at the center of Krakow, has a *kuna* affixed to an exterior wall above a low stone bench, in a niche with

> we separate them from the bosom of holy Mother Church, and condemn them with the anathema of the eternal curse, **that they may have no help of man nor any converse with Christians.** Let them be accursed in the city and accursed in the country. Accursed be their barns and the . . . seed of their lands, their flocks of sheep, and their herds of cattle. **. . . Let no priest say Mass for them, nor in sickness receive their confession, nor, unless they repent, grant them the sacrosanct communion even on their deathbed. But let them be buried in the grave of an ass . . .** that their shame and malediction may be a warning to present and future generations. (quoted in Henry C. Lea (ed.), *Studies in Church History* [Philadelphia: 1883], 333–39)

As late as the 18th century, English law mandated ignominious burial for suicides, see 4 William Blackstone, Commentaries 189. On ignominious punishments in Islam, see Christian Lange, *Justice, Punishment and the Medieval Islamic Imagination* (Cambridge: 2008).

13 See Deuteronomy 21:10–14; 2 Samuel 10:1–5 and Midrash Tanhuma (Warsaw), parashat Pinhas, §3; Isaiah 7:20.

ornate ironwork. The much plainer stone parish church of St Alexius in Przedborz has a *kuna* as well, in this case a simple ring; the chain is no longer extant. The institution of the *kuna* is well-documented in the Polish archaeological literature, and museums exhibit chains and other artifacts related to the *kuna*.

There is, of course, a Polish Wikipedia entry on the *kuna*.[14] But the phenomenon of the pillory in the church context was by no means limited to Poland, and was pervasive throughout Europe. Various types of church pillories were common in Scotland, Portugal, Spain, Germany, Switzerland, and Slovakia; they were also found in England, France, Italy and Scandinavia.

This is certainly due partly to the fact that it is a very inexpensive punishment in terms of the expense to the community — there is no need for the infrastructure of a prison, nor to maintain prisoners; and the offenders are not taken out of their routine — working to support their family, for instance. This makes the punishment attractive, especially to poor communities.

Note too that the institution of the *kuna* is not found only in the religious context, and is also a civic institution found in marketplaces, squares and town halls. Many civic pillories are stone columns to which offenders were chained; others, *kune*-style chains affixed to a ring on a wall of the town hall. The explanatory plaque on such a pillory in Ilmenau, Germany, reads:

> Pillory: For theft from gardens and fields, receiving stolen goods, blasphemy, libel, or in certain cases of adultery, the punishment of the neck-iron was imposed. Convicts usually had to stand one to two hours on the pillory, mostly on Sundays and market days, when deterrent effect was particularly strong. Until the introduction of the Criminal Code of 1839, this dishonorable punishment was meted out.

14 http://pl.wikipedia.org/wiki/Kuna_(narz%C4%99dzie_kary). This page can be translated into English by Google Translator. Wikipedia links its Polish "*kuna*" entry to its English-language entry for "Jougs" [http://en.wikipedia.org/wiki/Jougs], which it defines as follows: "The jougs, juggs, or joggs (Old French joug, from Lat. jugum, a yoke) is an instrument of punishment formerly in use in Scotland, the Netherlands and other countries. . . . an iron collar fastened by a short chain to a wall, often of the parish church, or to a tree. The collar was placed round the offender's neck and fastened by a padlock. The jougs was practically a pillory. It was used for ecclesiastical as well as civil offences." The page is illustrated by photos and hand-drawings of jougs at various Scottish churches.

In Poland, there were civic pillories in, among other cities, Vilna, Warsaw, Lvov, the Kazimierz section of Krakow, Szydlowiec, Wroclaw and Poznan.

Returning to the Jewish context, it can safely be said that the practice of putting offenders in the *kune* was practiced throughout eastern Ashkenaz. Synagogue *kune*s have been attested to in the following places: Bratislava, Gombin, Keidan, Krakow, Lezno (Lissa), Lublin, Lvov, Mattersburg (Mattersdorf), Mezeritch, Opatow, Ostrog, Pietrekow-Tribunalska, Pinchow, Pinsk, Przysucha, Przedborz, Przemysl, Radzyn, Sanok, Shklov, Siemiatycze, Slonim, Strzyzow, Tismenitz, Tykocin (Tiktin), Varka, Videshok, Vilna, Wyszogrod, and Zabludow. Cheder *kune*s for children were mentioned in recollections of Buczacz and Krynki.

Without any doubt, the *kune* is an emulation of a Gentile practice. There is, however, a talmudic "anticipation" of the pillory in tractate Ketubot of the Babylonian Talmud. In bKetubot 49b, addressing the case of someone who would not maintain his children, we find the following statement: "Rav Hisda used to say: 'Turn a mortar upside down for him in public, and let him stand [on it], and let him say, A raven cares for its young, but this man does not care for his children.'" That is to say, this man is to be stood on a platform, exposed to the public eye, and made to declare his shameful conduct. But certainly, this talmudic anticipation of the institution of the pillory cannot be regarded as a basis, textual or otherwise, for the *kune*, as it is never alluded to in the context of halakhic references to the *kune*. Furthermore, the alleged talmudic precedent is in essence a means of coercing the father to comply with his duties, and he can be "off the hook" at any moment if he expresses willingness to comply.

Our information about the *kune* comes from several different types of sources: literary works from the nineteenth and early twentieth centuries by Gottlober,[15] Goldfaden, I.L.Peretz,[16] and Nochem Meir

15 Abraham Ber Gottlober (Mehalalel) (Russia, 1811–1899), maskil, scholar, Hebrew poet and translator, wrote short stories and novels in Hebrew and Yiddish.

16 Isaac Leib Peretz (Poland, 1852–1915), Yiddish writer, folklorist, playwright, activist. One of his lesser known plays, written in 1908/09, is entitled "*In Polish oyf der Keyt: a holem fun a kloyznik*" ("Chained in the synagogue vestibule; a yeshiva-student's dream").

Shaykevitch (Shomer)[17]; journalistic reports; historical documents from the eighteenth to twentieth centuries; testimonies of individuals recalling their hometowns in Eastern Europe[18]; and extant archaeological evidence of *kune*s. There are also more recent literary sources: Sholom Asch, Isaac Bashevis Singer and Chaim Grade all mention the *kune* in various stories.

The institution of "standing in the *kune*"—"*shteln in kune*" — was internalized by Jewish communities, so much so that its Polish origin was suppressed or forgotten, even though the very same word was used in both cultures. Some readers may be familiar with the term "*kuni-leml*," the eponymous protagonist of Goldfaden's famous play "The Two Kuni-Lemls." The origin of the term "*kuni-leml*" is much discussed, but the term apparently invokes the notion of a lamb put in the *kune* to connote a duped innocent paying the price for something he did not do. My point is that the notion of the *kune* was deeply rooted in the folk consciousness. Gottlober,[19] writing in 1876, reflects on the *kune* — in a critical way, of course — as follows:

> I will not hide from you, dear reader, that I do not know the etymology of the word "*kune*," which is the popular term for the pillory. Does this term come from the root *kina* (קינה), lamentation, being a lament of the poor soul who is chained in this cage, and is suffering terribly, or does it, perhaps, come from *knia* (כניעה), surrender, for they certainly forced his sinful soul to surrender? Or does it come from *kana* (קנא), zeal, signifying a spirit of zealousness that overtakes the God-fearing, so they punish the sinners?[20]

This etymological discussion appears in the context of a story written by Gottlober about an incident in which a married woman happened to host a stranger for a few hours. As a punishment, she was put in the *kune*. Another reference to a woman being put in the *kune* is found in a passage from the memoirs of Isaac Joel Linetski, who describes the narrow-minded outlook of his hometown. He

17 Nochem Meir Shaykevitch (Lithuania c. 1849–US 1905), writer of sensationalistic melodramas much condemned by literary critics but popular among the reading public. See *Haboker Or* 4 (1879).

18 The *kune* is mentioned in remembrances of hometown synagogues in a number of Yizkor books, e.g., those for Mezritsh (Międzyrzec Podlaski), Przemysl, and Radzyn among others.

19 It is interesting to note that Gottlober taught Goldfaden when the latter was a young boy.

20 Abraham Ber Gottlober, "*Taanit hatulim*," *Haboker Or* 1 (1876).

sarcastically asks whether a woman who dared to preen in front of a mirror ought not be put in the *kune*.

To be sure, neither of these two anecdotes describes an actual case of a woman being put in the *kune*. However, there is a report of an actual case from turn-of-the-century Jerusalem. A rabbinical court there ruled that a woman who had confessed to having committed adultery was to be "put into the *kune* for three hours. And the whole congregation should gather to see her in her disgrace and humiliation. And afterwards, she is to be flogged thirty-nine lashes, and expelled from the city." This sentence was indeed carried out "in the presence of all the inhabitants of the city, and they even stood on the rooftops of houses — men, women, and children — and they all spit at her and cursed her, and many threw rotten eggs, eggshells, mouldy fruit and dirty rags. And whoever threw more, garnered more praise."[21]

From the various descriptions I have found, it seems that as a rule, the *kune* was situated inside the synagogue in the vestibule (*polish, pulish*) near the entrance to the main sanctuary. In at least one case, however — and it happens to be a case where the *kune* is still extant — the *kune* was outside, and moreover, its construction was fairly similar to that of the *kuna* at St Mary's Basilica in Krakow. I am referring to the *kune* of a synagogue in Przysucha (Pshishcha), Poland.[22] Beside the front entrance to the synagogue, which is constructed of brick, is an elaborate arched niche with a stone seat at the bottom, above which is affixed a *kune* ring.

Generally, though, the offender had to stand, sometimes in a rather confined space. This feature is emphasized in a memoir by a member of the famous An-ski ethnographic expedition, who provides the following description of the *kune* in the Maharsha shul in Ostrog:

21 Joshua b. David Yellin, *Memoirs of a Jerusalemite 1834–1918* (Hebrew), (Jerusalem: 1924). From Yellin's description, the Hurva synagogue's *kune*, which was located in a niche in the synagogue courtyard, had a slightly more elaborate design than the simple ring and chain: it consisted of two hooks that protruded from the wall several feet above the ground, with a bench underneath on which the offender stood. A metal piece (in another description, a chain) was then placed under his chin and through the hooks on either side, and fastened with locks.

22 This 18th c. limestone synagogue, which is still standing, though in precarious condition, has been designated for restoration and preservation by the Foundation for the Preservation of Jewish Heritage in Poland (FODZ); see http://fodz.pl/?d=5&id=93&l=en

> It is also important to recount that in the synagogue's antechamber (*pulish*), there stood a *kune*, which was a kind of tall narrow cabinet; the rabbinical court used to sentence transgressors to "stand in the *kune*." Only one person at a time could fit into the *kune*, and even then, only standing up, with his arms hanging down outside. In the upper part of the door to the *kune* there was an opening through which the offender's face was visible. It was by no means rare that when the guilty party had been sentenced to stand in the *kune* for a particularly grave sin, such as theft, informing, being caught with a married woman [adultery] and so on, the rabbinical court ordered that at the conclusion of the synagogue services, the worshippers, when leaving the synagogue, were to pass by the *kune* and, through the opening in the door, spit into the sinner's face, so as to increase the humiliation even more.[23]

Standing in the *kune* is depicted in a photograph taken in the beautiful wooden Gombin synagogue in 1919 and used to illustrate an article on the *kune* for a Warsaw Yiddish newspaper.[24] This *kune*, unlike the cabinet-style *kune* of the Ostrog shul, was a simple two-sided neck ring attached to a chain affixed to the wall; it looks virtually identical to the many pictures of jougs in Scottish churches. Although the *kune* in the picture is real, an accompanying photograph of a man locked in the *kune*, while children look on from no more than a metre or two away, is staged.[25] However, as the accompanying article explains, though the *kune* was no longer in use, it had been routinely used in the preceding centuries.

Although the photograph is staged, it nonetheless generates in the observer a feeling of great discomfort and shame. The photo calls to mind a passage from Hawthorne's *Scarlet Letter*:

> the pillory . . . so fashioned as to confine the human head in its tight grasp, and thus hold it up to the public gaze. The very ideal of ignominy was

23 Abraham Rechtman, *Jewish Ethnography and Folklore: a Memoir of Sh. An-ski's Ethnographic Expedition* (Yiddish), (Buenos Aires: 1959), 68.

24 The article was written by the rabbi of Gombin, R. Judah Leib Zlotnick (Poland 1887-Israel 1962), who was also an ethnographer. R. Zlotnick used the pen-name "Judah Elzet" for his ethnographic writings. An eminent biblical and talmudic scholar, in 1920 he left Poland for Canada, and later South Africa, in both countries serving as an educator and rabbinical leader, while continuing his scholarly pursuits. He later went to Israel, where he changed his name to Avida, and devoted himself to halakhic and philological research, and translation.

25 Judah Elzet, "*Unzer museum: di kune*" (Our museum: the kune), *Ilustrirte Velt* 2, Warsaw (1919).

> embodied and made manifest in this contrivance of wood and iron. There can be no outrage, methinks, against our common nature — whatever be the delinquencies of the individual — no outrage more flagrant than to forbid the culprit to hide his face for shame; as it was the essence of this punishment to do.

There is also an earlier picture — a hand-drawn illustration, not a photograph — of an offender locked in a *kune*. It depicts a noble and dignified, almost sage-like figure in the *kune* of Lvov's Great Suburban Synagogue (Wielka Synagoga Przedmiejska).[26] Presumably, the artist sought to present the *kune*, which was, we must not forget, a familiar and socially-sanctioned institution in the surrounding Gentile society as well — as a benign corrective institution.

The *kune* is mentioned, in passing, in *Journey to Poland*, a book-length account of a "roots" trip to Poland undertaken in 1924 by the famous Jewish novelist Alfred Doblin, author of *Berlin Alexanderplatz*, who was also a practicing neuropsychiatrist,

> In the evening, I see the groups of men emerging from small, brightly lit prayer rooms on the narrow streets of Kazimierz, the Jewish district of Cracow; they wear half-shoes, white stockings, colossal fur caps over their ears — the *shtreymls*. My companion is telling me — I lap up his stories — about a bizarre old man. . . . He used to be more liberal; now he eats no meat, wears prayer thongs [tefillin] and a prayer shawl outdoors, puts stones in his shoes. . . .
>
> When prayers are over, I enter the old synagogue. It used to be the library of "Emperor Kazimierz"; I saw a plaque outside: Kazimierz sitting as an angel; old Jews with Torahs thanking him for allowing them into Cracow. In the *pollish*, the ante-chamber of the synagogue, the chain still hangs on the wall — the chain for those condemned by the judge, the rebbe, and the pillory where they were spit at: theology as in the book at the Jagiellonian Library — a practical science.[27]

So cruel was this punishment perceived to be that an early nineteenth century Russian Jewish scholar and maskil, Isaac Baer Levinsohn, claimed that Jews converted to Christianity in order to avoid it: "Some abjured the faith of their forefathers for worldly gain;

26 Meir Balaban, *The Jews of Lvov at the Turn of the Seventeenth Century* (Polish), (Poland: 1909), figure 1:34 (drawing from the collection of the Pawlikowskich library [Lvov]).

27 Alfred Doblin, *Journey to Poland*, translated by J. Neugroschel (NY: 1991), 191. Originally published in Germany in 1926, it recounts the assimilated Doblin's experiences in Poland, especially in heavily-Jewish areas.

some, having transgressed certain enactments of the law, were afraid of the punishment of the Cuna, which the congregation would have inflicted on them, and therefore abjured their faith."[28] I do not wish to suggest that this constitutes historical proof that actual conversions took place due to fear of being subjected to the *kune* punishment, but it does show that such an assertion, even if extreme, was deemed plausible at the time, since Levinsohn was addressing readers who were familiar with the *kune*.

That communal officials themselves regarded the *kune* punishment as agonizing is evident in a ruling issued in the early eighteenth century regarding an ongoing dispute between the communities of Tykocin (Tiktin) and Siemiatycze. It stipulates that the rabbinical court may impose sanctions and fines as it sees fit, but "the severe punishment of *kune* ought be imposed only for a major offence."[29] This clearly indicates awareness that being locked in the *kune* and compelled to face the contempt of one's peers was a harrowing ordeal, not to be imposed lightly, and communities were well advised to exercise restraint in meting out this punishment.

Above, I mentioned the drawing of the *kune* in a Lvov synagogue in Meir Balaban's history of the Jews in Lvov. That *kune* was in the Great "Suburban" Synagogue built outside the old walled city in the early sixteenth century. Not far away, in the heart of the walled city, was the Taz synagogue, vestiges of which are extant. It was called the Taz synagogue[30] in honour of the eminent halakhic authority R. David Segal, the Taz.[31] A secondary source from mid-seventeenth century Lvov relates that at the outset of his rabbinical career, the Taz was put in the *kune* because he argued with the head of the local rabbinical court about a question of kashruth. The description of the *kune* focuses

28 Isaac Baer Levinsohn, *Efes Dammim, A Series of Conversations at Jerusalem between a Patriarch of the Greek Church and a Chief Rabbi of the Jews . . .*, trans. Louis Loewe (London: 1841), 107. *Efes Dammim* itself was a defense against the blood libel that had been leveled against the Jews of Zaslavl (Zaslaw), in Volhynia, in 1830.

29 Israel Halperin, *Acta Congressus Generalis Judaeorum Regni Poloniae* (Minutes of the Council of the Four Lands) (1580–1764) [Hebrew], (1945), §527, 249.

30 Also known as the Golden Rose synagogue and the Nachmanowicz synagogue, it has been digitally reconstructed and can be viewed at http://www.youtube.com/watch?v=-Z1sWxnLP4k.

31 R. David Halevi Segal (1586–1667), author of the *Turei Zahav* commentary on the *Shulhan Arukh*.

on its putative spiritual objective, a point to which I will return at the end of this article.

> To put him in the place of shame, under an iron lock . . . and its purpose was to put in it every sinner and offender, with chains of iron on their wrists, as a signal to the rebellious that they should hearken and fear. And this is what is popularly known as the *kune*.[32]

In addition to the literary, memoiristic, and incidental references to the *kune* detailed above, we also have legal enactments and concrete court decisions imposing the punishment of *kune*; let me bring a few examples.

i

An enactment was issued in Tiktin (Tykocin) in 1716 regarding debtors who claim they cannot return loans. The enactment instructs the court that, in addition to other punishments, such a debtor "is to be put in the *kune*. And no mercy is to be shown for the self-respect of the family or for [the debtor's] own self-respect, even if he is a member of a prominent family, who are the pillars of the world (*sfunei olam*), for all people are equal, with one law and one Torah for all, both great and small."[33]

32 *Anshei Shem*, p. 58, quoting Gabriel b. Naftali Hertz Sochostow, *Matzevet Kodesh* (Lemberg: 1860), part 3, letter "a." Another version of the story about the Taz is found in R. Judah Altusky's *Hegyonei Yehudi* (NY: 1940), vol. 2: Exodus, 40. It is also mentioned in Israel Bekmeister, *Sipurei Niflaot Migdolei Yisrael* (Tel Aviv: 1969), 14, and in Rafael Nahman b. Baruch Hakohen, *Shmuot Vesipurim Miraboteinu Hakedoshim* (Israel: 1964), story 142, 130–32. I am mentioning these hagiographic legends, not as historical evidence of recourse to the *kune*, but to show that the institution of the *kune* was a matter of common knowledge, and regarded as an integral part of Jewish life.

33 "Takana of the holy community of Tiktin, 17 Tevet 5476 [1716], regarding a debtor who claims he cannot return a loan," in Mordechai Nadav (ed.), *Minutes Book of the Jewish Community Council of Tykocin 1621–1806*; hand copied by Israel Halperin (Hebrew), (Jerusalem: 1996), vol. 1, §460 (2), p. 313. In another incident in Tiktin, from 1785, a butcher was sentenced by the "heads and leaders of the community, with the approval of the honorable head of the court and rabbi of our community" to "stand in the *kune*"; he and his son would then "be expelled from our community" (vol. 1, §974, p. 656).

ii

The next example is a legal ruling issued in Krakow in 1772, sentencing an offender to be put in the *kune*, again, along with other punishments:

> And thus we have issued a final ruling that he is totally unfit to serve as a witness or swear an oath, and he is to be excommunicated and banned in all the synagogues . . . and the iron chain is to be put around his neck.[34]

iii

Another document, recounting a case that took place in Zabludow in 1748, tells of a judgment meted out to someone who assaulted his fellows: "the hand that struck should be placed in the *kune* on the Sabbath, from the beginning of the synagogue prayers to the end."[35] Here too, this was in addition to other punishments meted out to the offender. This source indicates that the *kune* was used on the Sabbath, which I find astonishing, but was apparently the standard procedure. This mirrors the Christian practice of putting offenders in a pillory at the entrance to the church on Sundays.

Interestingly, a book on the magnificent wooden synagogue of Zabludow, no longer extant, mentions the *kune* punishment as well:

> . . . in the old Pinkas, there is a story about a young man, a butcher, who ate on a day of fast at a Christian's place in the nearby village of Trashtchenky. Before minkha [the afternoon service], the rabbi and other men of the community waited for him and gave him lashes on the stone. They made him stand by the "kouna." At the end of the prayer, everyone of them walked by him and spit and in this way the man atoned for his sin.[36]

iv

In his campaign against Hasidism, the Vilna Gaon attempted to have an important member of the Vilna community who had become a Hasid put in the *kune* (other sanctions were also to be imposed). The communal leaders, however, refused to do so, though "they punished

34 "Register of the Cracow Jewish Community, 1772" (Hebrew), *Measef*, St Petersburg (1902), 64–5.

35 Simha Assaf, "From the library archives: Pinkas Zabludow" (Hebrew), *Kiryat Sefer* 1 (1925), 317.

36 Michael Lifshitz, *Our Ancient Synagogue in Zabludow*. First published 1925; translated from Hebrew by Daphna Brafman, available at: http://www.zabludow.com/Chosenpagesancientsynagoguelifshitz.html

him very severely with other punitive measures."[37] The fact that the communal leaders refused to comply with the Vilna Gaon's instruction to put the rebel in the *kune*, though they went along with his directive that other severe punishments, including lashes, were to be imposed, attests to the fact that they considered the punishment of standing in the *kune* to be very harsh.

v

In Lublin, a certain Sender, who had been charged with falsifying documents and slandering R. David Lida of Amsterdam,[38] was — "in order to publicize his shame" — sentenced to be "put in the *kune* in front of the great synagogue in Lublin for the entire duration of the morning service."[39]

vi

The Lubavitch records of the notorious case of "Shimon the Heretic" state:

> In the middle of MarHeshvan, the verdict was issued: he and his family were to be expelled from the city, led away in a humiliating procession, as was customary in those days. But first, he would be placed in the stocks for three hours a day over the next three days, while all passersby would spit in his face. On Thursday, 23 MarHeshvan [November 24, 1796], the sentence was carried out; Shimon the Heretic and his family were led out of town in a humiliating procession.[40]

Reference to a "humiliating procession" is also found in other sources and merits further research.

Spitting was, indeed, an integral part of the punishment of *kune*.

37 *Zmir Aritzim Veharvot Tzurim* (Cutting Down of the Tyrants and Swords of Flint), compiled and published by R. Arie Leib, scribe of the Brody "Kloyz," in 1772. Reprinted in Mordechai Wilensky, *Hasidim and Mitnagdim: the Polemic between them from 1772 to 1815* (Hebrew), (Jerusalem: 1970), 1: 66.

38 A well-known Kabbalist suspected of Sabbatean sympathies.

39 Aaron Freimann, "R. David Lida and his self-defence in *Beer Esek* [*The Well of Contention*]" (Hebrew), *Nahum Sokolow Jubilee Volume* (Warsaw: 1905), 476.

40 "Shimon of Zamut," in R. Joseph Isaac Schneersohn, *Branches of the Chassidic Menorah*, vol. 2, *Biographical Stories*, trans. Shimon Neubort (NY: 1998).

vii

The following colorful passage from the work *Aliyot Eliahu*, which describes the life of the Vilna Gaon, mentions yet another *kune* incident. The various exaggerations do not negate the element of truth in the report about the *kune*:

> I was brought to the entrance of the synagogue to stand in front of all the people, and my neck was put into the clasp, the metal rings that are fastened to the walls of the synagogue. And above my head they pasted a paper on which it was written that this man is being punished for having ridiculed the words of our holy masters. And everyone who came to pray the afternoon prayer service would come and stand there. And they called me "wicked Israelite" and did not spare my face their spittle, and they spat at my face so much that there was almost a puddle streaming in front of me like the Jordan river. . . . When the afternoon prayer service was over, they took me outside the town and sent me on my way.[41]

The element of spitting transforms the punishment of *kune* into one in which the community as a whole is actively involved in the process of shaming.

## IV Conclusion

To sum up, recourse to punishment by putting someone in the *kune* was apparently meted out on an ad hoc basis rather than in accordance with a fixed list of offenses. The offenses that were punished by being put in the *kune* were sometimes minor, sometimes serious (adultery, informing). Sometimes the offense was specified on a piece of paper that was affixed to the wall beside the *kune*. At times, standing in the *kune* was a sole punishment; generally, though, it was imposed in addition to other penalties. In most cases, the punishment of *kune* was for a very limited period only — one day or several days. Sometimes the offender was to be expelled from the community altogether once he finished his stint in the *kune;* in such cases, the question of how the offender would feel in resuming his normal routine did not arise. But imagine how difficult it must have been for an individual to face his fellows and resume social relations after the mortification of the *kune*

41 Letter describing how someone who derided the Midrash was put in the pillory by order of the Vilna Gaon, in R. Joshua Heschel Lewin, *Aliyot Eliahu*, edited by Nahman b. Tzvi Hirsch (Vilna: 1856), 61 n 33. On an attempt to identify the individual in question, see *Hacarmel* (1871), 234; a different account is found on p. 462.

experience. What I find most remarkable, though, is that hardly any objections to recourse to the *kune* were ever voiced by the halakhic authorities in an effort to eliminate or at least reduce this practice. When it vanished, this was not due to internal disapproval, but rather to a change in the surrounding society's attitude to shame punishment.

Was the *kune* intended to humiliate the offender, induce him to repent — self-mortification to achieve this end is quite familiar to us[42] — or, as the historian Salo Baron contends, to correct his conduct?[43] This question can also be asked of the other forms of shame punishment. In the surrounding Christian culture, the atonement explanation prevailed: the harshness of the means was seen as mitigated by the desirable end. It will be recalled that above, I quoted the view of Gabriel b. Naftali Hertz Sochostow to the effect that the objective of the *kune* was to convey "to the rebellious that they should hearken and fear." My impression, however, is that in the Jewish context, the element of humiliation is primary. Certainly, judging from the works I examined, the punishment of *kune* was perceived by the community, and often, its leaders, as cruel and lacking any redeeming spiritual value.

Whatever the community perception, or for that matter, my own impression, the function of shame punishment within Jewish legal culture, and indeed, in general, remains to be clarified.[44]

42 See, e.g., Jacob Elbaum, *Repentance and Self-flagellation in the Writings of the Sages of Germany and Poland 1348–1648* (Hebrew), (Jerusalem: 1992).

43 Salo Baron, *The Jewish Community — Its History and Structure to the American Revolution* (Westport CN: 1972), 2:224.

44 I would like to thank Nessa Olshansky-Ashtar for superlative research assistance. I would also like to thank Dr. Eric Stepien for providing me with translations of Polish sources in the early stages of my research.

*The Jewish Law Annual*, Vol. XIX

# Refusal to Give a *Get*: Tort Damages and the Recalcitrant Spouse in Contemporary Jewish Law

Dov I. Frimer*

## 1 Introduction

How can we free a woman from the chains of *igun*, the bonds of marriage to a husband who refuses to grant his wife a Jewish bill of divorcement, a *get*? This has been one of the most pressing and difficult challenges confronting halakhic authorities throughout the generations.[1] In fact, Jewish law compares the heavy rabbinical responsibility surrounding the release of an *agunah*, a "bound woman," to the degree of responsibility generally associated with deciding cases involving capital crimes.[2] Thus it is not only a pressing matter,

* Rabbi and practicing lawyer; Adjunct Professor at the Hebrew University of Jerusalem Faculty of Law; Associate Professor at Fuchsberg Law Center, Touro College, New York.

1 See, e.g., the comments by the noted Galician halakhic authority, R. Shalom Schwadron (1835–1911), who writes at the conclusion of an oft-cited responsum (*Responsa Maharsham*, 1:84): "Therefore for all these reasons, I agree in this matter . . . to release a woman from the chains of *igun* and to allow her to be married under Torah law. As is explained in *New Responsa Bakh*, end of #64, 'he who releases even one *agunah* in these times is as if he had rebuilt one of the ruins of the supernal Jerusalem.' . . . And it is also thus stated in *Nahal Kedumim* on the scroll of Lamentations, in the name of R. A. Hayun. Therefore, I pressed myself to complete this responsum today [on Tisha B'Av!], on the day of the fast for the destruction of the House of our Glory. . . . "

2 See bGitin 66a, which states that if a rabbi has been "cast into a pit" and ordered that a bill of divorce be written, he does so, even though he is unable to identify the husband giving the order, for "in a time of danger, one writes [a *get*] and gives it [to the woman] even though one does not recognize him"; cf. *SA*, EH 121:3. Rashi on bJebamot 122a emphasizes that a woman's very status as an *agunah* is considered tantamount to a matter of life and death: "For this is like a time of danger, for if one does not believe this voice [an echo attesting to the woman's status, though the speaker is no longer present] . . .she will remain an *agunah*." R. Menahem Hameiri on bGitin 66a further notes: "And we have learned that [even] when there is

but a sensitive and complex one as well.[3] Moreover, the question is certainly not whether to act to free a woman from the chains of being an *agunah*, but how to do so.

Despite the clear importance of the issue, we can state with confidence that all contemporary halakhic authorities concur that suing a husband for tort damages for recalcitrance — even in a Jewish civil court — is not the proper way to release a woman from her shackles. As to other devices used to preempt recalcitrance and prevent *igun*,

no danger [that someone who can attest to a woman's marital status will die], in the case where he [the husband] lives in another country, and we do not recognize [the person giving the testimony], this matter is also [considered] like a time of danger, for if not now, when? Perhaps something will happen and it will be delayed — and such things happen every day." In the Meiri's view, even a temporary postponement is considered danger, lest this temporary postponement become permanent. Similarly, R. Joel Sirkes maintains that: "Wherever there is reason for concern that she will remain an *agunah* her entire life, this is considered like a time of danger" (*New Responsa Bakh*, #92). Consequently, R. Sirkes rules that if the husband is an apostate, "we are concerned that he may suddenly turn his eyes away and flee. . . as is his practice. . . or perhaps he may be killed and his wife will be considered an *agunah* her entire life. Therefore, without any doubt, for this reason it is considered like a time of danger, and one writes a divorce . . . even though they do not know [with certainty] the place of the writing [or] that the person issuing the divorce is her husband. . . . We treat it like a time of danger. . . . And certainly the edict of the Sages is thus, and in such cases we certainly say that 'Whoever marries a woman does so in accordance with the concurrence of the Rabbis'" (ibid.). See also R. Ezekiel Landau, *Responsa Noda Biyehuda*, 2nd edition, #123, and R. Abraham Hirsch Eisenstadt, *Pithei Teshuva*, Sidur Get, #18. Due to this consideration, among others, the decisors were generally lenient as to the proofs required to release an *agunah*, accepting forms of evidence and testimony that are generally not halakhically acceptable; see *SA*, EH 17. This last point, however, requires elaboration that is beyond the scope of this article.

3 The halakhic gravity of the matter can be deduced from the serious consequences that can ensue from the **improper** release of an *agunah*. E.g., mJebamot 10:1 rules: "[In the case of ] a woman whose husband went overseas [and all trace of him was lost], and [witnesses] came and said, 'Your husband has died,' and she remarried, and thereafter her husband came [back] — she is to be divorced both by this one and that one [the first and second husbands], and she requires a *get* from this and from that one . . . and the children born from this one and that one are deemed offspring of an incestuous or adulterous union (*mamzerim*)." See R. Judah Freis, *Sefer Yad Yehuda*, EH 4:16.

such as the signing of a prenuptial agreement, there is disagreement among the halakhic decisors about their effects on the validity of a subsequent *get*.[4] All decisors and rabbinical court judges, however, are in rare agreement that a tort claim predicated on the refusal of a husband to grant his wife a *get* renders invalid any *get* given in its wake. In the brief framework of this article, I will attempt to outline the main principles underlying this halakhic ruling, basing myself primarily on decisions of the rabbinical courts of the State of Israel.

## 2 Marriage and divorce: contractual model v. status model

In contradistinction to the marriage and divorce laws of most Western countries, which are generally based on status theory, in Jewish law, matters of marriage and divorce are based on a contractual model. On the status model, the State, or some authorized instance on its behalf,

4 See, inter alia, the articles in *Tehumin* 21 (2001) by R. Solomon Dichovsky, 279–87, R. David Mishelov, 288–323, R. Elyashiv Knohl, 324–39; and R. Abraham Scheinfeld's article in *Tehumin* 22 (2002), 148–56, with notes by R. Solomon Dichovsky; articles in *Tzohar* 20 (2005) by R. David Ben-Zazon, 79–82, Rachel Levmore, 83–91, R. David Bass, 93–103 and 125–27, R. Uriel Lavi, 105–14, R. Shimon Yacobi, 115–16, R. Eliezer Igra, 117–20, R. Eliezer Melamed, 121–24; articles in *Tzohar* 21 (2005) by R. Uriel Lavi, 155–61, R. Itai Elitzur, 163–69. See too Appeals File 47/5716, Counter Appeal 71/5716, SRC [Supreme Rabbinical Court, Jerusalem] (rabbis Isaac Nissim, Joseph Shalom Elyashiv and Bezalel Zolty) 2 PDR 9 (1956); R. Bezalel Zolty, "On the 'chained wife' enactment" (Hebrew), *Ha-Pardes* 57 (1983), 6–8; R. Shalom Messas, *Responsa Tvuat Shemesh*, EH, #66; idem, *Responsa Shemesh Umagen*, 1:11–12 and 2:36; R. Elijah Bakshi Doron, *Responsa Binyan Av*, 3; 63; R. Solomon Moses Amar, *Responsa Shema Shlomo*, 6:20; R. Uriel Lavi, *Ateret Devora*, 1:75; Rachel Levmore, *Mini Einayikh Midima* (Jerusalem: 1999); *Sefer Yad Yehuda*, n. 3 above, EH 134:4.

It appears that in 1954–1955, Israeli Chief Rabbi Isaac Herzog was one of the first contemporary halakhic authorities to seriously consider the use of prenuptial agreements to alleviate the problem of the recalcitrant spouse. He advocated inclusion of a "penalty" or "compensation" clause in the agreement, rather than the increased support payments commonly used today. On the other hand, R. Herzog makes these financial obligations conditional on the rabbinical court's having **obligated** the husband to grant a *get* (*hiyuv get*), and the husband's having refused to comply. See the series of letters included in R. Isaac Herzog, *Constitution, Laws, and Enactments of the Chief Rabbinate*, vol. 3 of I. Warhaftig (ed.), *Constitution and Law in a Jewish State according to the Halacha* (Hebrew), (Jerusalem: 1989), 200–210.

creates the marriage, and it is the State or authorized instance that terminates the marriage. The contractual model, on the other hand, takes the involved parties themselves to create the marital bond,[5] and they themselves terminate the marriage by means of their own actions.[6]

In classical Jewish law, therefore, the presence of a rabbi at the marriage ceremony, or the presence of the rabbinical court at a Jewish divorce, is required merely to ensure proper performance of the procedure in question. The rabbis, however, are not an integral part of the legal procedure itself.

Jewish law recognizes at least two general sets of circumstances in which a contractual relationship may be terminated: (a) when the parties involved agree to terminate it; or (b) when one party has fundamentally breached the terms of the contract. Similarly, a Jewish marriage may be terminated: (a) when there is agreement between the husband and wife to terminate the marriage[7]; or (b) when there has been a breach of the marriage. Such breaches are referred to as "grounds for divorce" (*ilot geirushin*).[8]

In the case of agreement, the free and voluntary consent of each of the parties, without any compulsion or pressure, is required.[9] On the other hand, where there are justified grounds for divorce, then should one side refuse to be divorced, it is possible to obligate, or even to coerce, that party to execute the *get*. The halakhic term for such

5 See Justice Haim Cohn in C.A. 337/62, *Reizenfeld v. Jacobson*, 17 PD 1009, esp. 1018 (1963). See also R. Koppel Kahane, *The Theory of Marriage in Jewish Law* (Leiden: 1966) and *Birkat Kohen* (Jerusalem: 1972), 101–23; Shalom Albeck, *The Principles of Marriage and Family Law in the Talmud* (Hebrew), (Ramat Gan: 2010).

6 Cohn, ibid. See also Justice Isaac Kahan in HCJ 661/77, *Haber v. Supreme Rabbinical Court of Appeals*, 32(3) PD 324, 328–29 (1977).

7 According to Torah law, the husband may divorce his wife even without her consent, provided that he pays her the sums specified in her *ketuba*. However, in the late Geonic period (c. 1000), the great halakhic leader of Franco-Germany, Rabbenu Gershom, issued an edict requiring the wife's agreement to the act of divorce as well, except in certain exceptional cases. See Rema, EH 119:6; File 98/5713 Jerusalem Rabbinical Court (rabbis Jacob Adas, Joseph Shalom Elyashiv and Bezalel Zolty), 1 PDR 193, esp. 198 (1953); Benzion Schereschewsky, *Family Law in Israel* (Hebrew), 4th ed. (Jerusalem: 1992), 278–79.

8 For a summary of the grounds for divorce, see Schereschewsky, ibid., 295–327.

9 See Schereschewsky, ibid., 327, and the sources there cited.

coercion is *isui* (compulsion); a *get* issued under **unlawful** compulsion is thus known as a "*get meuse*," a forced or compelled divorce.[10]

"Compulsion" in this context includes both "physical compulsion," such as physical abuse or imprisonment, and "monetary compulsion," such as when the husband is compelled to pay certain sums of money should he refuse to divorce his wife.[11]

## 3 Lawful and unlawful compulsion

The precise determination of the grounds that justify the use of "compulsion" to bring about a divorce is itself a complex and sensitive issue. In general, the option of using compulsion to bring about a Jewish divorce will be entertained only where the grounds for divorce are of significant gravity. Moreover, as a rule, "one does not compel [a divorce] except in those cases of which the Sages spoke [explicitly]."[12] Accordingly, rabbinical court judges, *dayanim*, will look to precedent when considering the use of compulsion in a particular case. In cases where the *dayanim* find sufficient legal basis to allow the use of compulsion to obtain the *get*, the coercion will be deemed "lawful compulsion." Absent such grounds, however, the force utilized will constitute "unlawful compulsion." Unlawful compulsion is not only improper as a means, but may also render the *get* void *ab initio*.[13]

10 bGitin 88b. For a summary of the various halakhically recognized grounds and means of coercing a divorce, see Zerach Warhaftig, "Coercion of a *get* in theory and in practice" (Hebrew), in *Studies in Jewish Law* (Hebrew), (Ramat Gan: 1985), 148–208.

11 See R. Solomon Adret, *Responsa Rashba*, 4, #40, in the name of Rabbenu Hananel. R. Menahem Hameiri, bGitin 88b, similarly writes: "And this compulsion [which disqualifies the *get*] . . . is not only when they beat him and strike him so as to make him [grant the divorce], but it includes any compulsion, even monetary compulsion, for instance, if they seized his property until he divorces her, or imposed a penalty on him." R. Joseph Colon, *Responsa Maharik*, #63, concurs, writing that: "It is an obvious matter" that monetary coercion is considered compulsion. See also R. Shimon b. Zemah Duran, *Responsa Tashbetz*, 1, #1 and R. Jehiel Mikhel Epstein, *Arukh Hashulhan*, EH 134:22, R. Moses Feinstein, *Responsa Igrot Moshe*, EH 4:106 (at the beginning). The issue is discussed at length in *Sefer Yad Yehuda*, n. 3 above, EH 134:4. See too Schereschewsky, n. 7 above, 327–31; R. Joseph Goldberg, *Get Meuse* (Jerusalem: 2003), 43–55, and the sources there cited.

12 *SA*, EH 154:5.

13 Schereschewsky, n. 7 above, 327–28 and the sources there cited.

In addition to the need for good legal grounds to compel a recalcitrant spouse to grant a divorce, the Mishnah teaches that there is a further requirement — proper authority: "A *get* compelled by [a court of] Israel is valid and by [a court of] heathens is invalid."[14] Only a rabbinical court constitutes an accepted halakhic authority for compelling a *get*. In the language of the Talmud: "Heathens are not [halakhically] competent to apply compulsion (*bnei isui*)."[15] The Talmud proceeds to link the two requirements — good legal grounds and proper authority — concluding that even when the compulsion is carried out by a competent Jewish court, if it does so "on good legal grounds, [the divorce] is valid, but if not on good legal grounds, then it is invalid."[16]

For compulsion to be lawful, and the ensuing *get* valid, therefore, at least two parties must satisfy conditions stipulated by the halakha: the party being compelled — that is, the husband — and the party carrying out the compulsion — that is, the authority enforcing the *get*. The husband's behavior must give rise to grounds that halakhically justify divorce and the use of coercion to bring it about. In addition, the executing authority that is lawfully compelling the divorce must be halakhically recognized as "competent to lawfully compel," and further, must use means of compulsion acceptable to the halakhic system. Deviation from either of these conditions creates the reality of an unlawfully compelled *get* — a *get meuse* — which, as we said, is invalid.

14 mGitin 9:8.

15 The Talmud (bGitin 88b) explains: "A bill of divorce given under compulsion [exercised] by an Israelite court on good legal grounds is valid, but if not on good legal grounds, then it is invalid but it still disqualifies [the woman from marrying a priest (*kohen*)]. If [the compulsion is exercised] by a heathen court on good legal grounds, it is invalid, but disqualifies [her nonetheless, as if she were truly divorced]; if without good legal grounds, it doesn't bear even the slightest resemblance to a bill of divorce [lit., there is not even the 'smell' of a *get*] [hence the woman is not disqualified from marrying a priest in the future]." The Talmud then discusses whether the invalidation of non-Jewish coercion is biblical or merely Rabbinic. See R. Samuel Feivush of Witoslaw, *Beit Shmuel*, EH 134, #10 and #13; and *Arukh Hashulhan*, EH 134:3, which rule that despite some differences of opinion among the Early Authorities on this matter, the law is in accordance with the majority view that the disqualification is biblical. See also *SA*, EH 134:7ff., and EH 150. For a contemporary application of these principles, see R. Menashe Klein, *Get Meuse Bearkhaot* (NY: 1994).

16 bGitin 88b; see also *SA*, EH 134:7–8.

The fourth generation Babylonian Amora Abbaye questioned the competence of the Babylonian rabbinical courts of his day to compel a *get*, even when justified grounds for such compulsion existed. After all, he argued, the *dayanim* were not truly qualified rabbinical judges, as they were not properly "ordained" in accordance with Jewish law. The necessary authority to compel a *get* requires ordination from the rabbis in the land of Israel, who themselves were ordained in an unbroken chain of tradition commencing with Moses and continuing from teacher to student.

> Abbaye encountered R. Joseph sitting [in court] and compelling [a husband to grant] a divorce. He [Abbaye] said to him: Surely we [judges in Babylonia] are only laymen [i.e., not fully ordained, full ordination being possible only in the land of Israel], and it has been taught . . . "These are the judgments which you shall set before them" (Exod. 21:1) — before them, and not before heathens. Another explanation: before them, and not before laymen. He [R. Joseph] said to him: We serve as agents [of the Sanhedrin in the land of Israel].[17]

Although he defends reliance on contemporary Jewish courts for *get* compulsion, R. Joseph's response acknowledges the validity of Abbaye's fundamental premise. Were it not for the fact that the Babylonian rabbinical courts, and all subsequent "lay" rabbinical courts, were authorized and empowered by the ordained rabbis of the land of Israel to implement the latter's rulings, they would indeed — like Gentile judges — lack the necessary authority to compel a *get*.[18]

It must be stressed that the legal and halakhic ramifications of "unlawful compulsion" are extremely severe: the *get* is void,[19] the couple is still considered halakhically married, even retroactively, and the woman's subsequent children from another man would be

17 bGitin 88b.

18 In other words, despite the fact that, unlike the judges of earlier generations, contemporary judges are not "ordained" (*smukhin*), contemporary judges act as the agents of earlier judges, and therefore have the authority to coerce a divorce lawfully. See also *SA*, HM 1. Accordingly, Maimonides rules: "Someone who can be legally compelled to divorce his wife, but does not want to do so — a Jewish court in any place and at any time may lash him until he says, 'I want to do it.' He may then write a bill of divorce (*get*), and it is a valid bill of divorce" (*Code*, Laws concerning Divorce 2:20). For a summary of the various views on the basis and nature of this agency, see R. Samuel Tzvi-Hirsh Gartner, *Kefia Baget* (Jerusalem: 1999), 114–17.

19 See n. 15 above.

considered offspring of an incestuous or adulterous union (*mamzerim*).[20] These are not consequences that any responsible rabbinical authority can take lightly. Therefore, any decision to compel a husband to grant a *get* must be weighed very carefully.

## 4 Can suing for tort damages be considered "lawful compulsion"?

A court order requiring a husband to pay his wife tort damages due to his recalcitrance may clearly compel him to grant his wife a *get*. Even in a case in which the husband would otherwise refuse to divorce, the financial pressure created by his need to pay significant sums unless he gives his wife a *get* will often supersede all other considerations. Indeed, it is usually this intended result that motivates the wife to initiate the tort suit. What are the halakhic implications of such a lawsuit, and how does it impact a *get* issued in its wake? In light of what we have seen thus far, the halakhic ramifications of the tort suit can be best addressed by distinguishing between two situations.

### i Where there is no rabbinical court ruling requiring a *get*

Unless the wife can successfully demonstrate to a rabbinical court that halakhically valid grounds for divorce exist, no rabbinical court will order the husband to grant his wife a *get*. Absent such a divorce order, a valid *get* requires the consent of the parties involved; that is, the *get* must be the product of full and voluntary agreement, without any pressure or compulsion whatsoever. Compelling the husband to grant a *get* without his agreement will constitute "unlawful compulsion," which in turn can lead to invalidation of the divorce.

As a rule, Jewish tort law does not award damages for pain and suffering — that is, injury that is neither monetary nor corporal.[21] Consequently, the type of damage that generally results from a husband's refusal to grant his wife a *get*, and which can perhaps constitute a cause of action in secular tort law, does not constitute a sufficient basis to support a tort claim under Jewish law. This is particularly true when no obligation to divorce the wife exists under Jewish law, that is, when there is no rabbinical court ruling obligating the husband to give his

20 See n. 3 above.
21 See *SA*, HM 420:32ff. See also R. Abraham Sheinfeld, *Torts* (Hebrew), (Jerusalem: 1991), 302–307 and the sources there cited.

wife a *get*. Thus, from the perspective of Jewish law, a claim for tort damages based on a husband's refusal to grant a *get* is viewed as a frivolous attempt by the wife to unlawfully extract monies from her spouse.

Let us consider, by way of analogy, the example of a woman who steals her husband's car, and only agrees to return it on condition that her husband gives her a *get*. Assuming that there is no rabbinical court ruling obligating the husband to give his wife a *get*, it seems quite clear that the wife's behavior under these circumstances constitutes unlawful coercion. Accordingly, even should the husband "agree" to grant the divorce in exchange for the car, the financial pressure created by the wife's actions would render the *get* invalid.[22]

In light of this analysis, it would appear that a tort action predicated on a husband's failure to deliver a *get* to his wife would constitute "unlawful" pressure, which would in fact invalidate any *get* granted in its wake.[23] In the eyes of Jewish law, monies owed as a result of a secular court's award of damages are comparable to the stolen car and similarly constitute unlawful compulsion and pressure. An ensuing *get* will be invalid even if the husband consents to give it in exchange for return of the damages paid.[24]

### ii When there is a rabbinical court ruling requiring a *get*

When there is a ruling by an authorized rabbinical court requiring a *get* — that is, a ruling that recognizes the presence of valid grounds for divorce — the husband, depending on the precise circumstances of

22 See *Kefia Baget*, n. 18 above, 397–445; *Get Meuse*, n. 11 above, 43–55; *Sefer Yad Yehuda*, n. 11 above, and the sources there cited.

23 See File 766955–21–1 Jerusalem District Rabbinical Court (rabbis Matityahu Shrem, Abraham Kilav and Abraham Sheinfeld) (2004) (unpublished); File 54568514–28–1 Netanya District Rabbinical Court (rabbis Chaim Shaanan, Michael Amos and David Bardugo) (2007) (unpublished); File 7041–21–1 SRC (rabbis Hagai Izirer, Menahem Hashai and Tzion Algrabli) (2008) (published on Nevo); File 272088/6 Netanya District Rabbinical Court (rabbis Michael Amos, Shneur Pardes and Ariel Yanai) (2011) (published on Nevo).

24 See *Ateret Devora*, n. 4 above, 1:76, 486–90, where R. Lavi argues that even were there appropriate civil legislation empowering courts to award damages in the case of recalcitrance, the award would constitute unlawful coercion since the legislation is clearly designed to compel the spouse to give the *get*.

the case, may properly be considered "one who can lawfully be compelled."

However, as noted earlier, that determination alone is insufficient. "Lawful compulsion" requires that the party actually compelling the husband to act be properly qualified and authorized; the executing body must be "competent to lawfully compel." As we saw above, only a rabbinical court that conducts itself in accordance with the halakha is authorized by Jewish law to execute lawful coercion and compulsion. Thus, in theory, were an authorized rabbinical court to order a husband to pay damages in accordance with Torah law with the intent of coercing him to give a *get*, such compulsion would be legal and the *get* would be valid. This would not be the case, however, if the award for damages emanates from a civil court. From the vantage point of Jewish law, a secular civil court, whose substantive law and procedure accord with secular and not Torah law, cannot qualify as a body "competent to lawfully compel." Even if the civil judges are incidentally Jewish, their halakhic status would be equivalent to that of unauthorized "lay" rabbinical court judges who, like Gentile judges, lack the proper jurisdiction and power to compel a divorce. Hence, any compulsion that the civil court might execute is considered unlawful, rendering the subsequent *get* invalid — notwithstanding the fact that the husband is obligated to give the *get*.[25]

25 See R. Lavi, ibid., 481. For a summary of the various rabbinical views on the status of Jewish secular courts, see Eliav Shochetman, "The halakhic status of Israeli courts" (Hebrew), *Tehumin* 13 (1992/93), 337–70. R. Lavi, 486–90, further argues that although there exists a rabbinical court ruling requiring a *get*, and although legislation in conformity with halakhic requirements empowers courts to award damages in cases of recalcitrance, the secular court damages awarded would nonetheless constitute unlawful coercion. While R. Lavi specifically discusses damage awards issued by secular courts, a careful review of his argument seems to leave no room for distinguishing between such awards made by secular courts and those ordered by rabbinical courts. But cf. R. Solomon Dichovsky, "Monetary enforcement measures against recalcitrant husbands" (Hebrew), *Tehumin* 26 (2006), 173–79, who maintains that if there exists a rabbinical court ruling requiring a *get*, and the rabbinical court itself rules — in accordance with its duly legislated authority — that the husband is required to pay fines until he divorces his wife, such coercion would be lawful and the pursuant *get* valid. Let me add that if R. Dichovsky's view is adopted, then even if the execution and enforcement of the rabbinical court ruling were turned over to another authority (such as the civil court or the governmental collection agency), the *get* would still be valid. In such a case,

## 5 Does cancelation of the tort suit constitute removal of the compulsion?

Let us take this analysis one step further. Let us assume that the wife has filed a tort claim with the civil court, or even that the civil court has already awarded tort damages in favor of the woman, damages that have yet to be collected. At the request of the husband or the rabbinical court, the wife then agrees to cancel her lawsuit or to forego the damages prior to execution of the *get*. Would Jewish law still maintain that the executed *get* is invalid? Here, too, we will address this question by distinguishing between two different situations.

### i When there is no rabbinical court ruling requiring a *get*

If there is no rabbinical court ruling requiring that the husband grant his wife a *get*, one might argue that the *get* is invalid — despite the fact that the actual lawsuit or award has been canceled — as long as there remains a concrete possibility that the woman will renew her tort suit should the husband change his mind and not give the *get*. The very existence of such a possibility can, in and of itself, constitute unlawful compulsion, thus invalidating the *get*.[26]

---

the state authorities would be acting on behalf of the rabbinical court. Regarding such cases, the Mishnah states that "if heathens beat him and tell him, 'Do what the Jews tell you to do,' the *get* is valid" (mGitin 9:8). Accordingly, if the husband refuses to divorce his wife, contrary to a valid halakhic ruling, the rabbinical court may give the wife permission to submit a suit for tort damages to the secular courts in order to force the husband to divorce her, and such a suit will not lead to invalidation of the *get*. See R. Isaac Herzog, *Responsa Heikhal Yitzhak*, EH, 1, #1 (end) and #2, reprinted in *Pesakim Ukhtavim*, EH, 7:157 (end) and 158; and "On concerns about unlawfully compelled divorce" (Hebrew), in R. C. Chavel and R. N. Rabinovitch (eds.), *Collected Essays from HaDarom in the First Decade of its Publication* (Hebrew), (NY: 1966), 42–67. Note, however, that R. Herzog emphasizes that his practical conclusions relate only to the use of reasonable spousal support by the rabbinical courts as a means of encouraging the husband to grant his wife a *get*. See too Warhaftig, n. 10 above, 157–62, and the sources there cited. On the effect of civil court support orders on the validity of a *get*, see *Responsa Igrot Moshe*, EH 1:137 and 4:106 (end); R. Isaac Jacob Weiss, *Responsa Minhat Yitzhak*, 8:137; R. Solomon Moses Amar, *Responsa Shema Shlomo*, 1, EH, 11.

26 See File 54568514–28–1, n. 23 above. See also *Ateret Devora*, n. 4 above, 489–90, which states that this issue is the subject of debate among the halakhic authorities. On threats as coercion, see *Get Meuse*, n. 11 above, 120–30.

However, where it is possible to ensure that after the wife relinquishes her claim and cancels her suit she can no longer sue her husband — even were he to renege on his agreement to grant the *get* — the giving of the *get* by the husband would be considered a freely-willed act, performed without compulsion, and therefore valid. But as long as the threat of a repeated tort action continues to hang over the husband, the *get* is presumably invalid.[27]

### ii When there is a rabbinical court ruling requiring a *get*

If a rabbinical court has already issued an order requiring the husband to grant his wife a *get,* there is a dispute among rabbinical court judges as to whether or not the *get* is valid. Some *dayanim* maintain that since the husband has been ordered by a rabbinical court to give a *get,* the threat of a possible renewed tort suit in the future is not of sufficient force to override the judicial order and invalidate the *get*. Consequently, these rabbis would allow for execution of a *get,* provided that the tort suit and the award for damages have been canceled prior to the actual granting of the *get* by the husband.[28] Others disagree and argue that even though there is a ruling requiring the husband to give a *get,* any threat inconsistent with Jewish law that impacts the husband's free will invalidates the *get*.[29]

27 Consequently, in File 54568514–28–1, the Netanya District Rabbinical Court required that prior to the *get,* the wife's tort claim be dismissed with prejudice. See also *Get Meuse Bearkhaot,* n. 15 above, 47. However, R. Lavi's view in *Tomer Devora* (490) is that since the wife knows that should she reinstate her claim for damages, the rabbinical court will refuse to arrange the *get,* the chances that she will in fact reinstate the civil suit are slim. Therefore, it suffices, in R. Lavi's opinion, for the wife, prior to execution of the *get,* to have her claim dismissed even without prejudice. R. Ariel Yanai, in File 272088/6, n. 23 above, apparently also deems dismissal without prejudice to be sufficient. He adds, though, that should the wife reinstate her tort claim after the *get* is granted, the *get* will retroactively be voided as having been secured under false pretenses.

28 See R. Hashai, File 7041–21–1, n. 23 above; R. Lavi, ibid. This also appears to be the view of R. Avraham Kilav in File 766955–21–1, n. 23 above.

29 See R. Algrabli and R. Izirer, File 7041–21–1, n. 23 above. R. Sheinfeld, File 766955–21–1, n. 23 above, seems to concur, unless the rabbinical court has issued a ruling not merely requiring the husband to give his wife a *get* (*"hiyuv get"*), but authorizing actual compulsion as well (*"kefiat get"*).

In practice, it seems that in both cases, namely, where the rabbinical court has issued a ruling requiring a *get* and where it has not, the *dayanim* approach this issue on a case-by-case basis. The rabbinical court will examine each matter in terms of its own particular facts in order to ascertain whether or not the husband is giving the *get* of his own free will, independent of the possible future threat of a tort suit. Only if the *dayanim* are satisfied that the husband is indeed granting the *get* altogether freely, will the divorce be recognized as halakhically valid.[30]

## 6 Conclusion

The idea of compelling a husband to grant his wife a *get* by means of monetary pressure is not a new one. In fact, rabbinical scholars worldwide have discussed and analyzed the matter in great depth for over eight hundred years. Even the more recent manifestation of this idea, focusing on compensatory tort damages, is not truly new; it was discussed — and rejected — by leading halakhic authorities some twenty-five years ago in connection with legal developments in this area in France.[31] A review of this literature reveals that the rabbis are extremely hesitant to recognize the validity of any *get* granted as a result of such financial pressure.

In 2008, Israel's Supreme Rabbinical Court in Jerusalem issued a lengthy and well-reasoned decision invalidating any *get* given in the wake of a claim for tort damages.[32] Despite criticism from certain quarters, the Court's decision was not at all surprising and, in truth, was to be anticipated from the very onset. I would venture to say that the Court's conclusion was the only conclusion that could be reached by examining the halakhic sources with intellectual honesty.[33]

30 See the concluding instructions of File 7041–21–1, n. 23 above; *Get Meuse*, n. 11 above, 52–54. See also R. David b. Zimra, *Responsa Radbaz*, 4:2095: "And the responsibility falls on the neck of the sage who arranges the *get*, for he knows whether or not the compulsion has been removed or not, and he can sense it for himself."

31 See *Responsa Minhat Yitzhak*, 7:136; R. Samuel Halevi Wosner, *Responsa Shevet Halevi*, 5:210.

32 File 7041–21–1, n. 23 above.

33 See, however, the suggestion of R. David Bass, "*Get* refusal and tort damages" (Hebrew), *Hatzofe*, January 14, 2005, magazine, 11–12. Some of R. Bass's points are reiterated in the article by R. Dichovsky cited in n. 25 above.

The tragedy of the *agunah* deserves the serious attention of Jewish communities around the world, and a sincere attempt to develop effective means with which to address this very troubling phenomenon. Nonetheless, civil tort claims and damage awards issued by secular courts are not, in our opinion, appropriate tools for this task.[34]

34 The author would like to thank his close friend and colleague, R. Judah Freis, for his comments on the substance of the issues treated in this article, their supporting references, and presentation. The author would also like to thank his law partner, Joseph B. Gellman, for helpful editorial suggestions.

*The Jewish Law Annual*, Vol. XIX

# Ruth's Conversion: Then and Now

Bernard S. Jackson*

This article reflects on some legal issues in the Book of Ruth in light of academic and traditional rabbinical analysis, and on a citation of Ruth in a recent case decided by the new Supreme Court of the United Kingdom. While the historical and comparative material may appear somewhat far removed from current politico-halakhic controversies concerning conversion, I would suggest that it alerts us to the conceptual issues underlying these controversies.

Ruth's four-word reply to Naomi is well known: "*Ameikh ami veelohayikh elohai*," rendered in most modern translations as, "Your people will be my people and your God my God."[1] The fact that in Hebrew, this utterance includes no verb, however, may prompt us to consider alternative translations, such as, "Your people **are still** my people and your God my God." Indeed, there is a minority rabbinical tradition that Ruth had already converted when she married.[2]

> R. Pedas asked the son of R. Yosi, man of Soko: Since Ruth converted [when she first married], why did they not give her a new [Jewish] name? He said to him: I received a tradition that she had another name. When she married Mahlon . . . they called her Ruth, for she converted when she

* Professor of Law and Jewish Studies, Liverpool Hope University; Chair, Jewish Law Association.

1 Ruth 1:16. I have consulted 16 modern translations, including ESV, JPS, KJV, NASB, NJB, NIV, RSV; with one exception, they all adopt future tense translations. The one exception is the 19th c. Young's Literal Translation: "Thy people **is** my people, and thy God my God" (emphasis in original). Interestingly, both the LXX and Vulgate render the phrase without a verb, as in the Hebrew.

Note that Ruth 1:16 contains the only instance in the Hebrew Bible of the root from which the term "*agunah*" is derived.

2 I am indebted to R. Shear-Yashuv Cohen for alerting me to the discussion of this issue in the rabbinical sources, and for drawing my attention to the *Yalkut Shimoni* on Ruth, see n. 9 below.

married Mahlon and not afterwards. He responded: But it says ". . . where you lean [your head], so I will lean; where you go, I go; your people is my people and your God is my God!"[3]

The rabbinical commentators assume that any prior conversion, whether before or after Ruth's marriage, must have complied with the traditional halakhic requirements (in this case, immersion in a ritual bath (*mikvah*) and acceptance of the commandments (*mitzvot*),[4] a rabbinical court being, in theory, unnecessary). If Orpah also converted properly, how could Naomi have suggested that her daughters-in-law return to their original idol-worshipping communities?

One answer that has been proposed is that the pre-marital conversions were "conditional" on a later show of sincerity, and were tested precisely by the circumstances of the deaths of the two husbands.[5] This answer avoids the need to speculate about a retrospective annulment of the conversion.

There may, however, be a far simpler answer to the question. In a society where status was still a matter of patrilineal descent, so that marriage to a foreign wife had no effect on the status of children,[6] it was

3 Zohar, Ruth 79a (II, 25b), quoted by R. Meir Levin at http://www.torah.org/learning/ruth/class15.html. In other sources, the deaths of Mahlon and Khilyon are regarded as divine punishment for intermarriage; see bBaba Batra 91b. See also Rashi on Ruth ch.1, who maintains that Ruth did not convert before marriage, and R. Eliezer Waldenberg's remarks in *Responsa Tzitz Eliezer* 17:42.

4 Indeed, Targum Ruth (S.H. Levey translation, http://targum.info/meg/ruth.htm) emphasizes acceptance of the commandments (*kabalat mitzvot*) in its rendering of the conversation between Naomi and Ruth: "But Ruth said, 'Do not coax me to leave you, to turn from following you, for I desire to become a proselyte.' Said Naomi, 'We are commanded to keep the Sabbaths and holidays, not to walk more than two thousand cubits.' Said Ruth, 'Wheresoever you go I shall go.' Said Naomi: 'We are commanded not to spend the night together with non-Jews.' Said Ruth, 'Wherever you lodge I shall lodge.' Said Naomi: 'We are commanded to keep six hundred thirteen commandments.' Said Ruth, 'That which your people keep, that I shall keep, as though they had been my people before this.' Said Naomi, 'We are commanded not to worship idolatry.' Said Ruth, 'Your God is my God.'" Cf. bJebamot 47b, where this verse is R. Eleazar's prooftext that "He [a prospective convert] is not to be persuaded or dissuaded too much."

5 R. Levin, n. 3 above, quoting R. Moses Shternbuch, *Moadim Uzmanim* 4, 316.

6 In which case there would also be no distinction between descent from priests and others.

assumed that an incoming foreign woman simply adopted the domestic religion of the household,[7] certainly when the marriage was patrilocal.[8] In this period, conversion was, like many other aspects of family law, "weakly institutionalized."[9] Like marriage and divorce, it was very much a matter of coming and going. Indeed, Ruth's language, whether she confirmed that "your people *are still* my people and your God my God" or that "your people *will be* my people and your God my God," emphasizes the nature of the adherence represented by this early form of "conversion" — it is adherence to people (here, a particular family) and their domestic cult, rather than to theological dogma or a comprehensive system of religious law. Obviously, the story of Ruth takes place after the giving of the Torah, and the Torah's directives should therefore be in force. However, the Book of Judges stresses that at this time, "there was no king in Israel and everyone did what he thought was right in his own eyes" (Judges 17:6, 21:25).[10]

A different legal problem in the Book of Ruth has attracted far more interest from modern biblical scholars, in large part because of its relationship to the Levirate law in Deuteronomy.[11] The relationship

7 That this is not explicitly regulated is consistent with biblical law's greater interest in "vertical" rather than "horizontal" relationships within the family; see my "Gender critical observations on tripartite breeding relationships in the Hebrew Bible," in D. Rooke (ed.) *A Question of Sex?: Gender and Difference in the Hebrew Bible and Beyond* (Sheffield UK: 2007), 39–52.

8 Interesting questions arise in matrilocal marriages, such as those of Jacob to Rachel and Leah. One such question concerns Rachel's motivation for stealing her father's *terafim* when leaving his household (Gen. 31:19). The traditional interpretation, namely, that she did so to wean her father from idolatry, presupposes that Rachel and Leah adhered to the religion of Jacob's household, notwithstanding that this was a matrilocal marriage.

9 See B. Jackson, "The 'institutions' of marriage and divorce in the Hebrew Bible," in G. Brooke and C. Nihan (eds.), *Studies in Biblical Law and its Reception* (Oxford: 2010). In this context, see the remark by R. Abbahu in *Yalkut Shimoni* on Ruth, §701: "Come and see how beloved are converts to the Holy One, Blessed be He. As soon as she [Ruth] made the decision to convert, Scripture compared her to Naomi, as it is written: 'So the two went until they came to Bethlehem' (Ruth 1:19)."

10 Cf. Judges 18:1.

11 I am preparing a full analysis of this issue in light of the modern literature. My initial observations on the problem can be found in my review of Bernard M. Levinson, *Legal Revision and Religious Renewal in Ancient Israel* (Cambridge and New York: 2008), in *Journal of Hebrew Scriptures* 10 (2010),

between the Levirate process described in Ruth and that mandated in the Bible is considered problematic, because Ruth appears to conflate the (Deuteronomic) Levirate law with the (Levitical) laws of redemption of land. Furthermore, in the *halitzah* ceremony described in Deuteronomy, it is the woman who removes the man's shoe, whereas in the Book of Ruth it appears to be the redeemer who removes his own shoe. Indeed, some suggest that the Book of Ruth itself attempts, anachronistically, to explain the apparent anomaly:

> Thus formerly it was done in Israel in cases of redemption and exchange: to validate any transaction, one man would take off his sandal and hand it to the other. This was the practice in Israel. (Ruth 4:7)

Thus the legal details in the Book of Ruth are often attributed to post-exilic confusion.[12]

Rather than deconstructing the Book of Ruth in light of the pentateuchal passages, I suggest that we reverse the process, and reconstruct our understanding of the Deuteronomic law in light of the information supplied by the author of Ruth. The key to understanding the matter lies in our interpretation of the verse describing removal of the shoe: "So the near kinsman said unto Boaz: 'Buy it for yourself.' And he drew off his shoe" (Ruth 4:8). Who removed whose shoe? This question interested the early rabbinical commentators far more than modern Bible scholars.[13] These commentators clarified that although the beginning of the verse quotes the rejecting redeemer, the subject of the second clause is Boaz, for it is he who, in terms of the previous verse, is performing the redemption that requires validation. This is one opinion cited in the Talmud,[14] as well as the view of the Targum Ruth: "When the redeemer said to Boaz, 'Put forth your hand for the act of acquisition, and buy it yourself,' Boaz took off his glove and made the purchase."[15]

---

online at http://www.arts.ualberta.ca/JHS/reviews/reviews_new/review454.htm.

12 The general *tendenz* is apparently opposition to Ezra's reforms of family law.

13 Honorable exceptions are E.F. Campbell, *Ruth* [Anchor Bible] (Garden City NY: 1975), 149–50, citing Targum Ruth and Ruth Rabbah, ad loc.; Y. Zakovitch, *Ruth: Introduction and Commentary* (Hebrew) [Mikra Leyisrael], (Tel Aviv: 1990), 108, also citing bBaba Metzia 47a.

14 bBaba Metzia 47a.

15 Levey translation, n. 4 above. Ruth Rabbah 7:12 debates the related (but not identical) question of **whose** sandal was removed.

What did Boaz redeem? Both the widow, Ruth, and the land of her deceased husband.[16] Although the Levirate law explicitly commands only that the man take the widow as a wife, the purpose of the Levirate law is to ensure that "that his [the deceased's] name may not be blotted out of Israel" (Deut. 25:6). This language is very similar to that of the plea of the daughters of Zelophehad: "Why should the name of our father be taken away from his family, because he had no son?" (Num. 27:4) and that context clearly refers to succession to a portion of the promised land.[17]

This perspective generates a better understanding of the *halitzah* ceremony. In the situation described in Deuteronomy, a brother who is qualified to carry out Levirate marriage (*yibum*) stands in the position of a Levirate redeemer (*goel*). But he refuses, and — in contrast to the situation in the Book of Ruth — there is apparently no one to take his place. Had he indeed carried out the Levirate marriage, we may infer from Ruth 4:7 that he would have done so by taking off his own sandal. Because he refuses to do so and there is no one else to take his place, he has violated the law. The humiliation that he must endure as a punishment is thus doubly talionic: first, the woman spits[18] (representing the **absence** of semen), and second, the sandal that he ought to have

16 Cf. David Daube's brilliant account of the interplay, in the trick played by Boaz on the kinsman, of the Levirate law and land redemption. According to Daube, Boaz led the redeemer to assume that the woman he was to marry in order to redeem the estate was Naomi, who would not be able to provide more than a single son, and that son would stand in the place of Avimelekh. When the redeemer refused and Boaz took his place, Boaz revealed that the Levirate widow was in fact Ruth (whom Naomi had set up to be an ersatz widow of Elimelekh to persuade Boaz, who had himself been reluctant initially, thinking that the woman he had to redeem was Naomi). See D. Daube, *Ancient Jewish Law* (Leiden: 1981), 37–43, reprinted in idem, *New Testament Judaism: Collected Works of David Daube*, edited by Calum Carmichael, vol. 2 (Berkeley: 2000), 492–99; cf. idem, *The Deed and the Doer in the Bible: David Daube's Gifford Lectures*, edited by C. Carmichael, vol. 1 (West Conshohocken PA: 2008), 204–47.

17 Zelophehad's family situation is already mentioned in the census in Numbers 26:33; that census was connected to distribution of the land.

18 On the spitting, see D. Daube, "The culture of Deuteronomy," *Orita: Ibadan Journal of Religious Studies* 3 (1969), 27–52, reprinted in idem, *Biblical Law and Literature: Collected Works of David Daube*, edited by Calum Carmichael, vol. 3 (Berkeley: 2003), 995–1013, especially 1001–1003.

removed to acquire the widow (and the property) is removed by the woman he has slighted.[19]

Thus, the narrative in Ruth complements rather than deviates from pentateuchal law. Both are concerned with the linked issues of widowhood and the descent of family property[20]; both entail redemption (or its absence); and both presuppose a signification of acquisition through removal of the acquirer's sandal.

~ ~ ~ ~ ~ ~ ~ ~

Ruth's declaration made a strange reappearance in twenty-first century legal history. The new Supreme Court of the United Kingdom has ruled that a Jewish school's use of the halakhic definition of a Jew in its admission criteria constitutes illegal discrimination on the grounds of ethnic origins under the Race Relations Act.[21] The case revolved around a question of conversion: the Jews Free School (JFS), a state-aided Jewish day school, had rejected a boy who was born to an Italian Catholic mother who had converted to Judaism under Masorti auspices before the boy's birth. The school had followed the guidelines set down by the Chief Rabbi, who does not accept Masorti conversion as valid; the boy was thus considered born to a non-Jewish mother.

The Race Relations Act 1976 (as amended), s.1, reads, "A person discriminates against another . . . if — (a) on racial grounds he treats that other less favourably than he treats or would treat other persons." "Racial grounds" is defined as including "colour, race, nationality, or ethnic or national origins." By a majority of 5 to 4, the Supreme Court maintained that the boy was excluded on the grounds of his ethnic

19 Note that the Levirate law appears in Deuteronomy immediately before an explicitly talionic rule — Deuteronomy 25:11–12.

20 Numbers 36 similarly seeks to ensure that succession by daughters does not result in alienation of property from the tribe.

21 R (on the application of E) *v.* Governing Body of JFS and the Admissions Appeal Panel of JFS and others, [2009] UKSC 15, [2009] EWCA Civ 626. On the first instance decision (in favor of the school), see Anat Scolnicov, "A question of faith," 69 *Cambridge Law Journal* (2010), 220–23. The complete texts of the Supreme Court judgment are available at www.supremecourt.gov.uk/docs/uksc_2009_0105_judgmentV2.pdf. For a fuller account of the case, see Frank Cranmer, "Who is a Jew? Jewish faith schools and the Race Relations Act 1976," 164 *Law & Justice* (2010), and my "Jewish law and state law: some comparative perspectives from England," in the forthcoming Fordham Conference Volume (provisionally: *Jewish Law Association Studies* 22).

origins,[22] notwithstanding the fact that the immediate issue was the criteria for conversion.[23]

Delivering the leading judgment for the majority, Lord Phillips[24] quoted an essay on conversion published a few years earlier (in an unrelated context), in which he wrote:

> What is conversion? People often refer to the case of Ruth the Moabite. It is from Ruth's reply to her mother-in-law Naomi that the basic principles of conversion are derived. She said: "Where you go, I will go. Where you stay, I will stay. Your people will be my people, and your God my God." That last sentence — a mere four words in Hebrew — defines the dual nature of conversion to this day. The first element is an identification with the Jewish people and its fate ("Your people will be my people"). The second is the embrace of a religious destiny, the covenant between Israel and God and its commands ("Your God will be my God").

Of course, Lord Phillips was unaware of the fact that this source is aggadic and not halakhic. Moreover, it long precedes the classical halakhic development of conversion (*gerut*),[25] so that the "ethnic" or "identificational" (sociological) aspect of conversion has since become completely separate from the halakhic, and plays no part in it, despite the attitudes voiced in certain ultra-Orthodox (haredi) circles.

Against this, in the minority opinion supporting the school, Lord Rodger[26] argued as follows:

22 Against the view that the grounds for discrimination were religious rather than ethnic, the majority, following the Court of Appeal, distinguished between "grounds" and "motives."

23 Against the view of Lady Hale that the admission was rejected because the boy's mother's ethnic origins were Italian Catholic, Lord Rodger remarked, "His mother could have been as Italian in origin as Sophia Loren and as Roman Catholic as the Pope for all that the governors cared. The only thing that mattered was that she had not converted to Judaism under Orthodox auspices."

24 Lord Phillips is quoted as saying that his mother's parents "were Sephardic Jews and had eloped to this country from Alexandria because they understood that England was a country in which they would enjoy freedom." See http://thejc.com/lifestyle/how-jewish-is/how-jewish-lord-chief-justice-phillips.

25 Notwithstanding its use as a prooftext in bJebamot 47b: see n. 4 above.

26 Alan Rodger was, like the present writer, a doctoral student at Oxford under David Daube. Though not Jewish, and a student of Roman rather than Jewish law, his close connection with Daube undoubtedly provided him with the halakhic sensitivity manifest in his judgment in this case.

> From the standpoint of Orthodoxy, no other policy would make sense. This is because, in its eyes, irrespective of whether they adhere to Orthodox, Masorti, Progressive, or Liberal Judaism, or are not in any way believing or observant, these are the children — and the only children — who are bound by the Jewish law and practices which, it is hoped, they will absorb at the School and then observe throughout their lives. Whether they will actually do so is, of course, a different matter.

So much for conversion as viewed in English law.[27] The case has, however, prompted much internal debate within the Jewish community, and not only on denominational grounds (where it may be possible to argue that the underlying conception of conversion among some of the non-Orthodox denominations is closer to that of the Book of Ruth than to the halakhic conception). Although there are haredi schools in the UK, the school in question is mainstream Orthodox, and welcomes children from non-observant (and even atheistic) homes, provided they are halakhically Jewish. Indeed, it has traditionally applied a "first come, first served" policy, which has resulted in some observant children being excluded in favor of non-observant children. The school's underlying philosophy, which does not necessarily reflect the motives of the parents in sending their children there, is that of outreach (*kiruv*). It seems apparent that, in rejecting this particular student, the school was not discriminating against those who accept non-Orthodox standards, but rather applying the established criteria of Jewish identity to determine eligibility for the school's educational services. Against this, it could be argued that the scope for outreach (and even Orthodox conversion, when necessary and desired) may be greater among committed members of non-Orthodox families. Furthermore, admission to the school constitutes no certification of halakhic status, and there is no halakhic objection to teaching such "non-Jewish" children alongside Jewish children.

The effect of all this has been to require Jewish schools in the UK to introduce "religious practice" tests rather than apply the halakhic criteria of Jewish identity. This has already resulted in the exclusion of one halakhically-Jewish child from a school that cannot fill its places with Jewish children. Nor is it clear that all kinds of religious practice tests will avoid the restrictions of the Race Relations Act, which applies

27 On this matter's relationship to issues of transformative accommodation, see my "'Transformative accommodation' and religious law," 11 *Ecclesiastical Law Journal* (2009), 131–53 and "Jewish approaches to law (religious and secular)," 164 *Law & Justice* (2010), 63–74.

a concept of indirect as well as direct discrimination.[28] Moreover, the ambit of "religious practice," and its relationship to trends in Diaspora Jewry, also raises concerns. There is clearly cause for concern in Israel as well, as is attested by the recent furor over the school in Emmanuel.[29]

28 One mainstream Orthodox school, the King David High School in Manchester, has rejected any religious practice test as overly intrusive, and now admits students on the basis of Orthodox synagogue membership of mother and child. Accordingly, it has offered a place to a child rejected by the King David High School in Liverpool for failure to fulfil the religious practice test (provision of rabbinical certification of synagogue attendance). See *Jewish Chronicle*, July 23, 2010 (http://thejc.com/news/uk-news/36095/liverpool-mum-joins-shul-school-place). However, since the criteria for membership in an Orthodox synagogue are themselves those of the halakhic definition of a Jew, the school may be liable to action on the basis of **indirect** discrimination. Here, however, there is a possible defense on the grounds that the discrimination is "a proportionate means of achieving a legitimate end" (as discussed in the Supreme Court judgments).

29 A version of this paper was delivered at the opening session of the Jewish Law Association's 16th Biennial Conference, held at the Netanya Academic College June 21–24, 2010.

*The Jewish Law Annual*, Vol. XIX

# The End of Life in Jewish Law

Alfredo Mordechai Rabello*

## 1 Introduction

The development of modern medical technologies has made bioethics a much discussed area of Jewish law. In fact, this aspect of halakha in particular has exerted great influence on the rulings of Israeli's Supreme Court,[1] especially in contexts that are not explicitly covered by Israeli law.[2]

Religious law in general must confront the apparent conflict between the responsibility to help others and the view that illness is an act of God, and Jewish law is no exception. The Midrash relates how R. Akiva, one of the Tannaitic Sages, provided a sick man with the name of a doctor and wished him a speedy recovery. A farmer who witnessed the encounter was amazed by R. Akiva's attitude, considering it contrary to the will of God, who had presumably sent the illness as a punishment. R. Akiva explained that he, in turn, was surprised that the farmer was carrying a hoe on his shoulders: after all, if God so desired, the earth would bring forth its produce without any intervention on the part of the farmer! R. Akiva explains that man must take part in the divine work of creation, and that the Bible itself establishes that doctors have an obligation to heal the sick.[3]

* Alfredo Mordechai Rabello is an emeritus professor at the Hebrew University of Jerusalem, and teaches at Zefat Academic College and at the University of Milan (Goren Goldstein Foundation).

1 See, e.g., C.A. 88/506, *Yael Shefer v. State of Israel*, PD 48(1), 87–199 (1994), authored by Justice Menachem Elon. See also Y.M. Bar Ilan, "Revisiting the problem of Jewish bioethics: the case of terminal care," *Kennedy Institute of Ethics Journal* 13:2 (2003), 141ff.

2 See Article 1 of Israel's *Foundations of Law Act, 5740–1980*: "Where the court, faced with a legal question requiring decision, finds no answer to it in statute law or case-law or by analogy, it shall decide it in the light of the principles of freedom, justice, equity and peace of Israel's heritage."

3 Midrash Shmuel, 4; Midrash Temura, 2, quoted in *Sefer Hapardes*; cf. C. Kahn's introduction to A. Steinberg (ed.), *Sefer Assia* 2 (1981), 5;

The verse cited by R. Akiva, "he shall cause him to be thoroughly healed" (Exod. 21:19), is traditionally understood as more than simply a general dispensation for doctors to intervene, as it were, in the work of God. Rather, it establishes a duty for physicians to cure the sick, or at the very least alleviate their pain. The verse has also been interpreted as commanding the physician to cure and do nothing else — a doctor is not permitted to voluntarily take the life of another human being.[4]

Having established the physician's authority, and responsibility, to engage in healing, Jewish law must confront bioethical questions that arise in the course of healing patients. Many of these issues are relevant to the inception and conclusion of human life.[5] As we will see, the guiding principle of Jewish law in this context is that "man must always direct his heart and all his actions solely toward knowledge of God, blessed be He."[6]

## 2 Preserving life

The halakhic approach to treating terminal patients is based on Judaism's foundational "sanctity of human life" principle.[7] The Bible

M. Halperin, "Modern perspectives on medical halacha," in *Assia — Jewish Medical Ethics* 1 (1989), 17, available at http://medethics.org.il/articles/JME/JMEB1/JMEB1.9.asp. The English-language journal *Assia — Jewish Medical Ethics*, edited by M. Halperin, covers the interface between halakha and medicine, and often features important articles on scientific and medical issues.

In Jewish law, the legal dimension is inextricably linked to the moral and religious domains; see A. Lichtenstein, "Does Jewish tradition recognize an ethic independent of halakhah?" in M. Kellner (ed.), *Contemporary Jewish Ethics* (NY: 1978), 102ff.; D. Sinclair, "Law and morality in halakhic bioethics," in B. Jackson (ed.), *Jewish Law Association Studies* 2 (Atlanta: 1986), 143ff.

4 See S. Goren, "The physician's responsibility for the life of his patient" (Hebrew), 7 *Dine Israel* (1976), 13ff.

5 See J.D. Bleich, "Ethico-halakhic considerations in the practice of medicine," 7 *Dine Israel* (1976), 87ff.; I. Jakobovits, *Jewish Medical Ethics* (NY: 1959). See also A. Steinberg, *Encyclopedia of Jewish Medical Ethics* (Jerusalem: 2003).

6 Maimonides, *Code*, Laws concerning Ethics 3:2.

7 On this principle, see M. Tendler and F. Rosner, "Quality and sanctity of life in the Talmud and in the Midrash," *Tradition* 28 (1993), 18ff. For a discussion of issues arising from adherence to this principle during the Holocaust, see I. Rosenbaum, *The Holocaust and the Halakha* (NY: 1976);

stresses that man was created in the "image of God," and it is this attitude that underlies the original prohibition against taking the life of another person: "And surely your blood of your lives will I require; at the hand of every beast will I require it.... Whoever sheds man's blood, by man shall his blood be shed; for in the image of God made He man" (Gen. 9:5–6.)[8] While this prohibition predates the revelation at Sinai and is considered one of the seven Noahide commandments, the value of human life is, of course, reiterated in the Ten Commandments: "Thou shalt not murder" (Exod. 20:13).

According to this moral conception, the principle of the sanctity of life would seem to be virtually unlimited; no person's life is more or less valuable than another's, as every person was created in the image of God. It would thus be impossible to assign specific valuations to the lives of, say, a great scientist, a newborn child, and a patient with only a few more hours to live, respectively.

Yet though Jewish law ascribes great value to human life, it is not an absolute value; other important values may, in fact, override it. In most cases, the Talmud teaches, a Jew is instructed to violate a commandment in order to preserve his life or that of someone else, as indicated by the verse, "And live by them."[9] But a Jew is to forfeit his life rather than violate the three cardinal precepts, which prohibit murder, adultery, and idolatry.[10] Moreover, despite the danger to life, there is a duty to go to war, as well as a duty to sacrifice one's life to sanctify the Divine Name.

Thus, although the sanctity and preservation of human life is clearly a halakhic value, there are other values that override it.[11] This gives rise to various bioethical dilemmas. Could consideration of a

---

E. Ben-Zimra, "Halakhic decisions relating to the sanctity of life and martyrdom in the Holocaust period" (Hebrew), *Sinai* 80 (1977), 151ff.; R. I.M. Lau, *Responsa Yahel Yisrael*, #55, 81.

8 The literal translation of the verse is "whoever sheds the blood of man in man," and has also been interpreted as prohibiting abortion — the killing of man "in" man.

9 Leviticus 18:5; Ezekiel 20:11, 13, 21; see also R. Ovadia Yosef, *Responsa Yabia Omer*, YD 13.

10 See bPesahim 25b; bSanhedrin 56a; jHagiga 76:3; Maimonides, *Book of Precepts*, negative precept 63; R. Joseph Caro, *Beit Yosef*, EH 178:19.

11 See A. Steinberg, "The terminally ill: secular and Jewish ethical aspects," *Israel Journal of Medical Science* 30 (1994), 130ff.; idem, "Report of the Public Committee on the Terminally Ill Patient" (Hebrew), *Assia* 69–70 (2002),

patient's suffering override the duty to preserve and extend life? If so, what is the threshold for such suffering?[12] Must life be preserved at all costs and risks? Is it preferable for a patient to undergo an operation that will endanger his life, but may also enable him to live longer, if he otherwise will live for only a short time?[13]

These questions have become particularly acute in the contemporary era, with the invention of medical technology that enables doctors to preserve human life far longer than was previously possible. Until relatively recently, most people died within a few days, and in their own homes. Today, many people die in hospitals, generally connected to machines that extend life, and after prolonged suffering. Modern doctors are faced with the dilemma of choosing between the principle of the sanctity of life and the duty to alleviate their patients' suffering.

For example, if a patient's kidneys are not functioning properly and he has such difficulty breathing that even an oxygen mask is unable to help him, must the doctor connect him to an artificial respirator so that he will be able to live for a few days or weeks?[14] Is it permissible to refrain from connecting him to the machine? Might it be forbidden to connect him, as it will extend his suffering? Once the

---

5–23; idem, "The halakhic basis of the draft *'Terminally Ill Patient'* law" (Hebrew), *Assia* 71–72 (2003), 25ff.; O. Navot, "The concept of sanctity of human life as a fundamental principle of modern medicine in Israel" (Hebrew), ibid., 40ff.

12 See R. M. Feinstein, "Withholding therapy from a terminally ill and suffering patient" (Hebrew), *Halachah Urefuah* 4 (1985), 102ff.; A. Steinberg, "A comparative moral approach to suicide: a Jewish perspective" (Hebrew), *Israel Journal of Medical Science* 23 (1987), 850ff.; M. Weinberger, "Intense suffering in relation to medical decisions" (Hebrew), in M. Halperin (ed.), *Emek Halakha — Assia*, vol. 1 (Jerusalem: 1985), 53ff.

13 See R. M. Feinstein, "Sacrificing *hayei shaa* for potential life-extending therapy *(hayei olam)*," (Hebrew), *Halachah Urefuah* 1 (1980), 131ff.

14 See, e.g., J.D. Bleich, "Treatment of the terminally ill," *Tradition* 30 (1996), 51ff.; C.D. Halevi, "Disconnecting a terminal patient from artificial respiration" (Hebrew), *Tehumin* 2 (1981), 304ff.; *Responsa Yahel Yisrael*, #81; D. Sinclair, "The interaction between law and morality in Jewish law in the areas of feticide and the terminally ill individual," 11 *Criminal Justice Ethics* (1992), 76ff.; idem, *Tradition and the Biological Revolution: The Application of Jewish Law and the Treatment of the Critically Ill* (Edinburgh: 1989). See also A.S. Abraham, *The Comprehensive Guide to Medical Halachah* (Jerusalem-NY: 1996), 190ff.

patient is connected to the machine, may the doctors disconnect him, thereby causing his death?

The Bible explicitly commands, "Neither shall you stand idly by the blood of your neighbor" (Lev. 19:16) — and the Talmud[15] and Maimonides[16] accordingly rule that one must do his utmost to save a dying person, even if he has only a few hours left to live. Since another person's life does not belong to us, we may never countenance shortening it, even when that person is close to death; we may not assign relative worth to human life under various circumstances.[17] It is thus forbidden to perform any act that may precipitate death, even if the patient is in agony, even if there is no hope of saving his life, and even if the request comes from the patient himself.[18] A doctor must not act directly to bring death about, nor must he suggest to the patient ways in which he could take his own life.

There is a distinction, however, between actively causing death and failing to extend life. As King Solomon proclaimed in his wisdom, "There is a time to be born and a time to die."[19] Jewish law concurs, establishing that there are situations in which it is prohibited to extend the life of a terminal patient,[20] and others in which it is permitted, or even considered a duty, to remove external impediments to death (*lehasir et hamoneia*).[21] Thus, if a woodcutter's rhythmical chopping prevents someone from dying in peace, the woodcutter should be

15 bSanhedrin 63a.

16 Maimonides, *Code*, Laws concerning the Sabbath 2:18.

17 Jakobovits, n. 5 above, 152.

18 On the problem of patient autonomy, see R. M. Feinstein, "Coercive treatment against a patient's will," *Halachah Urefuah* 4 (1985), 111ff.; Z. Schostak, "Is there patient autonomy in halacha?" in *Assia — Jewish Medical Ethics* 2 (1995), 22ff.; D. Shatz, "Concepts of autonomy in Jewish medical ethics," 12 *Jewish Law Annual* (1997), 3ff.; D. Sinclair, "Patient's autonomy: the right to choose" *Le'eyla* (Sept. 1994), 15ff.; idem, "Patient autonomy in modern Jewish law" in Y. Dinstein and F. Domb (eds.), *Israel Yearbook on Human Rights* 29 (2000), 35ff.; A. Steinberg, "Informed consent: ethical and halakhic considerations," 12 *Jewish Law Annual* (1997), 137ff. See also A. Carmi (ed.), *Informed Consent* (Haifa: 2003). D. Sinclair (ed.), 15 *Jewish Law Association Studies* (2005), Jewish Biomedical Law, section D, Coercive Life-saving Medical Therapy and Patient Autonomy, examines *Yosef Kurtam v. State of Israel*, and assesses Israel's *Patients' Rights Law, 5756–1996*, §15(2)e.

19 Ecclesiastes 3:2; see *Responsa Tzitz Eliezer* 13:89, 14:80.

20 See *Sefer Hasidim*, para. 234.

21 See, e.g., *Responsa Tzitz Eliezer* 14:80–81 and Justice Elon's decision in the *Shefer* case, n. 1 above, 63ff. ("Passive euthanasia") and 91ff.

asked to leave the vicinity.[22] Similarly, one need not place salt on the tongue of a sick person, a once-common practice thought to prevent demise, and one may remove salt that has already been placed on the tongue. On the other hand, if one who is dying says that he is unable to die unless he is moved elsewhere, he must not be moved. While removal of external factors preventing death is permissible, actively enabling death is not.

## 3 The moment of death

Death is defined as the irreversible absence of life. From a biological point of view, death is generally a process in which the cells, tissues, and organs die — at different stages, depending on their sensitivity — from lack of oxygen and energy supply.

The exact moment of death is a social, philosophical, legal, and religious construct. Some determinations establish a person's death on the basis of formal standards, even if some parts of the body may continue to be "alive."[23] Hence there are a number of different definitions of death: 1. death of all cells in the body (biological death); 2. absolute and irreversible loss of all cardiac activity, blood circulation, and respiratory activity (cardiopulmonary death); 3. absolute, complete, and irreversible loss of all cerebral activity, including that of the cerebral cortex (brain death).

Until recently, it was assumed that a death could be certified the moment respiratory and cardiac activity ceased. Over the past few decades, scientific and technological advances in medical science have changed the way the medical establishment determines the moment of death. As a result of improved means of reanimation, artificial respiratory and cardiac activity can be maintained for an extended period, enabling time to elapse between the absence of independent breathing and regular cardiac activity, and actual cessation of breathing and heartbeat. Moreover, new surgical technologies have made tremendous strides in saving human lives through organ transplants, but organ

22 *Sefer Hasidim*, para. 723.

23 For an overview, see "Moment of death" in *Encyclopedia*, n. 5 above, 6:18ff. See too the articles on "Ascertainment of the state of death in relation to organ transplantation" in *Sefer Assia* 7 (1993), 123–238; M. Halperin (ed.), *Establishing the Moment of Death* (Hebrew), (Jerusalem: 2007).

harvesting is only possible when the heart is beating, at least artificially. In the 1960's, doctors first defined the concept of "brain death," a situation in which it is verified that all cerebral activity, including independent respiration, has ceased irreversibly, notwithstanding the continuation of cardiac activity and blood circulation.[24]

The position of Jewish law with regard to determining the moment of death is complex and subject to debate. While sources in the Mishnah and the Talmud indirectly identify the elements relevant to establishing the moment of death,[25] the first halakhic definition of death was articulated in 1837 by R. Moses Sofer, the Hatam Sofer: "One who is reduced to the state of a silent stone, with no heartbeat: if breathing then stops — our holy Torah teaches that he is dead."[26] This

24 In Israel, the first regulations concerning brain death date back to a circular issued by the director-general of the Ministry of Health in 1969.

25 See bYoma 85a: "'If a building falls down' [and someone is found in the debris] — Our Rabbis taught: How far does one examine [him]? Up to his nose. Some say: Up to his heart. . . . Should we say that these Tannaim are engaged in the same dispute as the following Tannaim, for it was taught: From what place does formation of the embryo begin? From its head. . . . Abba Shaul says: From the navel, which sends out its limbs in every direction. You may even say that [the first view is in agreement with that of] Abba Shaul, for Abba Shaul holds his view only with regard to formation [of the embryo], because everything is formed from its middle, but regarding the saving of life even Abba Shaul would agree that the essential life force [manifests itself] through the nostrils, as it is written, 'All in whose nostrils was the breath of the spirit of life' (Gen. 7:22). R. Papa said: The dispute is only [if the victim is uncovered] from below upwards. But if [the victim is uncovered] from above downwards, then since he has been examined as far as the nostrils, one need not examine any further, as it is said, 'All in whose nostrils was the breath of the spirit of life'"; see the commentaries of Rashi and the Meiri ad loc. See also bJebamot 120a; jYoma 8:5; mOhalot 1:6 and the Gra's commentary thereon; Maimonides, *Code*, Laws concerning Corpse Uncleanliness 1:15. See also M. Halperin, "Is heart transplantation authorized by the halakha?" (Hebrew), *Sefer Assia* 5 (Jerusalem: 1986), 55ff., especially 63ff.; "Moment," n. 23 above, 30ff.; Sinclair 2005, n. 18 above, section E, The Definition of Death and Cardiac Transplants, examines *Belker v. State of Israel*, a seminal case. And see http://text.rcarabbis.org/the-brain-death-debate-a-methodological-analysis-part-1-yoma-passage-by-daniel-reifman.

26 *Responsa Hatam Sofer*, YD 338. The Hatam Sofer emphasizes that burial should take place soon after this point, as Jewish law demands that there be no unnecessary delay in burial.

statement has been interpreted as referring to three elements that must be present to establish death — a deep coma ("reduced to the state of a silent stone"), absence of cardiac activity and blood circulation ("with no heartbeat"), and absence of respiration ("breathing then stops"). According to this interpretation, the Hatam Sofer's definition is based on the clinical indications of death accepted in his day, namely, cardiopulmonary death.[27]

Others interpret the Hatam Sofer's ruling as implying that there is only one necessary condition that establishes death — the absence of breathing. On this reading, the other two elements are simply indicators of the irreversibility of the absence of breathing. Hence on this reading of the Hatam Sofer's definition, someone can be declared dead even if some of his organs are still alive. Halakhic decisors remain divided, however, as to which organ's death is sufficient to establish death.

R. Moses Feinstein notes that traditional sources considered breathing to be the element that determines whether one is alive or dead, hence the moment of death is established by the absence of independent respiration, even if there is still cardiac activity, as long as it is clear that the situation is absolute and irreversible.[28] Since it is possible that the absence of breathing is only temporary, obtaining a doctor's opinion is, according to this view, essential, as only a doctor can determine that respiration has ceased or that cerebral activity, which controls respiratory activity, has completely ceased. On this view, the brain is not the determining factor in and of itself, but only insofar as it controls respiration.

R. Eliezer Waldenberg maintains that it is necessary for both breathing and cardiac activity to cease.[29] Until the heart stops beating, it is necessary to continue trying to heal a sick person, or at least not

27 A. Steinberg, "Establishing the point of death with reference to heart transplantation" (Hebrew), *Sefer Assia* 7 (1993), 209ff.; idem, "Organ transplantation and definition of the moment of death — Jewish perspectives," available at http://www.hods.org.

28 *Responsa Igrot Moshe*, YD 2:174. The Commission on Transplants appointed by Israel's Chief Rabbinate also based itself on the Hatam Sofer's ruling, proposing that, "death is halakhically established by the cessation of respiration." See Halperin, n. 3 above. On the Israeli Rabbinate's decision, see section 4 below.

29 *Responsa Tzitz Eliezer* 9:46; see also other decisors quoted in "Moment," n. 23 above, 39 n. 86.

to alter his situation.[30] R. Solomon Zalman Auerbach maintains that the complete death of the brain, in all its parts and cells, is the necessary indicator of death.[31]

R. Joseph Shalom Eliashiv rules that in light of these criteria, it is forbidden to disconnect a patient from an artificial respirator.[32] R. Auerbach, however, maintains that the respirator is comparable to an object that is preventing a sick person from dying, and thus the patient may be disconnected. Once he is no longer ventilated, the patient's heart will stop beating after several minutes. In the meantime, however, it is forbidden to carry out any activity that will precipitate the death of the patient, such as extracting an organ for transplantation.[33] R. Moses Feinstein and R. Isaac Weiss rule that it would similarly be forbidden to extend the life of a terminal patient so as to be able to use his organs for transplantation.[34]

Other authorities maintain that death can be established simply by ascertaining that blood circulation has ceased, as the connection between blood and life (and lack of blood and loss of life) appears in biblical sources. Similarly, lack of blood flow to the organs that the Sages considered vital for life — the heart, brain, and liver[35] — is a sufficient indication of death, even though blood may continue to flow in other organs.[36]

## 4 Position of the Israeli Rabbinate

In 1985, Prof. Dan Michaeli, director-general of Israel's Ministry of Health, requested that Israel's Chief Rabbinate formulate its position on determination of the moment of death in relation to the problem of

30 On the definition of a sick person, see Abraham, n. 14 above, 19ff. Abraham upholds R. Waldenberg's definition of death: "Death is established only when spontaneous respiration, heartbeat and brain function have all ceased" (191).

31 See "Moment," n. 23 above, 39ff.

32 Ibid.

33 Ibid., 40 n. 88.

34 *Responsa Igrot Moshe,* YD 2:174; *Responsa Minhat Yitzhak* 5:8. See also "Organ transplantation," *Encyclopedia,* n. 5 above, 2:223 n. 87.

35 Maimonides, *Code,* Laws concerning Valuations and Things Votive 2:1, referring to organs without which one cannot live.

36 This is the opinion of R. Hershel Schachter, "Determining the time of death," *Journal of Halacha and Contemporary Society* 17 (1989), 32ff.; objections to this view are voiced in "Moment," n. 23 above, 40 n. 90.

heart transplantation: Given that it is more a religious problem more than a medical one, was it possible, from the halakhic perspective, to consider death of the brain's respiratory center to be equivalent to death of the entire body? The Rabbinate appointed a commission of rabbis and doctors, and consulted experts in the fields of neurology, anesthesia, surgery, cardiology, transplants, and neurophysiology, publishing its decision at the end of 1986. The report noted that electroencephalography (EEG), the method commonly used to establish death, was not foolproof, nor could it establish brain death, and more advanced methods were available.[37] Basing itself on the talmudic passage cited above,[38] the decision of the Hatam Sofer,[39] and the opinion of R. Feinstein,[40] the Rabbinate declared that "death is determined by irreversible cessation of breathing (*neshima*). Therefore, concerning a donor, it should be ascertained that the cessation of breathing is irreversible. This can be determined by proof of complete brain destruction, including the brain-stem, which controls autonomous breathing."[41]

37 H. Somer, "The medical basis for ascertainment of the state of death," *Sefer Assia* 7 (1993), 129ff.

38 bYoma 85a; Maimonides, *Code*, Laws concerning the Sabbath 2:18, 19.

39 *Responsa Hatam Sofer*, YD 338.

40 *Responsa Igrot Moshe*, YD 3:132; see R. M. Tendler, *Responsa of Rav Moshe Feinstein*, vol. 1: *Care of the Critically Ill* (Hoboken NJ: 1996). Steinberg 1993, n. 27 above, 209ff., accepts the principle that death coincides with the cessation of respiration, noting that this normally coincides with cessation of cardiac activity. When the patient is connected to a respirator, death is established on the basis of brain death, which attests to the cessation of independent breathing. Steinberg, a member of the Rabbinate's commission on transplantation, also discusses this subject in *Or Hamizrah* 130–131, 280ff., where he shows that the cessation of breathing can be verified via either the brain or the heart. In the same journal, A. Soloveitchik (298ff.) maintains that death can be established only by the cessation of breathing and heart activity. See too the discussion of this issue in *Assia* 53–54 (1994), 5ff.

41 The ruling is available at http://www.hods.org/pdf/Chief%20Rabbinate%20of%20Israel.pdf. For a discussion of the subject along the lines of the approach adopted by the Israeli Rabbinate, see R. M. Tendler, "Moment of death and organ transplant" (Hebrew), in A. Steinberg (ed.), *Emek Halakha — Assia*, vol. 2 (NY and Jerusalem: 1989), 213–19. *Sefer Assia* 7, n. 23 above, has two articles on R. Moses Feinstein's responsum on brain death (YD 3:132), one (137ff.) by R. M. Halperin, who also sat on the Chief Rabbinate's commission on transplantation, and one (149ff.) by R. Shabtai

The Rabbinate has thus adopted the brain death definition. To confirm death, chemical tests of the brain are performed, along with a BAER test (the brain-stem auditory evoked response procedure), in which acoustic stimulation is sent to the auditory system, and the electro-cerebral waves are then analyzed. If the first wave that originates from the inner ear is detected without the presence of electrical waves coming from the cerebral cortex, it is a sign that the ear is functioning but the cerebral cortex is dead.[42] In such a case, a patient who is not breathing independently is considered no longer able to breathe, and is thus considered dead according to the halakha.

As noted, harvesting of organs for transplantation requires maintenance of blood flow to the donor's organ and, of course, that the donor no longer be alive. The halakhic authorities who contend that brain death, established with the clinical tests, is considered death according to the halakha, are thus favorably disposed to transplantation.[43] However, so as not to leave the decision to harvest an organ for transplant in the hands of doctors alone, the Chief Rabbinate requested that a rabbi be present as well when such a decision was made.[44]

---

Rapoport, who edited the last two volumes of R. Feinstein's responsa. See too I.M. Lau, "Establishing the moment of death," *Assia* 53–54 (1994), 32ff., and see *Assia* 56 (1995), 21ff.

42 E.F. Wijdicks, "Determining brain death in adults," *Neurology* 45 (1995), 1003ff.; Somer, n. 37 above.

43 See M. Halperin, "Heart transplants in Jewish law," *Sefer Assia* 5 (1986); idem, "The legal significance of the Israeli Chief Rabbinate's directives concerning heart transplants" (Hebrew), *Assia* 47–48 (1989/1990); I. Jakobovits, "Brain death and heart transplants: the Israeli Chief Rabbinate's directives," *Tradition* 24 (1989); R. S. Goren, "Concerning brain death" (Hebrew), *Hatzofe* (Aug. 21 1992), p. 5; "Organ transplantation," n. 34 above, 199, 224ff.

44 See sources cited in nn. 23 and 41 above, and the articles in *Sefer Assia* 7 (1993), esp. S. Yisraeli, "Permissibility of heart transplant" (Hebrew), 167ff. See also the new decision of the Israeli Chief Rabbinate Council (4 Tishre, 5770/Sept. 22, 2009), which records the ruling of Chief Rabbi S. Amar in the name of former Chief Rabbi Ovadia Yosef. This decision confirms that the *Brain — Respiratory Death Law, 5768–2008* is in keeping with Jewish law and that it is thus possible to implement the Chief Rabbinate's 1986 ruling permitting organ donation on condition that death is established in accordance with the halakhic criteria. For the text of the law, see *Assia* 87–88 (2010), 70–99. The law formulates the requirements for establishing brain death, and is accepted by physicians and the halakhic authorities who accept the brain death definition of death. See http://kartisadi.org.il/eng/halaha.html.

Halakhic authorities who maintain that brain death is insufficient, on the other hand, do not permit heart or liver transplants.[45]

## 5 Euthanasia

Jewish law takes a negative view of euthanasia.[46] It is absolutely forbidden to carry out "mercy killings," and anyone who kills a terminal patient or precipitates his death[47] has committed a deed no less heinous

45 In particular, R. S.Z. Auerbach and R. E. Waldenberg.

46 See I. Jakobovits, n. 5 above, 146ff.; A. Dagi, "The paradox of euthanasia," *Judaism* 23 (1975), 164ff.; Y. Weinberger, "Euthanasia in Jewish religious law" (Hebrew), 7 *Dine Israel* (1976), 99ff.; H. Halevi, "Disconnecting a terminal patient from an artificial respirator" (Hebrew), *Tehumin* 2 (1981), 304ff.; D. Frimer, "Euthanasia" (Hebrew), *Halachah Urefuah* 4 (1985), 281ff.; B.Z. Firer, "Use of a respirator for terminal patients," *Tehumin* 7 (1986), 219ff.; Sinclair, n. 14 above; idem, "The terminal patient in Jewish law, with comparative reference to English law, American law, and Israeli law," 12 *Tel Aviv University Studies in Law* (1994), 283ff.; R. Z.N. Goldberg, "The terminally ill — halakhic questions," in M. Halperin (ed.), *Proceedings of the First International Colloquium on Medicine, Ethics, and Halakha* (Hebrew), (Jerusalem: 1993), 292ff.; Bleich, "Treatment of the terminally ill", n. 14 above; Z. Falk, "Jewish perspectives on assisted suicide and euthanasia," 13 *Journal of Law and Religion* (1998/99), 379–84; Abraham, n. 14 above, 193ff. See A. De Vries and A. Carmi (eds.) *The Dying Human* (Ramat Gan: 1979); A. Carmi (ed.), *Euthanasia* (Berlin: 1984); R. Misbin (ed.), *Euthanasia: The Good of the Patient, the Good of the Society* (Frederick MD: 1992); R. Cohen-Almagor, "A circumscribed plea for voluntary physician-assisted suicide" in idem (ed.), *Medical Ethics at the Dawn of the 21st Century*, Annals of the New York Academy of Sciences, vol. 913 (NY: 2000), 127ff.; H. Biggs, *Euthanasia, Death with Dignity, and the Law* (Oxford: 2001).

47 E.g., it is forbidden to remove the pillow from under the head of a dying person in order to hasten his death; see Rema, YD 339:1. The issue of precipitating death, or not extending a suffering patient's life, will be addressed in section 6, which discusses the talmudic case of R. Hanina b. Tradyon. See also E. Dorff, "Assisted suicide," in 13 *Journal of Law and Religion* (1998/99), 263–87; S. Resnicoff, "Jewish law perspectives on suicide and physician-assisted dying," 13 *Journal of Law and Religion* (1998/99), 289–349; M. Elon's opinion in *Shefer v. State of Israel*, n. 1 above, 54, s.v. "The principle of preventing pain and suffering"; R. Cohen-Almagor and M. Shmueli, "Can life be evaluated? The Jewish halachic approach vs. the quality of life approach in medical ethics: a critical view," *Theoretical Medicine and Bioethics* 21 (2000), 117–37.

than homicide. Similarly, a patient who "euthanizes" himself actually commits suicide.

According to preeminent halakhic authorities, there are certainly instances in which it is best not to connect a patient to a machine that will help prolong his life if there is no real chance of recovery and if prolonged survival will entail great suffering.[48] Once a patient is connected, however, it is difficult to permit disconnection. As noted above, most halakhic authorities take the position that it is forbidden to disconnect the patient, even in order to save another patient who is in need of the same (and maybe only) machine.

Recently, however, some have concluded that if, and only if, the doctors are absolutely certain that it is no longer possible to save the patient, it is permitted, and in some cases even a duty, to disconnect him from the machine.[49] Upon learning of the widespread practice in some American hospitals of extending a patient's life to earn more money from his hospitalization, R. Feinstein expressly forbade doctors from performing any action to extend human life if this would cause the patient to suffer. The first duty of doctors is to heal, not to prolong suffering. R. Feinstein similarly concluded that it is forbidden to extend a patient's life, thereby causing him to suffer, in order to harvest his organs for transplantation into another patient.[50]

48 Firer, n. 46 above.

49 Halevi, n. 46 above, 297ff.

50 *Responsa Igrot Moshe*, YD 2:174. Jakobovits, n. 5 above, 49, writes: "If and when to apply or suspend artificial respiration must be determined in the interests of the patient alone, and not for purposes of obtaining a vital organ for transplantation, since it would be reprehensible to manipulate one life for the benefit of another." His conclusions regarding euthanasia are that "Jewish law unreservedly rejects euthanasia in its strictest sense. It condemns every active and voluntary action that precipitates death purely and simply as an act of homicide, whether the doctor acts with or without the patient's consent. Judaism judges suicide even more severely than homicide from several points of view, since there is no way to atone through repentance for self-destruction. With regard to **passive euthanasia**, in the final phases of a life that is dragging on, contemporary rabbinical opinions differ. Some do not allow one to suspend efforts, even artificial and hopeless, which are directed at extending life. Others, however, do not require doctors to resort to **heroic means**; they allow one to stop administering medication or using machines which serve solely to extend the terminal patient's suffering, as long as natural means of sustenance (for example, food) are not eliminated."

Former Chief Rabbi of Israel R. Shlomo Goren explored the Sages' positions regarding various issues related to euthanasia, and reached the following conclusions: 1) it is considered a pious act to pray for a terminal patient who is suffering greatly and for whom there is no hope of recovery, so as to hasten his end and free him from suffering; 2) it is forbidden to practice any form of euthanasia at the request of the terminal patient, even if it is known that he does not have long to live; 3) one must refuse a terminal patient who is in great agony and requests that the artificial devices that are keeping him alive be disconnected in order to allow him to die a natural death. If his oxygen supply and feeding tubes need replenishing, one must, out of respect for the patient's present life, not accede to the patient's request that they not be refilled. The commandments, "That your brother may live with you" (Lev. 25:36) and "Neither shall you stand idly by the blood of your neighbor" (Lev. 19:16)[51] apply even when the patient asks for his death to be precipitated; 4) the patient may, however, refuse to take an experimental medication; 5) in the case of a terminal patient in his death throes (*goses*), who we know will not recover and who is connected to life-support devices that prolong his pain, one is not allowed to disconnect him from the devices, but eminent halakhic authorities, such as the Beit Yaakov and Shvut Yaakov, have ruled that one is allowed, in such a case, not to refill his feeding tubes and thereby leave him to die a natural death.[52]

## 6 The example of R. Hanina b. Tradyon

There is a talmudic passage that may help us understand the reasoning behind the decisors' decisions. The Babylonian Talmud describes in detail the martyrdom of the Tanna R. Hanina b. Tradyon.[53] The story takes place in Palestine at the beginning of the second century CE, during the reign of the emperor Hadrian, but its significance extends beyond its temporal and geographical limits.

These were particularly difficult times for the Jews of Palestine, which was then ruled by the Roman Empire. The Temple in Jerusalem was destroyed by Titus in 70 CE, the Jewish revolt during the reign of the emperor Trajan (115–117 CE) was harshly put down, and the great Bar Kokhba revolt a few decades later was also subdued, by Hadrian,

51 See Rashi's commentary ad loc.

52 See S. Goren, *Torat Harefua* (Jerusalem: 2001), 27–78.

53 bAvoda Zara 18a.

with great loss of life. Hadrian, influenced by Hellenism, adopted a policy of complete intolerance for Jewish observance. Roman sources describe how laws such as *Lex Cornelia de sicariis*, the law that punished murderers, were adduced to punish practices of the Jews in Palestine related to the observance of certain precepts (in particular, circumcision).[54] The Romans hoped that repressing Judaism would put an end to revolts against the empire.

The pervasive religious persecution is reflected in a comment in the *Mekhilta De-Rabbi Yishmael* on the biblical verse, "And showing mercy unto the thousandth generation for them that love Me and keep My comandments" (Exod. 20:6), R. Nathan, son of the exilarch of Babylonia, who arrived in Palestine at the time of the revolt against Hadrian, commented that this verse refers to the Jews who live in the land of Israel and put their lives at risk to observe the commandments.

> Why were you condemned to death? Because I circumcised my son. Why were you burnt alive? Because I read the Torah. Why were you crucified? Because I ate unleavened bread. . . . These blows have caused me to be beloved to my Father who is in the heavens.[55]

R. Hanina b. Tradyon continued to hold public meetings in order to teach Torah, though this was forbidden. The Talmud recounts the story of R. Hanina's visit to R. Jose b. Kisma, who was ill. R. Jose addresses R. Hanina:

> Hanina, my brother, do you not know that it is heaven that has ordained that this [the Roman] nation shall reign? For though it has laid waste His house, burnt His Temple, slain His pious ones, and caused His excellent ones to perish, still it is firmly established. Yet, I have heard that you sit and occupy yourself with the Torah, address public assemblies, and keep a Torah scroll in your bosom! He said to him: Heaven will have mercy. He said to him: I am making a serious point, and you say, "Heaven will have mercy!" I would not be surprised if they burn you together with the Torah scroll![56]

54 A.M. Rabello, "The ban on circumcision as a cause of Bar Kokhba's rebellion," in idem (ed.), *The Jews in the Roman Empire: Legal Problems, from Herod to Justinian* (Aldershot UK: 2000).

55 *Mekhilta De-Rabbi Yishmael*, introduction, s.v. *bahodesh*. Despite his intolerance of Jewish practices, Hadrian was interested in Judaism as a philosophy, and engaged in dialogue with the Rabbis on various subjects (see, e.g., Genesis Rabbah 10:3).

56 bAvoda Zara 18a. The halakhic authorities explain that in dangerous situations, including illness, one should act reasonably and not rely solely on divine intervention. See R. Abraham Isaac Kook, *Responsa Ezrat Kohen*, EH #37.

Indeed, not long after the death of R. Jose b. Kisma, the Roman authorities arrested R. Hanina and sentenced him to death: he was to be burned alive for studying Torah. To prolong the Sage's torment as much as possible, the Romans wrapped him in the parchment of his Torah scroll and placed on his flesh tufts of wool that had been soaked in water, so that the fire would burn slowly. R. Hanina's students, suffering as they watched the atrocities committed against their Master, asked him: "What do you see, Master?" Continuing to teach up until the last moment of his earthly life, R. Hanina replied, "I see the scroll burning, but the letters are flying upwards."[57] When the students could no longer bear their teacher's pain, they suggested that he hasten his death—"Open your mouth, so that the fire will enter within you!" R. Hanina refused to precipitate his death, however, as if to declare that his earthly mission had not yet come to an end: "Let He who gave me [my soul] take it away, but no one should injure himself." The Roman executioner (*quaestionarius*) who was supervising the death sentence was struck by the rabbi's suffering. "Rabbi," he asked, "if I increase the flame and take away the tufts of wool from over your heart, will you cause me to enter the world-to-come?" R. Hanina swore that he would. Immediately, the centurion stoked the fire, removed the wet wool, and, as the flames grew higher, threw himself into the fire. A celestial voice was then heard saying, "R. Hanina b. Tradyon and the centurion have been called to life in the world-to-come."

This episode is often presented as an illustration of the great power of repentance, *teshuva*, which has the power to save both the Jew and the pagan. Indeed, in one moment of repentance and self-sacrifice, the Roman soldier gained the world-to-come that R. Hanina b. Tradyon had earned by conducting his entire life with sanctity! Of course, R. Hanina's strength of will at a time of great suffering is highly edifying, demonstrating how man must be prepared to serve God with love and self-abnegation.

> R. Jacob used to say: One hour of repentance and good deeds in this world is better that the entire life of the world-to-come, and one hour of spiritual bliss in the world-to-come is better that the entire life of this world.[58]

57 R. Hanina's point was that although our persecutors may succeed in striking us with physical blows — in burning our bodies and Torah scrolls — they will not succeed in breaking our spirit, in destroying the biblical teachings themselves.

58 mAvot 4:17.

Who can say what takes place in the human soul in its final hours? Who can know what purifying effect suffering might have? Indeed, in his final moments of inexpressible torment, R. Hanina transformed the life of a Roman executioner whose career up to that moment had been dedicated to the cruel obliteration of the Jewish people; the transformation enabled this cruel torturer to disobey orders and alleviate his prisoner's pain. The Sage and the centurion were united in an instant of sincere and overwhelming repentance, remorse that rendered the Roman worthy of life in the world-to-come.[59]

R. Hanina's death teaches us a practical lesson in medical ethics as well. R. Hanina resisted his students' suggestion that they hasten his death, affirming that one cannot know what will happen in the little time one has left to live, and therefore has no right to precipitate his own demise.[60] Halakhic authorities find this passage problematic, however. R. Hanina told his students that we may not use human means to interfere with the divine will, but R. Hanina's disciples were also presumably conversant in halakha. Why were they unaware of this rule? Is this a statement of a general rule or a standard that applies only to the exceptionally pious (*midat hahasidut*) and those who wish to emulate them? Furthermore, if R. Hanina maintained that it was forbidden to hasten his death, why did he accept the Roman soldier's offer?

The *Tosafot* present two readings of this passage.[61] According to the first view, it is permitted to precipitate one's death when one is suffering unbearable pain. Rabbenu Tam, however, severely qualifies this dispensation, limiting it to the case where one fears that one will not be able to bear the suffering and will, as a result, transgress a serious prohibition.

59 "Great is repentance, which draws man closer to God . . . . Last night, he was considered odious in the presence of God, and today he is beloved" (Maimonides, *Code*, Laws concerning Repentance 7:6).

60 R. J. Reischer, *Responsa Shvut Yaakov*, 3:11, writes that on the basis of this passage, it is prohibited to commit suicide or precipitate death. In contrast, R. Jacob Emden asserts: "There are some who choose to endanger their lives in order to save themselves from terrible suffering, such as those who undergo an operation because of stones in the gall bladder or ducts, or kidney stones. This is very painful, like death itself; the Merciful One should save us. We allow them to do as they please, without objections, since sometimes they are relieved and cured" (*Mor Uketzia*, OH 328, cited in Justice Elon's decision in *Shefer*, n.1 above, 54ff).

61 *Tosafot*, bGitin 27b.

Others suggest a variant of the first view: the students advised R. Hanina to perform a permitted act in light of his great suffering, but he wished to act in a particularly pious manner and therefore refused to make use of this dispensation, despite his terrible suffering.[62] In refusing to precipitate his demise, he was manifesting conduct in accordance with the standard of the pious, and did not intend to establish a general rule.[63] As to the soldier, on this view, though R. Hanina himself refused to hasten his own death, the Roman soldier was not obliged to act in accordance with R. Hanina's standard, and could therefore act as he did.[64]

The majority of halakhic authorities, however, uphold Rabbenu Tam's reading, according to which R. Hanina's attitude reflects the halakhic rule that all must follow, provided there is no fear that they will transgress the commandments under torture.[65] That is, one may **not** precipitate one's death when suffering unbearable pain. How, then, can the Roman soldier's intervention be explained? After all, a non-Jew (Noahide) is forbidden to commit homicide. Some explain that the soldier's removal of the water-soaked sponges was comparable to the removal of an external object that is preventing death, which is permitted, given that the sponges were only there to prolong R. Hanina's suffering.[66] Some maintain that such an act is forbidden to a Jew but

62 *Ein Yaakov*, bAvoda Zara 18a.

63 See "Terminally ill" (*note lamut*), in *Encyclopedia*, n. 5 above, 4:362.

64 *Responsa Tzitz Eliezer* 18:48.

65 E.g., R. M. Feinstein, *Responsa Igrot Moshe*, HM 2:74, argues that this talmudic passage teaches that it is forbidden to open one's mouth to admit flames and hasten death. See also *Responsa Tzitz Eliezer* 10:25, which maintains that R. Hanina established the general rule — "for us his words are established halakha" — thereby establishing that it is forbidden to shorten one's own life and to shorten the life of another. According to R. Feinstein and R. Waldenberg, since there was no danger that R. Hanina would succumb to idolatry, his conduct complied with the general rule, and his students were mistaken. Others maintain, however, that Rabbenu Tam's comment did not refer specifically to R. Hanina, and we therefore cannot assert that Rabbenu Tam considered it prohibited to open one's mouth to admit fire. On this latter opinion, see Firer, n. 46 above, 223ff.; R. Z.N. Goldberg, "Discontinuation of artificial respiration (choosing a patient in the event of insufficient equipment)," in Halperin 1985, n. 12 above, 73ff.

66 Firer, n. 46 above, 219ff; I. Jakobovits, "The law relating to the precipitation of death of a terminally ill and suffering patient" (Hebrew), *Hapardes* 31 (1957), 28ff; R. S. Kook, "Killing a suffering individual" (Hebrew), *Torah*

permitted to a non-Jew, either because the matter was extremely beneficial for R. Hanina — "the speed of death being a great good"[67] and because he was dying an unnatural death[68] — or because the soldier did not consider his actions to be a homicide.[69] Others maintain, however, that we may not emulate the act of the Roman soldier. On this view, R. Hanina permitted the soldier to remove the sponges only because of the particular situation in which he found himself.[70]

The talmudic passage in bAvoda Zara 18a has generated an ongoing discussion that adduces other biblical, talmudic, and post-talmudic texts. What are the implications of the story about R. Hanina for our attempt to resolve the problem of suffering caused by continued medical treatment? A solution to this problem requires familiarity with

---

*Shebeal Pe* 18 (1976), 82ff., esp. n. 76; R. Y. Weiss, *Responsa Minhat Yitzhak* 5:8, states that it is permitted to precipitate death in cases of suffering, but without reaching a clear decision. The opinion that the sponges were comparable to an external impediment to death that it is permissable to remove is not shared by all the halakhic authorities.

67 *Responsa Igrot Moshe*, HM 2:74. R. Feinstein argues that just as it was forbidden for R. Hanina to open his mouth, it was forbidden for him to remove the sponges.

68 Ibid., YD 2:174; R. Feinstein indicates, however, that the matter requires further study.

69 *Responsa Tzitz Eliezer* 8:48. R. L.Y. Halperin notes that in all likelihood, it was the attending soldier who prepared the fire and added the sponges to begin with; a murderer may change his method of killing after deciding on one course, certainly if he switches to a less painful method. Thus, the act that was permitted to the soldier was certainly not permitted to any other observer, nor to the victim. On this analysis, there is no contradiction between the two parts of the talmudic passage. See his comment on R. Z.N. Goldberg's article, n. 65 above, 73ff.

70 In other words, it was an exigency ruling (*horaat shaa*), that is, a ruling that is valid for that specific moment in time, due to precarious circumstances, and cannot be considered valid as a general rule. See A. Weingort, *Responsabilité et sanction en droit talmudique et comparé* (Paris: 1998), 158.

The view that the dispensation given by R. Hanina to the Roman soldier was a *horaat shaa* is voiced in *Responsa Igrot Moshe*, HM 2:73:3. In a private conversation, R. Feinstein's nephew, R. S. Rappoport, himself a halakhic authority, explained that one can deduce the motivation for the special dispensation from the fact that the soldier changed his attitude to R. Hanina. According to R. Rappoport, there is no difference between removing the sponges and intensifying the flames, and both actions are, in general, prohibited.

both the halakhic sources and real-life situations.[71] In this article, I have endeavored to articulate some of the relevant principles and how they are applied, but the subject clearly calls for more in-depth study.[72]

71 In December 2005, the Knesset passed the *Terminally Ill Patient Law 5766–2005*, which to a great extent incorporated the findings of the committee headed by Steinberg (see n. 11 above). A critical view of the law is expressed in Y.M. Bar Ilan, "Is the clock ticking for terminally ill patients in Israel? Preliminary comments for a proposal for a bill of rights for the terminally ill," *Jewish Medical Ethics* 30 (2004), 353ff. See also both articles in Sinclair 2005, n. 18 above, section F, Treatment of the Terminally Ill. One examines *Shefer v. State of Israel* (n. 1 above); the second is D. Sinclair, "The report and draft law of the Committee concerning the Terminally Ill Patient (Steinberg Committee), 2002." And see A. Steinberg and C.L. Sprung, "The dying patient: new Israeli legislation," *Intensive Care Medicine* 32 (2006), 1234–37.

72 An Italian version of this article, "Problemi connessi con la fine della vita e l'eutanasia alla luce del Diritto Ebraic," appeared in Erminia Camassa and Carlo Casonato (eds.), *Bioetica e confessioni religiose. Atti del Convegno tenuto presso la Facoltà di Giurisprudenza dell'Università di Trento il 12 maggio 2006* (Trento: 2008), 29–58.

*The Jewish Law Annual*, Vol. XIX

# Man as a Synthesis of Body and Spirit: A Jewish Perspective

Nahum Rakover*

The notion that man is a synthesis of body and spirit can be considered from various points of view — philosophical, psychological, religious, and legal. This article will focus on the latter perspective.

According to the Jewish view, man's uniqueness, the essential element that distinguishes him from the rest of creation, is the fact that he was created in God's image: "And God created man in His own image, in the image of God He created him" (Gen. 1:27). According to the story of Creation, man was created as a synthesis of body and spirit, a combination of the "Divine breath" and the dust of the earth: "Then the Lord God formed man of the dust of the ground, and breathed into his nostrils the breath of life" (Gen. 2:7.). The Midrash expands on this concept: "[God] made him from the lower worlds and from the upper worlds — the body from the lower worlds and the soul from the upper" (Gen. Rabbah 12:7).

The link between the spiritual soul — the Divine breath — and the physical breathing that signifies life was noted by the Sages. Commenting on the verse, "Let every soul (*neshama*) praise the Lord" (Ps. 150:6), the Sages taught: "For every single breath (*neshima*) that a person takes, he must praise his Creator" (Gen. Rabbah 14:11). Underlying this homily — which may be construed as simply a play on words — is the idea of the intimate bond between soul and breath, a bond that was forged at the time of Creation, but lasts for all eternity. In light of this bond, man must give thanks to the Creator of his soul and the Creator of his breath.

Throughout the ages, the rabbinical authorities recognized the miraculous nature of this bond between the physical and the spiritual. R. Moses Isserles (Rema) regards the phrase "and does wondrously"

* Prof. Nahum Rakover, former Deputy Attorney General of Israel, is Chief Researcher at the Jewish Legal Heritage Society, and has written widely on Jewish law and its relationship to Israeli legislation.

in the benediction, said each morning, "Blessed art Thou ... who heals all flesh and does wondrously," as an expression of thanks for this miraculous bond:

> It seems to me that the phrase "and does wondrously" refers to the soul that [God] placed in man; and it is a great wonder that a spiritual entity, originating in the upper worlds, is able to exist in a material entity, the body of man, which originates in the lower worlds.[1]

The recognition that man was created in God's image determines man's unique position in the created sphere. It is the basis of the Jewish concern for humanity, as expressed in various commandments regarding the protection of human life and dignity. Indeed, the Bible links this recognition with the punishment inflicted on one who sheds human blood: "Whoso sheds man's blood, by man shall his blood be shed; for in the image of God made He man" (Gen. 9:6). Humankind's special status is similarly expressed in the severity with which any assault on human dignity was viewed by the Sages: "Whosoever shames his fellow man in public, it is as if he spills blood."[2] In our own time, this source was cited as a basis for the declaration of the Israel Supreme Court that one's honor is no less worthy of protection than is his or her right to life.[3]

Because it views man as a synthesis of body and spirit, Jewish law is highly sensitive to the protection of various spiritual values, such as the protection of the individual's rights to his or her literary or artistic work (copyright laws) and protection of the right to privacy. Mechanisms have thus evolved within the corpus of Jewish law to protect not only the human body, but the human spirit as well.

Preservation of the Divine image in man is so important that it applies even to offenders. The principle is invoked by the Sages to provide an explanation for the difference in the penalty imposed for stealing an ox and that imposed for stealing a sheep: whereas one who steals a sheep must pay four times the sheep's value, one who steals an ox is required to pay five times its value. According to the Sages, the reason for the lower penalty in the case of a stolen sheep is that the thief usually carries it away on his shoulders, thereby demeaning himself.

1 *Darkhei Moshe*, OH 6:1.
2 bBaba Metzia 58b.
3 F.H. 9/77, *Israel Electric Corp. Ltd.* v. *Haaretz Newspaper Publishing Ltd.*, 32(3) P.D. 337.

In this context, R. Johanan b. Zakai says: "The Holy One, blessed be He, is mindful of the dignity of His creations."[4]

Preservation of the Divine image in all people, including criminals, is alluded to in the Bible itself:

> And if a man has committed a sin worthy of death, and he is put to death, and you hang him on a tree, his body shall not remain all night upon the tree, but you shall surely bury him the same day. For he that is hanged is a reproach to God; that you defile not your land, which the Lord your God gives you for an inheritance. (Deut. 21:22–23)

Explaining the words "for he that is hanged is a reproach to God," the Sages cite a parable of identical twins, one of whom became a king while the other took to highway robbery. After some time, the latter was caught and hanged, and passersby exclaimed that it seemed that the king had been hanged. In the same sense, the hanged criminal, who was endowed with the image of the "King," is "a reproach to God."[5]

The same verse is interpreted by the sixteenth century commentator R. Obadiah Sforno in the spirit of medieval Jewish thought:

> Every essence distinct from matter is called Divine, and of this category is the essence of the intellectual soul in man, which is called "the image of God." . . . Now, since the dishonor done to a dead person after death is a dishonor of the intellectual soul, which is the distinct essence that remains after bodily death, [the Torah] said that it is "a reproach to God," for to leave the corpse hanging overnight without burial is a dishonor to that same eternal essence, which is called Divine.[6]

This concern for human dignity in connection with criminal offenders may seem surprising, but in fact goes to the heart of the concept of creation in the image of God. When one honors someone who is entitled to honor because of his merit, one honors that individual's singular qualities. But when one honors someone who has no such qualities, his only claim to dignity lies in his being human, and it is on this basis that he deserves a measure of respect. Moreover, while the dignity of an ordinary person may on occasion be violated by others, a criminal, having violated his own dignity, **invites** the contempt of others. Despite this, he is not therefore excluded from the scope of the law; on the contrary, in the dictum quoted above,

4 bBaba Kama 79b.

5 tSanhedrin 9:7; bSanhedrin 46b.

6 Sforno, commentary ad loc.

R. Johanan b. Zakai explains that the law seeks to restore to the criminal the human dignity that the criminal himself has caused damage to.

The wording of R. Johanan b. Zakai's dictum seems to point to the very origin of the concept of human dignity. The Hebrew word he uses is not *"adam,"* "man," but *"briyot,"* "creations" or "creatures," a term frequently used in rabbinical sources to designate humankind in general. It is derived from the verb root bet-resh-aleph (create), alluding to the fact that all human beings are the work of the Creator (*borei*) of the entire world. Human beings as such — not only those who are righteous, and of course, not only Jews, were created by God in His own image. This is implied by the verse: "This is the book of the generations of Adam; on the day that God created man, in the likeness of God He made him" (Gen. 5:1) — **all** human beings were created in God's image and therefore merit respect.

The halakhic authorities stressed that we must beware of shaming any person, since man is made in the likeness of God. This is expressed by Maimonides in his great code, the *Mishne Torah*:

> Do not belittle human dignity, for it overrides a negative commandment enacted by the Rabbis. How much more so the dignity of the children of Abraham, Isaac, and Jacob, who adhere to the true Torah.[7]

While it is the soul that explicitly expresses the Divine element of man, the physical body is also the work of God, as we say in the Penitential Service (*Selihot*) during the High Holy Day season: "The soul is Yours and the body is Yours. . . . The Soul is Yours and the body is Your work." This principle imposes certain limits upon what one is allowed to do to his or her own body.

In his commentary on Maimonides' *Code*, R. David b. Zimra, the Radbaz, elucidates another implication of the idea that man is created by God in His own likeness. Explaining why a confession is admissible in civil, but not criminal, cases, he writes:

> One can explain this to some extent as follows: Since man's soul is not his own possession, but that of the Holy One, blessed be He, as it is written in Scripture, "Behold, all souls are mine" (Ezek. 18:4), therefore, one's admission concerning something that is not one's own is of no avail. . . . On the other hand, material possessions are one's own, and we therefore say [in civil matters] that "the litigant's own admission is equivalent to testimony of a hundred witnesses."[8]

7 Maimonides, *Code*, Laws concerning the Sanhedrin 24:10.
8 Radbaz (1479–1573), Laws concerning the Sanhedrin 18:6.

The idea that human dignity stems from the fact that man is a creation of God has yet another implication — a special attitude to the entire universe. All of God's creations — inanimate, vegetable, and animal — also merit dignity on the same grounds. This sentiment is well expressed by R. Moses Cordovero, the pre-eminent kabbalist in Safed prior to R. Isaac Luria (the Ari):

> One's mercy must extend to all oppressed creatures. One should not demean or destroy them, for the Supreme Wisdom extends to all created things: inanimate, vegetable, animal, and speaking. For this reason, we are admonished against defiling food. . . . On the same principle, one should not defile any entity, for all entities [were created] in Wisdom. And one should not uproot a plant, unless it is needed; nor should one slay an animal, unless it is needed.[9]

This outlook is exemplified in an anecdote related by R. Aryeh Levin many centuries later. While taking an afternoon stroll with R. Abraham Isaac Kook, one of the most venerable leaders of the Jewish community in the land of Israel during the first decades of the twentieth century, R. Levin plucked a twig or blossom. R. Kook, taken aback by this act, gently chided R. Levin, remarking that never in his life had he ever needlessly plucked even a blade of grass, in keeping with the Sages' teaching that there is not a single blade of grass here on Earth that does not have a heavenly force urging it to grow! Every creation utters its own song in praise of God. R. Kook's attitude to each individual plant and to creation in general reflects a comprehensive philosophical approach to man's relationship with nature, at the core of which is the notion that the physical and the spiritual are not separate realms, but intimately connected.

The integral connection between the body and spirit is expressed in the talmudic dictum, "Three things restore a man's spirit: [beautiful] sounds, sights, and scents. Three things expand a man's spirit: a beautiful dwelling, a beautiful wife, and beautiful garments."[10] R. Kook interprets the restoration of spirit through sounds, sights, and scents as representing renewed communion with nature, and the embracing of natural life through the sounds of birds, the sight of hills and forests, and the scent of flowers.

9 *Tomer Devora*, ch. 3.

10 bBerakhot 57b.

# Framing Jewish Law for the Contemporary Law School

Chaim N. Saiman*



## Introduction

At a conference on Catholic legal theory at Villanova Law School, Justice Scalia spoke about the impact of Catholicism on his role as a Supreme Court justice. To the chagrin of many in the audience, the Justice took a minimalist view, saying that just as there is no Catholic way to cook a hamburger, there is no Catholic way to decide questions of constitutional law. Certainly, no observant Jew could have made the parallel claim, for while scholars debate the question of whether there is a Jewish way to interpret the Constitution,[1] for the observant Jew,

* Chaim Saiman teaches at Villanova Law School. His areas of expertise are comparative private law and Jewish law.

1 See, e.g., E.A. Kleinhaus, "History as precedent: the post-originalist problem in constitutional law," 110 *Yale Law Journal* (2000), 121, whose solution to a "post-originalist problem" draws on Jewish law interpretive techniques; S. Levine, "Jewish legal theory and American constitutional theory: some comparisons and contrasts," 24 *Hastings Constitutional Law Quarterly* (1997), 441, which recognizes numerous parallels between Jewish theory and constitutional theory; idem, "Unenumerated constitutional rights and unenumerated biblical obligations: a preliminary study in comparative hermeneutics," 15 *Constitutional Commentary* (1998), 511, comparing the issue of unenumerated rights in Jewish and American constitutional law.

there is indeed a Jewish way to prepare, cook, eat, and recite the blessings over a hamburger.

Judaism is undoubtedly law-oriented. The *Shulhan Arukh*, the sixteenth century code of Jewish law, begins with the laws of "arising in the morning" (*dinei hashkamat haboker*) and the nomism continues through to the laws of mourning (*dinei aveilut*). Questions that other legal and religious traditions analyze from the perspective of moral theology, ethics, practical reasoning, divine inspiration, empirical observation, political elections, and bureaucratic administration are refracted in Judaism through the lens of the halakha.

The irony is that despite all this law — by which I mean the multitude of religiously-mandated rules that populate the halakhic landscape — there is much uncertainty as to what, if anything, this mass of legal tradition has to say to American law and contemporary public life. While few think the traditional yeshiva curriculum is a good fit for the secular and mostly non-Jewish audience of the legal academy, articulating the precise role of Jewish law has proven a difficult task.[2]

2 Prior investigations into this question can be found in S. Cohn, "Teaching Jewish law in a secular American law school," in Hillel Gamoran (ed.), 12 *Jewish Law Association Studies* (Atlanta: 2002), 50; S. Cohn, "Yale Rosenberg: the scholar and the teacher of Jewish law," 39 *Houston Law Review* (2002), 872; S. Levine, "Teaching Jewish law in American law schools: an emerging development in law and religion," 26 *Fordham Law Journal* (1999), 4; idem, "Teaching Jewish law in American law schools — part II: an annotated syllabus," 2 *Chicago-Kent Journal of International and Comparative Law* (2002), 1; idem, "Applying Jewish legal theory in the context of American law and legal scholarship: a methodological analysis," 40 *Seton Hall Law Review* (2010), 933; E.H. Rabin, "Symposium: the evolution and impact of Jewish law — foreword," *U.C. Davis Journal of International Law and Policy* (1995), 49; J.I. Roth, "Fraud on the surviving spouse in Jewish and American law: a model chapter for a Jewish law casebook," 28 *Case Western Reserve Journal of International Law* (1996), 101; A. Sokobin, "A program in comparative Jewish law," 33 *University of Toledo Law Review* (2002), 795.

A number of the methodological questions that will be addressed in the first section of this article have been explored in the context of the role of Jewish law in the Jewish State by Justices Izhak Englard, Menachem Elon, and Haim Cohen, and Professors Shalom Albeck and Bernard Jackson; see B.S. Jackson (ed.), *Modern Research in Jewish Law* (Leiden: 1980). The present article refers mainly to the American and European context. For a compelling analysis of the Israeli context, see A. Edrei, "Why teach Jewish law?" (Hebrew), 25 *Iyunei Mishpat* (2001), 467–87.

At the outset, it is worth contrasting the condition of Jewish law with the parallel question facing Christian legal scholars. On the one hand, Christians — Protestants in particular, but Catholics as well — have considerably fewer of the type of legal rules common to the halakha. On the other hand, the Christian tradition has far more to say about the relationship between religious doctrine and political authority, or what we typically refer to as questions of church and state. This is due in large part to the fact that Christianity has been debating the relative roles of *regnum* and *sacerdotium* since the investiture controversies of the twelfth century, perhaps earlier. The Christian tradition thus contains nearly a millennium of thinking about the theology, politics, and doctrines of church/state relations.[3]

The same is not true of Judaism. Due in part to a lack of Jewish sovereignty since late antiquity, and mutual hostility between political Zionists and the halakhic establishment in the modern era, questions of this type occupy far less space in the classical Jewish canon.[4] Moreover, whereas Christianity broadcasts its message to the entire human family, the vast majority of the halakha applies only to Jews. Returning, then, to our initial question, what does Jewish law have to say to contemporary American society, and how should we teach Jewish law in American law schools? While these may be separate questions, for the purposes of this essay, I will analyze them together.

3 See M. McConnell et al. (eds.), *Christian Perspectives on Legal Thought* (New Haven: 2001); R. Cochran, Jr. (ed.), *Faith and Law: How Religious Traditions from Calvinism to Islam View American Law* (NY: 2007); J. Witte Jr. and F. Alexander (eds.), *The Teachings of Modern Christianity on Law, Politics, and Human Nature* (NY: 2006); D. Skeel, Jr., "The unbearable lightness of Christian legal scholarship," 57 *Emory Law Journal* (2008), 1471, 1500, which notes that Christian legal scholarship has been primarily focused on First Amendment/church-state issues.

4 The exception is, of course, discussion of the *dina demalkhuta dina* principle, a conflict-of-laws principle used to mediate the boundaries between Jewish and secular law. Over time, this concept became the entry point into more theoretical halakhic discussions of the relationship between Jewish law and the state; see nn 38–43 below and accompanying text.

In the context of the creation of the State of Israel in the first half of the 20th century, rabbis and scholars associated with religious Zionism examined different proposals for fashioning a comprehensive legal/political system on the basis of traditional Jewish law. For the most part, these efforts were not implemented, but the goal remained. As the century wore on, the project was more or less abandoned even by the most optimistic proponents; see Edrei, n. 2 above, n. 19.

Since Jewish law has become part of the curriculum of many American law schools, scholars have pursued these questions, using a number of different approaches. In this article I will analyze and critique the three dominant approaches. I will also explore the concept of *talmud torah* — the idea that the study of law is a central religious obligation that plays an important cognitive role in rabbinical culture. Although rarely discussed in the scholarly literature,[5] *talmud torah* explains the centrality of study within rabbinical culture, and provides a useful framework for considering the place of Jewish law in the contemporary law school.

## 1 The substantive law model (classical *mishpat ivri*)

During the twentieth century, the most popular approach to Jewish law at American law schools was based on methodological premises of the *mishpat ivri* (Hebrew law) movement.[6] In broad terms, this movement seeks to systematize and reformulate material taken from the traditional halakhic corpus to make its rules of decision accessible and relevant to a contemporary polity.[7]

In the American context, this method of teaching and scholarship proceeds in two ways. An attempt might be made to illuminate an area of conflict between Jewish and American law, and *mishpat ivri* might be proposed as a framework for resolving the tension between the two systems.[8] Or a problematic area of American law may be identified,

5 The concept of *talmud torah* is not seriously considered in any of the more programmatic works on Jewish law in the law school context cited in n. 2 above.

6 On the movement's early years, and the choice of the neologism "*mishpat ivri*" over the more traditional "halakha," see A. Likhovski, "The invention of 'Hebrew law' in Mandatory Palestine," 46 *American Journal of Comparative Law* (1998), 339.

7 The classic expression of this outlook is Menachem Elon's *Jewish Law: History, Sources, Principles*, translated by B. Auerbach and M. Sykes (Philadelphia: 1994).

8 See, e.g., M. Broyde, *The Pursuit of Justice and Jewish Law: Halakhic Perspectives on the Legal Profession* (NY: 2007), analyzing conflicts between the obligations of halakha and the obligations of legal practice under American law; M. Grossman, "Is this arbitration? Religious tribunals, judicial review, and due process," 107 *Columbia Law Review* (2007), 169, calling for modification of traditional arbitration jurisprudence as applied to religious arbitration panels; M. Helfand, "When religious practices

after which the halakhic corpus is mined for either a decision rule or an analytical framework taken to be more attractive. On this variant of the *mishpat ivri* approach to teaching Jewish law, the scholar assumes — either implicitly or explicitly — that greater awareness of Jewish law would have a salutary effect on the current state of American law.[9]

These approaches conceptualize the halakha as primarily a body of law, and this view has substantial appeal. First, the material is presented in a familiar format and hence is accessible. Second, because the legal literature tends to adopt a conflict-of-laws or comparative law framework, the halakhic sources readily connect to otherwise familiar legal issues. Third, using this model, Jewish law fits into a well-known paradigm of legal teaching and writing, on which scholars draw on "outside" disciplines (such as economics, psychology, philosophy, critical studies) to critique and reform existing doctrine and theory. Finally, given the sheer volume of halakhic material corresponding to private, criminal, and family law, there is considerable

---

become legal obligations," 23 *Journal of Law and Religion* (2008), 101, advocating application of the "foreign compulsion defense" — typically applied to cases of foreign law — to obligations emerging out of religious law; B. Wolf, "Resolving the conflict between Jewish and secular estate law," 37 *Hofstra Law Review* (2009), 1171.

9 See, e.g., S. Levine, "An introduction to self-incrimination in Jewish law, with application to the American legal system: a psychological and philosophical analysis," 28 *Loyola of Los Angeles International and Comparative Law Review* (2006), 257, 277, asserting that consideration of Jewish law's insights into confessions and self-incrimination "may help facilitate . . . a reassessment of American law;" I. Merker Rosenberg and Y. Rosenberg, "Of God's mercy and the four biblical methods of capital punishment: stoning, burning, beheading and strangulation," 78 *Tulsa Law Review* (2004), 1169, comparing Jewish and U.S. positions on the death penalty and methods of execution; idem, "'Perhaps what ye say is based only on conjecture' — circumstantial evidence, then and now," *Houston Law Review* (1995), 1371, discussing use of circumstantial evidence in Jewish law and American law; Y. Sinai, "Changing the current policy towards spousal abuse: a proposal for a new model inspired by Jewish law," 32 *Hastings International and Comparative Law Review* (2009), 155, recommending American spousal abuse law adopt aspects of the halakhic approach; R. Rosenthal Kwall, "Intellectual property and Jewish law: a comparative perspective on absolutism," 22 *Yale Journal of Law and Humanities* (2010), 101, analogizing different methods of constitutional interpretation and intellectual property law to debates within Judaism regarding the status of the halakha. A more comprehensive survey of this literature can be found in Levine 2010, n. 2 above, nn 59–68.

appeal in bringing the wisdom of the halakhic tradition to bear on questions of contemporary law.

This tactic, however, is not without its drawbacks. The shortcomings generally fall under the rubric of what comparative lawyers call legal transplants,[10] or more sardonically, legal irritants.[11] In recent years comparative scholars have become more critical of the practice of lifting a rule from one system and inserting it into another, because in most cases the transplanter fails to account for how the rule is situated within the jurisprudential, linguistic, and social context of its system of origin.[12] While these issues are well documented in the comparative law literature, the most pressing question for Jewish law is the degree to which the halakha is a legal **system** as modern jurisprudence understands the term. Were the rules of the halakha actually applied, or do they reflect an ideal vision of what law should be? When did they apply? To whom did they apply and what problems did they in turn generate? These issues present themselves in every comparative exercise. Yet because the halakha was often administered and generated outside the framework of a sovereign entity, the disparity between the real and ideal is particularly pronounced.[13]

By way of example, the most difficult question faced by private law theorists is not how to reach a fair result in a particular case, but rather, how to reach a fair result in the particular case without also generating unfair results in future cases. For this reason, prior to transplanting any halakhic doctrine — even a responsum addressing an actual case — a legal theorist should be aware of the degree to which the system was forced to internalize the cost of its ruling. For example, law and economics scholars have shown that when a court lets a poor widow

10 See A. Watson, *Legal Transplants: An Approach to Comparative Law* (Athens GA: 1993).

11 See G. Teubner, "Legal irritants: good faith in British law or how unifying law ends up in new divergences," 61 *Modern Law Review* (1998), 1, 13, who deems legal transplants a "misleading metaphor" because it suggests that once transplanted, the law will "remain identical with itself, playing its old role in the new organism." Teubner prefers "legal irritants" because it reflects the fact that transferred rules/laws are fundamentally reconstructed in the new host system.

12 See P. Legrand, "Issues in the translatability of law," in S. Berman and M. Wood (eds.), *Nation, Language, and the Ethics of Translation* (Princeton: 2005). Legrand sees law as a "culturally-situated phenomenon" and rejects the image of transplants, which "purport to establish sameness of laws across legal cultures" (41).

13 See Edrei, n. 2 above, 472–75.

out of her contract with an aggressive lender, it becomes more difficult for other widows to obtain loans down the road.[14] Did the rabbinical authorities grapple with this problem? Was the halakhic ruling aspirational or actually enforced?[15] Was it meant to persuade the lender to commit an act of charity and to write off the loan as *tzedaka* (charity), or was the lender expected to follow the ruling in the ordinary course of business? Did this ruling encourage other lenders to "forum shop" for rabbis who held alternate views? Did it encourage private settlement or send litigants to non-Jewish courts or communal institutions less influenced by formal halakhic arguments? Were the rabbinical authorities speaking as religious/ethical leaders advising the parties of their obligations toward heaven, or as judges exercising temporal–civil authority? And to what degree are these roles differentiated? To consider more contemporary concerns, how do these principles pertain to a corporation, an entity that the halakha has great difficulty conceptualizing?[16] How do these rulings apply to Jewish firms that must compete with firms that do not adhere to the dictates of Jewish law? How Jewish law should address these issues internally is heatedly debated,[17] and certainly points to the difficulty inherent in transplanting halakhic principles into American law.

14 The classic case is *Williams v. Walker-Thomas Furniture Co.*, 350 F. 2d 445 (D.C. Cir. 1965). The law and economics discussion can be found in R. Scott and J. Kraus, *Contract Law and Theory* (4th edition 2007), 58–63; R. Korobkin, "A 'traditional' and 'behavioral' law and economics analysis of *Williams v. Walker-Thomas Furniture Company*," 26 *University of Hawaii Law Review* (2004), 441.

15 See S. Last Stone, "In pursuit of the counter-text: the turn to the Jewish legal model in contemporary American legal theory," 106 *Harvard Law Review* (1993), 813, 889–91, noting the tension between aspirational law and conventional forms of authority within Jewish law.

16 See M. Broyde and S. Resnicoff, "Jewish law and modern business structures: the corporate paradigm," 43 *Wayne Law Review*, (1998), 1685.

17 Cf., e.g., the (Orthodox) Rabbinical Council of America's *Jewish Principles and Ethical Guidelines*, online at www.rabbis.org/news/article.cfm?id=105521 (Jewish law and business ethics requires only that companies comply with secular law and regulations) with M. Pava, "Kosher 'ethical guidelines' sidestepped ethics," *Forward*, March 26, 2010, www.forward.com/articles/126676 (arguing for a more robust conception of Jewish business and corporate ethics) and the statement of the Conservative movement's Rabbinical Assembly, "*Hekhsher tzedek al pi din*" at http://magentzedek.org/wp-content/uploads/2009/05/hekhsher_tzedek_al_pi_din_july_2009.pdf (arguing for enhanced corporate ethical standards on the basis of the halakha).

Further, in sharp contrast to state-based secular law, engagement in the practice and study of Jewish law has religious significance.[18] The religious obligation to toil in the garden of Torah by day and night means that a good deal of the system's intellectual energy is directed toward connecting to the divine via the wisdom embedded in the Torah, rather than defining the decision rules to be applied in actual cases; factors that underscore the crucial distinction between halakha and halakha-to-be-applied.[19] The corpus of halakhic literature from the Mishnah through the ages is replete with discussions of ostensibly-legal material that is better characterized as theology (apprehending the nature of God and His law), philosophical speculation, and moral guidelines for spiritual living than as "law" understood as social regulation through rule-based directives.

Third, because advocates of the *mishpat ivri* approach may be introducing Jewish law to an audience that does not accept the foundational assumptions of halakhic jurisprudence, they often attempt to bracket out the halakha's religious claims and deal mainly with the topics common to both Jewish and Western law.[20] The interlocking structure of civil and religious laws, however, makes this separation nearly impossible. For example, a common feature of halakhic tort law is that tortious acts that do not meet the halakhic definition of what American law calls "proximate cause" are "not liable in the court of man but liable in the court of heaven"[21] — a legal standard that is difficult to integrate into a system lacking this theological grounding.[22]

18 See section 4 below.

19 The importance of this distinction is stressed in the work of H. Ben-Menahem; see his *Judicial Deviation in Talmudic Law* (Chur Switzerland: 1991); "Maimonides on equity: reconsidering the *Guide for the Perplexed* III:34," 17 *Journal of Law and Religion* (2002), 19; "The second canonization of the Talmud," 29 *Cardozo Law Review* (2006), 37.

20 Elon is, of course, aware of these difficulties, and addresses them in several sections of his aforementioned opus; see Elon, n. 7 above, 116–37, 145–66. My own view is that the systems' disparate forms of legal regulation and authority raise greater conceptual and administrative concerns than Elon suggests, and that the relatively weak reception of Elon's jurisprudence within the Israeli courts reflects this as well.

21 See, e.g., bBaba Kama 56a.

22 Similar reservations are voiced in I. Englard, "Research in Jewish law — its nature and function," in B.S. Jackson (ed.), *Modern Research in Jewish Law* (Leiden: 1980).

The interconnectedness of the various branches of Jewish law generates further complexity for the comparative project. As a matter of positive law, American law asks whether the defendant is liable or not. The issue of the defendant's social or moral standing — whether he will be pilloried in the press or will lose his client base and go out of business — is left to alternate mechanisms, on the assumption that the social sphere is not fully subject to state regulation.[23] By contrast, not only does the halakha regulate some of the most intimate forms of conduct — as demonstrated by the laws governing how one should conduct himself in the bathroom[24] — but this regulation occurs under the same doctrinal and interpretative rubrics as questions of tort law or criminal liability. And while the question of whether particular conduct is subject to court-enforced sanction is a relevant concern within the halakhic framework,[25] on the whole, questions of administration and enforcement play a relatively minor role in halakhic jurisprudence.

This is not to argue that Jewish law is sui generis or that its decisional rules cannot be meaningfully compared to American/Western law. Indeed, some work in comparative Jewish law engages in deep doctrinal and structural analysis, producing insights that illuminate both systems.[26] Nevertheless, given the different orientations, structural comparison requires a level of nuance that is generally

23 Scholars have considered the viability of alternative forms of sanction in American law; see, e.g., D. Kahan, "What do alternative sanctions mean?," 63 *University of Chicago Law Review* (1996), 591; idem, "What's really wrong with shaming sanctions," 84 *Texas Law Review* (2006), 2075.

24 *SA*, OH 3.

25 E.g., the Talmud frequently distinguishes between claims cognizable in court and those that are not, and between offenses that warrant the intervention of human agency and those left to divine punishment. Nevertheless, these discussions are often of greater academic than practical interest. As numerous scholars have pointed out, actual court/community-enforced punishments are both more and less restrictive than what is formally proscribed by halakha. See, e.g., E. Quint and N.S. Hecht, *Jewish Jurisprudence: Its Sources and Modern Applications* (Chur Switzerland: 1980), 154–78; Stone, n. 15 above.

26 See, e.g., S. Lifshitz, "Distress exploitation contracts in the shadow of [the] no duty to rescue [rule]," 86 *North Carolina Law Review* (2008), 315; idem, "Married against their will? Toward a pluralist regulation of spousal relationships," 66 *Washington and Lee Law Review* (2009), 1565; idem, "Oppressive contracts: a Jewish law perspective," 23 *Journal of Law and Religion* (2008), 425.

absent from scholarship that looks to Jewish law as a springboard for reforming and improving American law.

## 2 The religious ethics model

A second approach concentrates on how Jewish law approaches matters deemed to be "ethical" or "moral" questions, commonly associated with abortion and end-of-life issues.[27] This view rests on the premise that religious traditions can supply ethical guidance, especially in areas where scientific and technological developments, new conceptions of personal autonomy, commodification, and centrally managed health care raise difficult legal issues. On the Jewish-law-as-ethics model, the syllabus focuses on addressing bioethical and other "moral" issues from a Jewish perspective.

This approach tends to avoid some of the drawbacks of the *mishpat ivri* approach. Contemporary discourse is more receptive to deontological and non-consequentialist arguments (and their halakhic analogues) in the sphere of bioethics than in the case of commercial law. And given the unique factual and technological matrix through which the said questions arise, there is less concern that a rule developed for one context (e.g., the commercial law of medieval Spain) will be unreflectively transplanted into a very different one.

Nevertheless, this approach has its own difficulties. First, what qualifies as a "law and religion" issue has more to do with how Americans negotiate their denominational (mainly Christian) and secular identities than with the internal understanding of Jewish law. Thus, while a scholar who suggests that we ought to resolve difficult questions of contract, property, tort, or evidence law by examining Canon or talmudic law is greeted with bemusement (an irony, given that all of these issues have deep roots in medieval religious jurisprudence[28]), when it comes to abortion and end-of-life issues, the Christian perspective has gained considerable traction in the legal and political spheres.

27 See Levine 2002, n. 2 above, 1 n. 4, which observes that the "advent of new biotechnologies" has led to an increase in scholarship addressing Jewish law and ethics, and mentions law school courses with titles such as "Comparative social issues under Jewish law," "Jewish law and contemporary issues," and "Jewish law and ethics in comparative perspective."

28 See H. Berman, *Faith and Order: The Reconciliation of Law and Religion* (Grand Rapids MI: 2000), 187–208.

It seems artificial, however, for a course in Jewish law to have these matters as its primary focus. Unlike commercial and criminal law, which are discussed at length by the Talmud and its intellectual heirs, halakhic approaches to bioethical questions must be teased out of terse statements scattered throughout the rabbinical literature. While important work is being done by scholars in the field, the emphasis bioethics receives seems exaggerated relative to the role of these questions within the tradition itself.

On a more methodological level, I have qualms over use of the "ethics" rubric in such contexts as "Jewish medical ethics" and even "Jewish business ethics." Without undertaking a full account of the relationship between law and ethics, from Plato's *Euthyphro* through Kant's *Groundwork of the Metaphysic of Morals* to Rawls' *A Theory of Justice*, ethics is conceptualized as a discourse that guides, conflicts with, and even challenges the outcomes mandated by law. In the Western tradition, ethics is a forum where ideas about the right and the good are developed through a process of reasoning from (or to) first principles, where reason serves as the primary criterion for assessing arguments and conferring legitimacy. This realm can be distinguished from that of law, where norms are generated from the promulgation and interpretation of authorized texts, and the authority of texts and their interpreters functions as the core source of legitimacy. It is for this reason that one of the primary purposes of ethical engagement is to create a platform **outside** the law from which law can be critiqued and improved.

Though there is little doubt that ethical concerns motivate a number of halakhic norms and influence halakhic decision-makers,[29] the classical rabbinical canon does not contain a term that corresponds to the rubric "ethics."[30] Furthermore, even in its least positivistic

29 Some apparently dispute this claim; see J. D. Bleich, "Is there an ethic beyond halacha?" in N. Samuelson (ed.), *Studies in Jewish Philosophy* (Lanham MD: 1987).

30 The tension between Jewish law and ethics has occasioned considerable debate and commentary, much of which grapples with how to define "halakha," "ethics," and the line between them. Important works in this debate include A. Lichtenstein, "Does the Jewish tradition recognize an ethic independent of halakha?," in M. Fox (ed.), *Modern Jewish Ethics, Theory, and Practice* (Columbus OH: 1975); M. Silberg, *Talmudic Law and the Modern State* (NY: 1973), 61–92; E. Berkowitz, *Not in Heaven: The Nature and Function of Halakha* (NY: 1983), 59–87; E. Korn, "Legal Floors and moral ceilings, a Jewish understanding of law and ethics," *Edah Journal* 2

exemplifications, the halakha proceeds via the interpretation and application of authoritative texts, not via reasoning based on first principles. Numerous case studies on the interface between Jewish law and ethics demonstrate that ethical ideals manifest themselves in the halakhic system through the network of authoritative texts, which explains why the question of whether there is an ethic independent of the halakha is so enduring and contentious.[31] In these and many other ways, the halakha bears closer resemblance to "law" than to "ethics."

Moreover, much of what is taught and written under the rubric of "Jewish ethics" is the product of conventional modes of halakhic analysis as applied to what are deemed "ethical questions." For a number of influential scholars, there is no discernable line demarcating classical halakhic-legal questions (the measure of damages for breach of contract; which labors are prohibited on the Sabbath; whether a particular form of processing renders a food non-kosher) from those commonly presented as ethical (the circumstances under which abortions are permitted; whether human cloning and research on stem cells derived from embryos should be prohibited or allowed).[32] It is not clear to me why "Jewish law arising in the medical context" or "the halakha of medicine" is not a more accurate designation than "Jewish medical ethics." Moreover, when medical halakha is misclassified as medical ethics, this preempts a more serious discussion about the

---

(2002), 2. An issue of the *Journal of Textual Reasoning* was devoted to the question of halakha and morality; it is available at http://etext.virginia.edu/journals/tr/volume6/number1/index.html. The question is also latent in much of A. Kirschenbaum, *Equity in Jewish Law* (Hoboken: 1991).

31 See, e.g., M. Halbertal in *Interpretative Revolutions in the Making* (Hebrew), (Jerusalem: 1999). In a different vein, the move toward egalitarianism within contemporary Orthodox circles is presented as debating the parameters of the halakhic concept of human dignity (*kvod habriyot*). See, e.g., D. Sperber, *The Path of Halakha* (Hebrew), (Jerusalem: 2007), 35–44.

32 See, e.g., E. Zipperstein, *Business Ethics in Jewish Law* (Hoboken: 1983), the front cover of which features an image of the frontispiece of the *Shulhan Arukh* law code. See also M. Broyde, "Fighting for peace: battlefield ethics, peace talks, treaties, and pacifism in the Jewish tradition," in J. Patout Burns (ed.), *War and its Discontents: Pacifism and Quietism in the Abrahamic Traditions* (Washington DC: 1996); B. Herring, *Jewish Ethics and Halakha for Our Time: Sources and Commentary* (Hoboken: 1984); F. Rosner, *Biomedical Ethics and Jewish Law* (Hoboken: 2001); idem, *Contemporary Biomedical Issues and Jewish Law* (Hoboken: 2007); F. Rosner and J. David Bleich (eds.), *Jewish Bioethics* (Hoboken: 1999); A. Steinberg, *Encyclopedia of Jewish Medical Ethics* (Jerusalem: 2003).

descriptive and normative relationship between halakha, Aggada, and ethical dimensions of legal and social issues.[33]

## 3 The legal and political theory model

Partly as a response to the problems discussed above and partly because different scholars are attracted to different questions, a third group of scholars, inspired by the late Robert Cover, have mined the Jewish tradition for insights into central questions of American and general jurisprudence.[34] Classes taught in this mode operate as seminars in comparative legal theory, drawing on biblical, rabbinical, and scholarly sources to illuminate conversations taking place in the wider legal academy.

On the whole, this direction is the most promising, for several reasons. First, as this is an exercise in comparing how scholarly elites conceptualize their legal systems (often in somewhat idealized form),

33 An approach to bioethics that directly addresses these questions is N. Zohar, *Alternatives in Jewish Bioethics* (NY: 1997). A good discussion of this issue more generally can be found in Y. Lorberbaum, "Reflections on the halakhic status of Aggadah," 24 *Dine Israel* (2007), 29.

34 In legal theory, much of this work has been influenced by Robert Cover. See M. Minow et al. (eds.), *Narrative, Violence, and the Law: The Essays of Robert Cover* (Ann Arbor MI: 1992), a collection that includes Cover's groundbreaking "Nomos and narrative," originally published in 97 *Harvard Law Review* (1983). On Jewish law scholarship influenced by Cover, see, e.g., Stone, n. 15 above; 17 *Yale Journal of Law and Humanities*, a symposium dedicated to Cover's work; P. Dane, "The maps of sovereignty: a meditation," 12 *Cardozo Law Review* (1991), 959; D.R. Dow, "Constitutional Midrash: the rabbi's solution to Professor Bickel's problem," 29 *Houston Law Review* (1992), 543; S. Levine, "Of inkblots and omnisignificance: conceptualizing secondary and symbolic functions of the Ninth Amendment in a comparative hermeneutic framework," *Michigan State Law Review* (2009), 277; idem, "Halacha and Aggada: translating Robert Cover's 'Nomos and narrative,'" *Utah Law Review* (1998), 465; Jeanne C. Fromer, "Looking to statutory intertext: toward the use of the rabbinic biblical interpretive stance in American statutory interpretation," 115 *Harvard Law Review* (2002), 1456.

On the political theory front, much of the work is inspired by Michael Walzer's ongoing Jewish Political Tradition project, which is expressly devoted to identifying texts that discuss legal and political theory within the Jewish tradition. See Walzer et al. (eds.), *The Jewish Political Tradition*, vol. 1, Authority (New Haven: 2003), vol. 2, Membership (New Haven: 2006) (henceforth JPT).

theory v. practice issues are of less concern. Second, since these scholars are more interested in exploring the phenomenon of law than in championing specific legal positions, the difficulties of inter-systemic transplants are moot. Third, by casting the inquiry as a search for theoretical frameworks rather than decision rules, this approach side-steps the fact that Jewish law is understood to apply exclusively to Jews. Finally, it recognizes that the halakha is far more than a system of discrete rules; rather, as a central institution of Judaism, it tackles more abstract questions of social and religious life.

Moreover, if one of the main questions facing our constitutional democracy is how to read static texts across time, there are good reasons for American scholars to be interested in one of the oldest legal systems still in existence. In this sense, American law is a 200 year old version of what Jewish law has been doing for two millennia: R. Akiva and R. Ishmael, Rava and Abbaye, Rashi and the Rambam, R. Joseph Caro and R. Moses Isserles, all grappled with the questions of text, time, and context. The Jewish experience of reading both the Bible and the Talmud has potential to enrich contemporary discourse on legal theory and interpretation considerably.

Nevertheless, this approach, too, has its own difficulties, principally related to the status of any sort of "theory" within the halakha. Although virtually every legal question in Jewish law raises problems of textual interpretation, these questions are generally addressed without explicit theorizing. The rabbinical authorities rarely consciously reflect on their methodology, and are far more interested in the technical dimensions of the legal dispute than the broader questions of interpretive theory and practice.

The tension, however, runs deeper than the general lack of methodological awareness or theoretical terminology. The halakhic corpus does contain terms for a wide array of abstract legal categories — concepts such as *kim lei bederaba minei, hatikha naaset neveila, tuma lemafreia, breira*, and *bikhdei sheyaasu*. Yet these terms are so enmeshed within the technical rules of halakhic decision-making that they are scarcely translatable beyond their native context. On the other hand, the tradition has few terms corresponding to those that figure in theoretical discussions of law and politics. Notions such as: politics, polity, democracy, autonomy, individualism, universalism, particularism, culture, constitutionalism, rule of law, equality, equity, and pluralism — the key terms we use to conduct our legal and political discourse — receive only rudimentary treatment within the classical rabbinical sources, which lack the conceptual and philosophical orientation that renders these ideas useful. The portrayal of Jewish law as offering a perspective on these theoretical issues, without acknowledging that the tradition, whether consciously or not, leaves them unaddressed, thus itself fails to address one of the most salient features of halakhic thought.

Further, even when focusing on the talmudic passages that most directly address "jurisprudential" issues, I am skeptical about the student's ability to appreciate them. These narratives are provocative because they reside within a genre obsessed with doctrinal reasoning and otherwise devoid of abstract thought. Take, for example, what is likely the best known talmudic passage among legal theorists, the celebrated narrative about the "oven of Aknai" (*tanur shel akhnai*).[35]

35 See bBaba Metzia 59. A search of Westlaw's "Journal and Law Reviews" and Lexis' "Law Reviews Combined" databases using the terms "oven of a**nai," "oven of a*nai," "oven of o**nai," and "oven of o*nai" yielded 28 results. These databases do not cover books, book chapters, and specialty and foreign journals in which work on Jewish law is likely to appear. The search generates the following results: M. Silberg, "Law and morals in Jewish jurisprudence," 75 *Harvard Law Review* (1961), 308; Cover 1983, n. 34 above, 4; S. Last Stone, "Colloquy: Judaism and Postmodernism," 14 *Cardozo Law Review* (1993), 1681; idem, "In pursuit," n. 15 above, 813; D. Greenwood, "Beyond Dworkin's dominions: investments, memberships, the Tree of Life, and the abortion question," 72 *Texas Law Review* (1994), 559; idem, "Fictional shareholders: for whom are corporate managers trustees, revisited," 69 *S.C. Law Review* (1996), 1021; idem, "Akhnai," *Utah Law Review* (1997), 309; S. Levine, "Halacha and Aggada: translating Robert Cover's *Nomos and Narrative*," *Utah Law Review* (1998), 465; D. Nimmer, "Adams and bits: of Jewish kings and copyrights," 71 *S.C. Law Review* (1998), 219; C. Povarsky, "Regulating advanced reproductive technologies: a comparative analysis of Jewish and American law," 29 *University of Toledo Law Review* (1998), 409; C. Weisbrod, "Susanna and the elders: a note on the regulation of families," *Utah Law Review* (1998), 271; E. Kleinhaus, n. 1 above, 121; S. Werber, "Cloning: a Jewish perspective with a comparative study of other Abrahamic traditions," 30 *Seton Hall Law Review* (2000), 1114; C. Fishman, "Old Testament justice," 51 *Catholic University Law Review* (2002), 405; Sokobin, n. 2 above, 795; B. Visotzky, "The myth of divine law in secular society," 51 *DePaul Law Review* (2002), 1061; S. Feldman, "Reason and analogy: a comparison of early Islamic and Jewish legal institutions," 2 *UCLA Journal of Islamic and Near Eastern Law* (2003), 129; B. Ledewitz, "The openness of Talmud," 41 *Duquesne Law Review* (2003), 353; A. Soifer, "Secular sectarianism, perilous neutrality," 38 *Tulsa Law Review* (2003), 755; D. Luban, "The coiled serpent of argument: reason, authority, and law in a talmudic tale," 79 *Chicago-Kent Law Review*

What makes this such a compelling story is that within the talmudic canon, the rabbis are far more likely to focus on an issue such as the ritual status of an oven — a detail that is perceived, on the standard jurisprudential account of this passage, as distracting from the thrust of the text, than on issues such as the nature of halakhic discourse, the sources of halakhic authority, original intent versus evolving meaning, and other jurisprudential issues presented via this rich passage. The Talmud's seemingly insatiable appetite for debating questions pertaining to the ritual status of various entities, in this case, a clay oven — a mindset foreign to the contemporary American scholar — is far more characteristic of "rabbinic legal theory" than the theoretical ideas explored through this famous passage. I fear that when the syllabus is framed around passages such as the oven of Akhnai, the story of Moses visiting R. Akiva's classroom,[36] invocations of the dictum "both are the words of the living God" (*eilu veeilu*),[37]and similar texts, little of the unique structure of halakhic thought is conveyed to students.

There is no doubt that in the late Middle Ages, Jewish scholars in Iberia and Italy borrowed terms and concepts from Greek and Arabic philosophers, incorporating them into their works on Jewish philosophy, biblical interpretation, and to a lesser degree, Jewish law. But with the significant exception of Maimonides, halakhists did not, on the whole, attempt to translate the particularities of the halakha into universal categories, nor did they produce much of what we would identify as organized or comprehensive legal theory. This is illustrated by examining one of the few texts in the rabbinical corpus that goes

---

(2004), 1253; J.A. Robertson, "Causative vs. beneficial complicity in the embryonic stem cell debate," 36 *Connecticut Law Review* (2004), 1099; C. Stern, "The common law and the religious foundations of the rule of law before Casey," 38 *University of San Francisco Law Review* (2004), 499; A. Jacobson, "Publishing dissent," 62 *Washington and Lee Law Review* (2005), 1607; A. Chodorow, "Agricultural tithing and (flat) tax complexity," 68 *University of Pittsburgh Law Review* (2006), 267; C. Saiman, "Jesus' legal theory — a rabbinic reading," 23 *Journal of Law and Religion* (2008), 97; K. Yelpaala, "Legal consciousness and contractual obligations," 39 *McGeorge Law Review* (2008), 193; H. Ben-Menahem, "Is talmudic law a religious legal system?" 24 *Journal of Law and Religion* (2009), 379; S. Resnicoff, "Autonomy in Jewish law — in theory and in practice," 24 *Journal of Law and Religion* (2009), 507.

36 bMenahot 22b.

37 bEruvin 13b.

beyond the familiar rabbinical debates to explicitly theorize about the nature of Jewish law and its relation to governance.[38]

As is well known, talmudic rules of criminal procedure make it all but impossible for a court to impose criminal sanctions.[39] Writing in the fourteenth century, R. Nissim of Gerona (Ran) drew attention to the social maladies that would inevitably result from a legal system denuded of its deterrent effect. In response, the Ran proposed an innovative reframing of the halakhic constitutional order. The Ran distinguishes between the sphere of the pure halakha, which reflects the ideal mode of social ordering, and the sphere of civil administration, which serves as a corrective for imperfect reality. According to the Ran, the rules of criminal procedure outlined in the Talmud are designed to ascertain the absolute truth regarding a suspect's culpability. This ideal law is the mechanism through which God bestows grace on the Jewish people. At times, however — maybe even most times — these cumbersome procedures will have adverse social consequences. Hence a parallel system of civil governance is required. Initially, the Jewish king administered this system, but with the demise of the monarchy, administration was transferred to the rabbinical courts. The king and rabbinical courts are authorized to promote social order through legislative and executive acts that may contravene halakha.[40]

38 Menachem Lorberbaum, *Politics and the Limits of Law* (Stanford: 2001) deals primarily with Maimonides and the Ran, but also cites Nahmanides' *Mishpat Haherem* and several of the Rashba's responsa which foreshadow the Ran's more comprehensive and ambitious treatment. See also E. Nachalon, "Structural models of religion and state in Jewish democratic political thought," 22 *Touro Law Review* (2006), 613, which cites Maimonides and the Ran as providing the leading theoretical account of the nature of Jewish constitutional law; S. Morell, "The constitutional limits of communal government in rabbinic law," *Jewish Social Studies* 33 (1971), 87. While Morell cites numerous 12th to 18th century rabbinical sources that grapple with core questions of communal political authority and social governance, the majority of these sources are either works of halakhic exposition or responsa dealing with individual cases. Few of these sources even attempt a conceptual account of the relationship between halakha and political governance.

39 A good exposition of this issue, as well as its apologetic and polemical uses in the modern era, can be found in B. Berkowitz, *Execution and Invention* (NY: 2006).

40 The degree to which the Ran is articulating a broad statement of Jewish constitutional theory, as opposed to specifying a set of emergency powers that the political leadership may use under exigent circumstances, is a

The Ran's thought goes beyond the back-and-forth of talmudic analysis to present an idea that can legitimately be considered halakhic legal/political theory. It is important to appreciate where a text like *Derashot Haran* (Sermons of R. Nissim Gerondi) fits within the range of rabbinical writing on Jewish law. In contrast to the majority of medieval halakhic writings, the Ran produced a self-standing text whose declared purpose is to confront a core theoretical difficulty posed by the talmudic conception of law. The Ran himself understood that his work belonged to a different genre, for *Derashot Haran* employs terms not typically found in the talmudic literature,[41] and its tone and structure are unlike those of conventional halakhic writing. In fact, at one point there was serious debate as to whether the author of the famous *Derashot* could really be the same person who had written an influential and traditionally-structured commentary on Alfasi's *Halakhot*.[42]

As I said, the most significant feature of the *Derashot* is that it provides a cohesive and systematic account of a specific sphere of the law. In a culture that parses every jot and tittle of the Talmud's phrasing, few talmudic scholars had, prior to the Ran, offered such a systemic treatment of any legal sphere. Nor did the publication of the Ran's *Derashot* awaken a latent desire for a more holistic approach to halakhic analysis. It was not until the nineteenth century — when the possibility of Jewish sovereignty appeared on the horizon — that talmudic scholars returned to the Ran's ideas about Jewish constitutionalism.[43]

---

matter of scholarly debate. Cf. A. Kirschenbaum, "The role of punishment in Jewish criminal law," 9 *Jewish Law Annual* (1991), 123 (arguing for the latter interpretation) with Lorberbaum, n. 38 above, 131–34 (arguing for the former interpretation).

41 E.g., terms such as *nimusei umot haolam*, *tikun medini*, and *sibot hahavayot hativiyot*. See Lorberbaum, n. 38 above, 153–55.

42 See the introduction to Leon (Aryeh L.) Feldman's edition of *Derashot Haran* (Jerusalem: 1973), 1–8.

43 It appears that when rabbis Grodzinsky and Herzog debated the scope of the Ran's view, neither cited other authorities who had discussed it. See JPT, n. 34 above, 1:471–76. With the exception of the Herzog/Grodzinsky debate, JPT does not point to other sources that discuss the Ran's ideas. And aside from a brief comment by R. Isaiah Horowitz, a 16th century halakhic authority, in his *Shnei Luhot Habrit*, Lorberbaum cites no pre-19th century source that addresses the viability of the Ran's thesis; see Lorberbaum, n. 38 above, 190 n. 19.

In sum, part of the story of the jurisprudence of Jewish law is surely the relative lack of systematic thinking on the ideas central to understanding a system of law and its functioning in society.[44] The "burying one's head in the details" approach to law itself forms a kind of atheoretical legal theory[45] that deserves at least as much consideration as the rare overt discussions of legal theory found in the writings of Maimonides, the Ran, the Abravanel, and a very few other Jewish thinkers. A survey of Jewish law wherein only the Ran's *Derashot* is presented, but not his talmudic commentary, and the seminal works *Beit Yosef, Ketzot Hahoshen,* and *Yam Shel Shlomo* are presented solely by considering their relatively philosophical introductions, would generate a highly bizarre perspective on Jewish law. Any account of Jewish law must grapple with the issue of why "legal theory" is to be found only in the **introductions** of these works, that is, why it is relegated to the margins, so to speak, of halakhic jurisprudence.

The difficulties in conceptualizing the study of Jewish law can be traced back to questions regarding the genre of the Talmud itself. The Talmud is a layered text in which a single passage can incorporate multiple legal and literary styles. It routinely mixes tightly-wound legal analysis with narrative, folklore, biblical exposition, ethical

44 See JPT, n. 34 above. This impression is confirmed by the selection of texts presented in the volumes of the JPT. Leaving aside the exceptional case of Maimonides, most of the rabbinical sources presented are not self-standing theoretical treatments of the subject, but rather brief comments nestled within larger works of biblical and talmudic commentary or responsa. See, e.g., JPT, vol. 1, ch. 3, which discusses the role of the monarchy. In addition to the works of Maimonides and the Ran discussed above, JPT cites the commentaries of the Abravanel and the Netziv on Deuteronomy 17:14–20, as well as the Meiri's commentary on Sanhedrin, none of which present a self-standing or theoretical account (for or against) monarchic government. JPT's chapter on the authority of the Gentile state (vol. 1, ch. 9) gives the same impression. These materials consist largely of snippets of talmudic commentary and responsa, and are not self-standing works that offer a theoretical account of the relationship between Jewish and Gentile law.

45 A similar mindset is found in both the classical Roman jurists and the early common lawyers; see J. Gordley, *Ius Civile*: The Roman Jurists (chapter in forthcoming book on the Western legal tradition; manuscript on file with author); G. Postema, "Classical common law jurisprudence (part ii)," 3 *Oxford University Commonwealth Law Journal* (2002), 1, 5–6 (the non-systematic nature of early common law jurisprudence).

teachings, and speculative thought, without much concern for the boundaries between them. Indeed, the Talmud is not only the foundational source for all questions of black-letter law, it is also the central repository of Jewish thought on many other areas of human inquiry. Given its legal architecture, however, ideas we might otherwise classify as pertaining to philosophy and ethics, politics, or theology are often cast in the legal mold of the talmudic give-and-take.

The main problem with the three approaches detailed above is not so much that they are wrong, as that they are incomplete. The substantive law (*mishpat ivri*) perspective correctly focuses on the elements of the halakha that are analogous to state-based regulations, though often at the expense of Jewish law's ethical, theological, expressive, and ritual dimensions. The "ethics" approach explicitly focuses on the aspirational and applied aspects of the halakha, but is reluctant to confront how neither "law" nor "ethics" (nor their synthesis) adequately captures the halakhic methodology. Finally, the "theory" perspective correctly construes the halakha as a reflective discourse, but can offer no account of either its overall lack of theoretical architecture or its obsession with the precise boundaries of discrete legal categories. While each approach highlights relevant features of Jewish law, each fails to explain how the largely undifferentiated and unstructured discourse, characterized by recourse to the same legal concepts throughout, performs these different functions simultaneously.

## 4 Studying Jewish law as *talmud torah*

The halakha's multiple roles pose considerable challenges to its classification. Yet from the perspective of the law school, I believe that the most compelling aspect of Jewish law lies in confronting the question of how these multiple profiles can be reconciled. The central challenge for those writing and teaching in the field is to grasp how these conflicting features relate to each other, and then to assess the implications for the theory and practice of Jewish law.

Provision of a fully-developed account of this complex process exceeds the scope of this article. The more modest goal of this concluding section is to highlight the traditional role of *talmud torah* (studying the Torah, i.e. the law), in the context of academic analysis of Jewish law, and explain how this concept can provide a useful framework for understanding the different functions of halakhic discourse.

While the halakha puts forward a great number of legal principles, perhaps its most distinctive contribution lies not in any substantive rule, but in the centrality accorded to learning the law, classically reflected in the ideal of *talmud torah*. As used here, *talmud torah* refers to three related ideas: (1) Torah study has intrinsic value and is studied "for its own sake" (*torah lishma*);[46] (2) Torah study is a foundational devotional and religious activity equal to, and perhaps outweighing, all other religious obligations (*talmud torah keneged kulam*);[47] and (3) the obligation to study Torah is incumbent on each individual.[48]

Pursuant to the ideology of *talmud torah*, Torah study — classically centered on the Talmud's analysis of specific details of Jewish law — is not limited to knowing the rules of a given jurisdiction or even to understanding the law's underlying principles. Rather, *talmud torah* is understood to be the most pristine method of divine worship, surpassing not only alternative spiritual and intellectual pursuits (prayer, good works, philosophical contemplation), but virtually every other activity[49] — including earning a living![50] Even in its less extreme manifestations, Torah study is taken to be an expression of religious commitment and a primary mode of generating and transmitting Jewish identity.

Like most areas of Jewish law, the practice of *talmud torah* is not well theorized, nor has its practice been uniform or static.[51] Torah study is pursued to: fulfill the religious duty to study; learn how to implement halakha in practice; develop resources to resolve novel legal questions;

46 E.g., Sifre Deuteronomy 48; mAvot 6:1; bPesahim 50b. While *talmud torah* attained its fullest expression in the ideology of the 19th century Lithuanian yeshivas, the idea that study of the law is a religious experience as well as the primary Jewish educational focus has been traced back as far as the first century. See, e.g., S. Safrai, *The Jewish People in the First Century* (Philadelphia: 1988), 945–74. On the history and theology of *torah lishma*, see N. Lamm, *Torah Lishmah: Torah for Torah's Sake* (Hoboken: 1989).

47 See mPeia 1:1. In bMegila 16b, the Talmud explains that Torah study is greater than honoring one's parents, building the Temple, and even saving lives!

48 Maimonides, *Code*, Laws concerning Study of the Torah 1:8.

49 The classic sources on the conflict between "study" and "practice" are Sifre Deuteronomy 4; bKidushin 40a.

50 This is not recommended for the average person, but is an ideal to be aspired to by the select; see bBerakhot 35a.

51 For a good survey of contemporary approaches to the study of rabbinical texts, see J. Levisohn, "A menu of orientations towards the teaching of rabbinic literature," *Journal of Jewish Education* 71 (2010), 1.

familiarize oneself with the wisdom of the Rabbis; comprehend the Torah's rules; communicate Jewish values; build a shared communal discourse; accumulate the cultural capital conferred on those who demonstrate Torah erudition. Yet several common themes emerge, and exploring certain features of *talmud torah* furthers our understanding of Jewish law and its potential contributions to the law school.[52]

52 There is currently considerable debate regarding what texts and methodologies reflect the most appropriate and authentic forms of *talmud torah*. The traditionalist position, which focuses on conceptual analysis of the legal sections of the Talmud, is powerfully articulated by R. Joseph Soloveitchik and his son-in-law, R. Aharon Lichtenstein, leading practitioners and theorists of *talmud torah*. R. Soloveitchik's thesis is presented most fully in his *Halakhic Man*, translated by L. Kaplan (Philadelphia: 1983), 99–137, and in more anecdotal form in statements collected by A. Rakeffet-Rothkoff in his memoir, *The Rav* (Hoboken: 1999) , 2:193–208. The most concise presentation of R. Lichtenstein's view is found in his "Study," in A. Cohen and P. Mendes-Flohr (eds.), *Contemporary Jewish Religious Thought* (NY: 1987). Other scholars reject this Talmud-centric approach and advocate broadening the conception of Torah study to include and even emphasize Bible, Jewish philosophy, theology, liturgical poetry, Midrash, Aggada, and Kabbala.

Recently, a number of scholars (many of whom are students of either R. Soloveitchik or R. Lichtenstein, or their students) have charted a middle path. These writers typically concur with the traditionalist view that *talmud torah* should focus on legal issues emerging from the Talmud, but have expanded the sources and methodology used to understand this material, and explored different theologies and legal theories consistent with the values of *talmud torah*. See, e.g., Judah Brandes, *Applied Aggada: Studies on Family, Society and Worship* (Hebrew), (Jerusalem: 2005) and *Mada Toratekha: Ketubot* (New Milford CT: 2008); D. Flatto, "Tradition and modernity in the house of study: reconsidering the relationship between the conceptual and critical methods of studying Talmud," *Tradition* 43 (2010); A. Walfish, "Hermeneutics and values: issues in improving contemporary Talmud teaching," in J. Saks and S. Handelman (eds.), *Wisdom from All My Teachers* (Jerusalem: 2003); see also the essays collected in P. Socken (ed.) *Why Study Talmud in the Twenty-first Century?* (Lanham MD: 2009). This approach is also implicit in much of the scholarship cited in nn 56–63 below.

My own view is that in the law school context, one cannot assume the theological claims at the heart of the traditionalist position, nor should we be limited to its literary canon or methods. On the other hand, the law school (as opposed to the Jewish day school and the Jewish Studies department) is the appropriate forum to focus on the distinctive role of law within Judaism and on the bold claims made on behalf of study and observance of the law.

i Law as a way of knowing

In most Western systems, the task of knowing the law is assigned to lawyers, a subset of the population that sells (or donates) its legal knowledge to others. Although ignorance of the law rarely succeeds as a defense, individual citizens are not required to display familiarity with its many details. Legal education is similarly geared toward training professionals charged with mediating between citizen-clients and the set of institutions known as "the law." The study of law is thus typically instrumental, and even in its more expansive dimensions, focuses on educating more complete **lawyers** rather than cultivating more refined **citizens**.

*Talmud Torah*, by contrast, envisions a system in which legal study is incumbent on everyone — or at least every male. The law itself is understood as a way of knowing — knowing God and knowing His human creatures, who are commanded to live in accordance with it. Studying is thus understood as an obligation of citizenship, an expression of belonging to the community, and a way of absorbing and affirming its values.[53] Ironically, for all the jokes about Jewish lawyers,

53 This approach to Torah study parallels the account of law and legal education developed by various "legal humanists," most prominently J.B. White. In *Heracles' Bow* (Madison WI: 1985), White describes law as an "intellectual and cultural activity" (49) and stresses the "ethical and communal character of law" and its study (34). Learning the law is "study of the ways we constitute ourselves as individuals, as communities, and as cultures" (35). Finally, law is "literally and deliberatively constitutive. . . . it makes real a social world" (35).

White's reading of American law offers a valuable starting point for understanding the role of *talmud torah* in Jewish law. However, *talmud torah* does not fit at least two aspects of White's theory. First, White envisions a citizenry that is legally literate, appreciates the broad contours of the legal discourse, and understands how to function in a social world that is governed by law. But even at his most expansive, White does not envision the culture of *talmud torah*, wherein citizens are absorbed in study of detailed and technical rules of law. In the community White describes, this side of the law remains limited to professionally-trained lawyers who are called upon to use this knowledge in practice. There is no need for educated citizens to be well versed in the particulars of tort law.

Second, White's account of law calls on lawyers to become conversant with an array of different forms of human expression, most notably literature and the arts. White's vision of law is attained when the lawyer is able to step back from his cases and statutes, and immerse herself in great works of literature — texts that lie outside the legal canon. *Talmud torah*, by

traditional halakha does not envisage the idea of professional "lawyers" on the Western model. Ideally, each citizen sustains a personal connection to the law, cultivated through the spiritual and pastoral guidance of a rabbi/teacher, rather than the contractual relationship of lawyer/client. As such, every Jew is commanded to set time aside each day to master halakhic intricacies.[54] Through *talmud torah,* the citizen is invited to join the law's creative discourse, to be engaged in following the development of legal ideas, and even to participate in their formulation. The Torah-studying citizen is not only the addressee of the law, but also the addressee of its internal dialogue, its way of knowing. The objective of studying the law transcends the instrumental, and encompasses the desire to be part of rabbinical culture and to form one's character via reflection on rabbinical teachings. Law is a tool for ongoing education.[55]

This explains why *talmud torah* does not distinguish between topics of current practical relevance and matters that have not been practiced for thousands of years. From the instrumental perspective, study of a system that expends its energy on tort law that no longer applies, or rules of criminal procedure that may never have applied, would seem to be a waste of time. Moreover, without detailed knowledge of the surrounding social and historical facts, it is difficult to reconstruct or appreciate the interests and policies reflected in each legal decision. But if we perceive the study of the halakha as a religiously-sanctioned form of cultural literacy, the curricular choices become more understandable. Modern scholars have done an admirable job of unearthing the foundational ideas embedded in the not-often applied laws of the

contrast, is classically anchored in specifically legal texts, and many of its most ardent devotees discourage (and even prohibit) the study of non-rabbinical literature, including Jewish writings that lie outside the sphere of halakhic exposition. Classical *talmud torah* thus seeks to fulfill many of the roles White ascribes to legal culture, but by means of a more circumscribed set of legally-oriented resources. Nevertheless, recent calls to reintegrate Aggada and other forms of Jewish thought into study of the rabbinical literature, as well as the move to more comparative approaches to Torah study, are in line with the outlook endorsed by White.

54 Maimonides, Laws concerning Study of the Torah 1:8–12. In law 12, Maimonides describes the "working man" as someone who spends three hours of his day working and nine hours engaged in study!

55 See Devora Steinmetz, "Talmud study as a religious practice" in Socken, n. 52 above, ch. 4.

"wayward woman" (*sota*),[56] false prophets,[57] kings and courts[58]; the apparently never-applied laws of *ir hanidahat*[59] and criminal procedure[60]; and the more mundane (but to some degree practiced) laws of employment,[61] civil procedure,[62] and the establishment of fast days.[63] From the perspective of *talmud torah*, the primary question is not whether the law is implemented as studied, but whether the student becomes a more fully developed halakhic citizen through study.

### ii Unfinished texts

A second feature is that *talmud torah* manifests a preference for "unfinished texts." These texts do not present a worked-out thesis on a given topic, but instead provide the raw materials from which meaning is constructed anew by the student engaged in Torah study. A critical element of Torah study is the first-hand struggle of uncovering and creating meaning through an encounter with the sanctified text.[64] In the view of rabbinical thinkers, the ongoing process of attempting to finish the unfinished text, of merging into "the sea of the Talmud," transforms the act of study into a means of divine communion.[65]

56 Y. Rosen-Tvzi, *The Rite that Was Not* (Hebrew), (Jerusalem: 2008).

57 S. Last Stone, "Between truth and trust: the false prophet as self deceiver," available at http://www.cardozo.yu.edu/uploadedFiles/Cardozo/Profiles/sstone-474/between_truth_and_trust.pdf.

58 D. Flatto, "The king and I: the separation of powers in early Hebraic political theory," 20 *Yale Journal of Law and Humanities* (2008), 61.

59 E.g., Halbertal, n. 31 above, 122–45.

60 E.g., Berkowitz, n. 39 above, 12–17 and sources cited therein.

61 E.g., E. Levinas, *Nine Talmudic Readings*, translated by A. Aronowicz (Bloomington IN: 1990), 94–119.

62 E.g., H. Shapira, "The debate over compromise and the goals of the judicial process," 27 *Dine Israel* (2010), 183.

63 E.g., A. Walfish, "The poetics of the Mishnah," in A. J. Avery-Peck and J. Neusner (eds.), *The Mishnah in Contemporary Perspective* (Boston: 2006); S. Last Stone, "On the interplay of rules, 'cases' and concepts in rabbinic legal literature: another look at the Aggadot on Honi the Circle-drawer," 24 *Dine Israel* (2007), 125.

64 See A. Lichtenstein, *Leaves of Faith: The World of Jewish Learning* (Jersey City NJ: 2003), 10–16.

65 These ideas are elaborated on in the final section of R. Joseph Soloveitchik's *Halakhic Man*, n. 52 above, 99–137; see also comments by R. Soloveitchik cited in Rakeffet-Rothkoff, n. 52 above, 202–203.

The Talmud is, of course, the prototypical unfinished text, a text that is not "read" so much as it is "learned" in a way that reproduces its unique dialectical style. Most talmudic and biblical commentary is likewise unfinished, depending conceptually — and even graphically — on the text being interpreted. The commitment to unfinished texts is demonstrated most dramatically by the reception of Maimonides' *Code* (*Mishne Torah*), likely the most **finished** text in the halakhic literature.[66] Maimonides authored the *Code* to remedy the confusion generated by the unfinished nature of the Talmud, setting down the law governing all aspects of Jewish life.[67] Yet, the *Code* achieved prominence not because it was finished, but in spite of it. Later interpreters — even later codifiers — were almost unanimous in rejecting the *Code*'s methodology. Instead, the *Mishne Torah* spawned numerous commentaries that sought to "un-finish" the *Code*'s crystalline language and analytic structure, and reintegrate it into mainstream rabbinical discourse.[68]

Law schools are familiar with unfinished texts, and the process of piecing together several lines of precedent offers a close parallel to the talmudic encounter. Yet this method is typically limited to courses focused on legal doctrine. As one moves from the analysis of doctrine to the courses probing the law's wider dimensions, syllabi shift their focus from the "case crunching" of legal texts to more deliberately reflective and "finished" works of scholarship.

*Talmud torah* resists this move. While Jewish law contains few overtly theoretical discussions, a wealth of accumulated wisdom on law, legal theory, and legal practice lies within the Talmud's intricate and sometimes convoluted atheoretical and legal narratives. Rather than shy away from the unfinished and technically dense analyses of legal doctrine, an approach anchored in *talmud torah* encounters

66 In fact, nearly all the texts of the classical Rabbinic period — from the earliest Midrash through the Mishnah, Tosefta, both Talmuds, and the later Midrashim — are unfinished. These texts contain statements attributed to multiple authors, are redacted rather than authored, and do not develop a thesis via sustained argument. It would take until the Geonic period before halakhic authorities began to produce finished texts.

67 See Maimonides' Introduction to the *Mishne Torah*. A more complete analysis of Maimonides' motivations and goals in writing the most finished work in the rabbinical canon is provided in I. Twersky, *Introduction to the Code of Maimonides* (New Haven: 1980), 20–47, 61–81.

68 Cf. I. Twersky, "The *Shulhan Arukh*: enduring code of Jewish law," *Judaism* 16 (1967), 141–58.

them directly, "interrogating" their content to uncover the broader implications latent in specific legal doctrines. This approach also plays to the institutional strengths of the law school, as lawyers are not intimidated by dense networks of legal rules and are trained to evaluate the social and intellectual commitments these networks presuppose. The insights that would emerge from adopting this approach would be a welcome addition to the study of Jewish law, and offer intriguing possibilities for the legal academy more generally.

### iii Study and obligation

The third element of *talmud torah*, perhaps the most difficult to confront in the contemporary academic context, is its normative emphasis. Torah study traditionally centers on texts that articulate halakhic doctrine; focuses on particular details rather than general principles; favors rules over standards; and is taken to embody binding norms that demand compliance. Although in recent years scholars have noted that the nature of halakhic authority is more complex than often assumed,[69] the bulk of halakhic discourse is unambiguously engaged in defining the scope and application of specific halakhic directives.

Theory — and legal theory in particular — can be normative, but normative legal theory tends to think about how to balance conflicting priorities, set the regulatory agenda, and develop a template for resolving interpretive and doctrinal difficulties. A deep reading of Jewish law teaches that it can perform each of these tasks as well, but halakhic discourse focuses on discrete actions, employing a high degree of precision in policing the boundaries of its categories. This exacting normativity forms the foundation of halakhic discourse.

*Talmud torah*, conceived as a program of cultural literacy, self-actualization, and spiritual discovery, occurs within a framework of discrete legal discussion that assumes corresponding legal obligations. While the direct aim of study is not limited to establishing authoritative practice, a commitment to *talmud torah* generates behavioral demands that are substantially more concrete than even didactic readings of literature or philosophy. Torah study is not only about gaining

69 See, e.g., the writings of H. Ben-Menahem, n. 19 above; A. Rosenak, *Halakha as an Agent of Change* (Hebrew), (Jerusalem: 2009); A. Ravitsky and A. Rosenak (eds.), *New Streams in Philosophy of Halakha* (Hebrew), (Jerusalem: 2008); A. Sagi, *The Open Canon: On the Meaning of Halakhic Discourse*, translated by B. Stein (NY: 2007).

familiarity with the law or demonstrating membership in a community; it is a practice that generates a deep sense of obligation to the system as a whole,[70] a feature that is especially important to a regime with limited enforcement mechanisms. In fact, the traditional expectation was that those immersed in Torah study would display higher degrees of voluntary compliance with the halakha, and that the personal practice of the scholar would model behavior for the layman. In its ideal form, the intellectual process of evaluating and interrogating halakhic sources generates both a heightened appreciation of their underlying meaning and an increased commitment to their actualization. Hand in hand with the self-realization enabled by the tradition's deliberative nature is the call for submission to the law: "Great is study, for it leads to action!" (*gadol talmud hameivi lidei maase*).[71]

This is not to suggest that students in a Jewish law class, or scholars writing in the field, must adhere to the dictates of Jewish law. But it does suggest that articulation of the project of teaching Jewish law in the law school context must take into account the highly particularistic level at which halakhic legal regulation operates. For in the law school setting, Jewish law is taught alongside law and literature, law and philosophy, law and society, and methods of cultural study whose normative implications are situated at a substantially higher level of generality. The comparisons are real and illuminating, but they underscore the need to emphasize that *talmud torah* usually involves investigation, in great detail, of the particularities of specific precepts rather than overarching principles.

## Conclusion

For all the strengths of *talmud torah*, one shortcoming must be acknowledged. The classical Lithuanian understanding of *talmud torah* is currently under review even in its traditional setting, and cannot simply be transplanted from the yeshiva to the law school.[72] Historically, *talmud torah* has excluded women and non-Jews, and perhaps

70 This aspect of *talmud torah* is stressed by Lichtenstein, n. 64 above, 7–8.

71 See bKidushin 40b, which records the classic debate over the relative merits of Torah study and precept observance.

72 In recent years, educators have become increasingly attuned to the shortcomings of classical *talmud torah* in its traditional settings. See, e.g., A. Lichtenstein and J. Brandes, *Talmud Study in Yeshiva High Schools* (Jerusalem: 2007); Y. Unterman, "'If you seek Him with all your heart':

even prohibited their participation. At the substantive level, it hardly takes into account Midrash or Aggada, or how they inform the halakhic project more generally. It can be naive and woefully uninformed about the social processes through which legal texts are created, how decisions are made, and the ensuing consequences. *Talmud Torah* has generally ignored the historicity of its own texts, and has been closed off not only from the world of legal scholarship, but from the humanities and social sciences more broadly. Even for lawyers, its sights are trained too narrowly.

Nonetheless, *talmud torah* opens up possibilities for understanding why law is studied. It reminds us that in addition to being a mode of regulation, law is a method of knowing, and that although in many ways the halakha was never experienced as a regulatory regime, study of law can been taken as the noblest of all human endeavors: engaging in God's word.[73]

Furthermore, *talmud torah* is process-based. The spiritual work is accomplished through direct contact with texts engaging core issues of theology together with fine points of legal detail. Jewish ethics are communicated not only from the texts' substance, but from the process of putting them together, pulling them apart, and discerning the meanings latent within them. To the contemporary theorist, *talmud torah* suggests that theoretical questions be addressed via discussion of the law's particulars. Within the halakha, these conversations take place by participating in *talmud torah,* by inhabiting the halakha from within.

Although not often stated explicitly, some of the best work in Jewish law is already informed by the *talmud torah* perspective. In bringing this concept to the fore, I hope to engender further conversations regarding the nature of Jewish law and its relevance to the contemporary law school.

---

nurturing total individual growth in *yeshivah,*" in Saks and Handelman, n. 52 above; Walfish, n. 52 above; A. Ross, "Motivational Issues in the Study of Gemara Among American High School Senior Boys" (Ph.D dissertation, Yeshiva University, 2009).

73 This sentiment is most eloquently expressed by R. Soloveitchik: "Torah study is more than an intellectual performance. It is a total, all encompassing, and all-embracing involvement of the mind and heart, will and feeling — the very center of the human personality. . . . The study of Torah is basically, for me, an ecstatic experience in which one meets God" (cited in Rakeffet-Rothkoff, n. 52 above, 202–203).

*The Jewish Law Annual*, Vol. XIX

# Normative Transparency in Jewish Law: Maimonides, R. Moses Sofer and R. Abraham Isaac Kook

Daniel B. Sinclair*

## 1 The Maimonidean requirement of transparency in rabbinic legislation

The distinction between biblical and rabbinic law is not only historical and literary in nature, but normative as well. Biblical law is normatively superior to rabbinic law; thus, doubtful situations regarding biblical law are resolved stringently, whereas doubts regarding rabbinic law are settled leniently. Furthermore, factors such as prevention of severe economic damage and preservation of human dignity may mitigate rabbinic prohibitions, but not biblical prohibitions.[1]

The doctrine of normative transparency in Jewish law is based on a ruling by Maimonides, who asserts that rabbinic legislators must make it clear to the public that the legal status of their legislation is rabbinic and not biblical. He cites the biblical prohibition against adding to or detracting from the Torah as the source for this requirement:

> Since the court is empowered to make enactments and to forbid that which is permitted by the Torah for all time, and to permit that which the Torah forbids, on a temporary basis,[2] what is the significance of the biblical

* College of Management and Academic Studies Law School, Rishon Lezion; Wolff Fellow in Jewish Law and Visiting Professor of Law, Fordham University Law School, New York.

1 See I. Herzog, *The Main Institutions of Jewish Law* (London: 1967), 1:2–11; M. Elon, *Jewish Law: History, Sources, Principles* (Philadelphia: 1994), 1:208–23.

2 According to Maimonides (Laws concerning Rebels 1:1–2), the source for the Rabbis' legislative authority is the biblical verse, "You shall act in accordance with the instructions given to you . . . you must not deviate . . . either to the right or to the left" (Deut. 17:11). The ideal legislative forum in Jewish law was the Great Court, or Sanhedrin, which sat in Jerusalem prior to the destruction of the Second Temple. There is no strict doctrine of separation of powers in Jewish law, and the Great Court served as judiciary, legislator, and executor, and exercised extensive jurisdictional freedom in all three fields. See M. Elon, *The Principles of Jewish Law* (Jerusalem: 1974), 53–57, 561–65.

prohibitions: "You may not add [to the Torah] nor may you detract from it" (Deut. 4:2 and 13:1)? The answer is that these prohibitions serve as a warning to the court not to endow its additions or detractions with the status of biblical law, both in terms of laws written explicitly in the text of the Torah and in relation to oral laws attributed by tradition to Moses on Sinai.[3] For example, the Torah states: "You may not cook a kid in its mother's milk" (Exod. 23:19.)[4] According to the oral tradition, this prohibition extends to the flesh of both domestic and non-domestic animals,[5] but not to poultry. Any court that permits the flesh of a non-domestic animal with milk on the grounds that the prohibition is not biblical is guilty of detracting from the Torah,[6] and any court that prohibits poultry with milk on the grounds that poultry is included in the word "kid" and hence is biblically forbidden, is guilty of adding to the Torah. If, however, the court states that under biblical law it is permitted to cook poultry and milk together, but it is prohibiting it, and makes known to the public that the reason for this prohibition is to prevent people from erring as a result of a mistaken argument to the effect that in the same way that chicken is permitted with milk because it is not specifically mentioned in the Torah, so the flesh of a non-domestic animal is permitted because it is not specifically mentioned in the Torah, then the court is no longer in breach of

3 Such laws also possess biblical status; see Maimonides' *Introduction to the Mishnah* s.v. *hahelek harishon*.

4 According to Maimonides, it is obvious that this prohibition extends to eating a mixture of meat and milk, in addition to cooking it; see Laws concerning Forbidden Foods 9:2. The prohibition against deriving benefit from a mixture of meat and milk is mentioned by Maimonides in his *Book of Precepts*, negative precept 186, but the actual basis for this prohibition is unclear; see *Lehem Mishne*, Laws concerning Forbidden Foods 9:2.

5 There is some confusion regarding this point in Maimonides' *Code*. In the Laws concerning Rebels, Maimonides makes it clear that a mixture of meat of non-domestic animals and milk is forbidden by the oral tradition handed down at Sinai, which has the status of biblical law. In the Laws concerning Forbidden Foods 9:4, however, he implies that this type of mixture is forbidden only by virtue of a rabbinic decree. Various solutions have been suggested to harmonize this discrepancy. See *Kesef Mishne*, Laws concerning Rebels 2:9 s.v. *al ma shekatav*; Radbaz, Laws concerning Rebels 2:9 s.v. *aval yesh kushia gedola*; *Lehem Mishne*, Laws concerning Forbidden Foods 9:4 s.v. *vekhen basar haya*; *Mirkevet Hamishne*, Laws concerning Forbidden Foods 9:4 s.v. *vekhatav rabi meir*. See too E. Rosenthal, "For the most part" (Hebrew), *Perakim* 1 (1967/68), 185 n. 10. For the talmudic background, see mHulin 8:4; bHulin 104a.

6 According to the *Lehem Mishne*, this does not refer to actual permission. Rather, the word "permits" in this passage refers to the downgrading of the status of the prohibition from oral Sinaitic tradition to rabbinic legislation. See *Lehem Mishne*, Laws concerning Rebels 2:9 s.v. *hoil veyesh*.

> the biblical prohibition against adding to the Torah. Such a precautionary measure is, indeed, vital, since in its absence, a member of the public may very well compound this type of error, and suggest that since the only domestic animal mentioned by the Torah is a goat, the prohibition against cooking meat and milk is confined to the flesh of goats. Another such false argument would confine the prohibition to the milk of the species from which the meat originates, and yet another mistaken individual may argue that the prohibition against cooking meat and milk is confined to the literal meaning of the biblical verse, i.e., the meat of a goat's kid prepared in its mother's milk. In order to prevent all of the above errors, we are instituting a blanket prohibition against the cooking of all types of flesh with all types of milk. Such a detailed statement is necessary if the court is not to fall foul of the prohibition against adding to the Torah.[7]

Both in terms of its substance and in terms of its interpretation of the biblical prohibitions against adding to and subtracting from the Torah, the transparency requirement is an original Maimonidean contribution to Jewish law. Maimonides' interpretation is, in fact, entirely different from that found in the classic sources of Jewish law.

The prohibition, "You may not add to it, nor may you detract from it," appears twice in Deuteronomy. Although at first glance it would seem that the simplest explanation of the prohibition is that one may not add to, or eliminate, any commandment in the Torah, the prohibition is understood by the Sifre, compiled at the end of the 4th c. CE, as a directive not to add to the number of separate elements involved in the fulfillment of a biblical commandment.[8] The examples offered by the Sifre include adding a fifth species to the four mandated by the Torah to be ritually "taken" on the festival of Sukkot (Lev. 23:40)

7 Maimonides, *Code*, Laws concerning Rebels 2:9. The Radbaz (1479–1573), ad loc., provides another illustration of the requirement that, to avoid transgressing the biblical prohibition against adding to the Torah, rabbinic authorities fully explain any measures they impose to "safeguard" the law. The consumption of blood is forbidden under biblical law (Lev. 7:26), but this prohibition does not extend to human blood, which is only prohibited by virtue of a rabbinic decree (Maimonides, *Code*, Laws concerning Forbidden Foods 6:2). Were a rabbinic authority to maintain that human blood is biblically forbidden, he would be in breach of the prohibition against adding to the Torah, since such blood is biblically permitted. Conversely, were he to maintain that the blood of a non-domestic animal is biblically permitted, he would be guilty of detracting from the Torah, since such blood is covered by the biblical prohibition against consuming the blood of an animal (*Code*, Laws concerning Forbidden Foods 6:1).

8 Sifre, Parashat Ree, §82.

and adding a fourth Priestly blessing to the three written in the Torah (Num. 6:22–27). The prohibition against detracting from the commandments is also understood in this fashion — that is, it is forbidden to "take" fewer than four species on Sukkot or to recite fewer than three Priestly blessings. This is also the interpretation found in the Talmud,[9] and Rashi cites this approach in his commentary on both occurrences of the prohibition in the Torah.[10]

The Maharal of Prague explains that the Talmud interprets the prohibitions as relating to adding and subtracting elements of the commandments, rather than entire commandments, because the prohibition against detracting from the Torah is otherwise meaningless. Total non-observance of a biblical norm is an actual breach of Torah law, not merely "detracting" from the Torah:

> That would not be "detracting," but rather not fulfilling the commandment at all, and the Torah has admonished us many times to keep all the precepts, so why would there be a need to tell us, "You may not detract from it?" In a similar manner, the prohibition against adding must mean that you shall not add anything to the substance of a commandment, for example, five fringes instead of the four specified in the Torah (Deut. 22:12), or five compartments in the phylacteries[11] instead of the required four.[12]

Since the prohibitions against adding to and subtracting from the Torah appear in tandem, it is reasonable to maintain interpretative symmetry between them. Thus, just as the prohibition against taking away from the Torah must refer to taking away one element or component of a commandment, the prohibition against adding to the Torah refers to adding to the existing elements of a commandment, and not to the formulation of an entirely new precept.

The traditional understanding of the biblical prohibitions against adding to and detracting from the Torah, then, confines its scope to

9 bSanhedrin 88b; bRosh Hashana 28b.

10 I.e., Deuteronomy 4:2 and 13:1. The scope of the prohibition against adding to the Torah is expanded by both the Talmud and later halakhic authorities to include observance of precepts for a longer period than that specified in the Torah and observance by someone not specified in the Torah as obligated to do so. Observance of the same precept a number of times does not, however, constitute a breach of the prohibition against adding. See *Talmudic Encyclopedia* (Hebrew), 3:325–30.

11 bMenahot 34a.

12 Maharal (1512–1609), *Gur Arye*, Deuteronomy 4:2 s.v. *lo tosifu*.

changes made to the quantity of internal elements in any particular biblical commandment; it does not apply to rabbinic legislation. Indeed, there is a body of opinion to the effect that the prohibitions against adding to the Torah or subtracting from it are aimed solely at individuals acting on their own private initiative, and do not apply at all to rabbinic authorities acting in a legitimate legislative capacity.[13] Maimonides, however, breaks with this traditional understanding and applies the prohibitions to the entire range of rabbinic legislation, using them to ground a general transparency requirement in all areas of rabbinic law.

Maimonides' position regarding additions to or subtractions from the number of internal elements in specific commandments is not clear. On the one hand, it is possible that in his *Book of Precepts*,[14] he accepts the traditional approach as the core meaning of the prohibition, but adds a peripheral meaning in the form of the normative transparency requirement, which, as we saw in the passage from the *Mishne Torah* cited above, encompasses all rabbinic legislation. On the other hand, it might be argued that Maimonides does not regard adding an element to an existing commandment as biblically prohibited at all, and takes the entire force of the biblical admonitions against adding and detracting to be directed solely at the transparency requirement vis-à-vis rabbinic legislation.[15] But whether Maimonides' interpretation of the prohibition is intended to elucidate its primary meaning or a corollary meaning, it is clearly novel.

Maimonides' departure from tradition on this point did not go unnoticed, nor did it escape criticism. R. Abraham b. David, the trenchant critic of Maimonides' *Mishne Torah*, is not reticent about his disapproval of this deviation from the traditional approach. In the Rabad's view, Maimonides' words are "utter vanity." In truth, he asserts, the prohibition against adding to the Torah is restricted to

13 See Rashba, bRosh Hashana 16a s.v. *lama tokin umeriin*. R. Joseph Albo, in a lengthy critique of Maimonides' position from a philosophical perspective rather than a legal one, also takes this view (*Sefer Haikarim* 3:14). Albo's theory of the historical evolution of the halakha in accordance with the mood of the times requires wide scope for rabbinic innovations. This doctrine does not fit with what he perceives to be Maimonides' constrained approach to rabbinic legislation.

14 *Book of Precepts*, negative precepts 313–314.

15 See R. Zvi Hirsch Chajes, *"Maamar Bal Tosif," Kol Kitvei Maharatz Chajes* (Jerusalem: 1958), 1:86–87.

"positive commandments, such as the *lulav* [four Sukkot species], phylacteries, and fringes. Indeed, it will apply whether or not the rabbinic authorities explain the status of and the reason for their addition."[16]

The Rabad further notes that talmudic law empowers the rabbinic authorities to add preemptive enactments to the corpus of Torah law and to invoke biblical verses as support for doing so,[17] and are similarly permitted to detract from the Torah when such a step is necessary for the public good.[18] In neither case are the rabbinic authorities remotely troubled by the fact that they may be in breach of the prohibitions against adding and detracting. Moreover, he claims, the Talmud states that it is within the rabbinic authorities' jurisdiction to endow their additional legislation with something akin to the authority of biblical law.[19]

None of the Rabad's talmudic-law-based objections to the Maimonidean stance are particularly strong, and the commentators on the *Mishne Torah* have little difficulty refuting them. Maimonides does not deny that the rabbinic authorities are empowered to enact preemptive legislation or to suspend Torah law for the sake of the general welfare. Indeed, he provides a detailed treatment of these powers in the *Mishne Torah* itself.[20] Maimonides simply argues that when the rabbinic authorities engage in these perfectly legitimate forms of legislative activity, they must adhere to the requirement of normative transparency. In his commentary on the *Mishne Torah*, R. Joseph Caro notes that the Rabad's only sound criticism is that Maimonides deviated from the traditional interpretation of the biblical prohibitions. R. Caro responds to this point on purely logical grounds: "Surely if someone states that fowl is included in the biblical prohibition against [mixing] meat and milk, even the Rabad must admit that he is adding to the Torah!"[21] This also seems to be the approach of the other major commentators on the *Mishne Torah*.[22]

16 Rabad (1125–1198), *Hasagot Harabad*, Laws concerning Rebels 2:9.
17 Such use of biblical verses is known as *asmakhta*; see bJebamot 21a; bHagiga 4a. Also see *Talmudic Encyclopedia* (Hebrew) 2:105–108.
18 bJebamot 90b; Elon, n. 1 above, 519–20; 533–36.
19 bKetubot 84a; Elon, ibid., 214–15.
20 This emerges from a careful reading of Maimonides' wording in Laws concerning Rebels 2:4 and 2:9.
21 R. Joseph Caro (1488–1575), *Kesef Mishne*, Laws concerning Rebels 2:9.
22 See, e.g. Radbaz and *Lehem Mishne* on Laws concerning Rebels 2:9.

The purely logical force of R. Caro's argument strengthens the assumption that Maimonides' call for transparency in rabbinic legislation is indeed an original contribution to Jewish law. Maimonides typically finds support for his innovative positions in biblical verses interpreted in an idiosyncratic fashion,[23] and normative transparency is but one such example.

Maimonides' insistence on transparency accords well with one of his main goals as a legal codifier, which, in true Aristotelian fashion, is preservation of the formal features of the law. Classification of laws as either biblical or rabbinic is one of the most important formal features of Jewish law, and therefore Maimonides takes great pains to ensure that the line between the two is never blurred.[24] There is, in fact, something strikingly modern and democratic about Maimonides' insistence that legislators strive to be as open as possible about their activities; they may not abuse their position by resorting to "normative upgrading" of a particular enactment, no matter how appropriate such upgrading may be in their eyes. As we will see below, this was a point of contention in later centuries.

Once the transparency requirement became part of Jewish law by virtue of Maimonides' codification, other halakhic authorities also referred to it in the context of the biblical prohibitions against adding to and detracting from the Torah. In the generation after Maimonides, Nahmanides[25] refers to the transparency requirement in his commentary on the Torah. After presenting the traditional understanding of the prohibitions against adding to and detracting from the Torah as they appear in the Sifre and Rashi, Nahmanides offers his own opinion: "If someone invents a commandment — for example, Jereboam, who instituted an entirely new festival[26] — he is also guilty of breaking the

23 See I. Twersky, *Introduction to the Code of Maimonides* (*Mishne Torah*), (New Haven: 1980), 145–50.

24 See ibid., 238–320. According to Twersky, "The ruling passion of Maimonides' life was order, system, conceptualization and generalization, and this received its finest expression in the *Mishne Torah*" (257).

25 1194–1270.

26 I Kings 12:33: "And he went up. . . in the month which he had devised of his own heart, and he ordained a festival for the Children of Israel." This case of the addition of an entirely new commandment is cited in a late $11^{th}$-century Midrash known as *Midrash Lekah Tov* or *Pesikta Zutrata* as an illustration of a breach of the biblical prohibition against adding, and Nahmanides may very well have taken it from this source.

prohibition against adding."[27] He goes on to cite passages from both the Babylonian[28] and the Jerusalem[29] Talmuds, from which it is evident that the prophets of Israel were careful not to add to the commandments of the Torah.

Neither of Nahmanides' examples deals with rabbinic legislation; the first refers to an addition made by an evil king, and the second to the authority of a prophet in the legal sphere.[30] The requirement of transparency in rabbinic legislation is only mentioned at the end of the passage, where Nahmanides asserts:

> The rabbis are permitted to legislate by virtue of a biblical directive,[31] on condition that they make known that what they are doing is erecting a fence around the Torah and that their legislation is not part of the Divine law, nor does it possess the status of such law.

In all likelihood, this short sentence is a brief summary of Maimonides' lengthy and detailed description of the transparency requirement in the *Mishne Torah.*

Although, as noted above, the Maharal of Prague opens his comments on the prohibition against adding by explaining the logical force of the traditional approach to the prohibition, toward the end of his remarks he proceeds to incorporate Maimonides' innovative stance:

---

The search for sources for what appear to be entirely novel rulings in the *Mishne Torah* is an ongoing dimension of Maimonidean scholarship. Whether or not this Midrash was also Maimonides' source is a matter of conjecture. Maimonides certainly made extensive use of the Midrash in his codification of Jewish law; see Twersky, n. 23 above, 150–54. But even if there is an earlier source for the notion that the prohibition against adding extends to any addition, and not only an addition to the essential elements of an existing law, Maimonides' detailed and expansive formulation of the transparency requirement is nonetheless novel in its own right.

27 *Commentary on the Torah,* Deuteronomy 4:2.

28 bMegila 14a.

29 jMegila 1:6.

30 In commenting on Deuteronomy 13:4, Nahmanides similarly emphasizes that a prophet has no authority to add a law to those of the Torah. If he does so, there is no obligation to act in accordance with his words, and he may be considered a false prophet, who is subject to the death penalty.

31 Leviticus 18:30; bJebamot 21b.

> No rabbinic precept constitutes an addition to the Torah, since the prohibition against adding applies only when the addition is equated with the Torah itself; fences and safeguards do not constitute additions since they are not on a par with the biblical laws.[32]

In his commentary on the Torah, R. Elijah of Vilna, the Gra, explains the two-fold repetition of the Torah's prohibitions against adding and subtracting as referring to the traditional and the Maimonidean approaches, respectively. The first appearance of the prohibitions forbids legislative additions to the Torah unless they are accompanied by the sort of clarification called for by Maimonides, while the second discourages individuals who might aspire to add to the internal elements of a biblical commandment, even if they desire to do so as an expression of piety.[33]

In the mid-nineteenth century, R. Zvi Hirsch Chajes published a short monograph on the biblical prohibition against adding to the Torah, most of which is devoted to justifying Maimonides' position and rebutting his critics. R. Chajes marshals a significant array of talmudic sources, concluding the first part of his monograph, "We have now made clear the opinion of our teacher, Maimonides, and rendered it free of any possible contradiction."[34]

The remainder of this article will examine two cases in which rabbinic authorities chose not to adhere to Maimonides' normative transparency standard. As we shall see, other authorities continued to defend that standard despite the arguments against it.

## 2 R. Moses Sofer's policy of "upgrading" the status of rabbinic prohibitions

In the late eighteenth century, fear of premature burial led governments in several European countries to pass laws requiring a mandatory waiting period of three days between the establishment of death

32 N. 12 above.

33 R. Elijah of Vilna (1720–1798), *Aderet Eliyahu*, Deuteronomy 13:1.The Gra also explains how each verse reflects the interpretation he espouses.

34 See n. 15 above. R. Chajes (1805–1855) had an unusually broad education for a rabbi of his time and milieu, and developed a highly systematic approach to halakhic literature and its legal categories. See M. Hershkovitz, *Rabbi Zvi Hirsch Chajes* (Hebrew), (Jerusalem: 1972).

and burial. Waiting stations were set up all over Europe to accommodate bodies awaiting burial and to provide an opportunity for each one to be examined by a physician before being placed in a coffin.[35] These delayed burial laws posed a problem for Jews, who traditionally buried their dead as close to the time of the establishment of death as possible.

One such law promulgated in Mecklenburg in 1772 prompted the leading rabbis of Germany to turn to Moses Mendelssohn with a request that he intercede with the local duke on behalf of the Jewish community, and persuade him to grant the Jewish community an exemption from the three-day waiting period. Mendelssohn did so, but at the same time, he initiated a debate within rabbinic circles as to the halakhic propriety of insisting on early burial in light of the new awareness that some people were, in fact, being buried alive. Mendelssohn argued that in such circumstances, delaying burial was halakhically justifiable, and marshaled various halakhic sources to prove his point. The leading German rabbis of the time, however, rejected his halakhic arguments, insisting that early burial was a strict requirement of Jewish law that must be upheld even in the face of the apprehension about premature burial that motivated the ducal edict.[36]

In 1836, a responsum on this issue was penned by R. Moses Sofer, the highly influential leader of Hungarian Orthodoxy. In the responsum, the Hatam Sofer categorically rejects any attempt to rule leniently on this matter. In his view, there is a biblical prohibition against delayed burial: "You shall not leave his corpse on the tree overnight, but you shall surely bury it on the same day."[37] Although this verse clearly refers to the body of a criminal executed by the court and then hanged as a deterrent to others, R. Sofer has no hesitation in

35 So great was the fear of premature burial in this period that some coffin makers equipped their coffins with an elaborate system of bells and flags that could be activated by the slightest movement in the erstwhile corpse's chest. Any such movement would release a spring that would open the coffin, admitting air and light. At the same time, a flag would wave, a bell would ring for a half hour, and a lamp would burn if the event occurred after dark. See K. Iserson, *Death to Dust* (Tucson: 1994), 31–38.

36 See A. Altmann, *Moses Mendelssohn: A Biographical Study* (Tuscaloosa AL: 1973), 288–93; M. Samet, "Delayed burial" (Hebrew), *Asufot* 3 (1989), 413–65.

37 Deuteronomy 21:23; mSanhedrin 6:4.

declaring that it is the source for a biblical prohibition against delaying the burial of an ordinary corpse as well.[38]

As we already noted above, biblical prohibitions are generally unassailable, whereas rabbinic prohibitions may be overridden by considerations ranging from the prevention of severe economic loss to the preservation of human dignity. The classification of delayed burial as a biblical prohibition makes it virtually impossible to override unless its continued observance constitutes a clear and immediate threat to human life.[39] R. Sofer takes pains to explain that this is not the case with regard to Jewish burial, since burial-society (*hevra kadisha*) members are well-trained in the establishment of death, and only they are allowed to prepare corpses for burial.[40]

The Mishnah and the major codes of Jewish law state that "whoever leaves his dead unburied transgresses a negative commandment."[41] Nevertheless, it is not clear that this phrase refers to a full-fledged biblical norm. The Talmud records two versions of a statement by R. Johanan regarding the extension of the biblical prohibition against leaving the corpse of a criminal hanging overnight to the corpse of an ordinary decedent.[42] The first version does, indeed, equate the two categories, and thus classifies a delay in the burial of an ordinary corpse as the breach of a biblical commandment. The second version, however, states that the biblical verse concerning delayed burial serves only as a "hint" vis-à-vis prohibiting delay in the case of an ordinary decedent; it does not constitute a basis for prohibiting such a delay on biblical grounds. Both R. David b. Zimra[43] and R. Abraham

38 R. Moses Sofer (1763–1839), *Responsa Hatam Sofer*, YD #328. In addition to discussing the normative status of the prohibition against delaying burial in general, the responsum also engages in a more nuanced discussion of the positive and negative elements of the biblical commandment regarding timely burial. On delayed burial, see *Talmudic Encyclopedia* (Hebrew), 9:434–44.

39 Jewish law mandates that the saving of life overrides all but three biblical prohibitions: the prohibitions against murder, idolatry, and unlawful sexual relations; see Leviticus 18:5; bYoma 85a.

40 In his responsum, R. Sofer explains that the burial society's expertise is based on an ancient tradition which may have been transmitted to Moses at Sinai.

41 mSanhedrin 6:5; Maimonides, *Code*, Laws concerning the Sanhedrin 15:8; Laws concerning Mourning 12:1; *Tur*, YD 357:1.

42 bSanhedrin 46b.

43 Radbaz, Laws concerning Mourning 12:1; cf. *Responsa Radbaz*, #780.

di Boton[44] contend that according to the second version of R. Johanan's statement, there is no formal biblical prohibition against delaying the burial of an ordinary corpse. Since the Talmud does not make a definitive decision in favor of one of these versions, both have normative status.[45]

There is thus some doubt regarding the definitive talmudic position on the normative status of the prohibition against delaying the burial of a non-criminal corpse. In fact, a clear statement to the effect that delaying the burial of an ordinary corpse does not constitute violation of a biblical prohibition appears in the responsa of R. Yair Bacharach:

> If not for the fact that I feared that it would place me beyond "the center of truth,"[46] I would say that the phrase "whoever leaves his dead unburied transgresses a negative commandment" does not refer to an actual biblical commandment, since in the Torah the precept that burial is not to be delayed is confined to the body of a criminal executed by order of the court. The phrase "whoever leaves his dead unburied transgresses a negative commandment" used in the Mishnah is mere hyperbole. Indeed, there are numerous examples of this usage in the Talmud. For example, "One who engages in profane talk . . . R. Aha b. Jacob says he transgresses a negative commandment"[47]; "R. Eleazar said: Whoever counts Israelites transgresses a negative commandment"[48]; "R. Joshua b. Levi said: Whoever accepts hospitality from men of niggardly spirit transgresses a negative commandment"[49]; "R. Judah said: Whoever goes up from Babylon to the land of Israel transgresses a positive commandment."[50] In all these instances, although biblical verses are cited as a basis for these "commandments" . . . none of them qualify as authentic biblical precepts. In a similar vein, the talmudic statement, "Rav said: Whoever is unyielding in a dispute transgresses a negative commandment"[51] is accompanied

44 *Lehem Mishne*, Laws concerning Mourning 12:1.
45 R. Nissim Gerondi (14th c.) limits the second version of R. Johanan's statement to the method of burial; the requirement that the corpse be interred in the ground and not above the ground is "hinted" at, whereas the requirement of immediate burial is clearly biblical in nature; see Ran, bSanhedrin 46b s.v. *tikberenu*.
46 Presumably, this rather obscure phrase means rabbinic consensus, as opposed to legal truth. R. Bacharach is aware that his opinion is not shared by the majority of his colleagues.
47 bYoma 19b.
48 Ibid. 22b.
49 bSota 38b.
50 bKetubot 110b.
51 bSanhedrin 110a.

> by a scriptural proof-text that is explained by Maimonides[52] as "a mere scriptural peg (*asmakhta*) upon which to hang this rabbinic precept. It does not make it into a genuine biblical commandment."[53]

R. Bacharach's view is cited by R. Zvi Hirsch Chajes in his glosses on the Talmud,[54] and it is also shared by R. Aaron of Worms.[55]

In light of the halakhic uncertainty regarding the normative status of the prohibition against delayed burial, and in particular in view of R. Bacharach's responsum, R. Chajes wrote to R. Sofer requesting an explanation for his definitive presentation of the prohibition as a biblical norm. R. Sofer answered him as follows:

> I wrote that delaying burial constitutes infraction of a biblical norm since Nahmanides holds this view.[56] In any case, in the present era, the normative status of a prohibition must not be allowed to have any effect on its binding nature, and it is good to augment prohibitions. You base your case on the generally rejected view of the author of *Havat Yair*, who maintains that the entire prohibition against delaying burial for ordinary bodies is only rabbinic in nature. This view should not be revealed to the public because, due to our many sins, many of our coreligionists now claim to be bound solely by biblical law, and they ignore rabbinic norms, which, they argue, do not emanate from a Divine source. Indeed, due to our many sins, the *gaon*, the author of *Responsa Noda Biyehuda*,[57] erred in this matter, when in order to prevent severe financial loss to many Jewish families, he permitted a non-Jew working in a Jewish factory to write on the Sabbath, in reliance on the rejected view cited by the Rema that writing in Latin or

52 Maimonides, *Book of Precepts*, eighth root.

53 R. Yair Bacharach (1638–1702), *Responsa Havat Yair*, #139. The question submitted to R. Bacharach concerned the need to ransom the body of a Jewish criminal who had been executed by the non-Jewish authorities.

54 *Hagahot Maharatz Chajes*, bSanhedrin 46b. In this gloss, R. Chajes refers to his monograph on the prohibition against adding to the Torah in which, inter alia, he justifies Maimonides' interpretation; see n. 15 above.

55 R. Aaron of Worms (1754–1836), *Meorei Or, Hagahot Ken Tahor*, Sanhedrin 46b. A similar approach is taken by R. Baruch Halevi Epstein, *Torah Temima*, Deuteronomy 21, n. 160.

56 Commentary on the Torah, Deuteronomy 21:22; *Hasagot* on Maimonides' *Book of Precepts*, first root; cf. *Torat Haadam*, Inyan Hakevura s.v *benigmar hadin*.

57 R. Ezekiel Landau (1713–1793), *Responsa Noda Biyehuda*, vol. 2, OH #29. On the social and economic background of this and another responsum (#33) on running Jewish-owned factories on the Sabbath, see J. Katz, *The "Shabbes Goy"* (Philadelphia: 1989), 121–32.

> other languages is not biblically prohibited.[58] The decision of the author of *Noda Biyehuda* is halakhically accurate, since asking a non-Jew to perform a merely rabbinically-interdicted act on the Sabbath is permitted.[59] Nevertheless, with all due respect, the evil-doers use this as a justification for writing in non-Hebrew languages on the Sabbath, claiming that they are only transgressing a rabbinic norm. . . . And in this regard, the Sages are warned[60] to pay careful attention to what they say.[61]

The entire thrust of R. Sofer's response to R. Chajes is to justify normative obfuscation of the halakha. He begins by arguing that it is good to enhance the status of the prohibition against delaying burial because rabbinic law must be viewed as just as binding as biblical law. Delayed burial, as far as R. Sofer is concerned, is but another example

58 R. Moses Isserles (1520–1572), Rema, OH 306:11. The view referred to is that of R. Isaac b. Moses in *Or Zarua*, Laws of the Sabbath, #76. R. Isaac rules that writing in Latin or other languages is only rabbinically prohibited. His source is a statement in the Jerusalem Talmud (jShabat 12:3) according to which only writing in Hebrew or ancient Greek contravenes the biblical prohibition against writing on the Sabbath, while writing in other languages only violates a rabbinic prohibition.

Later authorities were, indeed, unhappy with R. Isaac b. Moses' ruling and sought to dismiss it as a minority view. See *Arukh Hashulhan*, OH 306:22; *Mishna Brura* 306:47 and *Biur Halakha*, ad loc. Clearly, R. Sofer's fears were well founded, and his policy of downplaying the difference between biblical and rabbinic prohibitions was adopted by later halakhists who sought to shore up Orthodoxy against the inroads of Reform.

59 The Rema uses the *Or Zarua*'s view to explain the law permitting a non-Jew to draw up a bill of sale for a house in the land of Israel on behalf of a Jewish purchaser on the Sabbath. Since both asking a non-Jew to carry out an act prohibited on the Sabbath and writing in a language other than Hebrew or ancient Greek are only rabbinically prohibited, the rabbinic edict is twice removed from the biblical prohibition it is protecting ("*shvut deshvut*"). In such a situation, there is room for leniency in the face of an important competing value, such as enabling Jewish settlement in the land of Israel. The *Noda Biyehuda* applies this logic as well: arranging with a non-Jew prior to the Sabbath to write on the Sabbath is only forbidden by rabbinic law, and the act of writing in a non-Hebrew language is similarly prohibited solely on the basis of rabbinic decree. Since the closing of the factory on the Sabbath would destroy the livelihoods of hundreds of Jewish families, R. Landau held that the prevention of enormous financial loss outweighed the rabbinic prohibitions.

60 mAvot 1:1.

61 Cited in Maharatz Chajes, *Darkhei Hahoraa*, in *Kol Kitvei Maharatz Chajes* 1:269–70.

of the insidious process of chipping away at the foundations of the halakha in response to changes in general society.[62] Accepting the view that delayed burial is only rabbinically forbidden, and therefore should not stand in the way of accepting the new legislation requiring a waiting period between establishment of death and burial, would send out a negative signal to the effect that rabbinic law is normatively inferior to biblical law. This would invite abuse by modernists and reformers, and threaten to destroy the traditional Orthodox way of life. It must therefore be fought, even at the cost of halakhic normative transparency.

In the Hatam Sofer's view, the exigencies of the hour required drastic action. He saw Orthodoxy as a "package deal" consisting of both biblical and rabbinic law, and felt that every effort must be made to ensure that this was understood and internalized by the Jewish public. To defend Orthodoxy against the inroads of the Reform movement, and keep the flock within the Orthodox fold, R. Sofer was prepared to ignore the Maimonidean doctrine of legislative transparency and to "upgrade" the status of rabbinic prohibitions.

It is important to emphasize that R. Sofer's critique of R. Landau's responsum regarding the operation of Jewish-owned factories on the Sabbath is not at all substantive. Indeed, he himself states that the actual decision was correct. What he deemed problematic was the fact that R. Landau published a halakhic position that provided modernists and reformers with an excuse for writing on the Sabbath in non-Hebrew languages. Once again, the thrust of the argument is the danger posed by halakhic transparency.

R. Sofer's reply did not satisfy R. Chajes, who wrote the following critical note on the responsum:

> In my view, his decision to "upgrade" the status of prohibitions . . . is incorrect . . . . Presenting a rabbinic prohibition as biblical contravenes the biblical prohibition, as defined by Maimonides, against adding to the Torah. . . . It is also a breach of the biblical precept, "Keep afar from a false matter" (Exod. 23:7), notwithstanding that there is a good reason for the falsehood. Moreover, the rabbis in the Talmud constantly take pains to distinguish between biblical and rabbinic law, even in cases where the distinction is of no practical significance.[63]

62 R. Sofer is known for his adage, "New things are forbidden by the Torah," which he invokes at the beginning of his responsum to R. Chajes; see the sources cited in n. 66 below.

63 See n. 61 above.

There is no evidence of any further correspondence between R. Sofer and R. Chajes on this point, and the debate over delayed burial continued to engage European halakhic authorities for some time.[64]

This exchange is representative of a broader disparity between R. Sofer's and R. Chajes's respective approaches to modernity in general. While R. Sofer believed in fighting it at all costs, R. Chajes was generally welcoming of modernity and the application of scientific methodology to the study of Jewish law.[65] R. Sofer argued that defending Orthodoxy took precedence over the normative transparency requirement, R. Chajes disagreed.[66]

R. Sofer clearly felt bound only by the classical talmudic understanding of the prohibition against adding to the Torah, on which it is confined to adding to the number of separate elements involved in the fulfillment of a given biblical commandment, or extending the obligation to observe it to those exempt from doing so under biblical law.[67] Nevertheless, he attempted to justify his prophylactic policy in terms of the Maimonidean approach, distinguishing between his time and the ideal period of which Maimonides wrote. The prohibition against portraying a rabbinic commandment as biblical applies in a perfect generation in which there is no need to take any prophylactic measures to preserve halakhic practice. But in sinful times such his own, R. Sofer argued, it is necessary to "add" so as to erect a protective fence around the Torah.[68]

64 See Samet, n. 36 above.

65 See n. 34 above.

66 A broader study of these two halakhic authorities is beyond the scope of the present article. On R. Sofer, see J. Katz, "Contributions towards a biography of the Hatam Sofer," in F. Malino and D. Sorkin (eds.), *From East and West: Jews in a Changing Europe, 1750–1870* (Oxford: 1990), 223–66; M. Shapiro, "Aspects of R. Moses Sofer's intellectual profile," in *Be'erot Yitzhak: Studies in Memory of Isadore Twersky* (Cambridge MA: 2005), 285–310; A. Schreiber, "The Hatam Sofer's nuanced attitude towards secular learning, maskilim, and reformers," *Torah U-Madda Journal* 11 (2002/2003), 123–73; M. Kahana, "The Hatam Sofer: the self-image of a *posek*" (Hebrew), *Tarbiz* 76 (2007), 519–56. On R. Chajes, see Hershkovitz, n. 34 above.

67 This is the only sense in which the prohibition against adding to the Torah figures in R. Sofer's responsa; see *Responsa Hatam Sofer*, OH #167; EH, vol. 2, #90.

68 This idea is cited in the name of R. Sofer by a prominent disciple, R. Moses Schick, in his commentary on mAvot 1:1.

The wisdom of applying R. Sofer's policy in a secular age came up some seventy years later, and is the topic of our final section.

## 3 R. Kook on the perils of halakhic opacity in a secular age

Eating leavened products (*hametz*) during Passover is strictly forbidden under biblical law.[69] Only products made from five types of grain — wheat, barley, oats, spelt, and rye — are capable of undergoing leavening. Leavening is thus irrelevant with respect to other grains, such as rice.[70] When the aforementioned five grains are cooked at an extremely high temperature, in a process known as *halita*, there is no possibility that they will become leavened.[71] Hence to ensure that products made from the said five types of grain do not become leavened, grain products are prepared in a special way, which involves keeping them dry and baking them at high temperatures for a very short period of time.[72]

According to biblical law, one may take a grain that is not one of these five types, such as rice, and mix it with water, make it into dough, allow it to expand as a result of warmth and moisture, and then eat the "risen" rice-cake on Passover, as rice can never become leavened.[73] Indeed, this is the practice of many Sefardic Jews to this day. Ashkenazic Jews, however, follow a custom that apparently originated

69 Exodus 12:15. But it is a biblical commandment to eat unleavened bread (*matza*) on Passover (Deut. 16:3).

70 Leavening (or "rising," as it is more commonly known), is a basic stage in the manufacture of all breads and baked goods. All dough made from the five grains contains the enzyme Amylase B. When this enzyme comes into contact with water at a moderate temperature, it is activated and breaks down the polysaccharides in the grains into sugars and carbon dioxide. The carbon dioxide then expands and causes the dough to rise. This process is accompanied by whitening of the dough and the appearance of cracks on its surface. Only the said five types of grain contain Amylase B, thus leavening is impossible in dough made from anything else.

71 Amylase B is deactivated at very high temperatures, preventing the leavening process. *Halita* is approved of in the Talmud (bPesahim 32b), but is prohibited in practice because of uncertainty regarding the temperature necessary to prevent leavening. See Maimonides, Laws concerning Leavened and Unleavened Bread 5:3.

72 See Maimonides, Laws concerning Leavened and Unleavened Bread, ch. 5, for the principles involved in preparing non-leavened products from the five grains for consumption on Passover.

73 Maimonides, Laws concerning Leavened and Unleavened Bread 5:1.

in the Middle Ages, according to which the baked products of all grain-like species are not eaten on Passover. These species are referred to by the general term "*kitniyot*," roughly translated as "legumes." This category includes, inter alia, rice, millet, beans, lentils, peas, sweet corn, buckwheat, and sesame.[74] Prominent Ashkenazic authorities also extended the custom to oils derived from *kitniyot*.[75]

In 1912, R. Abraham Hakohen Kook[76] and his rabbinic court issued a certificate of kashruth attesting to the halakhic acceptability of sesame oil made by a local Jewish manufacturer for use by Ashkenazic Jews during Passover. The reason for R. Kook's approval in this case, despite the custom of refraining from consumption of *kitniyot* oils, was the nature of the manufacturing process. Up until that point, sesame oil had been produced by soaking the sesame kernels in salt water and then removing the oil. A new machine, which R. Kook witnessed in action, used a completely dry process and functioned at a very high temperature and speed, both of which inhibit leavening in products made from the five types of grain. In R. Kook's view, use of the oil was clearly permitted: since products made from the five types of leaven-able grains baked under these conditions would be permitted during Passover, given that no leavening was possible, sesame oil, which is only a *kitniyot* derivative, should certainly be permitted under

74 The Ashkenazic custom began in order to avoid confusing *kitniyot* products with those made from the five types of grain that can become leavened, and because sacks of legumes may contain some kernels of the five grains, which may then be inadvertently made into a leavened product and consumed during Passover. See *Mordekhai*, Pesahim 2, ̄588; *Beit Yosef*, OH 453. Originally, the Ashkenazic custom of refraining from eating *kitniyot* on Passover applied to un-boiled *kitniyot* only, since boiling at a high temperature prevents leavening, as explained in n. 71 above. See R. Samuel of Falaise, cited in *Or Zarua*, Laws of Passover #256; *Hagahot Rabbenu Peretz*; *Sefer Mitzvot Katan*, §222. Eventually, it became customary not to eat any *kitniyot*, regardless of how they are prepared; see *Mordekhai*, ibid.; *Arukh Hashulhan*, OH 453:5. Several prominent authorities opposed this Ashkenazic practice, regarding it as an entirely unnecessary stringency; see R. Yeruham, *Toledot Adam Vehava*, path 5, part 3; *Tur*, OH 453; S. Eider, *Halachos of Pesach* (NY: 1998), 49–51.

75 Rema, OH 453:1; *Terumat Hadeshen*, #113; *Shulhan Arukh Harav*, OH 453:5; *Nishmat Adam*, Laws of Passover, #32; *Responsa Melamed Lehoil*, OH #87; *Mishna Brura* 453:10.

76 R. Kook (1865–1935), the first Ashkenazic Chief Rabbi of the Jewish community in the land of Israel, left Europe in 1904 to become the rabbi of Jaffa.

the same conditions. It would be highly illogical to be more stringent regarding a *kitniyot* derivative than with regard to actual *hametz*!

R. Kook wrote to the judges of the rabbinic court of the ultra-Orthodox Ashkenazic community in Jerusalem (Badatz), requesting that they accept his decision and approve use of the Jaffa sesame oil during the upcoming Passover festival. Much to his surprise, his request was refused. Moreover, the Badatz requested that he publicly withdraw his permissive ruling, despite the cost to his personal pride. R. Kook refused to do so and took pains to emphasize that this was solely because he was absolutely convinced of the halakhic integrity of his argument. Personal pride had nothing to do with his stance:

> Know that I am not one of those who are ashamed to admit their mistakes. If I felt even to the slightest extent that my view was mistaken, I would admit as much before tens of thousands. In this case, however, the halakha is crystal clear. I would, therefore, request that you take into account the honor of the Torah, my insignificant reputation, and the honor of my rabbinic colleagues on the Jaffa rabbinical court. Also, the fact that everything which we did was for the sake of heaven. . . . My request is that you do not provoke an uproar over this matter, since, in any case, there are enough arguments and disputes involving the rabbinate at present without adding more. . . . Kindly cooperate with us this year by issuing a public document supporting the decision of our rabbinical court and explaining the difference between the new process for producing sesame oil and the old one. We will then discuss the matter at length next year, and the view of the majority will prevail. . . . In this way, the Name of Heaven will be sanctified and the honor of the Torah upheld. . . . Finally, I must implore you to take pity on the unfortunate manufacturer, who invested heavily in raw materials on the basis of our permissive ruling and is liable to become bankrupt if he cannot sell his oil this Passover. We should take the prospect of his great financial loss into account in this matter.[77]

The Badatz, however, remained obstinate, and R. Kook wrote a second and lengthier responsum to the court on this issue.[78] In this responsum, he developed the halakhic arguments in greater detail and repeated his conviction that if the Badatz judges were to visit Jaffa and witness the operation of the new sesame oil machine, they would immediately agree with him.

R. Kook also rebutted a number of methodological criticisms directed against his ruling. First, he noted that his use of the term

77 *Orah Mishpat*, Laws of Passover, #111.
78 Ibid., #112.

"custom" to categorize the Ashkenazic prohibition against consuming *kitniyot*, rather than "legislation," was fully justified in terms of the classical halakhic sources on the issue,[79] and it would be wrong to "upgrade" the prohibition to the level of rabbinic legislation. This was especially true given that *kitniyot* are eaten by Sefardic Jews, and "even Ashkenazic authorities permit their consumption in times of famine . . . in accordance with the circumstances." Second, R. Kook took issue with the Badatz's argument that the fact that a previous decision did not allow sesame oil must forestall any possibility of the Badatz's now ruling permissively on the matter.[80] Citing the talmudic principle that previous rulings must always be carefully analyzed before applying them in new cases,[81] R. Kook emphasized the difference between the earlier decision, which apparently turned on the issue of whether or not the prohibition against *kitniyot* applied to sesame oil, and the present case, in which the core issue was the new machine, which yielded a product that would be legally permitted even if it were made from the five species of grain that leaven. R. Kook also emphasized that his rabbinic colleagues should use their halakhic expertise to help improve economic conditions in the Jewish community in the land of Israel, and in particular the material circumstances of the machine owner, who stood to earn enough to live on for several months over the week of Passover, provided his oil received a recognized kashruth certification.

The issue of *kitniyot* was discussed by R. Sofer as well. In the early nineteenth century, the Jewish Consistory of Westphalia allowed the Jews living in that part of Germany to eat *kitniyot* during Passover. In a responsum written in support of R. Abraham of Glogau, the chief opponent of the Consistory's ruling, R. Sofer began by suggesting a possible justification of the dispensation: if the choice is between eating *kitniyot* or actual *hametz*, permitting *kitniyot* is certainly the lesser of two evils. He argued that even in such a situation, however, the *kitniyot* should be boiled at a very high temperature to satisfy the medieval

79 See the sources cited in n. 74 above.

80 See *Responsa Melamed Lehoil*, OH #87, for a reference to this earlier Badatz ruling and comments on the practices of both the Ashkenazic and the Sefardic communities of Jerusalem regarding the use of sesame oil on Passover for cooking purposes and as a source of light.

81 bBaba Batra 130b; see also Elon, n. 1 above, 2:960–68.

halakhic stipulations on this issue.[82] R. Sofer observed that he himself would routinely advise Jewish soldiers serving in non-Jewish armies to eat boiled *kitniyot* on Passover, as the only other option for them was to eat leavened bread in breach of biblical law, or to starve. The innovation introduced by the Consistory was, however, an entirely different matter, he maintained. The Consistory wished to abolish the custom of not eating *kitniyot* in its entirety, and this was a step R. Sofer absolutely refused to condone.

Most of R. Sofer's responsum discusses the question of abolishing customs, and here he engaged in normative "upgrading" by blurring the line between custom and rabbinic edict, designating the Ashkenazic practice of abstaining from *kitniyot* "a rabbinic edict designed to erect a fence around the Torah."[83] Under this description, the practice would be virtually impossible to abolish without the unanimous approval of all the Ashkenazic communities and their rabbis.[84] R. Sofer also finds ample support in the rabbinic literature for an absolute ban on the use of rice by Ashkenazic Jews except during a famine or military service.[85] At the end of the responsum, R. Sofer concludes that "there is no way in which the prohibition against eating rice on Passover may be entirely dispensed with. . . . and the leaders of Westphalian Jewry have no halakhic basis for their decision to permit the eating of *kitniyot* by the general public."

Acknowledging that R. Sofer's approach was influential vis-à-vis the attitude of the Badatz court, R. Kook argued that R. Sofer's policy of "upgrading" the status of prohibitions may have been justified in his time, but at present, normative obfuscation was counterproductive:

> And in truth, it is evident from his writings that the reason the brilliant Hatam Sofer, of blessed memory, adopted a stringent approach in these matters was that in his time, the need of the hour was to combat the Reform movement, which was constantly attempting to make drastic changes, God forbid, to Judaism. Any authorized abrogation of a well-established custom merely served as ammunition for their cause. As a

82 See the sources cited in n. 74 above.

83 *Responsa Hatam Sofer,* OH #122. As we saw, R. Kook's unequivocal characterization of the ban on *kitniyot* as a mere custom was also opposed.

84 See *SA,* YD 228:28. R. Sofer distinguishes between a measure adopted to safeguard a biblical prohibition, as is the case of *kitniyot,* and a measure intended to promote extra piety, which might be more easily abolished; see *SA,* YD 114:1.

85 See *Pri Hadash,* Minhagei Isur #9.

> result, he opposed all change, even regarding a mere custom. . . . In our times, however, this threat no longer exists, since, as a result of our many sins, those who wish to ignore halakha do so without seeking rabbinic justification. Today, no one outside of the Orthodox camp takes the issue of changing halakhic rules seriously. Hence, there is no problem with allowing that which is permitted by the Torah even if it was previously forbidden by custom. . . . Moreover, it is clear to me that as far as the present generation is concerned, it is important to demonstrate complete transparency in our halakhic rulings. We should permit everything that is permissible from a halakhic standpoint so that it will be understood that what we do is dictated solely by halakhic norms and nothing else. . . . If it emerges that there are practices that are halakhically permissible, but the rabbis do not permit them, even though permitting them would spare people trouble and discomfort, the result will, God forbid, be a serious profanation of God's name, since it will then be said with regard to many fundamental halakhic prohibitions that if the rabbis wanted to, they could permit them [as well]! This is the greatest disservice that we can do to the halakhic cause.

R. Kook observes — with great prescience — the pernicious effects of halakhic obfuscation on a generation for whom halakhic authority is no longer as binding as it was in the past, even within the Orthodox community. In such an era, absolute integrity is a *sine qua non* for maintaining the dignity and standing of the rabbinic establishment.[86] Such integrity requires absolute transparency along the lines laid out by Maimonides. In its absence, the halakhic cause will only suffer. Transparency is a prerequisite for preservation of the halakha as a normative system, and we ignore it at our peril.

86 The Midrash sees the peril of favoring pastoral politics over normative integrity in the biblical account of the Garden of Eden (Gen. ch. 3). God told Adam not to eat of the fruit of the Tree of Knowledge on pain of death. Because he did not trust Eve, Adam upgraded the prohibition, telling her that she could not even touch the fruit. The serpent forced Eve to touch the fruit; when she did not die as a result of doing so, he was able to convince her that she would similarly not die if she ate the fruit. The tragic result was that Adam and Eve were expelled from Eden. From this story, R. Hiya learned an important lesson for all rabbinic authorities: "Do not make the fence more [important] than the principal thing, lest it fall and destroy the plants" (Gen. Rabbah 19:3). In other words, rabbinic overkill in attempting to protect the Torah may, in fact, lead to its weakening. Rashi, commenting on Genesis 3:3, cites the maxim that the effect of adding may well be to diminish.

*The Jewish Law Annual*, Vol. XIX

# The Tort of Negligent Misrepresentation in Investment Planning: A Comparative Analysis

Ronnie Warburg*

The tort of negligent misrepresentation refers to communication, in the course of one's employment or profession, of an unintentional false representation of information for the guidance of others in their commercial transactions. In contrast to fraud, which entails a willful intent to deprive another of his legal rights, negligent misrepresentation involves failure to meet standards of care and competence recognized within the industry **without** the intent to perform a wrongful act. Over the years, American courts have significantly expanded the parameters of this tort. To assess this issue in a specific context, this essay analyzes a pronounced shift in the standard of care owed by an investment planner to a client who relies on his planner's statements and representations for commercial purposes, such as securities offerings and corporate acquisitions.[1]

The purpose of this article is twofold. I first review the state of American law regarding negligent misrepresentation.[2] What is the extent of a financial planner's liability? Is his responsibility limited to his client, or does it include others as well? I then explore how Jewish law has addressed this issue of privity or an equivalent relationship between a planner and his client, and examine the halakhic grounds for liability.

* Ronnie Warburg serves on the Beth Din of America and is a research scholar at the Institute of Jewish Law, Boston University School of Law.

1 Legally, an investment advisor or financial planner acts solely in the best interests of his clients, while a broker may recommend a portfolio that serves his own interests, in the form of increased commissions, at the expense of the client's best interests. Despite this distinction, liability for negligent advice is recognized and applied in cases involving all types of securities dealers. Therefore, despite their differing roles and obligations in other areas, the terms "broker," "investment advisor," and "financial planner" are used interchangeably in relation to this tort.

2 There is little case law, as most claims for negligent misrepresentation are referred to arbitration.

## 1 American case law

Traditionally, advisors could only be sued for negligence by parties with whom they were in privity of contract and in cases in which their non-contractual obligations extended no further than a duty to refrain from committing fraud. Two interrelated harms resulted — third party plaintiffs were denied compensation and planner misconduct was not deterred. Courts feared, however, that an expanded negligence standard would expose financial planners to a degree of liability so extreme and indeterminate that it would threaten their economic existence.

Nonetheless, over the course of time, courts have embarked on what Justice Benjamin Cardozo called an "assault on the citadel of privity."[3] Non-contractual obligations are now generally viewed as extending to third parties who the broker knows will rely on his opinion or to any foreseeable parties who rely on the advisor's work, provided that the user received the information from the planner for commercial purposes. Even more broadly, the scope of the duty may encompass all those whose reliance was foreseeable, rather than specifically foreseeable. In effect, since such parties may include every present or future investor, brokers may be liable to the entire investment world. In certain jurisdictions, time-honored precedents limiting or denying the existence of the tort of negligent misrepresentation have been abandoned in regard to a financial consultant's malpractice.

The 1931 opinion by Justice Cardozo of the New York Court of Appeals in *Ultramares Corp. v. Touche, Niven and Co.*[4] is the watershed case in New York establishing the rule that accountants are liable for negligence only to those individuals with whom they are in privity. The defendant was a firm of certified public accountants employed by Fred Stern and Co., Inc. to audit a yearly balance sheet. Touche was aware that Stern would use the certified balance sheet in its business affairs with third parties, such as investors. While the balance sheet reflected a healthy business, the audit negligently overvalued the assets of the company, which in fact was insolvent. The plaintiff, who had loaned money to Stern based on the balance sheet he had furnished, successfully sued Touche, advancing claims of fraud and negligence. According to the court's holding, the auditor's duty is owed not only to those he is in privity with, but equally to those who

3 *MacPherson v. Buick*, 111 N.E. 1050–1051 (1916).
4 *Ultramares Corp. v. Touche, Niven and Co.*, 255 NY 170, 174 N.E. 441 (1931).

are **known beneficiaries** at the time of the auditor's undertaking. As an alternative to strict privity, the duty is extended to non-contracting parties whose reliance on the accounting company's work was **actually foreseen** by the firm.

On appeal, however, Justice Cardozo absolved the accountants:

> If liability for negligence exists, a thoughtless slip or blunder . . . may expose accountants to a liability in an indeterminate amount for an indeterminate time to an indeterminate class. The hazards of a business conducted on these terms are so extreme as to enkindle doubt whether a flaw may not exist in the implication of a duty that exposes to these consequences.[5]

Specifically, the opinion required the plaintiff to establish either privity of contract or "[a] bond . . . so close as to approach that of privity."[6] Cardozo acknowledged that in the usual course of business, the audit sheet would be exhibited by Stern's company to investors, creditors, banks, and the like, but he nevertheless invoked the privity doctrine rather than expanding reliance based on the foreseeablity doctrine that he himself had propounded in his earlier decisions in *MacPherson v. Buick Motor Co.*[7] and *Glanzer v. Shepard.*[8] Thus, the accounting company's duty of care is circumscribed by the formal contract with the client. The court grounded its holding on a concern as to where protection of the economic interests of third parties would end, and thus refused to hold the auditor liable for negligent misrepresentation.

The *Ultramares* privity doctrine has been upheld by a number of jurisdictions for decades as the standard for defining the scope of auditor liability.[9] Nevertheless, the privity or close to privity doctrine has never been extended to investment broker liability for negligent misrepresentation. Privity and near privity essentially would have taken broker liability cases out of the realm of tort law and placed them within the sphere of contract law.

5 Ibid. at 179–80, 174 N.E. at 444.
6 Ibid. at 182–183, 174 N.E. at 446.
7 *MacPherson v. Buick Motor Co.*, 111 N.E. 1050–1051 (1916).
8 *Glanzer v. Shepard*, 233 NY 236, 135 N.E. 275 (1922). It is arguable that Cardozo's argument in *Glanzer* is not one of forseeability; despite the absence of a contract between the parties in that case, the plaintiff's reliance on the information directly communicated by the defendants created a bond that was so similar to one of privity that it was indistinguishable.
9 See, e.g., *Credit Alliance Corp. v. Arthur Andersen & Co.*, 483 N.E. 2d 118–19 (NY 1985).

Criticism of the privity standard led to the Restatement (Second) of Torts Section 552, which resulted in broader liability for those who are "in the business of supplying information." The standard set forth in the Restatement provides:

> One who, in the course of his business, profession or employment, or in any other transaction in which he has a pecuniary interest, supplies false information for the guidance of others in their business transactions, is subject to liability for pecuniary loss caused to them by their justifiable reliance upon the information, if he fails to exercise reasonable care or competence in obtaining or communicating the information.[10]

Which service providers are subsumed under the category of individuals who are "in the business of supplying information"? The court stated in *Rankow v. First Chicago Corporation*:

> A great many businesses involve an exchange of information as well as of tangible products — manufacturers provide operating or assembly instructions, and sellers provide warranty information of various kinds. But if we ask what the product is in each of these cases, it becomes clear that the product (a building, roofing material, computer, or software) is not itself information, and that the information is merely incidental.[11]

At the other end of the spectrum are those individuals who are in the business of providing information:

> Real estate brokers and termite inspectors would seem to fall fairly clearly into a category at the opposite end of a continuum beginning with manufacturers dealing only in tangible goods; brokers and inspectors arguably provide information only. If we ask what the product is in these cases, the answer is obviously "information," whether about the housing market or about termite infestations.[12]

The court continued:

> Between these two extremes lie the more difficult cases, involving defendants whose business it is to provide both tangible goods (or other non-informational goods or services) and information. Financial services such as those provided by banks and stockbrokers present a particularly difficult problem, because there is a very thin line between an exchange of information about finances and actual financial transactions. . . . That is why . . . it is particularly important in these settings to examine the particular information and transactions involved case by case.[13]

10 Restatement (Second) of Torts Section 552(1) (1977).
11 *Rankow v. First Chicago Corporation*, 870 F. 2d 356, 364 (7th Cir. 1989).
12 Ibid.
13 Ibid.

In short, the case of a financial advisor presents a hybrid situation. Is he considered to be offering "information" regarding an investment or simply serving as a selling agent for another party, a sort of informational conduit?

Once a court arrives at the conclusion that a financial planner is "in the business of supplying information," pursuant to the Restatement approach, the scope of the advisor's liability for negligent misrepresentation includes classes of persons **actually known** to be foreseeable users of the information.

The adoption of the Restatement position reflects an intermediate standard between privity and user foreseeability. In a much-cited accountant liability case, the court stated:

> [Section 552] recognizes that liability should extend not only to those with whom the accountant is in privity or near privity, but also to those persons, or classes of persons, whom he knows and intends will rely on his opinion, or whom he knows his client intends will so rely. On the other hand ... it prevents extension of liability in situations where the accountant "merely knows of the ever-present possibility of repetition to anyone, and the possibility of action in reliance upon [the audited financial statements], on the part of anyone to whom it may be repeated." Restatement (Second) of Torts Section 552, Comment h. As such it balances, more so than the other standards, the need to hold accountants to a standard that accounts for their contemporary role in the financial world with the need to protect them from liability that unreasonably exceeds the bounds of their real undertaking.[14]

For example, in *Engle v. Dinehart*,[15] the defendant was acting in the course of his business when he planned and organized investment workshops, selected a third party as his representative and as the professional to lead them, and solicited the plaintiffs' reliance on this professional for investment advice. The defendant represented to the plaintiffs that the professional was an expert whom they could justifiably rely on for financial counsel. The plaintiffs relied on the third party and suffered losses as a direct result of his fraudulent advice. They thereafter filed a claim against the defendant for negligent misrepresentation, and the court granted relief. Following in the footsteps of the Restatement, the court limited liability to a specific class of

13 Ibid.

14 *Raritan River Steel Co. v. Cherry, Bekaert & Holland*, 367 S.E. 2d 609, 617 (NC 1988).

15 *Engle v. Dinehart*, 213 F. 3d 639, 2000 WL 554942 (CA 5 2000 (Tex.)).

persons that a service provider had **actually foreseen** would rely on his advice.[16] Numerous jurisdictions have invoked the applicable Restatement provisions and adopted this approach regarding the liability of securities advisors.[17]

In recent years, a number of courts have delineated the scope of an investment planner's liability to allow recovery whenever there is a "special relationship" of trust and confidence between the parties.[18] While there is generally no liability for words negligently spoken in casual conversation or a "curbside opinion," a greater degree of responsibility is demanded of an advisor when such a "special relationship" exists.

The genesis of the "special relationship" standard emerges from *Kimmell v. Schaefer*. In reply to the defendant's claim that he was not in privity or a relationship functionally equivalent to privity that would render him liable for negligent misrepresentation, the court wrote:

16 Restatement (Second) of Torts Section 552(2) (1977).

17 *Penrod v. Merrill Lynch*, 385 N.E. 2d 376 (IL. App. Ct. 1979); *Zurad v. Lehman Brothers Kuhn Loeb*, 757 F. 2d 129, 134 (1985); *Gutter v. Dow Jones*, 490 N.E. 2d 898, 901 (Ohio 1986); *Rankow v. First Chicago Corp.*, 678 F. Supp. 202 (N.D. IL 1988); *Rankow v. First Chicago Corp.*, 870 F.2d 356, 365 (7th Cir. 1989); *Rosengard v. McDonald*, 562 N.E. 2d 583, 586 (IL. App. 1 Dist. 1990); *Mason v. Burkett*, 756 F. Supp. 679 (Conn. 1991); *Lutheran Brotherhood v. Kidder Peabody & Co., Inc.*, 829 S. W. 2d 300, 309 (Tex. App.-Texarkana 1992); *Marchese v. Nelson*, 809 F. Supp. 880, 891 (D. Utah 1993); *Continental Leavitt Communications, LTD. v. PaineWebber, Inc.*, 857 F. Supp. 1266, 1270 (N.D. IL 1994); *Houlihan/Lawrence v. Michael Duval*, 228 A.D. 2d 560, 644 N.Y.S. 2d 553–554 (1996); *Securities and Exchange Commission v. Hughes Capital Corporation*, 124 F. 3d 449, 454; *Engle v. Dinehart*, 213 F. 3d 639, 2000 WL 554942 (CA 5 (Tex.)); *Stephenson v. Deutsche Bank AG*, 282 F. Supp. 2d 1032, 1061 (D. Minn. 2003); *Small v. Fritz Companies*, 30 Cal. 4th, 167, 174, 65 P. 3d 1255, 1259, 132 (Cal. Rptr. 2d 490, 495); *Washington Mutual Bank v. Advanced Clearing*, 679 N.W. 2d 207, 210 (Neb. 2004); *Maliner v. Wachovia*, 2005 WL 670293 (S.D. Fla.); *Fraternity Fund Ltd. v. Beacon Hill Asset*, 376 F. Supp. 2d 385 (S.D. N.Y. 2005).

18 *Suez Equity Investors, L.P. Associates v. The Toronto-Dominion Bank*, 250 FA. 3d 87, 103 (2d Cir. 2001); *Fleet Bank v. Pine Knoll Corporation*, 290 A.D. 2d 792, 736 N.Y.S. 2d 737 (NY App. Div. 2002); *Lynch v. McQueen*, 309 A.D. 2d 790, 765 N.Y.S. 2d 645 (NY App. Div. 2003); *Eternity Global Master Fund Ltd. v. Morgan Guar. Trust Co.*, 375 F. 3d 168, 188 (2d Cir. 2004); *Henneberry v. Sumitomo Corp. of America*, 532 F. Supp. 2d 523 (S.D. NY 2007); *J.A.O. Acquisition Corp. v. Stavitsky*, 863 N.E. 2d 585, 587 (2007); *Cahaly v. Benistar Property Exchange Trust Co.*, 864 N.E.2d 548, 559 (Mass. App. Ct. 2007).

> In the commercial context, a duty to speak with care exists when "the relationship of the parties, arising out of contract or otherwise, [is] such that in morals . . . the one has the right to rely upon the other for information" (*International Prods. Co. v. Erie RR Co.*, 244 N.Y. 331, 338, 155 N.E. 662). This reliance must be justifiable. . . .
>
> Liability for negligent misrepresentation has been imposed only on those persons who possess unique or specialized expertise, or who are in a special position of confidence and trust with the injured such that reliance on the negligent misrepresentation is justified. . .[19]

Whether the nature and caliber of the relationship between the parties is such that the injured party's reliance on a negligent misrepresentation is justified is an issue of fact. In determining whether justifiable reliance exists in a particular case, a fact finder must consider whether the person making the representation held or appeared to hold unique or special expertise, whether a special relationship of trust or confidence existed between the parties, and whether the speaker was aware of the use to which the information would be put, and in fact supplied it for that purpose.[20]

Pursuant to the holding in *Kimmell v. Schaefer*, which is representative of a number of New York court decisions, the components of negligent misrepresentation are: (1) recklessness in communicating words; (2) on which others were expected to rely; (3) on which they acted or failed to act; (4) to their loss. A service provider who possesses specialized expertise or who has a relationship of trust or confidence with the party knows that his words will be relied on by the person with whom he has a professional relationship or a duty of care, and is therefore liable for negligent misrepresentation.[21]

Assessing the parties' expectations based on a special relationship of trust or confidence between them is reminiscent of the oft-cited New York case, *Credit Alliance Corp. v. Arthur Andersen & Co.* In that case, the court articulated a three prong test that requires near-privity to impose liability for the negligent performance of an audit.

> Before accountants may be held liable in negligence to non-contractual parties who rely to their detriment on inaccurate financial reports, certain prerequisites must be satisfied: (1) the accountants must have been aware

19 Ibid., 453–54.

20 Ibid.

21 *White v. Guarente*, 43 N.Y. 2d 356, 401 N.Y.S. 2d 474, 478, 372 N.E. 2d 315 (1977); *Kimmell v. Schaefer*, 675 N.E. 2d 454 (1996); *Dallas Aerospace, Inc. v. CIS Air Corporation*, 352 F. 3d 775, 788 (2nd Cir. 2003).

> that the financial reports were to be used for a particular purpose or purposes; (2) in the furtherance of which a *known party or parties* was intended to rely; and (3) there must have been some conduct on the part of the accountants linking them to *that* party or parties, which evinces the accountants' understanding of *that* party or parties' reliance.[22]

In *Credit Alliance*, the court formulated a near-privity standard. Absent the existence of a contract, actual or constructive knowledge of a specific party's reliance on the audit will be sufficient grounds for mandating accountants' liability. This holding is consistent with earlier New York case law in *Ultramares* and *Glanzer*, which recognized in certain situations that a third party has such a close relationship with the auditing firm and the client as to constitute "near-privity." Moreover, the holding relied on the same precedent invoked by *Kimmell v. Schaefer*.[23] In effect, there is no clear conceptual difference between the near-privity rule and the special relationship doctrine. As noted in the recent New York case regarding a bank representation, *J.A.O. Acquisition Corp. v. Stavitsky*, "A claim for negligent misrepresentation requires the plaintiff to demonstrate the existence of a special or privity-like relationship imposing a duty on the defendant to impart correct information."[24] The interchangeability of terms ("special or privity-like relationship") demonstrates that there is no critical distinction between them.

The concept of "near-privity" may also be invoked via the concept of "a special relationship." As *Dallas Aerospace v. CSI Air Corporation* aptly noted:

> Dallas urges that *Kimmell* enunciated a new standard, exacting liability whenever the relationship between the parties is "such that in morals . . . the one has the right to rely upon the other for information." . . . This is a misreading of the case. . . . Indeed, the assertedly "new" standard stated in *Kimmell* was a quotation from a New York Court of Appeals decision that preceded it by seven decades.[25]

Similarly, after citing *Kimmell v. Schaefer's* doctrine of "a special relationship," the court in *JP Morgan Chase Bank v. Winnick* asserted: "A special

22 *Credit Alliance Corp. v. Arthur Andersen & Co.*, 483 N.E. 2d 110, 118 (N.Y. 1985). See also *Westpac Banking Corp.* v. *Deschamps*, 484 N.E. 2d. 1351–1352 (N.Y. 1985).

23 *White v. Guarente*, 372 N.E. 2d 320 (1977).

24 *J.A.O. Acquisition Corp. v. Stavitsky*, 863 N.E. 2d 585, 587 (2007).

25 *Dallas Aerospace v. CSI Air Corporation*, 352 F. 3d 775, 788 (2nd Cir. 2003).

relationship may be brought about by either privity or a relationship so close as to approach that of privity."[26]

In the final analysis, a third party claiming harm must demonstrate a relationship or a bond with the broker which sufficiently approaches privity based on some conduct on the part of the broker.

Thus, there are two alternative approaches to defining the parameters of advisor liability. One narrows liability to those in privity or an equivalent relationship, such as "a special relationship of trust or confidence" with the broker. The other extends liability to parties who are known or not specifically identified, and perhaps only foreseen. According to the first approach, the public part of the financial consultant's dual identity is secondary, so that only identified third party users should rely on it, whereas according to the second approach, the public part is sufficiently significant that third parties, known or foreseeable, should be able to rely on it.

## 2 Jewish law

How does Jewish law[27] address the scope of an advisor's liability for negligent misrepresentation?[28] Do "casual" statements made by a provider of financial services fall under the duty to speak with care, or is

26 *JP Morgan Chase Bank v. Winnick*, 350 F. Supp. 2d 393, 401 (N.Y. App. Div. 2004).

27 Jewish law is recorded in various authoritative sources: (1) the Talmud, the classical exposition of Jewish law; (2) *peirushim* (commentaries) and *hidushim* (novellae — discursive critical investigations); (3) *psakim* (codes); and (4) *sheeilot uteshuvot* (responsa literature) — juridical authorities' decisions on legal queries of litigants, judges, community leaders, and other concerned individuals. Juridical authorities have at their disposal five tools for arriving at legal decisions: *midrash* (canons of interpretation); *takana ugzeira* (legislation); *minhag* and *nohag* (custom and usage); *maase* (precedent); and *svara* (legal logic). For further elucidation of these sources and tools, see Menachem Elon, *Jewish Law: History, Sources, Principles* (Philadelphia: 1994).

28 See C.A. 86/76 *Amidar v. Aharon*, 32(2) PD 337 (Justice Menachem Elon's opinion); David Schonberg, "Aspects of the Jewish law of negligent misrepresentation," 13–14 *Dine Israel* (1986/1988), 31; Yaron Unger, "Negligent misrepresentation," Israel's Ministry of Justice, Weekly Torah Portion Series, no. 223. See too my "The investment advisor: liabilities and halachic identity," *Journal of Halacha & Contemporary Society* 58 (2009), 107–21 and "The multi-faceted halakhic identity of a Jewish investment broker," *Tradition* 43 (2010), 51–71.

liability for negligent misrepresentation imposed only on those persons who possess unique or specialized expertise? Is liability limited to those who are in a contractual relationship with the investment planner? Does Jewish law establish the rule that a third party can bring an action in negligence only if it can enforce the contract as a third party beneficiary? Does the Jewish legal system allow for such a suit in cases of near-privity? Is there a movement toward expanding the scope of a consultant's liability to include parties that are actually known by the planner to be users of the information, or does Jewish law embrace the foreseeable user standard, and hold investment planners liable to any reasonably foreseeable user of the information who received it for a business purpose? Or does Jewish law use an entirely different standard for liability?

Expounding the biblical verse "Before a blind person you shall not place a stumbling block; you should fear your God, I am God" (Lev. 19:14), the Sifra (*Torat Kohanim*), a halakhic compilation dating back to 120–140 CE, rules as follows: "If he takes advice from you, you shall not provide advice which is improper for him." [29]

Later authorities clarify that although it is forbidden to knowingly provide "bad advice," a violation of this prohibition entails no halakhic–judicial remedy. Jewish law recognizes the damage as remote (*gerama*), and the advisor would therefore not be held liable for any damage ensuing from his faulty advice.[30]

The following talmudic passage appears to implicitly challenge this conclusion:

> If one shows a dinar to a moneychanger [in order to determine whether it is good and he should accept it, and the moneychanger says it is good], but it turns out to be bad, the baraita states that if he is an expert, he is exempt from liability [for recurring damage resulting from his advice], while if he is a layman, he is liable. However, another baraita states he is liable regardless of whether he is an expert or a layman. R. Papa stated: The statement that an expert is exempt from liability relates to those like Dankho and Issur [who were exceptional experts], who have no need for further training. So what was their error? They erred in [appraising] a new coin which recently had been minted. . . .

29 *Torat Kohanim*, Leviticus 19:14.

30 R. Jacob b. Asher (Germany, 14th c.), *Tur*, HM 306; R. Solomon Luria (Poland, 16th c.), *Yam Shel Shlomo*, Baba Kama 6:4; R. Moses Isserles (Poland, 16th c.), *Darkhei Moshe* and *Rema*, HM 306:3. An expression of reliance is required before an advisor's liability commences; see *Rema*, HM 129:2.

> Resh Lakish showed a dinar to R. Eliezer. He said it was good. Resh Lakish said to R. Eliezer: "See, I rely on you."[31]

In talmudic times, the value of a coin was dependent on its weight, shape, and the manner in which was minted. A flawed coin was worth much less than a non-flawed coin. Individuals consulted moneychangers to appraise the value of their currency. In our case, the moneychanger informed the merchant that his coin was authentic, but it was later discovered that he erred; the civil authorities disqualified the currency. In reconciling the two baraitas, the Talmud concludes that a layman who proffers advice as a moneychanger is liable for any ensuing damages should his advice be acted on, and an expert moneychanger who is not exceptionally qualified is equally liable.

How can this be reconciled with the conclusion reached, on the basis of the Sifra, that one who offers bad advice is not held liable? One approach to resolving this apparent contradiction argues that the Sifra discusses an individual who gives a casual "curbside opinion" and is therefore not liable. He had no reason to assume that his opinion would be relied on when he offered it. In the moneychanger case, we are dealing with an exceptionally qualified expert who proffered mistaken advice. As the Talmud states, the coin must have been newly minted — in other words, it was an error beyond his control. However, a laymen and regular expert are held responsible for any errors in judgment.[32]

As noted by Resh Lakish at the end of the talmudic passage, in the absence of the client's clear reliance on the professional, no liability would ensue, whether the advisor is a layman or an expert.[33] During the Geonic period (7th–11th c.), this reliance doctrine is cited authoritatively as the main rule for defining the parameters of liability for negligent misrepresentation. An anonymous Gaon stated: "And Resh

31 bBaba Kama 99b–100a.

32 R. Joseph Caro (Israel, 16th c.), *SA*, HM 306:6; *Rema*, ad loc.; R. Shabtai Rappaport (Moravia, 17th c.), *Shakh*, ad loc. 12, in the name of the *Shiltei Giborim* and *Yam Shel Shlomo*.

33 For a different approach to explaining the apparent contradiction, see Nahmanides (Spain, 13th c.), *Kuntres Dina Degarmi* 47, as explained in *Shiurei Harav Aharon Lichtenstein: Dina Degarmi* (Israel: 2000), 36; R. Mordekhai b. Hillel (Germany, 13th c.), *Mordekhai*, Baba Kama 116; and R. Asher b. Yehiel (Spain, 13th c.), *Hagahot Asheri*, Baba Kama 9:16 (in the name of R. Efraim).

Lakish relied on him and it turned out that the dinar was bad, resulting in a loss caused by R. Eliezer, and this is *garmi*."[34] Because he explicitly relied on R. Eliezer, Resh Lakish was able to collect damages due to the direct causal nexus (*garmi*) between the professional advice offered and the ensuing damage. The nexus was created by the special position of confidence and trust that the professional held with respect to the injured party, such that reliance on the negligent misrepresentation was justified.

Decisors in the post-talmudic period further elaborated on the reliance doctrine. R. Isaac Alfasi invoked Resh Lakish's opinion as precedent: "We may conclude that a non-expert is liable to pay provided that he [the client] informed the non-expert that he is relying on him."[35] The view that reliance exists where the client explicitly states to the non-expert that he is relying on his investment advice was endorsed by numerous legists and codifiers throughout the ages.[36]

The Rif continues: "And if the circumstances demonstrate that there is reliance, he need not inform the non-expert that he is relying on him." That is, although Resh Lakish explicitly informed R. Eliezer that he was relying on his opinion, the Rif argues that verbal expression of reliance is not necessary. Subsequent authorities upheld the Rif's view, arguing that reliance may be inferred from the circumstances, even if

34 *Otzar Hageonim*, Baba Kama, p. 75.

35 R. Isaac Alfasi (Rif), (North Africa, 11th c.), bBaba Kama 100b. Some argue that in the opinion of the Rif, an expression of reliance is also required for an expert. See R. Solomon b. Benjamin (Salonika, 18th c.), *Responsa Lev Shlomo*, 83.

36 Maimonides (Spain and Egypt, 12th c.), *Code*, Laws concerning Hiring 10:5; R. Abraham b. Isaac (France, 12th c.), *Responsa Raavad of Narbonne*, #176; R. Solomon Aderet (Spain, 13th c.), *Responsa Rashba* 7:443 and *Responsa attributed to Nahmanides*, #240; R. Isaac b. Moses (France, 13th c.), *Or Zarua*, Baba Kama 9:410, in the name of R. Joel b. Isaac; R. Shimon b. Tzemah Duran (North Africa, 15th c.), *Responsa Tashbetz* 2:174; R. Joseph Habiba (Spain, 15th c.), *Nimukei Yosef*, bBaba Kama 100b; R. Bezalel Ashkenazi (Egypt and Israel, 16th c.), *Shita Mekubetzet*, bBaba Kama 100a, in the name of R. Meir Abulafia (the Rama) and the Rashba; *SA*, HM 306:6; *Rema*, HM 306:6; *Shakh*, HM 306:12. Cf. *Tosafot*, bBaba Kama 100a s.v. *ahvei*; R. Asher b. Yehiel (Spain, 13th c.), Baba Kama 9:16; *Rema*, ibid.; and *Yam Shel Shlomo*, Baba Kama 9:24, who argue that non-expert liability also extends to situations where there was no expression of reliance.

not stated explicitly.[37] For example, R. Yehiel Epstein, a leading Russian decisor at the beginning of the twentieth century, codified this as follows:

> If he [the advisor] says to the lender, "Lend to X, as he is sound," and he lent to him accordingly, and afterwards it became apparent to him [the lender] that he [the borrower] was not sound at the time of the loan, then he [the advisor] is liable to him, for, as a result of what he said, he gave him the loan, and there is no greater *garmi* than this. . . . And it seems to me that a ruling can be made that in the case where the lender asked him [the advisor] if X, who wants to receive a loan from him, is sound, and he [the advisor] answers, "He is sound," then, if the lender had not told him, "See, I rely on you," he cannot be found liable. For such is the way of the world, and perhaps he really thought that he was sound, and he did not check this thoroughly. But if [the advisor] came [of his own initiative] to the lender and said to him, "Lend to X, as he is sound," clearly he investigated it well, and he is liable if he was not sound at that time, even if he was not told, "See, I rely on you."[38]

According to R. Epstein, an expression of reliance in the form of oral or written communication engenders liability, as the advisor must then consider if he has investigated the matter fully enough to provide his opinion. In the absence of an explicit expression of reliance, a relationship of reliance is established if the advisor is the initiator of the offer of advice. We assume that the advisor researched the matter before approaching the prospective client to offer his unsolicited advice, and an expression of reliance is therefore unnecessary to engender liability. However, if the customer approached the advisor for counsel of his own accord, reliance of the former on the latter must be proven. Unless the client explicitly stated that he is relying on the advisor's advice, the advisor is not liable for any misrepresentation.

Another approach to determining reliance focuses on the advisor's financial expertise, as reflected in the baraita cited by the Talmud: "If he is an expert, he is exempt from liability, while if he is a layman, he is liable." R. Papa concludes that only an expert who requires no further

37 R. Meir Abulafia (Rama), (Spain, 12th c.), in *Shita Mekubezet*, Baba Kama 100a; *Responsa Rashba* 7:443; *SA* and *Rema*, HM 306:6; *Shakh*, HM 306:6:12. Cf. R. Jonathan Eybeschutz (Prague, 18th c.), *Urim Vetumin*, HM 129. Although the Rosh (Baba Kama 9:16), does not mandate an expression of reliance, he posits a minimal requirement that the existence of a relationship of reliance can be extrapolated from the circumstances; see *Responsa Rosh* 102:3.

38 *Arukh Hashulhan*, HM 129:3. This translation is from Schonberg, n. 28 above, 59–60.

training is not liable; all others would be liable. While the Talmud distinguishes between an expert and a non-expert regarding liability for negligent misrepresentation, it does not say whether the advisor's credentials are indicators of reliance or lack thereof.

Maimonides codified the tort of negligent representation as follows:

> The same [rule] applies when a person shows a coin to a money changer and he says that it is acceptable, and it is discovered to be unacceptable. If he charged for his services, he is obligated to pay even though he is an expert and does not require further training. If he did not charge, he is not liable, provided he is an expert and does not require further training. If he is not an expert, he must reimburse [the questioner] even when he does not charge for his services. [This applies when the questioner] tells the money changer, "I am relying on you," or it is obvious from the situation that he is relying on his opinion and he is not seeking another opinion.[39]

According to Maimonides, a paid financial planner who has an education, earned a license in financial planning, and has no need for further training may be classified as an expert (*mumhe*) who is justifiably trusted.[40] Given that he is an expert, those who avail themselves of his services rely on his advice, and he is exempt from liability only because he is viewed as under duress (*anus*).[41] If he is paid for his services, an expert would be held liable in the case of negligent misrepresentation, but this is not because payment is an expression of reliance.[42] On the

39 Maimonides, *Code*, Laws concerning Hiring 10:5. This translation is from Maimonides, *Mishneh Torah*, vol. 27, Mishpatim, edited by Eliyahu Touger (NY: 2000), 104.

40 *Netivot Hamishpat*, HM 306:12; *Arukh Hashulhan*, HM 306:13, concurs with this conclusion. The Maimonidean stance can be challenged on the grounds that reliance is due to payment for services rather the advisor's professional expertise; see text below at n. 46.

The burden of proof for demonstrating expertise in planning lies with the planner. See Maimonides, *Code*, Laws concerning Hiring 10:5; *SA*, HM 306:7; *Responsa Beit Halevi* 3:20 (2); R. Joseph Teomim (18th c.), *Pri Megadim*, YD 1:4; R. Abraham Karelitz (Israel, 20th c.), *Hazon Ish*, Baba Kama 7:18.

41 See *Tosafot*, bBaba Kama 99b s.v. *eima*; R. Vidal of Tolosa (Spain, 14th c.), *Magid Mishne*, Laws concerning Hiring 10:5.

42 *Netivot Hamishpat*, n. 40 above; *Shakh*, HM 306:6:12. According to the *Or Zarua*, Baba Kama 2:137, even an expression of reliance would not make the expert liable. The *Maharam Barukh* argues, however, that an expression of reliance will trump the investor's expertise; see *Shakh*, loc. cit. There is a dissenting opinion that requires a statement of reliance, in the case of an expert, for liability to ensue; see Maharih's view cited by *Hagahot Asheri* on Rosh, Baba Kama 9:16 and R. Joseph b. Shimon (Italy, 16th c.), *Shiltei Giborim*, bBaba Kama 99b.

other hand, a layman proffering advice would be liable regardless of whether he is paid. The communication of advice renders him a tortfeasor (*mazik*).[43] In short, professional expertise is a yardstick for the reliance relationship.

Finally, some legists maintain that one of the factors establishing reliance is "the pecuniary interest." In other words, receiving a professional fee for one's services indicates that the client is relying on the advisor's counsel. The earliest source for this approach is the Tosefta: "Someone who shows a dinar to a money changer and it turns out to be bad — he is obligated to pay because it is akin to someone who receives remuneration."[44]

Although this passage in the Tosefta invokes the notion of remuneration, it does not state that remuneration establishes a reliance relationship. The Talmud and numerous codifiers, such as Maimonides, the *Shulhan Arukh*, and the Rema, are equally silent regarding this matter.[45] R. Shimon b. Tzemah Duran (Tashbetz), however, states that "since he is an expert ... and he takes payment, he only takes payment so that he will be relied on, and he is thereby liable."[46] Similarly, R. Epstein states: "where payment is tendered, even where he [the inquirer] did not say, 'I rely on you,' he is liable — since as he took payment, it is clear that he [the inquirer] relied on him totally."[47]

Those decisors who take remuneration to be an element that establishes reliance argue that if the investment advisor receives money for his advice, whether or not he is an expert, he becomes liable.[48] In fact, one opinion states that this view is "eminently clear"

43 Cf. *Tosafot*, bBaba Kama 100a s.v. *ahvei*; *Rosh*, Baba Kama 9:16; and *Yam Shel Shlomo*, Baba Kama 9:24. See also R. Menahem Meiri (Spain, 13th c.), *Meiri*, bBaba Kama 56a; *Tosafot*, bBaba Kama 99b s.v. *vetanya*.

44 tNezikin 10:10 (Lieberman edition); *Tosefta Kifshuta*, Nezikin, Baba Kama, Baba Metzia, 118.

45 bBaba Kama 100a; *SA* and *Rema*, HM 306:6.

46 *Responsa Tashbetz* 2:174.

47 *Arukh Hashulhan*, HM 306:13.

48 Ibid. Even the possibility of payment is sufficient to establish reliance. See *Tarshish Shoham*, HM 99; Schonberg, n. 28 above, 52. To engender liability, this must be payment in exchange for the investment advice, rather than any other indirect benefit accruing to the advisor for servicing the customer. See R. Uziel Lachiah (Italy, 17th c.), *Mishkenot Haroim*, 70:105; Schonberg, 52–54. If the advisor receives no direct remuneration but nevertheless stands to benefit — for example, a bank officer or corporate officer who provides information regarding a company — liability would not ensue.

(*pashut*).[49] According to many authorities, however, this is a relevant criterion for establishing reliance only with respect to an expert advisor.[50]

In sum, there are four possible criteria that can be used to assess whether there was reliance on the advisor, and hence, a fiduciary relationship existed between the parties:

1. An explicit expression of reliance, such as Resh Lakish's statement to R. Eliezer.
2. Apparent reliance based on the circumstances, as in R. Epstein's case of the advisor who offered advice of his own initiative.
3. The advisor's expertise.
4. Payment to the advisor for his services.[51]

R. Solomon b. Aderet, the Rashba, argues that the last element, pecuniary interest, is not relevant, and rules: "Since [the money changer's profession] entails observation and expertise regarding the shape of coins, there is no room for error, and if he erred it was an accident . . . and even an expert who receives payment is exempt."[52]

Accordingly, payment for services rendered is irrelevant to the advisor's liability. Hence, a layman who proffers advice is liable for negligent misrepresentation whether or not he receives payment. On the other hand, we presume that an expert did his work with due diligence, and if he erred, it was an accident. He is therefore exempt under all circumstances, even if he was paid.

The more accepted view, however, is that receipt of payment makes the expert liable for negligent misrepresentation, while the layman whom the customer relied on is always liable, regardless of

49 *Netivot Hamishpat*, HM 306:11. See also R. Solomon Eger (Germany, 19th c.), *Responsa R. Solomon Eger*, #23; *Arukh Hashulhan*, HM 306:13.

50 *Rosh*, bBaba Kama 9:16; *Tur* and *SA*, HM 306:6. Cf. *Hidushei Harashba*, Baba Kama 99b s.v. *amar rav papa*, who argues that pecuniary gain does not entail liability for an expert or a layman.

51 Whereas my presentation advances the argument that there are four factors in establishing reliance, earlier treatments have either analyzed the concept of reliance separately from the concepts of expertise and payment for services, or concluded that only express or apparent reliance and pecuniary interest are indicative of reliance. See the sources cited in n. 28 above.

52 *Hidushei Harashba*, bBaba Kama 99b s.v. *amar rav papa*. See also *Yam Shel Shlomo*, Baba Kama 9:24.

whether he was paid. Relying on the views of Maimonides and the Rosh, R. Caro codified this position as follows:

> If he charged for his services, he is obligated to pay even though he is an expert and does not require further training. If he did not charge, he is not liable, provided he is an expert and does not require further training. If he is not an expert, he must reimburse [the questioner] even when he does not charge for his services.[53]

Unable to decide between the different opinions and reach a definitive ruling, R. Joseph ibn Lev, a sixteenth century Turkish legist, ruled: "In case of doubt, we do not extract money."[54] R. Joseph ibn Lev is implicitly invoking the stance of the Rosh, who argued that an arbiter who feels unable to render a decision should abstain from definitively deciding a case.[55] Ibn Lev would thus maintain that one cannot extract money from the financial planner.[56] On this view, one would be unable to file a claim in a rabbinical court against a negligent expert advisor who was paid for his services.

Relying on the opinions of Maimonides, the Rosh, and R. Caro,[57] R. Shabtai Rappaport (Shakh) demurred and argued that one may sue a negligent expert financial consultant who receives payment for his investment advice.[58] This position reflects normative Jewish law.[59]

53 Maimonides, *Code*, Laws concerning Hiring 10:5, *Rosh*, Baba Kama 9:16; *SA*, HM 306:6. Interestingly, although we would label this the majority view today (see R. Joseph ibn Lev, *Responsa Mahari ibn Lev* 3:30), in the fourteenth century, the majority view was that of the Rashba (bBaba Kama 99b) and the Rif (bBaba Kama 100b). See R. Yeruham b. Meshulam (southern France, 14th c.), *Sefer Meisharim*, 31:2; R. Jonathan Hakohen of Lunel (southern France, 12th c.), *Commentary of R. Jonathan Hakohen of Lunel on the Mishnah and Alfasi, Tractate Baba Kama* (Hebrew), (Jerusalem: 1969), 309 n. 806.

54 *Responsa Mahari ibn Lev* 3:30.

55 *Piskei Harosh*, Sanhedrin 4:6. Another view contends that inability to resolve a matter should mandate an arbiter's abstention from decision-making altogether; see R. Judah b. Joseph Hakohen (Moravia, 18th c.), *Kuntres Hasfeikot* 5:9.

56 This supports Morell's thesis that Mahari ibn Lev's judicial decision-making can be characterized as "a hesitancy to rule definitively in the legal controversies of earlier authorities." See Samuel Morell, *Precedent and Judicial Discretion: The Case of Joseph ibn Lev* (Atlanta: 1991), 12–13, 81.

57 Maimonides, *Code*, Laws concerning Hiring 10:5; *Tur*, HM 306; *SA*, HM 306:6.

58 *Shakh*, HM 306:11.

59 *Pithei Hoshen*, Hiring, 328–29, Damages, 170 n. 57.

Assuming that a claim for negligent misrepresentation for investment advice is justiciable in a rabbinical court,[60] how is an arbiter to determine which criteria will serve as guidelines for determining whether there was negligent misrepresentation by a planner? Invoking the Maimonidean position word for word, R. Joseph Caro asserts:

> The same [rule] applies when a person shows a coin to a money changer and he says that it is acceptable, and it is discovered to be unacceptable. If he charged for his services, he is obligated to pay even though he is an expert and does not require further training. If he did not charge, he is not liable, provided he is an expert and does not require further training. If he is not an expert, he must reimburse [the questioner] even when he does not charge for his services. [The above applies when the questioner] tells the money changer, "I am relying on you," or it is obvious from the situation that he is relying on his opinion and will not be seeking another opinion.[61]

Commenting on this ruling, the Rema writes: "And there are those who contend that even without an expression of reliance, the non-expert is liable. And I think that the first opinion is to be preferred."[62]

The Rema thus subscribes to the *Shulhan Arukh*'s position. Both contend that it is the advisor's expertise and the payment remitted to him for his professional services that create a relationship of reliance. On the other hand, a layman who offers his advice gratis is liable only provided that there was an expression of reliance — either an actual statement or apparent reliance based on the circumstances. In the absence of such an expression of reliance, the Rema concurs with the *Shulhan Arukh* that the non-expert would be exempt from liability.

The Talmud and subsequent commentaries, codes, and responsa all focused on the moneychanger scenario. A potentially far-reaching ruling of the Rema may expand the boundaries of the reliance doctrine well beyond the parameters of that situation. When executing a loan, a third party, the *arev* (guarantor), obligates himself to pay the debt should the borrower default on repayment of the loan. At the inception of the suretyship (*arevut*), the guarantor must articulate that he is obligating himself to the suretyship. For example, to establish the suretyship, he may say, "Lend to the borrower and I will pay you," or,

60 Procedurally, arbitrators in contemporary times are empowered to adjudicate cases of indirect damage, such as negligent misrepresentation. See *SA*, HM 1:4; *Arukh Hashulhan*, HM 1:5.

61 *SA*, HM 306:6.

62 *Rema*, HM 306:6.

"Lend to the borrower and I will be a guarantor to you."[63] Relying on precedent,[64] the Rema rules that if an advisor counsels a lender to lend money to a borrower, as he is financially secure, and the advice proves to be false, the advisor is liable to pay the lender as if he had guaranteed the loan.[65]

In effect, the advisor's liability results from the fact that the lender relied on his advice; the advisor is liable because he negligently portrayed the borrower as an individual of financial means,[66] a representation which caused the lender to lose his money. This is analogous to the case of a guarantor, who assumes liability due to the fact that the creditor parted with monies on the strength of his assurance. In other words, the Rema's position is not limited to the context of a loan transaction, but applies equally to establishing the liability of an advisor who negligently misrepresented the facts when giving investment advice.[67] The consultant is liable because the investor relied on him.

Although the Rema's words seem to indicate that the advisor's liability is based on the fact that a suretyship (*arevut*) relationship has been established, the source serving as grounds for the Rema's position,[68] and numerous other authorities, construe this position as

63 *SA*, HM 129:1–2. In addition, the guarantor must direct the lender to give the money to the borrower; see *SA*, HM 129:18.

64 R. Jacob Weil (Germany, 15th c.), *Responsa Mahari Weil*, #80.

65 *Rema*, HM 129:2. Some contend that a prerequisite for liability is that a fiduciary obligation has been created whereby the borrower communicated to the third party his reliance on him as a guarantor, or there is some proof that reliance is present. See *Shakh*, HM 129:7; R. Hayim Palagi (Izmir, 19th c.), *Responsa Hikekei Lev*, HM 31. Others argue that if the third party states to the lender that "the borrower is financially secure," such a statement is sufficient to generate liability. See R. Solomon Tabak (Hungary, 19th c.), *Erekh Shai*, HM 129:20; R. Sholom Schwadron (Poland, 19th c.), *Responsa Maharsham* 5:11. Clearly, the stance of the latter authorities is in line with the view of the Rema and his source (see below at n. 68).

66 The underlying premise of the Rema's position is that an obligation was undertaken; see Berachyahu Lifshitz, "Consideration in Jewish law — a reconsideration," 8 *Jewish Law Annual* (1989), 115, 122–23; idem, *Promise: Obligation and Acquisition in Jewish Law* (Hebrew), (Jerusalem: 1988), 214.

67 *Shakh*, HM 129:7; *Netivot Hamishpat* 129:2; *Arukh Hashulhan*, HM 306:14; R. Joshua Beneviste (Izmir, 17th c.), *Responsa Pnei Moshe* 2:119; R. Elijah b. Solomon (Vilna, 18th c.), *Biur Hagra*, HM 129:5; *Responsa Lev Shlomo*, #83; 9 *PDR* 16, 48. Cf. R. Joshua Ehrenburg (Israel, 20th c.), *Responsa Dvar Yehoshua*, HM 110.

68 See *Responsa Mahari Weil*, #80; *Darkhei Moshe*, HM 129:2.

arguing for liability based on the laws of damages (*dinei nezikin*).[69] Viewing this matter within the context of torts in general and *garmi* in particular, the ensuing damage from the faulty advice is inevitable (*bari hezeka*),[70] and the advisor is therefore liable. In the absence of deception, if the borrower becomes financially insecure subsequent to the guarantee, the guarantor is not liable.[71] Similarly, provided that the investment advisor performed his due diligence regarding the client's financial ability to execute the investment, if the client nonetheless incurred losses due to a sudden downturn in the market, the broker is not liable.

Assuming that we are dealing either with an expert advisor or a layman who is working gratis, why did the Rema rule that there is liability for negligent misrepresentation of the borrower's financial situation? As we noted, according to the Rema,[72] an advisor is exempt from liability in both cases in the absence of an actual expression of reliance or apparent reliance. As noted by another writer,[73] the *Arukh Hashulhan*'s innovative words, cited above, shed light on the Rema's position. The *Arukh Hashulhan* states that there is a crucial difference between cases in which the lender approached the advisor for counsel and those in which the advice was proffered at the advisor's initiative.[74] If the lender sought the advice and informed the advisor that he would be relying on the advice, and it subsequently turns out that the advice was unsound, the advisor is liable. In the absence of an expression of reliance, however, the advisor may legitimately say in his own defense, "I thought you would seek advice from others as well, and I was not offering my advice as a definitive recommendation."[75] However, should the advisor offer the counsel of his own initiative, he is liable for misrepresentation even if there was no actual or apparent reliance. Since he offered the advice of his own initiative, the advisor cannot say, "I did not intend that this advice be taken as definitive." We presume

69 *Netivot Hamishpat* 129:2; *Biur Hagra*, HM 129:5; *Shakh*, HM 129:7; *Erekh Shai*, HM 131:14. Some authorities, however, contend that the Rema's stance should be understood within the context of *arevut* rather than torts; see R. Isaac Ettinger (Lemberg, 19th c.), *Responsa Mahari Halevi* 16.

70 On use of this criterion to ascribe liability, see *Piskei Harosh*, Baba Kama 9:17; *Talmudic Encyclopedia* (Hebrew), "*Garmi*," section 2.

71 *Rema*, HM 129:2.

72 Ibid., HM 306:6.

73 Schonberg, n. 28 above, 60–61.

74 *Arukh Hashulhan*, HM 129:3.

75 *Erekh Shai*, HM 129:20; *Maharsham* 5:11.

that the advisor performed his due diligence prior to communicating information to the lender. Analogously, in the situation addressed by the Rema, the advisor performed his due diligence prior to communicating to the lender that the borrower was financially secure.

## 3 Comparison

Comparing the positions of Jewish law and American law is edifying from a number of perspectives. To sharpen the contrast, consider the following case:

A financial planner who received remuneration for his services prepared a newsletter featuring general commentary about the securities market and specific recommendations for buying, selling, and holding stocks. A subscriber to the newsletter relied on this investment advice and sold some stocks at a loss. Will he succeed in his claim against the broker alleging that the advisor, in preparing an inaccurate report, was negligent? Similarly, can an individual who relied on an educational financial planning seminar given by a professional advisor who received a fee for his service succeed in his claim that the broker was negligent in his presentation?

In American law, the privity doctrine dictates that recovery of economic loss due to negligent misrepresentation by a provider of information is possible only if there was a direct contractual relationship between the parties. According to the forseeability doctrine, the advisor may be held liable if the injured party was at least a possible beneficiary of the defendant's undertaking, even if he was not known to the provider in advance. The Restatement approach strikes a balance between the privity doctrine and foreseeability test, by limiting the advisor's liability to losses incurred by third parties that the provider has actually foreseen, rather than parties that are reasonably foreseeable.[76]

As I have shown, various jurisdictions have adopted either a near-privity approach, couched in the language and terminology of reliance, or endorsed the Restatement approach regarding the liability of an investment planner. Although the foreseeable user standard has been used in addressing the liability of other information providers, such as

76 See Jay Feinman, "Liability of accountants for negligent auditing: doctrine, policy, and ideology," 31 *Fla. St. U. L. Rev.* 17 (2003).

accountants,[77] courts have eschewed the foreseeable user approach for financial planners.

How does Jewish law delineate the scope of the tort of negligent misrepresentation for a broker? Shalom Albeck attempts to demonstrate that the concept of negligence (*peshia*) underlies all of Jewish tort law.[78] Albeck argues that the case of the moneychanger is to be understood in terms of the categories of negligence (*peshia*) and absence of fault (*ones*). Without elaborating on the scope of the foreseeability standard, Albeck posits that these criteria are operative in our case. Since the moneychanger could not foresee the sequence of events leading to the damage, he is exempt from liability: "And the moneychanger is exempt, according to all opinions, if he was unable to foresee that the inquirer would rely on his advice."[79]

This interpretation is problematic. By declaring that particular damage is not "proximate," an arbiter essentially communicates that recovery is impossible. In effect, this renders the idea of fault devoid of meaning.[80] My examination of this matter yields a conclusion very different from Albeck's. As I have shown, normative Jewish law takes the concept of reliance, with its component elements of professional expertise, pecuniary interest, and an expression of trust and confidence (actual or apparent), as the substantive guideline establishing an advisor's liability for negligent misrepresentation. Whereas American law views the subject through the lens of near-privity or foreseeability as defined by the Restatement, Jewish law subscribes to the notion of reliance alone.

Given the absence of privity or near-privity between the publisher of a brochure and a subscriber or reader, if we embrace the Restatement

77 See *H. Rosenblum, Inc. v. Adler*, 461 A. 2d 138 (NJ 1983); *Citizens State Bank v. Timm, Schmidt & Co.*, 335 N.W. 2d 361 (Wis. 1983); *Raritan River Steel Co. v. Cherry, Bekaert & Holland*, 367 S.E. 2d 609, 617 (NC 1988); *Bily v. Arthur Young & Co.*, 834 P. 2d 745 (Cal.), *modified*, 3 Cal. 4th 1049a (1992).

78 Shalom Albeck, *General Principles of the Law of Tort in the Talmud* (Hebrew), (Tel Aviv: 1965), 19–26. See also idem, "Law and history" (Hebrew), 3 *Iyunei Mishpat* (1974), 714–15.

79 Ibid., 58, 181.

80 I. Englard, "Research in Jewish law — its nature and function," in B. Jackson (ed.), *Modern Research in Jewish Law* (Leiden: 1980), 21, 62; Steven Friedell, "Some observations on the Jewish law of torts," 13–14 *Dine Israel* (1986/1988), 65, 74 n. 27. On Albeck's methodology, see Jackson, op. cit., and Berachyahu Lifshitz, "The theoretical basis of the condition in Jewish law" (Hebrew), 4 *Mishpatim* (1973), 636.

standard, the question is whether the erroneous information was published for a specific group with the knowledge that it would influence their investment decisions. As long as the communications between the parties remain entirely impersonal and do not develop into a fiduciary tie, a person-to-person relationship characteristic of investment advisor-client relationships, courts have generally taken the position that in arriving at financial decisions, exclusive reliance on a newsletter is not reasonable.[81] In the absence of applicable case law regarding liability for information delivered at an investment seminar, it would seem that this scenario is indistinguishable from liability for incorrect information negligently published by a newspaper.

Rejection of the privity requirement is implicit in the Rema's extension of the reliance doctrine (endorsed by various decisors from the seventeenth century on[82]) to cases in which a paid professional broker initiates the offer of advice.[83] This opens up the possibility of broker liability to creditors, shareholders, lenders, and — arguably — anyone else in the financial world. Indeed, R. Zalman Nehemiah Goldberg, an internationally renowned expert on Jewish civil law, has argued as follows:

> The moneychanger who inspected a dinar and found it bad is only responsible to the inquirer, rather than the entire world, unless his opinion was expressed in a public lecture. This position merits further elucidation.[84]

The financial advice found in an investment newsletter sent out to attract clients to a fee-based professional investment advisory service[85] or offered in a public setting is a contemporary scenario to which we can apply the Rema's view that an expert bears liability for losses resulting from advice proffered of his own initiative. We presume that the advisor performed his due diligence prior to communicating this information to the world, and he is therefore liable should he err.

81 *Lowe v. S.E.C.*, 105 S. Ct. 2557, 2572–2573 (1985); *Gutter v. Dow Jones & Co., Inc.*, 22 Ohio St. 3d 286, 490 N.E. 2d 898(1986); *Pittman v. Dow Jones & Co., Inc.*, 662 F. Supp. 921(E.D. La. 1987); *Ginzburg v. Agora, Inc.*, 915 F. Supp. 733 (D. Md. 1995).

82 See n. 78 above.

83 *Rema*, HM 129:2.

84 R. Goldberg's position was communicated orally to Dr. Itamar Warhaftig, who forwarded this communication to me on June 5, 2009.

85 Warhaftig suggests that R. Goldberg's opinion can be extended to an advisor's liability for the content of an investment report he prepared.

The attempt to correlate concepts of a religious system with those of a secular system risks serious anachronism and may give rise to invidious comparisons. Having analyzed the various elements underlying the tort of negligent misrepresentation relating to investment advice in Jewish and American law, I hope to have avoided Santayana's reproach that comparison "is the expedient of those who cannot reach the heart of the things compared."[86]

86 George Santayana, *Character and Opinion in the United States* (NY: 1920), 166.

*The Jewish Law Annual*, Vol. XIX

# On Conduct Rules and Decision Rules in Jewish Law

Shai Wozner*

## 1 Introduction

Legal thought distinguishes between two sets of rules: conduct rules, which are directed to the ordinary person, instructing him on how to behave, and decision rules, which instruct courts on how to make decisions on cases presented for judgment. "Do not steal" is a conduct rule addressing the individual, whereas the punishment specified for theft is a decision rule that the court is supposed to apply when convicting a defendant for theft. In a well-known paper, M. Dan-Cohen developed the model of "acoustic separation," noting that because the two sets of rules were thought to be complementary parts of a single entity, the distinction between them had been ignored in the legal literature. He argued that awareness of the distinction between the two types of rules, which address different audiences and have different content, can help clarify legal discussions and afford new legal insights. Moreover, the two sets of rules are not complementary, but point to an unexpected normative tension.[1]

The distinction is not unknown in Jewish law. Indeed, the Sages were clearly aware of it, although, as is characteristic of talmudic discourse in general, they did not state it explicitly. It seems that they even used the distinction's inherent vagueness to more efficiently control the behavior of the public. In this article, I analyze a number of specific legal questions, and show that awareness of the distinction is necessary for a proper understanding of halakhic dicta and their normative implications.

* Shai Wozner is a member of Tel-Aviv University's Faculty of Law.

1 M. Dan-Cohen, "Decision rules and conduct rules: on acoustic separation in criminal law," 97 *Harvard Law Review* (1984), 625–77; see also idem, *Harmful Thoughts: Essays on Law, Self, and Morality* (Princeton: 2002), ch. 2.

## 2 Jewish law v. secular law

Secular legal systems focus on decision rules. Western penal codes, for example, do not usually contain conduct rules such as "do not kill" or "do not steal," but rather decision rules stating the punishment for various felonies. It is assumed that the punishments will guide citizens in understanding how they are expected to behave. In this spirit, Hans Kelsen argues that from a jurisprudential point of view, law contains only decision rules addressed to the court, and conceptually speaking, conduct rules are not part of the law at all.[2]

In contrast, the primary legal instruments of the halakha are conduct rules, the vast majority of which are not backed by penal decision rules and the infringement of which does not lead to legal sanctions.[3] This is justified by the assumption that the addressees of the halakha obey its norms, even in the absence of institutionalized sanctions administered by the courts, due to the addressees' deep identification with the halakha and the halakhic community, as well as their apprehension regarding Divine punishment.[4]

2 H. Kelsen, *General Theory of Law and State* (Cambridge MA: 1945), 61. Cf. J.W. Harris, *Legal Philosophies*, 2nd edition (Cambridge: 1997), 69, summarizing Kelsen's view: "Both legal and moral norms contain 'oughts,' but a moral norm stipulates, for example, 'people ought not to steal,' whereas a legal norm stipulates 'if people steal, they ought to be punished.' Moral norms are addressed directly to citizens. Legal norms are addressed only to officials."

Hart argues, however, that a complete dichotomy is too radical, since the concept of punishment itself implies a sanction for the violation of a conduct rule: "A punishment for a crime, such as a fine, is not the same as a tax on a course of conduct, though both involve directions to officials to inflict the same money loss. What differentiates these ideas is that the first involves, as the second does not, an offence or breach of duty in the form of violation of a rule set up to guide the conduct of ordinary citizens" (*The Concept of Law* [Oxford: 1994], 39). For a fuller discussion of the disagreement between Kelsen and Hart, see Dan-Cohen, "Decision rules," n. 1 above, 626–29.

3 This characteristic of the halakha is noted several times by M. Silberg in *Such is the Way of the Talmud* (Hebrew), (Jerusalem: 1962): "Jewish law is a law without judges. It does not tell the judge how to rule, but tells men how to live" (52); "Jewish law on the whole, in both the penal and the civil spheres, is a legal system primarily addressing citizens, not judges" (56–59; 94–96).

4 See R. Cover, "The Supreme Court 1982; foreword: nomos and narrative," 97 *Harvard Law Review* (1984), 4–68.

Furthermore, even when the halakha does apply sanctions, it does not forgo explicit mention of the conduct rule. Indeed, twofold reference to decision rules and conduct rules is prominent in biblical law. For example, there are two scriptural chapters on incest; one (Lev. 18:6–24) defines the prohibition of incest and lists the forbidden relationships, the other (Lev. 20:8–21) reiterates the list from the decision-rule perspective, specifying the punishments incurred for violation of the conduct rules. This dual presentation did not go unnoticed by the Sages, prompting them to formulate the rule that "there is no punishment without forewarning."[5] In other words, punishment may not be imposed unless the offender was notified beforehand of a conduct rule explicitly forbidding the behavior in question.

The anonymous medieval author of the *Sefer Hahinukh* raises the question of why this duality was necessary. If the perpetrator is punished, is it not clear that the incest was prohibited? His answer is that from an analytical point of view, it is indeed impossible to deduce a categorical conduct rule from a decision rule. Punishment of a thief does not necessarily mean that stealing is forbidden. In the absence of a conduct rule, it may very well be that stealing is permitted, provided the prescribed price — the punishment — is paid. From the punishment imposed on the thief, we can only infer a hypothetical rule that one should not steal if one does not want to be punished.[6] This is why Scripture consistently indicates the desirable behavior by articulating categorical conduct rules; the punishments specified for violation of the conduct rules are only an instrument for enforcing their observance.[7]

5 bYoma 81a.

6 On the distinction between categorical rules and hypothetical rules, see Kant, *Fundamental Principles of the Metaphysic of Morals* (1785), translated by T.K. Abbott, 2nd edition (NY: 1949), second section, available at: http://ebooks.adelaide.edu.au/k/kant/immanuel/k16prm: "Now all imperatives command either hypothetically or categorically. The former represent the practical necessity of a possible action as [a] means to something else that is willed (or at least which one might possibly will). The categorical imperative would be that which represented an action as necessary of itself without reference to another end, i.e., as objectively necessary."

7 "For the mere mention of the punishment without a formal prohibition is not sufficient for us. And this is what the Sages meant by saying, 'This [verse] teaches the punishment; whence do we derive the formal prohibition?' The reason of the matter is that if God would not tell of His

## 3 The obligation to suffer punishment

The first issue we will consider can be termed "the Socratic dilemma from the halakhic perspective." Socrates was convicted and sentenced to death for his heretical doctrines and for corrupting the youth of Athens. Although he considered his sentence unjustified, and his disciples worked out an escape plan for him, Socrates refused to flee. In his Speech of the Laws,[8] he argued that it was in precisely such circumstances that true obedience and subordination to the rule of law was tested.

Let us examine a similar case from the perspective of Jewish law. Someone profanes the Sabbath, is prosecuted, and is sentenced to death by a court of twenty-three judges, as prescribed by Jewish law. While on death row, he has an opportunity to escape and thereby save his life. This individual is deeply religious and precept-observant, and only once failed to properly observe the Sabbath laws. Is he permitted to seize the opportunity to escape?[9] As far as I know, this question has not been explicitly discussed in the halakhic literature. Examining this question in the conduct rules/decision rules distinction context, however, may yield some suggestions as to where the appropriate answer might be found.

---

disapproval, but say, '[If you] do such-and-such a thing, you will be punished,' it would signify that anyone who was prepared to be punished and cared not about his suffering was permitted to transgress the commandments, and he would not be acting contrary to the will of God, may He be blessed, and His precepts. So the precepts would turn out to be something akin to commerce. That is, one who wished to do a certain thing had to pay a certain amount and then could do it, or expose his shoulders to suffer the lash and then do it. But this is not the intention of the commandments, but rather, for our own good, God forbade us to do certain things, and in a few cases, He let us know the punishment to be expected from His hand, in addition to acting against His will, which is the worst of all things. And this is what the Sages, of blessed memory, mean by saying, 'There is no punishment without forewarning [not to commit a given deed]' (bYoma 81a). That is, God did not tell us the punishment that will be incurred for transgressing a commandment unless He first let us know it was His will that we not do the deed that incurs the said punishment" (*Sefer Hahinukh*, precept 69).

8 Plato, *Crito* 50a6–54d1.

9 After all, Jewish law declares that escaping mortal danger supersedes almost every other law, in cases of both duress (i.e., where someone is coerced by someone else to commit a prohibited act), and necessity (i.e., where someone chooses to commit a prohibited act to escape mortal danger) — as in the present case.

As we noted above, statements imposing punishments are decision rules, not conduct rules. It is the duty of the court to punish the transgressor, but this decision rule by its very nature does not necessarily oblige the transgressor to suffer the punishment[10]; he does not break any law by escaping.[11] Indeed, while most legal systems include the explicit felony of escaping from custody, such a felony does not appear in Jewish law, neither as a decision rule nor as a conduct rule. It may therefore be inferred that escaping from death row is permitted.

This approach reflects the complexity of halakhic thinking, which is capable of embracing various and even opposed perspectives. On the one hand, courts must punish transgressors; on the other hand, the law does not obligate transgressors to cooperate and suffer punishment.[12]

It could be argued that punishment also has another function, that of inducing atonement. The sinner therefore must not escape, but rather willingly submit to the punishment he deserves, in order to gain atonement. But though it is true that punishments may bring about atonement, it is not certain that the sinner must suffer the punishment in order to achieve that goal; there is, after all, a better alternative — repentance. This idea is expressed in the following Midrash:

> As long as a man is alive, the Almighty expects him to repent. Once he dies, all his hopes are lost, as it is written: "When a wicked man dieth, his hope shall perish" (Prov. 11:7). This is comparable to a band of robbers locked up in jail. One of them dug a tunnel, and they all ran away except for one. When the jailer arrived, he beat him with his stick and said, You unfortunate fool! There is a tunnel and you did not run away! Similarly, the Almighty will tell the wicked, "There is repentance and you did not repent!"[13]

The Midrash appears to support our hypothesis: it does not object at all to the criminals' escaping punishment. Indeed, the point of the parable is not only that one should use every opportunity to repent;

10 Jewish law does not obligate sinners to seek punishment, and committing suicide is categorically forbidden even if one has been sentenced to death. See R. Moses Feinstein, *Responsa Igrot Moshe*, HM 2:69.

11 See R. A. Amiel, *Hamidot Leheker Hahahlakha* (Tel-Aviv: 1940), vol. 2, 25.

12 Thomas Hobbes puts forward a similar idea in *Leviathan*, chs.14 and 21. He argues that while capital punishment of criminals may be justified from society's point of view, it is equally justified for a criminal to try to escape; in his situation, the social contract that divests him of his right to resort to violence no longer applies.

13 Midrash Rabbah, Ecclesiastes 7:32.

that idea could have been expressed equally well using other analogies with less anarchic implications. For example, the Midrash could have portrayed a doctor telling his dying patient, "Fool! Why didn't you take your medicine? Now you will die!" The Midrash chose the analogy of criminals escaping from jail to illustrate that the sinner need not be punished in order to gain atonement. In fact, the Almighty would prefer that he repent and survive.

## 4 Conduct rules and court rulings

As noted above, Western legal systems generally focus on decision rules, whereas Jewish law emphasizes conduct rules. This impacts the role of the courts in the respective legal systems. Ordinarily, decision rules guide courts to their decisions post factum — in the situation that exists after an action has already been taken — because it is only at this stage that the parties present their grievances to the court and ask for legal redress. Hence in Western legal systems, most decision rules instruct the courts on how to decide cases where questionable conduct has already been exhibited. It is quite unusual for a Western court to address future behavior and to determine *ex-ante* whether a given behavior is permitted or not. Indeed, a citizen wondering about the conduct rule applicable in a given situation might consult a lawyer, but would find it difficult to attain aid from a court. He could only ascertain the answer to his legal question from an earlier judgment addressing a similar case, provided such a judgment existed.

Conversely, in the halakhic system, such inquiries are routine. To approach a halakhic judicial institution (such as a court, rabbi, or decisor) and ask how one ought to behave in the future is normative behavior. In such cases, the court is asked to define the conduct rule applicable in the given circumstances, not to apply the decision rule that would be pertinent after an action had been carried out.

Let me now focus on cases of this type, analysis of which will reveal an unexpected disparity between the conduct rules defined by the legislator and rulings handed down by the court.[14]

14 It is easier to identify normative disparities in a system in which conduct rules are explicitly stated, as in Jewish law, than in a system where they are not explicitly articulated, as in Western law. Nevertheless, though more difficult to pinpoint, similar disparities probably exist in these legal systems as well.

Suppose someone asks the court about the conduct rules applicable in a particular setting. Let us imagine that conduct rules and decision rules are recorded in two different books. The inquirer could have opened the book of conduct rules himself to find the appropriate rule for his particular circumstances, but did not do so; perhaps he feared that he lacked the ability to properly understand what was written in the book of conduct rules, and preferred to turn to the court to explain it to him. Which book would the court consult? Although the inquirer is interested in the applicable conduct rule, the court would consult the book of decision rules. Most of the time, we would assume, the decision rule will "match" the corresponding conduct rule, but it is conceivable that the answer in the book of decision rules differs from that in the book of conduct rules. In other words, had this individual consulted the book of conduct rules himself, he would have found answer "p," but since he consulted the court, which must respond on the basis of the book of decision rules, he will receive answer "q."

Such a disparity between the conduct rule and the answer given by the court may be reflected in the talmudic principle, "This is the law, but we do not rule in accordance with it."[15] In this case, the inquirer is, in a sense, misinformed by the court. This strange policy must be explained and justified.

In some cases, the conduct rule may be somewhat problematic; it may lead to unwanted, unexpected, or unforeseeable results, or create a "slippery slope." The court therefore does not make the conduct rule common knowledge, and does not instruct the public to adopt it. The law is indeed "p," but in deciding cases, the court does not invoke it, instead rendering its decisions in accordance with a safer, and usually stricter, stance. In this sense, the policy reflects a sort of acoustic separation, what Dan-Cohen calls "selective transmission."

There are other cases, however — more interesting in our context — in which the court has no such concerns, and the conduct rule per se is not deemed to be problematic. Nevertheless, the court does not decide in accordance with the conduct rule for reasons of policy and out of institutional considerations. Certain rulings, for instance, if handed down, might have an adverse effect on the court's image, and diminish public trust in and respect for the court. Furthermore, some things are best left unsaid by a legal authority; public discussion of these topics is not desirable.

15 *"Halakha veein morin ken"* (bShabat 12b and parallels).

In other words, having a certain question posed to the court, and the act of ruling on it, could be consequential in themselves, especially with regard to the image of the court subsequent to its ruling and the public discourse prompted by the judgment. The very fact that the court's opinion has been solicited introduces considerations that did not exist up to that point. In such cases, the court may not object to conduct rule "p," but will nevertheless not agree to condone it. The problem is not **conduct** that accords with "p," but the court's **issuing a ruling** that is in accordance with "p."

Let us now consider some concrete examples of the hypotheses I have advanced.

## 5 The case of the extradition

Terrorists threaten to kill a group of Jews unless one member of the group is handed over for execution. Is it permissible to hand over one of the group in order to save the rest? The Tosefta rules: "It is better that all of them die rather than hand over one Israelite."[16] The Tosefta goes on to say, however, that if the terrorists demand that a specific person be turned in, threatening the whole group with death if they refuse, it is permissible to hand over the named person in order to save the group. Apparently, the difference between the two cases is that in the former case, there is no way to decide who to choose, whereas in the latter, the choice has been made by the terrorists.

The Jerusalem Talmud recounts the story of a Jew by the name of Ulla bar Koshab, who was wanted by the Roman authorities on capital charges. To escape death, he sought refuge in Lydda, the town of R. Joshua b. Levi. The Romans laid siege to Lydda, threatening to destroy it if Ulla was not turned over to them. R. Joshua b. Levi persuaded Ulla to turn himself in, thereby saving the people of Lydda. R. Joshua b. Levi acted in accordance with the Tosefta's second rule, as the Romans had asked for Ulla by name. Nevertheless, the Talmud relates that the Prophet Elijah, who, prior to this incident, had often appeared to R. Joshua b. Levi, ceased making such visits after the incident. Perturbed by this, R. Joshua fasted for many days until Elijah relented and visited him once again. When R. Joshua asked why he had ceased his visits, Elijah answered, "Do you think I appear before traitors who hand over Jews to be killed!?" R. Joshua protested, "Have

16 tTerumot 7:23.

I not acted in accordance with the law?" To this Elijah responded, "Is that, indeed, the law of the pious?"[17]

What does piety have to do with this story? Conduct is said to be in accord with "the law of the pious" only when one is willing to act beyond the call of duty without causing harm to others. In the present case, had R. Joshua not handed over Ulla, the entire community would have been endangered. Would conducting himself in a manner that would bring death to all the town's inhabitants be deemed "conduct of the pious"?[18]

It is possible that this dilemma influenced Maimonides when he formulated this law in the *Mishne Torah*. Maimonides rules in accordance with the Tosefta — if the enemy demands that the Jews hand over someone of their own choosing, they are forbidden to do so, but if the enemy asks for a specific person, it is permitted to hand him over. But, Maimonides adds, "we do not instruct them to do so" (*veein morin lahem ken lekhathila*).[19]

The distinction Maimonides is making here is not that between the "regular" law and the law of the pious, but rather, that between conduct rules and decision rules. According to Maimonides, the halakha's conduct rules permit the group to hand over a Jew under such circumstances, but its decision rules instruct courts to refrain from issuing an explicit judgment to that effect. Apparently, Maimonides thought that pious conduct was expected of R. Joshua, not because handing over the wanted party was wrong, but because he was Lydda's leading rabbinical authority — judge. He therefore should have upheld the decision rule forbidding the surrender of individuals to hostile forces, in order to preserve the image of the court and its representatives. In other words, Maimonides argues that it was indeed permissible to extradite Ulla, and it was certainly the proper conduct in terms of saving the community, but in light of institutional considerations, it was not proper for the rabbi, acting in his judicial capacity, to issue an explicit ruling that a Jew was to be handed over to the enemy to be

17 jTerumot 8:11 (41b).

18 See *Taz*, YD 157:7; S. Lieberman, *Tosefta Kifshuta*, Terumot, 422. In the parallel version in Genesis Rabbah 94, Elijah continues, "You should have left others to hand over Ulla and not brought it about by yourself." As Lieberman notes, however, this does not solve the difficulty; Elijah seems to be suggesting that he ought to have left the dirty work to others, which surely is not "conduct of the pious."

19 *Code*, Laws concerning the Fundamental Principles of the Torah 5:5.

killed. It was not the act of extradition that was objectionable, but the court ruling condoning the act.[20] The court, if asked, must not rule that it is permitted, but rather withhold its ruling and let the people act in accordance with their own understanding, in the hope that they will, in fact, hand over the specified party.

## 6 The case of the fornicator

As our second example, consider the "law of the zealot": "one who has intercourse with a heathen [lit., Aramaean] woman — zealots may kill [lit., harm] him."[21] This law is extraordinary in recognizing the legitimacy of punishment by a private citizen outside the framework of the courts. Indeed, the punishment meted out is at variance with the law; from a purely halakhic point of view, intercourse with an Aramaean woman is not punishable, and it is certainly not a capital offense.

The source of this law is the biblical story of Phinehas and Zimri (Num. 25:1–15). The Israelites had fornicated with the daughters of Moab in Shittim, and were punished for this offense by being struck by a plague. Then Zimri appeared at the Tent of Meeting, together with his Midianite woman, Kozbi the daughter of Zur. Seeing this, Phinehas was filled with the spirit of zealotry, and killed both of them with his spear; the plague then stopped.

The Talmud makes three qualifications to the law of the zealot,[22] one being that if the zealot consults the court about what action he should take, he is not apprised of the law of the zealot. This case, then, also falls into the category of "This is the law, but we do not rule in accordance with it." Some have attempted to infer from this that the halakha does not actually endorse zealous murder, but merely accepts the zealot's emotional state as an excuse for his behavior. This explanation is doubtful, however. After all, Scripture praises and justifies Phinehas's act, and Maimonides says that a zealot who kills the profligate who fornicates with a heathen is "praiseworthy and

20 For another explanation of this case, see Hanina Ben-Menahem, "Some introductory remarks on Genesis Rabbah and the law," 16 *Jewish Law Annual* (2006), 145–47.

21 mSanhedrin 9:6.

22 bSanhedrin 82a.

assiduous."[23] But if the zealot's act is so praiseworthy, why does the court refrain from telling him to act thus?

I think that in this case as well, the answer is to be found in institutional considerations. In the opinion of the court, the zealot's act is indeed worthy, but the court cannot explicitly apprise him of this, because such an instruction might damage the court's standing. People might construe the ruling as anarchic and injurious to the authority of the law. They would not be able to accept the normative dissonance between the court's refraining from sentencing the profligate to death, and its instructing the zealot to kill him.

Once again, this is an example of a discrepancy between the system's book of conduct rules, which says that the zealot may kill one who fornicates with a heathen woman, deeming the act justified, and its book of decision rules, which says that if the court is consulted in such a case, it is not to explicitly permit the zealot to carry out such an act.

## 7 The case of the lovesick man

Our third example is based on a rather strange talmudic story.

> It happened that a man once set his eyes on a certain woman, and his heart was inflamed with lust [endangering his life]. And they went and consulted doctors, and they said: There will be no cure for him unless she submits to intercourse with him. The Sages said: He should die, but she should not have intercourse with him. [The doctors said:] Let her stand naked before him; [they answered:] Let him die, but she should not stand naked before him. Let her converse with him from behind a fence. Let him die, but she should not converse with him from behind a fence.[24]

The Amoraim debate whether or not the woman in this case was married. If she was not married, the Talmud notes, a relationship with the man would be permissible. What, then, was the reason for the stringent view of the Sages? The Talmud answers that they ruled this way to prevent the daughters of Israel from being promiscuous.

Maimonides takes the view that the woman in the case was not married, and rules:

23 Maimonides, *Code*, Laws concerning Forbidden Intercourse 12:4–5.
24 bSanhedrin 75a; see also jShabat 14:4 (14d). For a literary analysis, see Barry Wimpfheimer, "Love and law: the dialogical nature of talmudic legal narrative," available at http://papers.ssrn.com/sol3/papers.cfm?abstract_id=813849.

> If a man set eyes on a woman, falls ill and is near death, and the doctors say that there is no remedy for him unless she has intercourse with him — he should die, but she should not have intercourse with him, even if she is unmarried. Nor do we issue him a ruling that he may speak to her even from behind a fence. And he should die if the alternative is issuing a ruling that he may speak to her from behind a fence, so that the daughters of Israel will not be in jeopardy, and no breach of sexual mores will ensue.[25]

Maimonides notes twice that it is forbidden to rule permissively — not that the act itself is forbidden. Apparently, he regards this strict law as a decision rule, not a conduct rule. He does not say that the man must not talk to the woman from behind the fence; he rules only that the court must not permit him to do so. The courtship is not to be condoned.

Maimonides remains faithful to the talmudic precedent — "The Sages said. . . . Let him die, but she should not converse with him from behind a fence" — explaining that this precedent teaches us how courts should rule, but does not establish a conduct rule for the individual.

What is the reason for the disparity between the conduct rule and the decision rule in this case? Perhaps Maimonides thought that it would, in fact, be permitted for the lovesick man to talk to an unmarried woman privately, and even to have relations with her, in order to save his life. Moreover, it is likely that such activity, if it were to take place, would not cause the daughters of Israel to be promiscuous. What Maimonides emphasizes is that a court must not state publicly that it is permitted — not because of any objection to the act itself, but to ensure that it will not be said of the court that it permitted such conduct. In other words, to control public discourse.

This story may serve as an example for the broader realm of the laws of modesty. Modesty is manifested, first and foremost, at the level of public discourse. As the Talmud says, "We all know why the bride stands under the canopy," but there are things which need not — and should not — be said.[26] It is likely that some of the laws of modesty do not purport to control individual conduct in private, and their purpose is to model the norms of public discourse.

This thesis calls to mind the opinion of Lord Devlin in the famous debate over homosexuality in England in the 1960s, on the question of

25 Maimonides, *Code*, Laws concerning the Fundamental Principles of the Torah 5:9.

26 bShabat 33a.

whether morality should or should not be enforced by the law.[27] Devlin argued that the state could prohibit homosexual relationships between consenting adults in private because moral concepts promote social unity; if the law permitted immoral behavior (as homosexuality was then regarded), it would damage the fiber of society. Hart opposed that position, asking how an act conducted in private between consenting adults could possibly damage the fiber of society. Devlin could have responded by making the distinction we made above: the problem is not with private homosexual acts, but with a public ruling that they are permissible. The aim of the law, he could have argued, was to shape public discourse in accordance with the prevailing ethical standards, not to control people's behavior in private.

Similarly, I contend, the goal of the ruling regarding the lovesick man was not to prevent social interaction between men and women, but rather to **declare** it forbidden, with the intent of shaping public discourse about this sensitive realm.

## 8 The case of the abandoned wife

Elsewhere, I analyzed the law of the woman whose husband had disappeared at sea ("endless waters" in talmudic terminology), rendering her an *agunah*.[28] According to talmudic law, such a woman is not permitted to remarry, because her husband might have survived and may still be alive. If she breaks the law and remarries, however, she is not compelled to be divorced from the second husband.[29]

This law raises two dilemmas, which I have called the dilemma of consistency and the dilemma of effectiveness. With respect to consistency, the question is why the law changes its position vis-à-vis the forbidden marriage. By law, the second marriage is not to be contracted *ab initio*, yet after the fact, the law considers the marriage valid. Regarding effectiveness, R. Meir of Rothenburg asks the following question: if after the fact the marriage is considered valid, what justified preventing the *agunah* from remarrying in the first place? In the aforementioned article, I offered a number of solutions to these dilemmas. In

27 P. Devlin, *The Enforcement of Morals* (Oxford: 1965); H.L.A Hart, *Law, Liberty and Morality* (Oxford: 1963).

28 "Consistency and effectiveness in Jewish law as reflected by the *lekhathila–bediavad* distinction" (Hebrew), 20–21 *Dine Israel* (2000/2001), 42–100.

29 bJebamot 121b.

the present context, however, let us examine the case in terms of the distinction between conduct rules and decision rules.

Is the rule prohibiting the second marriage a conduct rule or a decision rule? The Early Authorities already noted that the second marriage is permissible according to biblical law, since biblical law addresses the usual case and formulates its norms on that basis, and in the usual case, someone lost at sea is indeed drowned. It is only a Rabbinic prohibition that prevents the second marriage, as there is a slight chance that the husband survived. Accordingly, I would suggest that this is a decision rule. The woman is permitted to marry even from the Rabbinic point of view; the Rabbinic prohibition against remarriage is not addressed to the woman, but is a decision rule for the court, instructing it how to decide when asked whether the wife of the apparently-drowned man may remarry. Thus, the Mishnah stating that she may not marry is instructing the court how to decide such a case; it is not a directive addressed to the woman or her prospective second husband.

If the woman is permitted to rely on the usual case — viz., assume her husband is dead — then given that probability is in her favor, why doesn't the court give her a straightforward dispensation to do so? I think the answer is simple. Were it the court's policy to permit such women to remarry, we could state with statistical certainty that in some cases, however few, a woman would inadvertently commit adultery because her first husband had in fact survived. A permissive court ruling might therefore give rise to a series of mishaps: if the first husband returned from sea, the woman would have to divorce both men, and her children from the second husband would be deemed offspring of an adulterous union (*mamzerim*). Such a result — caused by a court ruling — would surely damage the image of the court and expose it to strong public criticism. For this reason, the general policy of the court is to prohibit the second marriage.

As we said, however, this is a decision rule; the conduct rule allows the woman to rely on the usual case and remarry. Hence if she does remarry, the court does not compel her to be divorced. In such a case, the husband's potential reappearance would not damage the court's standing in the public eye, as the court was not asked whether the marriage was permissible in the first place and had no involvement in the mishap.

In this case, the disparity between the conduct rule and the decision rule originates from the disparate perspectives of the woman and the court. From the woman's point of view, the marriage is a single, discrete event, and she may rely on probability. From the court's point of view, however, the marriage is just one of many potential such events, and it must adopt a policy that maximizes "safe" legal outcomes, and avoids causing undesirable results to even one woman.

The Talmud, and subsequently, Maimonides, rule that a rabbi who permits such a remarriage is to be placed under a ban.[30] The Talmud does not, however, say that the woman is to be placed under a ban for remarrying, even if she did so willfully. We can thus confirm that the rule prohibiting the second marriage is a decision rule.

## 9 Conclusion

The distinction between conduct rules and decision rules demonstrates the complexity of halakhic thinking, and influences the interpretation of halakhic decisions. When a rabbi issues a halakhic ruling, we must ask whether it is a true reflection of the conduct rule, or if it reflects a decision rule. Ensuring that the right decision is made can only be achieved by independent assessment of the pertinent conduct rules, which court rulings do not necessarily reflect. Court decisions are influenced by institutional and public considerations that are not always relevant for the individual.

30 bJebamot 121a; Maimonides, *Code*, Laws concerning Divorce 13:20.

# HEBREW SECTION

# הבטחה–בין דין תורה לדין פרס

ברכיהו ליפשיץ*

I. בעבר הנהר ישבו בני ישראל שנים רבות, מחורבן בית ראשון וגלותם בבלה עד לסוף תקופת הגאונים. לפי המקרא וחז״ל, בעליית עזרא לא עלו עימו כל בני הגולה, אלא העולים היו מן הנחותים שבעם והבלתי מיוחסים שבהם,[1] ובפרס נותרו לפחות חלק מן ״החרש והמסגר״ שירדו לבבל,[2] שהיו תלמידי החכמים ובעלי ההלכה.[3] סביר אפוא להניח שידיעת התורה לא היתה בלתי מוכרת ליהודי בבל גם קודם לירידתו של האמורא רב וכי היו ביניהם תלמידי חכמים גדולים.[4] בין כך ובין כך, מתקופת האמוראים יש בידינו התלמוד הבבלי במלוא רחבותו ובמגוון הלכותיו; אפשר גם להניח שיהודי בבל ידעו את שיטת המשפט שנהגה בין יושבי הארץ שבקרבם הם חיו ושאיתם הם באו בקשרי שכנות ומסחר, על כל המשתמע מכך. לאחרונה הולך ומתרחב העיון בקשרים שבין ההלכה היהודית המשתקפת בתלמוד הבבלי לבין המשפט הסאסאני שנהג בבבל באותה תקופה, וזאת בזכות מחקריהם של יעקב אלמן ושל תלמידיו, המאירים את פניהן של סוגיות עמומות, או של כאלה שנחשבו בהירות אך באו כעת בפנים אחרות.[5] ההשוואה מתאפשרת בעיקר אחרי פרסומו של הספר

* הקתדרה על-שם הנרי ג׳ ופאני הרכבי למשפט השוואתי, הפקולטה למשפטים, האוניברסיטה העברית בירושלים.

1 קידושין סט ע״ב.

2 מלכים ב כד יד, ירמיהו כד א.

3 סנהדרין לח ע״א; וראו דברי פרקוי בן באבוי, *גנזי שכטר*, ב, עמ׳ 504 (תורתן של גאונים [י׳ יודלוב וש״ז הבלין, עורכים], ח״ב, ירושלים תשנ״ב, עמ׳ 687). אבל ראו דברי רבנו תם, *ספר הישר*, התשובות, מח, ו. ואכמ״ל.

4 כהלל ועוד, כפי שציין רי״א הלוי, *דורות הראשונים*, א, כרך ג. וראו גם י׳ גפני, *יהודי בבל בתקופת התלמוד*, ירושלים תש״ן, עמ׳ 91–20 ואילך; J. Neusner, *A History of the Jews in Babylonia*, vols. 1–5 (Leiden: 1965–1970), בייחוד בכרך שלישי, בפרקים III, IV. וראו מה שציינתי במאמרי ״׳אגדה׳ ומקומה בתולדות תורה שבעל- פה,״ *שנתון המשפט העברי* כב (תשס״א-תשס״ד), עמ׳ 270 הע׳ 92, על מסורות וספרים שהיו בידי יהודי בבל וחלקם עלו עימם לארץ ישראל, מקורות שלא נידונו שם. דעתי נוטה לכך שהייתה תורה בגולת בבל, ואף אם אפשר לפקפק בכל אחת מן הראיות שהובאו לכך, המכלול והסברה מטים לדעה זו. וראו גם הזהרתו של גפני (שם, עמ׳ 53) מפני הסתמכות על היעדר מקורות ספרותיים מאותה תקופה.

5 כבר לפני כמאה ושלושים שנה קרא י״ה שור לעסוק בחקר ההשפעה שהייתה לחוק הפרסי ולאמונה הפרסית על התלמוד הבבלי, והדגים זאת בעשרות רבות של דוגמאות

*The Book of A Thousand Judgments*,[6] שמבין פסקיו אפשר ללמוד משהו, אך בוודאי לא בשלמות, על הדין שנהג בתקופתן של ישיבות האמוראים והגאונים שבבבל.

בדברים שלהלן לא אעסוק בבירורה של הלכה פרטית שבתלמוד ויחסה לדין הפרסי, אלא בעמדה כללית העולה מכמה וכמה פסקים שבספר הפסקים הנזכר באשר למעמדה של ההבטחה בדין זה, ובהשוואתה עם מה שעולה מן

---

(הטעונות, כמובן, בירור לגופן) בהלכה ובאגדה–ראו מאמרו שבשני חלקים, "התורות," *החלוץ* ז (תרכ"ג), עמ' 1; שם, ח (תרכ"ט), עמ' 1 (וראו להלן מדבריו). וראו:
Y. Elman, "Acculturation to elite Persian norms and models of thought in the Babylonian Jewish community of late antiquity," in
י' אלמן ואח', (עורכים), *נטיעות לדוד, ספר היובל לדוד הלבני* (ירושלים: תשס"ה,) החלק האנגלי, עמ' 56–31;
idem, "Marriage and marital property in Rabbinic and Sasanian law," in C. Heszer (ed.), *Rabbinic Law in Its Roman and Near Eastern Context* (Tubingen: 2003), 242; idem,"Returnable gifts in Rabbinic and Sasanian law," *Irano-Judaica* 6 (2008), 150–95; idem,"'Up to the ears' in horses' necks (B.M. 108a): on Sasanian agricultural policy and private 'eminent domain,'" *JSIJ* 3 (2004), 95–149; idem, "Middle Persian culture and Babylonian Sages: accommodation and resistance in the shaping of Rabbinic legal literature," in C.E. Fonrobert and M.S. Jaffe (eds.), *Cambridge Companion to the Talmud and Rabbinic Literature* (Cambridge: 2007), 165–97; idem, "The socio-economics of Babylonian heresy," *JLAS* 17 (2007), 80–127; idem, "Babylonian Jews at the intersection of the Iranian economy and Sasanian law," in A. Levine et al. (eds.), *Economics and Judaism* (Oxford: 2010), 545–83.
הנ"ל, "ישיבות בבל ובתי דין פרסיים בתקופה האמוראית והבתר-אמוראית," בתוך ע' אטקס (עורך), *ישיבות ובתי מדרשות* (ירושלים: תשס"ז), עמ' 31–5; הנ"ל, "מעשה בשתי עיירות: מחוזא ופומבדיתא כמייצגות שתי תרבויות הלכתיות," בתוך ד' גולינקין ואח' (עורכים), *תורה לשמה, מחקרים במדעי היהדות לכבוד פרופ ש" י פרידמן* (רמת-גן וירושלים: תשס"ז), עמ' 8–3; וראו גם ב' ליפשיץ, "ערבות לגוף–הלכה ואגדה," בתוך א' אדרעי ואח' (עורכים), *מחקרים במדרש ובתלמוד, ספר זיכרון לתרצה ליפשיץ ז" ל* (ירושלים: תשס"ה), עמ' 231, שבו הוצגה עמדה שונה מזו של אלמן בעניין סוניית בבא בתרא קעג ע"ב, אך עולה לפיה הכרה עמוקה של החוק הפרסי על ניסוחו. וראו גם:
S. Secunda, "Talmudic text and Iranian context: on the development of two talmudic narratives," *AJS Review* 33 (2009), 45–69;
ושם בהערות 3–6 ציין למאמרים נוספים הדנים בקשר שבין התלמוד הבבלי לבין סביבתו הנוכרית, חוקיה והשקפותיה. ראו גם:
S. Friedman, "The 'plotting witness' and beyond," in C. Cohen et al. (eds.), *Birkat Shalom, Studies . . . Presented to Shalom M. Paul* (Winona Lake IN: 2008), 827 n. 81.
וראו גם הערתו של י' זוסמן, "'תורה שבעל-פה' פשוטה כמשמעה," *מחקרי תלמוד* ג (תשס"ה), עמ' 351 הע' 93.

6 ראו:
*The Book of A Thousand Judgments, A Sasanian Law Book*, Introduction, Transcription and Translation of the Pahlavi Text, Notes, Glossary and Indexes, by Analit Perikhanian (Costa Mesa CA: 1997); M. Macuch, *Rechtskasuistik und Gerichtspraxis zu Beginn des siebenten Jahrhunderts in Iran: Die Rechtssammlung des Farrohmard i Wahraman (Iranica I)*, (Wiesbaden: 1993).
מהדורה קודמת, פחות משוכללת ומלאה, יצאה לאור בשנת 1937. החיבור הוא מראשית המאה השביעית, אך כפי שהוכר, יש בו חומר הקדום אף למאה החמישית ובהתחשב באופיו השמרני של החוק אפשר להניח שהוא משקף מצב משפטי קדום יותר. וראו גם הפניות לחומר רלבנטי נוסף אצל סקונדה (לעיל, הע' 5).

התלמוד הבבלי באותן סוגיות. תכלית ההשוואה היא לברר את היחס שבין בעלי ההלכה לבין דין המקום, ואולי את מידת החשיבות שהעניקו לו בעת שערך של ההלכה התנגש בו. מובן שאין בכוונתי לטעון לוודאותו של הטיעון אלא להסתברותו, כרגיל.

II. בעבר תיארתי בהרחבה את השתלשלותה של המחלוקת בסוגיית תוקפה של ההבטחה במשפט העברי,[7] שהחלה בתקופת התנאים, המשיכה בתקופת האמוראים, עבור דרך תקופת הגאונים ועד להכרעת הראשונים. למחלוקת זו יש כמובן השלכות בכל תחומי המשפט, הן אלה שבמשפט הפרטי, הן אלה שבמשפט הציבורי והן אלה שבדיני המשפחה והירושה. את סיכום הדברים אנו יכולים למצוא בדברי הרמב״ם; וזו לשונו:

> *אם לא קנה עתה והתנה עימו שאם נתקיים תנאי זה יקנה*. . . *אף על פי שנתקיים התנאי–לא קנה, שזו אסמכתא היא, שהרי סמך קנייתו לעשות כך וכך*.[8]

III. להלן אצטט כמה הלכות מתחומי משפט שונים מספר הפסקים הסאסאני הנזכר, לפי סדר הופעתן בו, שעולה מהן לפי תומן ששיטה זו הכירה, כדבר מובן מאליו, בתוקפן של הבטחות.[9]

1. 10–7, **20** (עמ׳ 67)

If a father transmits to his wife and children (the estate which) he will receive and subsequently frees a slave (from servitude), then. . . the (former) slave cannot ("may not") be brought back from his (acquired status of) a "subject of the King of Kings."

השאלה עוסקת בעבד ששוחרר ובביטול שחרורו מכיוון שהמשחרר התחייב קודם לשחרור להעביר את הירושה, הכוללת את העבד, שהוא עתיד לקבלה לאחר מועד התחייבותו. בקשר לכך אנו נזכרים בהלכת התוספתא, שזה לשונה:

7 ראו: ב׳ ליפשיץ, *אסמכתא: בין קניין לבין התחייבות* (ירושלים: תשמ״ח) (להלן: *אסמכתא*, שתרגומה המדויק לעברית הוא ״הבטחה״); הנ״ל, *עובד וקבלן: בין קניין לבין התחייבות* (ירושלים: תשנ״ג); הנ״ל, ״מדוע אין המשפט העברי אוכף קיומה של הבטחה?״, *משפטים* כה (תשנ״ה), עמ׳ 179–161; הנ״ל, ״מתנה לחוד–בין קניין לבין התחייבות,״ דיני ישראל יב (תשמ״ד), עמ׳ קכה-קנה. כן עסקתי במאמרים נוספים בכמה וכמה השלכות של העמדה הסוברת שאין תוקף להבטחה.

8 הלכות מכירה פי״א, הי״ב. לרמב״ם שיטה משלו בטעמה של פרשה זו, בתפקידו של התנאי בה ובהיקפה (ראו *אסמכתא*, לעיל, הע׳ 7), אבל ניסוחו משקף את עיקר הדברים.

9 ראו גם מה שהובא ב- *Encyclopedia Iranica*, בערך Contracts. אין ספק שהסכמים כובדו, ואם לאו–נאכפו.

מה שאירש מאבא מכור לך–לא אמר כלום; ומה שתעלה מצודתי מכור לך–לא אמר כלום. מה שאירש מאבא היום, ומה שתעלה מצודתי היום מכור לך–מותר משום כדי חייו.[10]

בעבר ציינתי, שהמחלוקת בשאלה אם אדם מקנה דבר שלא בא לעולם אם לאו היא ביטוי אחר למחלוקת אם אסמכתא (=הבטחה) קונה אם לאו.[11] אם בכוחה של הבטחה, כשלעצמה (ראו להלן), ליצור קניין בעתיד, הרי שאי-הימצאותו עדיין בעולם של שהחפץ הנקנה במועד מתן ההבטחה אין בה כדי למנוע את תחולת הקניין כאשר החפץ יבוא לעולם או לבעלותו של המבטיח. כן הצבעתי שם על הימצאותה של הלכה זו בין סוגיות העוסקות בענייני ריבית ועל הקשר שיש בדרך הניסוח של הלכה זו (ואחרות) במקבילותיה, המדברת על איסור ועל היתר, מצד אחד, ועל מתן תוקף, או אי-מתן תוקף, לעסקה, מן הצד האחר. בין כך ובין כך, לפי הדין הפרסי אין מניעה מנתינת תוקף לעסקה כזאת של הקנאת נכסים שיבואו בירושה למקנה בעתיד. לכאורה אנו גם למדים מן הפיסקה הזאת, שאלמלי היה הנכס המובטח עבד ששוחרר, וזכה למעמד של "עבדי הם ולא עבדים לעבדים", הרי שנכס אחר היה מועבר למי שהבטיחו לו אף על פי שהועבר לצד שלישי.

2. **20**, 11–13 (עמ' 67)

> If a man concludes (the following) agreement with [x]: "I convey this thing to you after the passage of ten years", but [x] dies during this ten years, the thing does not pass to [x]'s wife, children and family.

הפסיקה מבוססת כנראה על פירוש ההבטחה, שלפיה ההקנאה תיעשה רק למי שהנכס הובטח לו, ולא ליורשיו. מכל מקום ברור שההקנאה לא נעשתה על אתר במועד מתן ההבטחה, כי במקרה זה הזוכה היה קונה את הנכס ומורישו ליורשיו במותו, ואילו היה הזוכה חי עד המועד הקבוע היה זוכה בנכס ללא כל צורך במעשה הקנאה אחר. לפי ההלכה התלמודית ברור שלעסקה זו אין תוקף כלל.[12]

10 בבא מציעא פ"ד ה"י (מהד' ליברמן, עמ' 83). וראו הדיון בתלמוד הבבלי בעניין זה, בבא מציעא טז ע"א.

11 *אסמכתא* (לעיל, הע' 7), עמ' 406 ואילך.

12 ראו *אסמכתא* (לעיל, הע' 7), עמ' 100. אך השוו לפסקים שמספריהם 3–5, **66**, שבעמוד 165; 14–17, **66**, שבעמוד 167. וראו גם מס' 13–16, **20**:

> "a thing which will pass into my personal possession ("property") shall belong to you."

מס' 3, 16–21 **20**. אכן, יש אי בהירות מסוימת לגבי מעמדם של נכסי הירושה, הנקראים על ידי המבטיח "the estate which belongs to me", אך הם יבואו רק לאחר זמן, ואז ייחשבו בתור "my personal property." ראו גם מס' 55, 3–7 (עמ' 143):

> "If he declares the following: 'A (share) value at. . . shall belong to you from the estate that belongs to me (now) and the estate that will belong to me (in the future).'"

3. 15–12, **56** (עמ' 147)

If he declares: "Let this thing belong jointly to (my) daughter when she comes of age and to [x], then I understand this in the following manner: Inasmuch as it is written: "(let it) belong jointly," then [x], too, shall obtain it (only) when the daughter attains her majority, for only then may (this thing) belong to her.

במועד ההתחייבות הבת הייתה קטינה ולכן היא לא הייתה יכולה לרכוש את הנכס אלא בהגיעה לגיל הכשרות המתאים, ולכן גם האחר, האמור להיות לבעלים משותף עם הבת, לא יזכה בנכס אף הוא אלא באותו מועד. לא כך הוא לפי ההלכה.[13]

4. 68–13, **67** (עמ' 169)

If he makes the following agreement with a man: "I shall convey such-and-such a thing to you against this sum of money," and (if) when the latter claims the thing, he declares: "I cannot convey to you a thing of this type, but I shall transfer to you another thing against that sum of money."

כאן ממשיך הפסק לדון באפשרויות שונות העולות מן העניין. אך ברור שהקונה יכול לדרוש את מימוש העסקה בנכס שלא היה מוגדר ומסוים אלא צוין באופן כללי בלבד.

5. 14–12, **68** (עמ' 171)

If he declares: "(Whatever) thing belonging to me valued at 200 (drachms) which you desire shall belong to you," and if the one to whom he made his declaration declares his selection of a thing and his approval of the disposition ... then the declaration ... has been made, the thing belongs to [him].[14]

גם כאן מימוש העסקה הוא בעתיד. החשיבות המיוחדת שיש בפסק זה היא שהוא מלמד אותנו על הכלל שההבטחה כשלעצמה, כשהיא נפגשת בהסכמת מי

---

נקבע שערך החלק בנכסים העתידים לבוא בירושה ייקבע לפי שוויים בעתיד, בעת השלמתה של העסקה.

13 כאמור, ההלכה אינה מאפשרת הקנאה בעתיד. וראו גם את הפסק שמספרו 14–12, 65, עמ' 165, על הקנאה לבן שכבר נולד ולבן העתיד להיוולד.

14 ראו גם הפסק שלאחר מכן, מס' 17, **68** (בעמ' 171):

If he declares: 'Whatever a certain man shall approve (=select) shall belong to you'

כלומר, ייחודו של נכס מסוים בידי אדם שלישי שהוא יעבור לבעלותו של המקבל. ראו גם הפסק שבעמ' 259 (17–13, **A7**) על קביעתו של אדם אחר למי יוקנה הנכס; ובעמ' 283 (13–9, **A199**) על זיהוי חפץ בידי אדם אחר לקניינו של הקונה. וראו גם עמ' 259 (12–7, **A8**).

שהבטיחו לו, יוצרת את העברת הזכויות בנכס מן הנותן אל המקבל, בין בהווה ובין בעתיד. כך היא גם דרך פעולתה של האסמכתא, לפי דעתם של מי שסוברים שאסמכתא קניא.[15] כלומר, בניגוד למבנה של החוזה המוכר לנו, שלפיו נוצר חוזה ואזי יש לקיים את ההבטחה הכלולה בו על ידי מעשה נוסף של ההקנאה, המבנה העולה מן הדין הפרסי ומן ההלכה, שונה. אנו נמצאים בכל ההליך בתחום דיני הקניין ופעולתם, ומעשה הקניין, שהוא ההבטחה עצמה, לשיטה הנותנת תוקף להבטחה, חל גם לאחר זמן. כאמור, זוהי איננה השיטה שהתקבלה להלכה, ונוסיף על כך עוד דברים להלן.

יש לצרף לדיון זה את הנלמד מן הפסקים 11–9, **104**; 17–15, **104**; 3–1, **105** (עמ׳ 235), שהעברת הזכויות נעשית בדברים בלבד, בהצהרה בלא "מעשה קניין":

> "Let the gold belonging to me belong to my wife."

כפי שציינתי, ההלכה הקדומה קבעה ש"בראשונה היו קונים בקצצה", דהיינו־בהסכמה.[16] ונראה שמשמעותה של קביעה זו הייתה הן שאין צורך במעשה קניין לעסקה שעל אתר והן שההסכמה לעתיד תקפה ופועלת קניין, כאמור לעיל. רק לאחר מכן נקבע, לשיטה אחת, שאין המכר נגמר בדברים, כלומר בהסכמה ובהתחייבות.[17]

6. 12–9, **71** (עמ׳ 177)

> If he declares: "I shall convey this thing to you . . . on day [x] (and) if I do not convey it I shall pay a fine . . . if he acts in a manner other than the one declared (in the agreement), he (=the other party) must wait three days (. . .before he demands the payment of the fine).

החיוב העצמי בקנס הוא גם הנושא של חמשת הפסקים הבאים בפרק XLV של ספר הפסקים הפרסי. קנס עצמי הוא גם עניינם של כמה מקרים שנידונו בתלמוד כסוגיות שמעורבת בהן בעיית האסמכתא, ובעקבותיהן של סוגיות אלה סברו כמה ראשונים שזהו הפגם הכרוך בהן, כלומר פגם בסמיכות הדעת.[18] כפי שהראיתי, לא זה הפגם אלא עצם היעדרו של הקניין על-אתר הוא זה השולל את תוקפן של הבטחות. אין

15 ראו *אסמכתא*, עמ׳ 394; 399.
16 ירושלמי קידושין פ״א ה״ה, ס ע״ג, וראו *אסמכתא* (לעיל, הע׳ 7), עמ׳ 335.
17 *אסמכתא* (שם), בפרק "דברים," עמ׳ 383 ואילך.
18 ראו *אסמכתא*, עמ׳ 28 ואילך.

הבדל בין ההתחייבות הראשית–לקיים–לבין ההתחייבות המשנית–לשלם את הקנס אם ההתחייבות הראשית לא תקוים. בדין הפרסי גם כן אין הבדל בין שתי ההתחייבויות, אלא שלפיו את שתיהן יש לקיים.[19]

7. 9–11, **109** (עמ׳ 243)

> If he declares (the following): "I have conveyed a thing to [x]," but [x] is not present; then, until [x] appears ("arrives") and declares: "not needed" (i.e. refuses to acquire it through transfer),[20] the *sturship* of the one who made the declaration in this fashion (=the *sturship* of the conveyer) is held up; (a *stur*) should not be appointed.

בעיה כעין זו עולה בתלמוד הבבלי בדברי ריש לקיש (שהוא אומנם אמורא ארץ ישראלי) בסוגיית כריתות כד ע״א, ובדבריו של רב ששת (שם) על מי שנתן מתנה למי שאינו יודע על כך ובעת שנודע לו הדבר הוא מסרב לקבלה, שכל המחזיק בה זכה במתנה. לפי העמדה הנזכרת של המשפט הפרסי אין בהקנאה כזאת כל קושי; לפי ההלכה התלמודית שהבטחה אינה קונה נמצא להלכה זו–המשקפת את העמדה שהבטחה אכן קונה–פתרון אחר (של שיעבוד עצמו).[21]

נראה שההלכה הקדומה, שרבים המשיכו להחזיק בה לאורך כל הדורות, הייתה שקונים בקצצה, ושההלכה הרווחת הייתה כר׳ יוסי, הסבור שאסמכתא קניא;[22] עמדה זו מצויה במקורות תנאיים רבים. הקשיים שמציבים מקורות אלה לשיטה הנגדית מיושבים בדרכים שונות, שאינן לפשוטן של משניות,[23] ואף על פי כן עושים חכמי בבל את המאמץ הפרשני הזה בגלל רצונם לפסוק כר׳ יהודה, הסבור שאסמכתא לא קניא אף על פי שאין זה לא על פי כללי הפסיקה ולא לפי מסורת ההלכה הפשוטה. הטעמים לנחישות זו אינם מפורשים, אך כעת אנו יודעים שנוסף לטעמים הפנים הלכתיים שלא לפסוק כר׳ יהודה הרי שהעמדה שהוצגה כמכריעה

19 מן הפסק שמספרו 3–5, **72** עולה שהתחייבויות למכור סוס או לשלם קנס יכולות להיות במדרגה אחת וחלופיות זו לזו לפי רצונו של המבטיח, היכול לבחור איזו מן השתיים יקיים. אם כך הוא, אין מקום כמובן לאכוף על המבטיח את דרך הקיום.

20 זו הערת המהדירה. מן האמור לעיל נראה שאין צורך בהעברת הנכס כדי להשלים את הקניין. העברתו תהיה רק כהעברת החזקה בלבד, ואילו הבעלות עברה בהבטחה. וראו הפסק שבעמוד 241 (5–7, **107**):

> "If a thing is given to the detriment (of the interests) of a minor with (his) father's consent, or a **transfer-agreement** is concluded, but the minor protests (against the transfer) when he comes of age, then. . . the agreement must be concluded".

21 ראו *אסמכתא* (לעיל, הע׳ 7), עמ׳ 187 ואילך.

22 בבא מציעא פ״ד מ״ה ובבלי שם סו ע״א; בבא בתרא קסח ע״א, *ואסמכתא* (שם), עמ׳ 4–6.

23 ראו: בבא מציעא סו ע״א; בבא בתרא ג ע״א; בבא בתרא קעג ע״ב.

בתלמוד הבבלי הייתה שונה גם מזו שנהגה בדין המלכות, דהיינו שהבטחה קונה. יש במעשים אלה כדי לחזק את הדעה ששיקולים מטה-הלכתיים הם שהיו ביסוד העמידה הנחושה למען השינוי הזה.[24]

IV. מסוגיות התלמוד אנו יכולים להסיק, במפורש ובמשתמע, שהיו חילוקי דעות איתנים בין החכמים בשאלה כיצד יש לפסוק בסוגיה זו. חלק מן המידע עולה ממחלוקות ישירות וחלקו מפעולות עקיפות של עריכה, כפי שאפרט.

א. בסוגיית בבא מציעא סו ע״א מובא שתחילה נחלקו רב הונא ורב נחמן בדבר תוקפו של התנאי הנזכר במשנה (בבא מציעא פ״ה מ״ג)–״הלווהו על שדהו ואמר לו: אם אי אתה נותן לי מכאן ועד שלוש שנים הרי היא שלי–הרי היא שלו. וכן היה ביתוס בן זונין עושה על פי חכמים.״[25] וממשיכה הסוגיה ואומרת:

> אמר רב הונא: בשעת מתן מעות–קנה הכל. לאחר מתן מעות–לא קנה אלא כנגד מעותיו. ורב נחמן אמר: אפילו לאחר מתן מעות קנה הכל.[26] עבד רב נחמן עובדא גבי ריש גלותא כשמעתיה, קרעיה רב יהודה לשטריה . . .[27] הדר אמר רב נחמן: אפילו בשעת מתן מעות לא קנה ולא כלום. איתיביה רבא לרב נחמן: ״אם אי אתה נותן לי מכאן ועד שלוש שנים הרי היא שלי–הרי היא שלו״! אמר ליה: אני אומר אסמכתא קניא ומניומי אמר אסמכתא לא קניא [=״הייתי רגיל לומר קנה הכל, דאסמכתא קניא, אבל מניומי חלוק עלי והחזירני מדברי״. רש״י שם, ד״ה ״אני אומר״].

24 ראו ניסיון להסביר את הטעמים השתוקים שעמדו מאחורי העמדה הזאת במאמרי ״מדוע אין המשפט העברי אוכף קיומה של הבטחה?״ (לעיל, הע׳ 7). שם הנחתי שהטעם הוא הרצון לשמור על מהותו של האדם כיצור שביכולתו להבטיח ולקיים או להפר את הבטחתו. אך בספרי *אסמכתא* העליתי אפשרות אחרת, והיא הרצון למנוע עבירה על איסורי ריבית דרבנן אם נאכוף מכירה בהבטחה כשהתשלום ייעשה בעת ההבטחה אבל שוויו יעלה, כמצופה, בעת מילוי ההבטחה.

25 גם ממשנה זו מוכח שהיא נוקטת בפשטות שיש תוקף להבטחה, וכי ההבטחה משמשת גם בתפקיד מעשה הקניין היחיד הנדרש להשלמת העסקה.

26 גם רב הונא וגם רב נחמן (עדיין) סוברים שהבטחה תקפה, ונחלקו רק בשאלה אם גם לאחר מתן מעות הלווה רציני בהבטחתו שיקנה המלווה את כל השדה אם לא יפרענו במועד גם אם היא שווה יותר מסכום ההלוואה, או שכוונתו למישכון רגיל. בסוגיית נדרים כז ע״א חשים שיש ליישב את דברי רב הונא עם העמדה הרווחת שאסמכתא לא קניא. וראו להלן.

27 ונראה שרב יהודה סבור היה כרב הונא. דברי רב הונא (בבא מציעא סו ע״ב): ״המוכר פירות דקל לחבירו, אמר רב הונא: עד שלא באו לעולם יכול לחזור בו״ מלמדים, שגם לשיטת הסוברים ״אסמכתא קניא,״ אין תוקף להבטחה כהבטחה אלא שהיא ״קונה,״ כלומר היא עצמה משמשת כמעשה קניין, והיא קונה בעתיד, לכשיבשילו התנאים לפעילותה כמעשה קניין. אך עד להשלמת מעשה הקניין יכול המבטיח לחזור בו מהבטחתו, ממש כפי שיכול הוא לחזור בו קודם להשלמת מעשה קניין אחר, כמשיכה והגבהה וכדומה (ואפילו תוך כדי דיבור מעשייתו של קניין סודר). הדבר משקף את העמדה הקדומה, ששליפת המנעל באה לקיים ״כל דבר,״ דהיינו הבטחה, ושבראשונה היו קונים בקצצה, כלומר: בהסכם. וצריך עיון.

ולמניומי קשיא מתניתין [כשאלת רבא דלעיל]! איבעית אימא מתניתין ר׳ יוסי היא דאמר אסמכתא קניא, איבעית אימא [כר׳ יהודה]: דאמר ליה קני מעכשיו.[28]

הנה כי כן, אנו עדים לחזרה מפתיעה של רב נחמן מעמדתו הקודמת ואין אנו יודעים מה שיכנע את רב נחמן לחזור בו מן העמדה המקובלת. זו תופעה שאיננה רגילה בתלמוד, והוא איננו מגלה לנו מה היו הראיות לטובת קבלת עמדתו של ר׳ יהודה, ולכן יש מקום לחשוב שלא היו אלה ראיות תלמודיות רגילות, אלא טענות שבמדיניות שיפוטית.[29]

ב. בבבא מציעא סו ע״ב אנו לומדים כך:

אמרו ליה מר ינוקא ומר קשישא בני דרב חסדא[30] לרב אשי: אמרי נהרדעי[31] משמיה דרב נחמן)!(: האי אסמכתא בזמניה קניא, בלא זמניה לא קניא.[32]
אמר להו: כל מידי בזמניה קניא בלא זמניה לא קניא, דלמא הכי קאמריתו . . . ולא היא–דאפילו בגו זמניה נמי לא קנה, והאי דקאמר ליה קני, קא סבר כי מטי זמניה לא ליתי ליטרדן.
אמר רב פפא: האי אסמכתא זימנין קניא וזימנין לא קניא:[33] אשכחיה דקא שתי שכרא–קני; דקא מהפך אזוזי–לא קני. אמר ליה רב אחא מדפתי לרבינא: דלמא לפכוחי פחדיה קא שתי? אי נמי, איניש אחרינא אסמכיה אזוזי? אלא אמר רבינא . . . אמר ליה רב אחא . . . דלמא . . . אלא אמר רב פפא . . . ואמר רב פפא . . .
אמר ליה רב הונא בריה דרב נתן לרב פפא: מי קאמר . . . ?
סבר רב פפא למימר: כי אמרינן אסמכתא לא קניא, הני מילי בארעא, דלאו לזבוניה קיימא, אבל חמרא, כיון דלזבוניה קאי–כזוזי דמי.
אמר ליה רב הונא בריה דרב יהושע: הכי אמר רבא[34]–כל דאי לא קני.

28 הקנאה מעכשיו מוציאה כמובן את העניין מהיותו הבטחה להקנות בעתיד.
29 על כך שחל שינוי בעמדתו אפשר אולי ללמוד גם מן הלשון שנקט חכם זה עצמו (בבא מציעא סו ע״ב): ״אמר רב נחמן: השתא דאמור רבנן אסמכתא לא קניא.״ וראו גם לעיל, שם: ״אמר רב פפא: אף על גב דאמור רבנן אסמכתא לא קניא.״ אחר זמן העיד על עצמו גם רב האי גאון שהחזיר את חותנו המפורסם, רב שמואל בן חופני גאון, מדעתו שיש לפסוק כר׳ יוסי דווקא, ראו אסמכתא (לעיל, הע׳ 7), עמ׳ 44. גם רב האי לא הסביר מה ראה רשב״ח לשנות מן הפסיקה הרגילה בין הגאונים וכיצד שכנע אותו רב האי לשוב אל הזרם המרכזי של הפסיקה. ראו גם י׳ עץ-חיים, ״שינויים בעמדה ההלכתית שהולידו סוגיות מוחלפות,״ סיני פט (תשמ״א), עמ׳ קפ, הע׳ 50.
30 ראו ח׳ אלבק, *מבוא לתלמודים* (תל-אביב: תשכ״ט ), עמ׳ 437.
31 ראו להלן.
32 זו עמדתו לפני שחזר בו, ראו לעיל. היא מתאימה למסורתם של חכמי נהרדעא, שאף רב נחמן החזיק בה.
33 ייתכן שזו הנוסחה הנכונה שהביעו בני נהרדעא, ובני רב חסדא הביאוה בפני רב אשי בחלקה הראשון של הסוגיה.
34 כך בכל כתבי היד; בדפוס: רבה.

לפנינו ניסיונות בלתי נלאים של רב פפא לחתור תחת הכלל הגורף שאסמכתא אינה קונה ולעשותו ליחסי, כאשר קנה המידה לתוקפה הוא לפי מידת סמיכות הדעת שיש לייחס למבטיח כפי שהיא נלמדת מן הנסיבות של עשייתה. באופן מהותי ההבטחה קונה אפוא, אבל הניסוח הוא לפי שיטת "אסמכתא לא קניא"; הוא מתכוון לכבוש את המלכה עימו בבית. מעתה, הקביעה מתי יש לייחס למבטיח סמיכות דעת מספקת ומתי אין לייחס לו כוונה רצינית להתחייב, תהיה על פי שיקול דעתו של בית הדין. וכך הוא גם בתופעה הבאה.

ג. בשלוש סוגיות נוספות אנו מוצאים את התופעה של צמצום העמדה שאסמכתא אינה קונה תמיד, ומייחסים לה את העמדה שאסמכתא אומנם קונה בנסיבות מסוימות, ואלו הסוגיות:

i. **בבא מציעא עג ע"א:**

אמר רב חמא: האי מאן דיהיב זוזי לחבריה למיזבן ליה חמרא, ופשע ולא זבין ליה–משלם ליה כדקא אזיל אפרוותא דזולשפט.
אמר אמימר: אמריתא לשמעתא קמיה דרב זביד מנהרדעא, אמר: כי קאמר רב חמא הני מילי ביין סתם, אבל ביין זה–מי יימר דמזבני ליה ניהליה?[35]
רב אשי אמר: אפילו יין סתם נמי לא. מאי טעמא? אסמכתא היא ואסמכתא לא קניא.
ולרב אשי מאי שנא מהא דתנן (בבא מציעא פ"ט מ"ג) "אם אוביר ולא אעביד אשלם במיטבא"?[36]–התם בידו, הכא לא בידו.

לפי הבנת הראשונים, בתירוץ מבחינים בין מקרה שבו סמכה דעתו של המתחייב, שכן הדבר בידו לעשותו, לבין מקרה שבו לא סמכה דעתו כיוון שהעסקה תלויה ברצונם של אחרים.[37]

ii. **בבא מציעא קד ע"ב:**

הוא גברא דקבל ארעא מחבריה, אמר: אי מוברנא לה יהיבנא לך אלפא זוזי. אוביר תילתא. אמרי נהרדעי: דינא הוא דיהיב ליה תלת מאה ותלתין ותלתא ותילתא.
רבא אמר: אסמכתא היא ואסמכתא לא קניא.

35 על עמדתם של אמימר וחכמי נהרדעא ראו להלן.
36 זהו קנס שמתחייב החוכר את הקרקע לשלם אם לא יעבד את הקרקע וכך יגרום נזק למחכיר שלא יקבל דבר באין יבול.
37 אכן, אין זה הפירוש היחיד לתירוץ זה; ראו *אסמכתא* (לעיל, הע' 7), עמ' 408.

ולרבא מאי שנא מהא דתנן "אם אוביר ולא אעביד אשלם במיטבא"?–התם לא קגזים, הכא כיון דאמר מילתא יתירתא–גוזמא בעלמא הוא דקגזים.

גם בסוגיה זו רבא מביע את עמדתו הנחרצת שאסמכתא איננה קונה, אך סתם התלמוד "מתרץ" את דבריו לפי שיטת "סמיכות הדעת", הנותנת תוקף להבטחה לפי הנסיבות שיש בהן ללמד על קיומה של סמיכות הדעת באותה עסקה.[38] כך גם בסוגיה הבאה:

iii. בבא מציעא קט ע"א:

ההוא שתלא דאמר להו: אי מפסידנא–מסתלקנא. אפסיד. אמר רב יהודה: מסתלק בלא שבחא.[39] רב כהנא אמר: מסתלק ושקיל שבחא. ומודה רב כהנא דאי אמר אי פסידנא מסתלקנא בלא שבחא–מסתלק בלא שבחא.
רבא אמר: אסמכתא היא ואסמכתא לא קניא.
ולרבא מאי שנא מהא דתנן "אם אוביר ולא אעביד אשלם במיטבא"?
התם–מאי דאפסיד משלם, הכא–מאי דאפסיד מנכינן ליה ואידך יהבינן ליה.

המבנה האחיד של הסוגיות מלמד על עריכתן באופן שתעלה מהן, כאילו בהכרח ומחמת הקושיה מן המשנה, השיטה שבסופו של דבר גם המתנגד הקשה של שיטת "אסמכתא זימנין קניא וזימנין לא קניא" מודה לה.[40]

ד. נדרים כז ע"א-ב:

ההוא גברא דאתפיס זכוותיה בבי דינא ואמר: אי לא אתינא עד תלתין יומין ליבטלון הני זכוותאי. איתניס ולא אתא. אמר רב הונא: בטיל זכוותיה . . .[41]
ולרב הונא מכדי אסמכתא היא ואסמכתא לא קניא!? שאני הכא . . . והתנן . . .
ואמר רב נחמן אמר רבה בר אבוה אמר רב: אין הלכה כר' יוסי דאמר אסמכתא קניא?! שאני הכא דאמר . . .
והלכתא אסמכתא קניא. והוא דלא אניס, והוא דקנו מיניה בבית דין חשוב.

בסוגיה זו יש חילופי נוסחאות, וכן במקבילה שבבבא בתרא קסח ע"א, והמפרשים עמלו ביישובן.[42] אך יהיה התירוץ אשר יהיה, ברור שמוצגים כאן חילוקי דעות

38 גם כאן ייתכן הסבר אחר, ראו ב' ליפשיץ, *משפט ופעולה* (ירושלים: תשס"ב) בערך "גזם"; *אסמכתא* (לעיל, הע' 7), עמ' 60.
39 ראו לעיל, הע' 27, שנראה שרב יהודה סבור שאסמכתא קניא.
40 יש מן הגאונים שהעמיד את המשניות הללו בקנס המאושר על ידי תקנת חכמים, ראו *אסמכתא*, עמ' 84 ואילך.
41 על עמדתו של רב הונא ראו לעיל, הע' 26.
42 ראו דקדוקי סופרים השלם לנדרים, שם ובהערות המהדירים. יש להדגיש את החילוף בדעתו של רב, אם הלכה כר' יוסי אם לאו. כן יצוין הניבוב של העמדות והסייגים.

מהותיים בשאלה כיצד לפסוק–כר׳ יוסי או כר׳ יהודה–ואם הלכה כרבי יהודה, האם לצמצמה לפחות לנסיבות המקרה הזה.[43]

ה. בבא בתרא קסח ע״א:

אמר רב נחמן אמר רבה בר אבוה אמר רב: הלכה כר׳ יוסי.
כי אתו לקמיה דרבי אמי אמר להו: וכי מאחר שרבי יוחנן מלמדנו פעם ראשונה ושניה הלכה כר׳ יוסי, אני מה אעשה.
ואין הלכה כר׳ יוסי.

גם כאן משתקפת כנראה עמדתו הראשונה של רב נחמן ליתן תוקף לאסמכתא,[44] אלא שמן העניין הוא לשים לב לעמדתו של ר׳ יוחנן שחזר ולימד שאסמכתא קניא, ומן הסתם עשה כן בגלל המבקשים לסטות מהלכה זו, וכך עולה גם מהתנצלותו של רבי אמי. ועל שהייתה זו מחלוקת גם בארץ ישראל אנו למדים מן הירושלמי בבא בתרא פ״י ה״ה, יז ע״ג.

V. עמדה יציבה וברורה השתמרה בידי חכמי נהרדעא לדורותיהם, לפני חורבנה ולאחר ישיבתה מחדש, והם המשיכו ופסקו כר׳ יוסי שאמר ״אסמכתא קניא״. זו הייתה עמדתו הראשונה של רב נחמן שהיה תלמידו של שמואל והיה ראש ישיבת נהרדעא קודם לחורבנה וקודם לבואו למחוזא, שבה שימש דיין בבית הדין של ראש הגולה[45]; זו הייתה גם עמדתם של רב חמא איש נהרדעא (סנהדרין יז ע״ב) ושל רב זביד, והיא נשתמרה במסורת שהביאו בני רב חסדא בשם נהרדעי; וזו הייתה גם עמדתו המפורשת של אמימר שהעיד על עצמו ״אנא נהרדעא אנא״ (בבא מציעא לה ע״א), בשאלת תוקפה של הערבות:

אמר אמימר: ערב דמשתעבד–מחלוקת ר׳ יהודה ור׳ יוסי. לר׳ יוסי דאמר אסמכתא קניא–ערב משתעבד, לר׳ יהודה דאמר אסמכתא לא קניא–ערב לא משתעבד.[46]

ערבות היא הבטחה של אדם לשלם לנושה אם החייב לא יפרע לו את חובו. המשנה, הנוקטת בפשטות ש״המלווה את חברו על ידי ערב לא ייפרע מן הערב״, היא,

43 ראו דברי הגאון (שהובאו *באסמכתא* [לעיל, הע׳ 7], עמ׳ 45), המעמיד את הסוגיה לפי ר׳ יוסי בלבד, והפקדת השטרות בבית הדין חשוב אינה מעלה או מורידה. הרמב״ם פסק לפי מסקנת הסוגיה, שההפקדה בבית דין חשוב מסלקת את הפגם של חוסר סמיכות הדעת שיש בכל אסמכתא–הלכות מכירה פי״א הי״ג.

44 וראו *תוספות שם*, ד״ה ״אמר רב נחמן,״ *ואסמכתא* (לעיל, הע׳ 7), עמ׳ 7–6, לחילופי הנוסח.

45 על הקפדתו של אבא, אביו של שמואל, לקיים את הבטחתו ראו *מדרש שמואל* (מהד׳ ליפשיץ), (ירושלים: תשס״ט) פרשה י, ג, עמ׳ 41 ובפירוש, שם עמ׳ 247.

46 בבא בתרא קעג ע״ב.

לדעתו של אמימר, כדעתו של ר׳ יהודה הסובר שאסמכתא לא קניא. אכן, אמימר עצמו יסבור שיש לערבות תוקף משום שהוא, כשאר חכמי נהרדעא, נוקט כר׳ יוסי, הסבור שאסמכתא קניא.[47] על אף עדותו של רב אשי (בבא בתרא שם), ש״מעשים בכל יום דאסמכתא לא קניא״, כלומר שהפסיקה שנהגה הייתה כר׳ יהודה, כנראה שכך פסקו בתי הדין היהודיים שבשאר חלקי בבל אך לא כך פסקו בנהרדעא. קשה לקבוע אם היה טעם מיוחד שכך נקטו חכמי נהרדעא בישיבתם הוותיקה והחשובה.

פסיקה זו שבכל יום, ובניגוד למשפט המדינה הנוהג, מעלה את השאלה בדבר היחס שבין הדין היהודי לבין הדין הפרסי ושאלת היקף הסמכות שהוענקה לבתי הדין היהודיים לדון לפי הדין היהודי. בשאלה זו דנו אשר גולאק,[48] משה בר,[49] יעקב אלמן ואחרים.[50] גולאק שיער שהיה הסכם בין ראש הגולה לבין השליט הפרסי שלפיו הכלל ש״דינא דמלכותא דינא״,[51] תקופת החזקה במקרקעין ומכירה בעקבות חוב של מס לשלטון יהיו תקפים גם בבתי דין של ישראל (בבא בתרא נה ע״א).

47 יש הסוברים בסוגיה זו שהערבות יסודה בהוראת הכתוב ורב אשי הסביר שיסודה של הערבות אינו בהבטחה אלא בהתחייבות על אתר, שהיא ״שיעבוד עצמו״–ראו אסמכתא (לעיל, הע׳ 7), עמ׳ 201.

48 *יסודי המשפט העברי*, ברלין תרפ״ב, ח״ד, עמ׳ 28–27. וראו ש׳ שילה, *דינא דמלכותא דינא* (ירושלים: תשל״ה), עמ׳ 6.

49 *ראשות הגולה בבבל בימי המשנה והתלמוד* (תל-אביב: תשל״ו), עמ׳ 89. וראו גם גפני (לעיל, הע׳ 4), עמ׳ 227, והערה 215, שם.

50 ״ישיבות בבל ובתי דין פרסיים״ (לעיל, הע׳ 5).

51 לדעתי, לא האמורא שמואל היה הראשון שפסק שדין המלכות הוא דין. הדבר נקבע כבר במקרא, בהיתר שנתן המלך הפרסי ארתחשסתא לעזרא הסופר לשוב לארץ ישראל ולהשיב את השלטון היהודי בה: ״ואנת עזרא כחכמת אלהך די בידך, מני שפטין ודינין דאנין לכל עמא די בעבר נהרה לכל ידעי דתי אלהך ודי לא ידע תהודעון. וכל די לא להוא עבד דתא די מלכא, אספרנא דינה להוה מתעבד מנה, הן למות, הן לשרשי הן לענש נכסין ולאסורין״ (עזרא ז כה-כו). כלומר, עזרא הוסמך לדון לפי דת האל ולפי דת המלך. וראו עזרא החיצוני (תרגום א׳ כהנא במהדורת הספרים החיצוניים שהוציא, א, עמ׳ תר [פרק ח כג-כד]): ״ואתה עזרא, כחכמת האלהים תמנה שופטים ודיינים ודנו בכל ארם וכנען ... וכל אדם אשר יעבר על דת אלהיך ודת המלך מהרה יענש אם מות ואם מלקות או ענש כסף או לבית האסורים.״ וכן הוא בדברי יוסף בן מתתיהו, קדמוניות היהודים, 11, 5, 1. וראו גם אסתר ג ח: ״ישנו עם אחד מפזר ומפרד בין העמים בכל מדינות מלכותך, ודתיהם שונות מכל עם ואת דתי המלך אינם עושים.״ יש שפירשו שתורת האל היא גם דת המלך, הואיל והיא אושרה על ידי המלך, אך רבים אחרים פירשו, וכך נראה, שהדין מורכב משניים: דין האל ודין המלך. וראו דברי הימים א כו לב: ״... לכל דבר האלהים ולכל דבר המלך״; שם ב יט יא: ״והנה אמריהו כהן הראש עליכם לכל דבר ה׳ וזבדיהו בן ישמעאל הנגיד לבית יהודה לכל דבר המלך.״ וראו המאמרים שכונסו בספר
J.W. Watts (ed.), *Persia and Torah, the Theory of Imperial Authorization of the Pentateuch* (Atlanta: 2001).
התלמוד הבבלי (מועד קטן טז ע״א) והרמב״ם (הלכות סנהדרין פכ״ד ה״ט) מסתמכים על הפסוקים שהובאו כדי לגזור מהם את הענקת הסמכויות הנזכרות בהם לכל בית דין. וראו ח״ה כהן, ״עיונים משפטיים בספר עזרא,״ *זר לגבורות, ספר היובל לכבוד זלמן שז״ר* (ירושלים: תשל״ג), עמ׳ 371. ההיקש, המסתמך על ההמשכיות של מנהגי השלטון, ילמדנו על מתן אוטונומיה לבני הדתות האחרות ועל הסמכות לאכוף את פסקי הדין שניתנו על ידי שופטיהן.

לדעתו, רק על יסוד הסכמה זו ניתן היתר לישיבות לדון לפי הדין היהודי. קשה לדעת מה היחס בין הכלל "דינא דמלכותא דינא", לבין שני הפרטים שבאים לאחריו,[52] ומדוע צוינו דווקא פרטים אלה. לדברי גולאק,[53] אילו לא היו חכמים מכירים בדין החזקה[54] הדבר "יכול היה להביא ערבוביא גדולה וסכסוכים רבים בקנין קרקעות"; ובאשר לגביית המיסים מן המקרקעין אסור היה להתערב בכך "וגם היה צריך להזהר שלא יעורר את קנאת בעלי האחוזות הגדולות."

מדברי גולאק עולה שהדיון המשפטי בסוגיות אלה נערך בין יהודי לבין פרסי, ואם כך הוא, והיה חשש לערבוביה ולסכסוכים, הלא שני הדינים הללו היו נדירים יחסית בהרבה מן הדיון היום-יומי היכול להתגלע בין צדדים להסכם כלשהו. כיצד יכולים אנו לתאר את חיי המסחר השגרתיים באין תוקף חוקי להבטחות? אכן, יהודי יכול היה לטעון כלפי פסק דינו של ראש הגולה שניתן בינו לבין חברו היהודי "גבי ריש גלותא דדאין דינא דפרסאי למה לי?", ולקבל פסק דין שונה מרב נחמן,[55] אך מה יענה לבעל דינו הפרסי? אכן, מדברי התלמוד בסוגיות השונות שכללו של שמואל נזכר בהן ומפירושי הראשונים עולה שהדיון היה בין יהודים דווקא, וגם אז היה צורך להחיל בסוגיות אלה את הדין הפרסי, ולא עוד אלא שהחילו את הדין הפרסי גם בעניינים אחרים, נוסף על אלה שנזכרו לעיל. יעקב אלמן סבור,[56] שחכמי ההלכה, ובמיוחד רב נחמן, ניסו למנוע מן היהודים הליכה לערכאות של פרסיים וניסו להיענות לאתגר שפסקיהם של בתי דין אלה העמידו בפניהם.[57] אך אף שייתכן שכך היה הדבר, הראיות המובאות לביסוסה של הטענה אינן מכריעות. מכל מקום, האם יש בידינו לומר דבר מה לעניין זה מפרשת פסקיו השונים של רב נחמן בעניין תוקפה ומעמדה של ההבטחה ומפרשת המחלוקת שבין האמוראים בשאלה זו?

מי שרוצה בביטולה של הבטחתו יעדיף לפנות אל ערכאה שאינה נותנת תוקף להבטחה, והמבקש שהבטחה שקיבל תקוים יעדיף להתדיין בערכאה הנותנת לה תוקף. נראה שבאופן כולל עדיפה שיטה המקיימת הבטחות-כך יש ביטחון בעסקות. והרי מי שירצה היום להשתחרר מהבטחתו ירצה מחר בקיומה של הבטחת זולתו שניתנה לו. כך אפשר להבין את ניסיונותיו החוזרים ונשנים של רב פפא להחזיר את עטרת ההלכה שאסמכתא קניא ליושנה-אך אין בכך כדי להסביר

52 ראו דברי שילה, לעיל הע' 46.
53 שם, עמ' 29 הע' 27.
54 ראו א"ש רוזנטל, "למילון התלמוד-בירורי מלים ועניני נוסח," *תרביץ מ* (תשל"א), עמ' 187.
55 בבא בתרא נח ע"ב.
56 לעיל, הע' 48, עמ' 32, 40, 47 ואילך.
57 בניגוד לעמדתו של בר, אין אלמן סבור ש"דינא דפרסאי" הוא כינוי גנאי לדין זה. אף אני מסכים לכך, ראו מאמרי שצוין לעיל, הע' 5.

את השינוי שחל בעמדתו של רב נחמן ואת עמדתם של כל מי שפסקו בעקשנות שלא כר' יוסי.

עוד יש לשאול בענייננו, מדוע לא נזכרה בכל הדיונים שהיו בסוגייתנו טענה כעין זו שבאה בתלמוד בעניין אחר (בבא בתרא נד ע"ב): "והאמר שמואל דינא דמלכותא דינא, ומלכא אמר לא ליקני ארעא אלא באיגרתא!"–האם גם בזאת יש ראיה לשיטת הראשונים הסוברים שהכלל ש"דינא דמלכותא דינא" חל רק על מקרקעין, כי הארץ היא של המלך,[58] וזה המכנה המשותף של המקרים שהוזכרו בהקשר זה בתלמוד? וייתכן שהיו הוראות של המלך שלא הייתה כוונה שיבואו במקום ההוראות של שלטון המקומי אלא יחולו לצידן תוך מתן אפשרות לאמצן. עניין זה נובע באופן מהותי ממהותו של שיטת המשפט הכפולה שנהגה באימפריה הפרסית.[59]

VI. אך מעבר לדמיון שבשיטות המשפט אנו צריכים להביט גם אל הפן הדתי והתרבותי,[60] כי תרבותה של חברה המקיימת הבטחות בצל המשפט שונה מתרבותה של זו שבה הבטחות אינן נאכפות. על הפן המשפטי העולה מן הדין הפרסי כבר עמדנו, ועל כך יש להוסיף את הפן הדתי, המתגלם בדמותו של האל מיטרא, שמשמעות שמו היא ככל הנראה "חוזה, הבטחה".[61] למעשה, החוזה הוא

58 ראו שילה (לעיל, הע' 46), עמ' 69.
59 הבעיה מצויה גם כן בהלכה, המכירה במשפט התורה ובמשפט המלך שלצידה. ואכמ"ל.
60 להשראה התרבותית בין שכבות העילית האליטות הפרסיות ליהודיות ראו אלמן, "Acculturation to elite Persian norms," (לעיל, הע' 5). וראו דיונו של י' גפני וציוניו (לעיל, הע' 4), עמ' 149–176. וראו א' אחדות, "הפולמוס היהודי-זורואסטרי בתלמוד הבבלי," *איראנו-יודאיקה* 4 (2000), עמ' יז.
61 ראו בערך Mithra ב–*Encyclopedia Iranica*. ויש אומרים שהוא מלשון שטר (Vertrag), והם הם הדברים. במסורת הדתית ההודית אנו מוצאים את הצמד Mitra, חוזה, ו-Varuna, דיבור של אמת. החוקרים נחלקו בשאלה, האם פולחנו של מיטרא, המוכר מן העולם הרומי ואשר אופיו עטוף מסתורין, הוא המשכו של הפולחן הפרסי–ראו:
F. Cumont, *The Mysteries of Mithra*, trans. T.J. McCormack (NY: 1903); M.J.Vermaseren, *Mithras, the Secret God* (London: 1963); M. Clauss, *The Roman Cult of Mithras, the God and his Mysteries*, trans. R. Gordon (NY: 1990.)
האל הזה מתואר באומנות בת-הזמן כמי שנאבק עם השור. וראו י"ה שור, *החלוץ ז* (לעיל, הע' 5), עמ' 16, על האל Tir, שהוא הממונה על המטר וגופו שדומה לשור (וראו גם שם, ח, עמ' 18, אות יג, ועמוד 62). וציין לתענית כה ע"ב, שהמלאך הממונה על הגשמים דומה לשור, או לעגל, וראו רש"י יומא כא ריש ע"א. וכן הוא במדרש כונן. וראו י' ליבס, "מידותיו של אלהים," *עלילות אלהים*, ירושלים תשס"ט, עמ' 151.
בין האלילים הרומיים היה האל Semo Sanctus, הוא Dius Fidius, הוא האל של הנאמנות, היושר והשבועות; בכך הוא כיסה חלק מן התחומים של מיטרא. על מיטרא כשופט ראו:
S. Shaked, "Mihr the judge," *Jerusalem Studies in Arabic and Islam* 2 (1980), 1–31.
יש שרצו לראות השפעה של תורת הניגודים הזורואסתרית (שבה יש טוב ורע, והטוב מתאפיין בשמירת הבטחות) על בני קומראן שבהם הטוב הוא האמת, והיא בידי נסיך האור, והרע הוא השקר והמרמה–ראו:
בשמירת הבטחות) על בני קומראן שבהם הטוב הוא האמת, והיא בידי נסיך האור, והרע הוא

האנשה של האל הזה. קיומו של החוזה הוא קיומו של האל, וכיבודה של הבטחה היא כבודו של האל. מיטרא מוכר גם כאל של החוזים. הוא מקיף את העולם כולו,

---

D. Winston, "The Iranian component in the Bible, Apocrypha, and Qumran: a review of the evidence," *History of Religions* 5 (1966), 183–216, esp. 200 ff.
וראו הסתייגותו של ר״נ פריי:

R.N. Frye, "Qumran and Iran, the state of studies," in J. Neusner (ed.), *Christianity, Judaism and Other Greco-Roman Cults*, 3 (Leiden: 1975), 3:167–73.
על תיאורו של האל כשמש וכאור ראו:

M. Goodman, "The Jewish image of God," in R. Kalmin and S. Schwartz (eds.), *Jewish Culture and Society under the Christian Roman Empire* (Leuven: 2003), 134–45.
ראו גם:

S. Shaked, "Qumran and Iran: further considerations," *Israel Oriental Studies* 2 (1972), 433–46; idem," Iranian influence on Judaism: first century BCE to second century CE," *Cambridge History* of *Judaism* 1 (1991), 308–25.
במאמר זה דן שקד גם בשאלת חופש הבחירה בדת הזורואסתרית (עמ׳ 319), שנותרה בלתי ברורה ויש לה חשיבות לקשר שבין אי-האכיפה של ההבטחה לפי הסוברים כך, ראו מאמרי שצוין לעיל, הע׳ 7. תהיה מידת ההשפעה ההדדית כאשר תהיה, קשה להתעלם מן הדמיון הרב. וראו בראשית רבה א ז: ״ר׳ יצחק פתח: ׳ראש דברך אמת׳ וגו׳ (תהלים קיט קס). אמר ר׳ יצחק: מתחילת ברייתו של עולם ראש דברך אמת–׳בראשית ברא אלהים׳ (=סופי תיבות אמת), ׳וה׳ אלהים אמת׳ (ירמיהו י י). לפיכך ׳ולעולם כל משפטי צדקך׳ (תהלים שם שם), שכל גזירה וגזירה שאתה גוזר על בריותיך הן מצדיקין עליהם את הדין ומקבלין אותו באמונה (!), ואין כל ברייה חלוקה לומר ב׳ רשויות נתנו את התורה, ב׳ רשויות בראו את העולם; ׳וידברו אלהים׳ אין כתוב כאן אלא ׳וידבר אלהים׳, ׳בראשית בראו׳ אין כתוב כאן אלא ׳בראשית ברא׳.״ וראו גם שם ט; שם ח ה: ״אמת אומר אל יברא ... נטל אמת והשליכה לארץ ... מה את מבזה אלטיכסייה (=חותם) שלך? תעלה אמת מן הארץ!״ וראו גם ישעיהו מה ז. והשוו השמות ״בעל ברית״ (שופטים ח לג, ט ד), ו״אל ברית״ (שופטים ט מו). לדעת אולברייט, ״בעל ברית ואל ברית אינם אלא כינויים לאל חורון, הממונה כנראה על שמירת הבריתות, שהרי בכתובת כנענית שנתגלתה במיסופוטמיה נאמר על חורון אש תם פי, כלומר: אשר פיו נאמן״ (אנציקלופדיה מקראית, א, טור 286, ערך ״בעל ברית״). וראו גם השם, שעלה מבבל, ״כל חזה״ (נחמיה ג טו, יא ה). והשוו מלכים ב יז יג, וצ״ע.

יש הרואים במטטרון/מיטטרון, המלאך הגדול במיסטיקה היהודית, את בן דמותו של מיטרא (ראו דברי הנרחבים של ח״י קאהוט בערוך השלם, ערך ״מיטטרון,״ ושם קבע שעיקר הכתיב הוא מיטטרון; ר״ר מרגליות, *מלאכי עליון* (ירושלים: תשכ״ד), עמ׳ פה, פח, ושמו נובע מהיותו ממונה על הגשמים). וראו *תיקוני הזוהר*, נז (מהד׳ מרגליות), (ירושלים: תשל״ח), צא ע״ב: ״לזמנין אתקרי מיטטר״ר בזמנא דאממנא על מטרא.״ מטטרון מזוהה גם כאליהו, מלאך הברית, ואשר בידו נמסר מפתח של גשמים. וריש לקיש אמר ששמות המלאכים עלו בידן מבבל (ירושלמי ראש השנה פ״א ה״ב, ו ע״א, *ומלאכי עליון*, שם, עמ׳ כא). וראו פירושו של רמב״ן לשמות יב יב ומה שצוין שם, *ערוך השלם*, ערך ״מטטר״; וראו חגיגה טו ע״א, שהיה כותב זכויותיהם של ישראל. וראו י׳ דן, *תורת הסוד של חסידי אשכנז* (ירושלים: תשכ״ח), עמ׳ 219–224; הנ״ל, ״ענפיאל, מטטרון ויוצר בראשית,״ *תרביץ* נב (תשמ״ג), עמ׳ 447. ראו גם מ׳ אידל, ״חנוך הוא מטטרון,״ *דברי הכנס הבינלאומי הראשון לתולדות המיסטיקה היהודית: המיסטיקה העברית הקדומה* (ירושלים: תשמ״ז), עמ׳ 151. *בספר החשק*, לבוב ,1865 הכולל שבעים שמות המיוחסים למטטרון לפי תכונותיהם, אין נזכרות השמירה על ההבטחות והמלחמה בשקר. וראו גם *תורה שלמה* לשמות כג כ, עמ׳ 227 ואילך. אך מטטרון הוא גם המלאך המכונה ״ה׳ קטן,״ ששם הוויה בקרבו. וראו סנהדרין לח ע״ב: ״מטטרון ששמו כשם רבו . . . אי הכי נפלחו ליה (=אם כך, יעבדוהו?) כתיב: ׳אל תמר בו׳, אל תמירני בו . . . הימנותא בידן דאפילו בפרוונקא (=כשליח) נמי לא קבילניה.״ וראו רש״י לשמות ו ג וויקרא יט כו, על שם הוויה, שהוא המציין את המידה של קיום הבטחות. (על ההבחנה בין הבטחת האל לבין נבואות ראו ״גור אריה,״ בראשית לב, ז;י.) וראו גם שבת נה ע״א ורש״י שם, ד״ה ״חותמו.״ וראו י״ה שור, *החלוץ* ח (לעיל, הע׳ 5), עמ׳ 3.

ועיניו משוטטות בכל לחפש אחרי דוברי שקר ומפירי ברית המפרים את הבטחותיהם ואת החוזים שכרתו ובכך גורמים נזק לעולם כולו, כי כל קיום של הסכם הוא קיום העולם והפרתו היא הריסתו.[62] לכן המפרים ייענשו על ידיו והמקיימים יתוגמלו בין השאר בירידת גשמים.[63] ילדים וילדות היו נקראים על שמו של מיטרא (בגרסתו הקדומה של השם) ובכינוי "הבטחה".[64] חגו של האליל הזה

62 ראו *ילקוט שמעוני* בראשית, רמז ג: "אותיות של אמת בשתי רגלים ושל שקר ברגל אחד. כל שעושה אמת–מקוים." וראו שבת קד ע"א. אין זה ביטוי לתפיסה של "אמנה חברתית" בדבר הצורך בחיברות לשם הקיום האנושי, אלא עיקרון המונח בתשתיתו של העולם.

63 ראו שיר התהילה למיטרא אצל I. Gershevitch, *The Avestan Hymn to Mithra* (Cambridge: 1967); M.W. Meyer, *The 'Mithras Liturgy'* (Misoula MO: 1976) וראו תענית ט ע"ב: "כי היכי דמשקרי בבלאי משקרי מיטרייהו"! (כלומר, היו עננים שנראו כענני גשם, ולבסוף לא ירד הגשם.והשוו ברכות נט ע"א: "טמיא כדיב הוא ומיליה כדיבין"). וראו שמות רבה מב א: "מי שהוא אומר [=מבטיח] ליתן מתנה לחברו ואינו נותנה למה הוא דומה? לנשיאים ורוח וברקים שהם באים–וגשמים אינם יורדים." כלומר, השקר והמטר-מיטרא תלויים זה בזה. סביר שהמימרה הזאת משקפת היכרות עם עולם האמונות הפרסי, ואולי היא צופנת לעג: הבבליים שקרנים ואלילָם– מיטרא– מכזב, לעומת האמור "כי לא איש אל ויכזב" (במדבר כג יט). וראו ויקרא רבה כו א (מהד' מרגליות, עמ' תקפז):" אמרות ה' אמרות טהורות [תהלים יב ז]–אמרות ה' אמרות, אמרות בשר ודם אינן אמרות." וראו *פסיקתא רבתי* יד, נז ע"א ואילך); "אל אמונה ואין עול" (דברים לב ד); "דבר שקרים לא יכון לנגד עיני" (תהלים קא ז); לא אחלל בריתי ומוצא שפתי לא אשנה" (תהלים פט לה); "חותמו של הקב"ה אמת" (שבת נה ע"א), ועוד. [וראו *חידושי אגדות* למהר"ל מפראג, ראש השנה ח ע"ב, ד"ה "אפילו."] בכך דומות מאוד מידותיו של אלוהי ישראל לאלו המיוחסות על ידי הפרסים לאליל מיטרא. כן יש לציין שגם המקרא משווה בין ירידת הגשמים לבין קיום ההבטחות, "הדברים": "כי כאשר ירד הגשם והשלג מן השמים ושמה לא ישוב כי אם הרוה את הארץ והולידה והצמיחה ונתן זרע לזרע ולחם לאכל. כן יהיה דברי אשר יצא מפי לא ישוב אלי ריקם כי אם עשה את אשר חפצתי והצליח אשר שלחתיו" (ישעיהו נה י-יא). וראו גם תהלים קמז טו "השולח אמרתו ארץ, עד מהרה ירוץ דברו," המצוי בהקשר של ממטרים. והשוו גם ברכת גבורות. וכך מסרו בשם ר' אמי (תענית ח ע"א): "אין גשמים יורדים אלא בשביל בעלי אמנה, שנאמר אמת מארץ תצמח וצדק משמים נשקף." כלומר, בשל מי שמקיימים את הבטחותיהם, שאין "אמנה" אלא הבטחה כעולה מהמשך הדברים, שם, במעשה בחולדה ובור וברש"י ד"ה "מחולדה ובור": "שנתן אמונתו." וראו אסמכתא (לעיל, הע' 7), עמ' 162 ואילך. [וראו על סוגיה זו דברי מהר"ל מפראג, נתיבות עולם, נתיב האמונה, פרק א. על טעמים אחרים לעצירת גשמים ראו שם ז ע"ב. על תפילות וצומות בשל עצירת גשמים בארץ ישראל ובבבל ראו שם כד ע"א]. ואפשר לציין כאן למלאך "אף ברי," שלפי מסורת קדומה נזכר באיוב לז יא, והוא המלאך הממונה על העננים (רש"י, שם). וראו פיוטו של ר' אלעזר הקליר לתפילת הגשם המתחיל במילים אלה, ושם הוא שר המטר, העלול להימנע מהמטרת גשמים למי שנאשמים ב"נשיון שטר," כלומר בהפרת התחייבות (וראו "אגדה" [לעיל, הע' 4], הע' 246). לפיוט זה הפנו בתוד"ה "מלאך" בנידה טז ע"ב. וראו י"ה שור, *החלוץ* ח (לעיל, הע' 5), עמ' 7. ומיד לאחר מכן הזכיר שור את המלאך Bereja, כלומר בְּרֶיָה, הממונה על בישול הפירות. שמו מזכיר את ברי. ap/ab הוא "מים" בפרסית.

64 peiman. הדגשת חשיבות האמת בדת הזורואסתרית מתבטאת גם בריבוי השמות הפרטיים, המכילים את המרכיב של האמת. החינוך לאמירת האמת ולאהבתה החל מגיל צעיר–ראו י"ה שור, *החלוץ* ז [לעיל, הע' 5], עמ' 25. מן השם "מוהרנקי" בא המוהר, המוכר בערבית ובעברית. והשוו "מהר ימהרנה לו לאשה" (שמות כב טו), שפירוש "מהר" שם הוא עצם הלקיחה ולא התשלום עבור הנערה, ראו במפרשים. וראו בהערה 66 להלן. וראו עבודה זרה עא ע"א: "אמר אמימר: משיכה בעובד כוכבים קונה. תדע, דהני פרסאי משרי פרדשני להדדי ולא הדרי בהו. רב אשי אמר: לעולם אימא לך משיכה בעובד כוכבים אינה קונה, והאי

היה בשישה עשר בתשרי–שבו חל גם חג הסוכות, הוא החג שבו נידונים על המים– והוא נזכר בתלמוד הבבלי (עבודה זרה יא ע״ב) בלשון זה: ״ודפרסאי מאי? מוטרדי וטוריסקי, מוהרנקי[65] ומוהרין״.[66] הזכרתו של אליל זה הייתה בענידת טבעת, המסמלת את יצירת הקשר והאהבה וההחברות בין המתקשרים בה.[67] לפי דברי הינלס,

"To the Persians, Persia was naturally the land of Contract."[68]

VII. מן החיבור הזורואסטרי, המכונה Vandidad/Vendidad/Widēwdād אנו למדים על מידת החשיבות שיוחסה בדת זו להבטחות; וזה לשונו:

---

דלא הדרי בהו–דרמות רוחא דנקיטא להו.״ כלומר, דעתו של רב אשי היא שהפרסים אומנם אינם חוזרים בהם מהבטחתם להקנות, שהרי משיכה שאינה תקפה הרי היא כהבטחה בעלמא, על פי בבא בתרא ג ע״א. אך הוא מייחס זאת, משום מה, לא לחובה החוקית והמוסרית המוטלת עליהם לקיים את הבטחתם אלא להיותם בעלי רוח רמה, גאים. ואולי סבר שמעיקרם בני בבל שקרנים הם (לעיל, הע׳ 63). וראו ניסוח זה המובא משמו של רב אשי לעניין אחר, ויש לשקול אפשרות של העברה בעלמא. וראו קידושין ע ע״א ניסוח כעין זה משמו של שמואל. וראו ראשונים על סוגיית עבודה זרה הנ״ל, וראו *חידושי הרשב״א*, שם, ד״ה ״הא דאמר.״

65 כך צריך להיות, ראו *בערוך השלם* בערכו ובערך ״מוהרין״ ובהערות המהדיר בערך ״מסרדי,״ והוא החג הידוע כ-mihrgan.

66 ראו גם *תשובות הגאונים*, הרכבי, סי׳ מו (עמ׳ 22): ״ואלו אידיהן של פרסים אשר הוזכרו מוסרדי ומיהרקאני טריאסקי ומהרוז (מהרון?). ועכשיו מוסרדי וטריאסקי אינן נוהגין, אבל מהרקאני עד עכשיו אלו הדילומיים [נוהגין] בם בבבל ונקראין מהרנאן בראש הקיץ ובראש החורף. ומהרוז הוא יום החודש . . . גוים שבשדות ושבמדברות . . . היו להם ימי אד שנוהגין הן בהן יום. מוהרי שנותנין חותמות בשידוכי אשה, וימי אקניאתא, יום שאדם קונה שדהו אותו היום עשאוהו יום טוב ובאין ושותין אצלו ומזמרים לע״ז עד שמעמידין״ (וראו הערתו של י״ה שור על תשובה זו בביקורתו על מהדורתו של הרכבי, *החלוץ* יג [תרמ״ט], עמ׳ 73). וראו חילופי הנוסח בדקדוקי סופרים ומה שציין ר״ש אברמסון במהדורת מסכת עבודה זרה מכ״י ביהמ״ד לרבנים שהוציא לאור, ניו-יורק תשי״ז, עמ׳ 150, ובמבואו, שם, עמ׳ xix. וראו בפירושו של רבנו חננאל, שגרס ״מהרוז״ ויש שתיקנו בו ״מהרין״ והסתייגותו של ר״ש אברמסון (שם) מכך. וכן מצינו רשימת אידי הנוכרים בבבל ובמדי בירושלמי עבודה זרה פ״א ה״ג, לט ע״ג: ״ר׳ בא בשם רב: שלשה זמנים בבבל–מהורי וכנוני וכנוותא. שלשה במדיי–נוסרדי ותירייסקי ומהירקנה.״ וראו י״ה שור, *החלוץ* ז (לעיל, הע׳ 5), עמ׳ 51. וראו:
B.H. Taqizadeh, "Iranian festivals adopted by the Christians and condemned by the Jews," *BSOAS* 10 (1940), 632–53; M. Boyce, "Persian religion in the Achemenid Age," *Cambridge History of Judaism* 1 (Cambridge and NY: 1991), 284, 303, 305;
שם נטען כי החגיגה של חגים אלה לא הייתה בגדר חובה. וראו גם:
R. Brody, "Zoroastrian themes in Geonic responsa," *Irano-Judaica* 4 (2000), 181–82.
בכרכי כתב העת הזה יש כמה וכמה מאמרים העוסקים בקשרים שונים שיש לדת פרס לגלגוליה עם תחומים שונים של היהדות (ראו למשל מאמריהם של ש׳ פינס, ר׳ ברודי וש׳ שקד שבקובץ השני; ושל ג׳ סטרומזה ושל ק׳ איראני בקובץ השלישי, ועוד).

67 בני בבל אינם מקדשים בטבעת, כדברי ספר *חילוף מנהגים בין בני בבל לבני ארץ ישראל* (מהד׳ מילר, וינה תרל״ח, עמ׳ 24; מהד׳ מרגליות, עמ׳ 139). וראו מאמרי ״סיטומתא–בין קניין לבין התחייבות,״ בתוך ר׳ הורביץ ואח׳ (עורכים), *ספר הזיכרון לפרופסור זאב פלק* (ירושלים: תשס״ה), עמ׳ 59. טבעות אלו הן ה״חותמות״ שהיו נותנים בשידוכי אישה, כאמור בתשובת הגאון שנזכרה בהערה הקודמת.

68 ראו: J.R. Hinnels, *Persian Mythology* (London: 1973), 78

2. How many in number are thy contracts, O Ahura Mazda? Ahura Mazda answered:

> "They are six in number, O holy Zarathustra. The first is the word-contract; the second is the hand-contract; the third is the contract to the amount of a sheep; the fourth is the contract to the amount of an ox; the fifth is the contract to the amount of a man; the sixth is the contract to the amount of a field, a field in good land, a fruitful one, in good bearing."

3. The word-contract is fulfilled by words of mouth. It is canceled by the hand-contract; he shall give as damages the amount of the hand-contract.
4. The hand-contract is canceled by the sheep-contract; he shall give as damages the amount of the sheep-contract.

The sheep-contract is canceled by the ox-contract; he shall give as damages the amount of the ox-contract.

The ox-contract is canceled by the man-contract; he shall give as damages the amount of the man-contract. The man-contract is canceled by the field-contract; he shall give as damages the amount of the field-contract.
5. If a man breaks the word-contract, how many are involved in his sin? Ahura Mazda answered: "His sin makes his Nabanazdishtas answerable for three hundred (years)."
6. If a man breaks the hand-contract, how many are involved in his sin? . . . "His sin makes his Nabanazdishtas answerable for six hundred (years)."
7. If a man breaks the sheep-contract, how many are involved in his sin? . . . "His sin makes his Nabanazdishtas answerable for seven hundred (years)."
. . .
12. If a man breaks the hand-contract, what is the penalty that he shall pay? Ahura Mazda answered: "Six hundred stripes with the Aspahe-ashtra, six hundred stripes with the Sraosho-charana."
13. If a man breaks the sheep-contract, what is the penalty that he shall pay? Ahura Mazda answered: "Seven hundred stripes with the Aspahe-ashtra, seven hundred stripes with the Sraosho-charana."
. . .
15. O Maker of the material world, thou Holy One! If a man breaks the man-contract, what is the penalty that he shall pay? Ahura Mazda answered: "Nine hundred stripes."
. . .
44. If men of the same faith, either friends or brothers, come to an agreement together, that one may obtain from the other, either goods, or a wife, or knowledge, let him who desires goods have them delivered to him;

let him who desires a wife receive and wed her; let him who desires knowledge be taught the holy word. . . .
54. Down there the pain for that deed shall be as hard as any in this world: to wit, the deed of a man, who knowingly lying, confronts the brimstoned, golden, truth-knowing water with an appeal unto Rashnu and a lie unto Mithra.
55. O Maker of the material world, thou Holy One! He who, knowingly lying, confronts the brimstoned, golden, truth-knowing water with an appeal unto Rashnu and a lie unto Mithra, what is the penalty that he shall pay in this world? Ahura Mazda answered: "Seven hundred stripes with the Aspahe-ashtra, seven hundred stripes with the Sraosho-charana."[69]

VIII. אנו יכולים אפוא לתאר לעצמנו את נוכחותו המתמדת, כביכול, של מיטרא בחיי המעשה ואת האווירה שהייתה רוויה בתחושת החובה הדתית, המשפטית והפילוסופית שהבטחות יש לקיים. בניגוד לכל אלה, פעל רבא, הגר במחוזא והמושפע מהלכי הרוח של שכבות העילית הנוכריות בנות המקום,[70] לשינוי ההלכה המקובלת והורה שאסמכתא לא קניא, ורב נחמן, המקורב לראש הגולה והמכהן כדיין בבית דינו, חזר בו מדעתו והורה כדעתו של רבא. גם רב חלק על עמדתו של ר׳ יוחנן ולימד ש״דברים אין בהן משום מחוסרי אמנה״, דהיינו שהחוזר בו מהבטחתו אינו מתכנה בתואר המבזה ״מחוסר אמנה״, שהוא מי שאין ממש בהבטחתו (בבא מציעא מט ע״א. אך ראו גיטין יד ע״א);[71] וכשהקשו על כך מדברי רבי יוסי בר יהודה: ״מה תלמוד לומר ׳הין צדק׳, והלא הין בכלל איפה היה? אלא לומר לך שיהא הן שלך צדק ולאו שלך צדק!״, ענה על כך אביי, בן דורו וחברו של רבא: ״ההוא שלא ידבר אחד בפה ואחד בלב״ (שם). כלומר, בשעת ההבטחה צריך שתהיה הכוונה לקיימה, אבל אפשר אחר כך לחזור מן הקיום![72] ואת הברייתא הבאה פירש רבא פירוש מצמצם:

69 התרגום הוא משל ג׳ דרמשטטר, משנת 1898. י״ה שור, *החלוץ* ח (לעיל, הע׳ 5), עמ׳ 39, מביא מפירוש לסעיף 44 שיש מחלוקת מהו דינו של החוזר בו מהבטחה שנתן למי שאינו בן אמונתו, והוא מפנה למחלוקתם של רב ור׳ יוחנן (בבא מציעא מט ע״א) אם החוזר בו מדברים יש בו משום מחוסר אמנה אם לאו. וראו *חידושי הריטב״א החדשים*, בבא מציעא סג ע״א, ד״ה ״אמר רב עושים אמנה בפירות.״ וראו ח׳ ילון, *פרקי לשון*, עמ׳ 339–340, אך יש לחלוק על דבריו, כי ״חסד,״ ״טוב,״ ו״ישר״ הן לשונות של הסכמה ואין הן מציינות עשייה לפנים משורת הדין, כדעתו של ילון.

70 ראו אלמן, לעיל, הע׳ 59.

71 בירושלמי שביעית (ראו ההערה הבאה) אמרו שלמידת חסידות לא היה חוזר בו, אבל ממידת הדין אפשר לחזור. ובבבלי הבחינו בין מקבל עני לבין מקבל עשיר.

72 כך היא גם עמדת חכמי ארץ ישראל, ראו ירושלמי שביעית פ״י ה״ט, לט ע״ד: ״בשעה שאמר צריך לומר בדעה גמורה. מבתר כן אין חזר ביה-(לא) חזר ביה״; בבא מציעא פ״ד ה״ב, ט ע״ג: ״בשעה שאמר הין-שלצדק היה.״ וראו פסחים קיג ע״ב: ״שלשה הקדוש ברוך הוא שונאן: המדבר אחד בפה ואחד בלב.״ אבל ראו סוכה מו ע״ב: ״ואמר ר׳ זירא: לא לימא איניש לינוקא דיהיבנא לך מידי ולא יהיב ליה משום דאתי לאגמוריה שיקרא, שנאמר ׳למדו לשונם דבר

רבי שמעון אומר: אף על פי שאמרו טלית קונה דינר זהב ואין דינר זהב קונה טלית, מכל מקום אמרו כך הלכה, אבל אמרו מי שפרע מאנשי דור המבול ומאנשי דור הפלגה ומאנשי סדום ועמורה ומצרים בים הוא עתיד ליפרע ממי שאינו עומד בדיבורו. והנושא ונותן בדברים–לא קנה.[73] והחוזר בו אין רוח חכמים נוחה הימנו.

ואמר רבא: אנו אין לנו אלא "אין רוח חכמים נוחה הימנו". דברים ואיכא בהדייהו מעות–קאי ב"אבל"; דברים וליכא בהדייהו מעות–לא קאי ב"אבל".[74]

---

שקר׳." וראו שתי מימרותיו של רבי אלעזר בסנהדרין צב ע"א: "כל המחליף בדיבורו כאילו עובד עבודה זרה"; "לעולם הוי קבל וקיים." י"ה שור, *החלוץ* ח (לעיל, הע׳ 5), עמ׳ 39, ראה בדברי אביי עדות ל"פחיתות מעמדם המוסרי" של חכמי אותם הימים. וראו דברי מהר"ץ חיות על פירושו של רש"י לבבא מציעא מט ע"א הנ"ל. כדברי הירושלמי ואביי נקט גם תומס אקווינס (*Summa Theologica*, שאלה 110, iii, תשובה להתנגדות החמישית) "אדם אינו משקר ככל שבדעתו לקיים את אשר הבטיח, כי הוא אינו אומר דברים בניגוד למה שבדעתו. אך אם אין הוא שומר את הבטחתו, הוא נראה כפועל שלא בנאמנות בשנותו את דעתו." אכן, אקווינס סבור שהבטחות יש לקיים. והשוו גם דברי אריסטו, *אתיקה ניקומכאית*, ד, ז. וראו גם רש"י לכתובות פו ע"א, ד"ה "פריעת בעל חוב מצוה": "מצוה עליו לפרוע חובו ולאמת דבריו, דכתיב הין צדק–שיהא הן שלך צדק ולאו שלך צדק," ובהערת בעל *גליון הש"ס*, שם, מסוגיית בבא מציעא הנ"ל. וראו סנהדרין צז ע"א: "אמר רבינא: מריש הוא אמינא ליכא קושטא בהאי עלמא אמר ליה ההוא מרבנן . . . ואי יהבי ליה כל חללי עלמא לא הוי משני בדיבוריה. כי איקלע להיא אתרא וקושטא שמיה ולא הוו משנינן בדיבורייהו." מן הסוגיה משמע ששינוי הדברים כאן הוא שקר. והשוו מלאכי ג, ו: "ואני ה׳ לא שניתי."

73 "הנושא ונותן בדברים" הוא זה ש"נושא ונותן באמונה," כלומר שהוא קונה ומוכר בהבטחות, כמשמע המקורי של הצירוף "משא ומתן," שהרי אין "אמונה" אלא "אמנה"–"הבטחה"; ראו *אסמכתא* (לעיל, הע׳ 7), עמ׳ 162 ואילך. ועל כך ראוי שתהיה תחילת דינו של אדם, ששואלים אותו גם אם קבע עתים לתורה, אם ציפה לישועה, פלפל בחוכמה, הבין דבר מתוך דבר ואם נשא ונתן בהבטחה וקיים את דברו (שבת לא ע"א), שזה כל האדם, ראו המאמר שצוין לעיל בהערה 24. (השאלה היא שאלת הבחירה החופשית, ואכמ"ל.( וראו נידה ע ע"ב, ששם המליצו לרוצה להעשיר להרבות בסחורה ולשאת ולתת באמונה. ייתכן, כמובן, שהסוחר ביושר זוכה ללקוחות רבים יותר וכך יתעשר, אך לאור האמור נראה שהמסחר בסחורות שעתידות לבוא מרחיבות את היקף הסחורה הנסחרת גם על זו שתבוא בעתיד, וכך יגדל העושר. וראו מגילת ברית דמשק, מהד׳ קימרון, (ירושלים: תש"ע), עמ׳ 48, שורות 16–18: "ואיש מכל באי ברית אל ישא ואל יתן לבני השחת כי אם כף לכף (=במשיכה). ואל יעש איש דבר למקח ולממכר כי אם הודיע למבקר אשר במחנה ועשה בעצה [קמרון; לפי רבין: "באמנה"]. פיהם של בני השחת דיבר שווא, ועל כן אין לישא וליתן עימהם באמנה, מה שאין כן עם בני הברית. וראו הלכות דעות לרמב"ם פ"ב ה"ה, פ"ה הי"ג. וראו רבנו בחיי בר אשר, כד הקמח, אות א, אמונה: "וכבר שמענו כי יש ארצות בעולם שאין להם תורה כלל ומדרך השכל יש להם אמונה גדולה במשאם ומתנם עם כל אדם"; וראו שם תיאורו. וראו דברי רבנו נסים בהקדמתו לספר המפתח ושו"ת אבני נזר, חושן משפט, סי׳ לב בשם בעל חידושי הרי"ם על הטעם מדוע מזכירים בקללת "מי שאינו עומד בדיבורו" את דור המבול. חכמים מאוחרים התקשו לגשר על הפער שבין הביטויים המחייבים קיומן של הבטחות לבין האפשרות ההלכתית לחזור מהן ולא לקיימן, ראו: *שו"ת אבני נזר*, יורה דעה, סי׳ שו; *שו"ת* אהל משה, ב, סי׳ קלח.

74 בבא מציעא מח ע"א. וראו תוספתא בבא מציעא פ"ג הי"ד (מהד׳ ליברמן, עמ׳ 76). וראו שם, בהמשך ההלכה: "והנושא ונותן בדברים אין לו עליו אונאה, אבל אמרו חכמים כל המבטל את דבריו אין רוח חכמים נוחה הימנו." ובהלכה כ"ה: "כשם שאונאה במקח ומכר, כך אונאה בדברים. ועוד מרובה אונאת דברים מאונאת ממון, שבאונאת [ממון] הוא אומר ׳ולא תונו איש את אחיו׳, ובאונאת דברים הוא אומר ׳לא תונו איש את עמיתו ויראת מאלהיך.׳" ולכאורה הכוונה לאונאה בהבטחה, כפירושו של המונח "דברים" בכל המקורות האחרים. ואחר כך

רבא צימצם אפוא את הבעת הגנאי למי שאינו עומד בדיבורו רק לכך ש״רוח חכמים אינה נוחה הימנו״–ואין בו משום ״מחוסר אמנה״. בוודאי שאין מקללים אותו.[75] הקללה בידי האל–״מי שפרע״–לבד ובלא כפייה בידי בית הדין, באה רק על המוכר שקיבל ממון וחזר בו מעסקת המכר–כי לפי דין תורה מעות קונות ורק חכמים תיקנו שלא יקנו–ולא על הקונה, ולא במקרה שניתנה הבטחה למכור בלי שהמוכר קיבל דמים מן הקונה. גם הדין וגם ההשקפה משקפים עתה את העמדה שאין חובה לאדם לעמוד בדיבורו. והלוא דבר הוא! ואף שחכמים הביעו חוסר נחת ממי שאינו עומד בדיבורו, ואף שיש להניח שהבריות קיימו בדרך כלל את הבטחותיהם, בכל זאת ״מעשים שבכל יום [היו] שאסמכתא לא קניא״.

IX. אך חכמים לא פירשו את דבריהם בפרשה זו ואין אנו יכולים לדעת אם ירדנו לסוף דעתם.[76] אך בגלל הקושי הגדול מוטל עלינו להעלות השערות אפשריות כדי להסביר את פשר התופעה הזאת. ייתכן שהסיבה לכך תלויה בריבוי הכשפים שהיו בבבל ובשכיחותם של ה(א)מגושים שהיו המכשפים ובעלי השפעה גדולים.[77] לשיטתם של אלו, הדיבור הוא הדבר כשלעצמו;[78] וכשם שהכישוף מתקיים כך גם החוזה–ההבטחה היוצאת מפיו של אדם–יקוים כאילו אין הדבר תלוי ברצון

---

מוסיפה התוספתא עניינים אחרים היוצרים פגיעה בדיבור פה. ואכמ״ל. וראו מאמרי ״תשובה–בין תשובה גמורה לבין קבלה להבא״ (בדפוס).

וראו חידושי הר״ן לפסחים עב ע״א, ד״ה ״אהדרינהו,״ בשם הרב דוד, שאדם ״צריך לקיים התחייבותו ולעמוד בדיבורו אע״פ שלא יתחייב מן הדין.״ וראו גם ספר המנהיג, מהדורת י׳ רפאל, הקדמה, עמ׳ יט, על החיוב להיות דובר אמת גם בלבבו. וראו גם אמרי בינה, דיני דיינין, סימן מז.

75 ראו *שיטה מקובצת* על אתר מדברי הרשב״א והרא״ש. וכך גם בירושלמי בבא מציעא, שצוין בהערה 71. והשוו דברי המהרש״א על שפיהם של הגויים דיבר שווא ואילו שארית ישראל לא יעשו עולה ולא ידברו כזב. וראו גם *חידושי מהר״ץ חיות* על אתר. על ״מי שפרע״ ראו בהרחבה ר״ש קליינמן, ״קללת ׳מי שפרע׳; דת, משפט וחברה,״ *מחקרי משפט* כו (תש״ע), עמ׳ 179.

76 לתופעה דומה באנגליה של ימי הביניים ראו:

M.S. Arnold, "Fourteenth-century promises," *Cambridge Law Review* 35 (1976), 321: "All this supports the proposition that an important tenet of medieval morality was that promises ought to be kept. Yet the common law of promises was curiously retarded, thus creating what seems an odd gap between law and morality."

פער זה נעשה מוזר עוד יותר אם זוכרים שקודם למאה הארבע עשרה נהגו בתי המשפט באנגליה לאכוף הבטחות גם אם לא לבשו את הצורה הפורמלית של חוזה, כפי שעוצבה לאחר זמן.

77 על האמגושים ומלחמתם של חז״ל בהם ראו:

J. Neusner, "Rabbi and Magus in third-century Sasanian Babylonia," *History of Religion* 6 (1966/7), 169–78.

78 ראו ניסוחו של לאוטרבך:

J.Z. Lauterbach, "The belief in the power of the word," in idem, *Studies in Jewish Law, Custom, and Folklore* (NY: 1970), 143: "whatever is spoken . . . comes true and actually happens, that is to say, the word becomes fact."

המתחייב. באו חכמים להודיענו שבבחירה הדבר תלוי, ואין דיבורו של הקב״ה, שהוא כמעשה,[79] כדיבורו של האדם, שהוא בעל בחירה ויכול הוא גם לכזב.[80] ואולי נוספה על כך גם נוכחותו המתמדת של האל מיטרא ובתי הדין שגם כפו בפועל קיומן של הבטחות וגם הם שללו בכך את מהותו של האדם כבעל בחירה.[81] לכן צמצמו חכמים את כוחה המחייב של המילה היוצאת מן הפה רק למקרים שניתנו מעות, וגם אז לא הייתה זו אכיפה מלאה והסתפקו בקללת ״מי שפרע״. כאמור לעיל. מן הסתם הנימוקים הללו היו חשובים בעיניהם מן החובה לקיים הבטחה.

---

כידוע, המילה ״דבר״ משמשת לציון הן של דיבור והן של חפץ מוחשי. והוא הדין למילה ״חפץ״ עצמה: רצון וכלי. היחס בין הדיבור, הבעת הרצון ובין היצירה הממשית הוא רב משמעות.

79 ראו בראשית רבה מד כב (מהד׳ תאודור-אלבק, עמ׳ 445): ״אף מאמרו של הקב״ה מעשה.״ וכעין זה במדרש תהלים מב ג: ״אלא מאמרו של הקב״ה הוא מעשה. אמר הקב״ה: אמרתי דבר הרי מעשה נעשה.״

80 ראו דברי הרמב״ם: ״הן מין זה שלאדם היה אחד בעולם, ואין לו מין שני דומה לו בזה העניין: שיהא הוא מעצמו, בדעתו ובמחשבתו יודע הטוב והרע ועושה כל מה שהוא חפץ ואין לו מי שיעכב על ידו מלעשות הטוב או הרע.״ וכן ראו *בפירוש המשניות* של הרמב״ם, הקדמה למסכת אבות, פ״ח.

81 ראו מאמרי ״מדוע אין המשפט העברי אוכף קיומה של הבטחה?״ (לעיל, הע׳ 7).

# מעמדם של שני עדים לשיטת הרמב״ם

יובל סיני*

## הקדמה

״על פי שני עדים או על פי שלשה עדים יקום דבר״ נאמר בתורה.[1] ואכן, מקובלת התפיסה שעל פי המשפט העברי שני עדים כשרים הם ראיה מושלמת ולעדות שני עדים מעמד בכורה במסגרת דיני הראיות (בבחינת ״מלכת הראיות״), וכפי שכתב אשר גולאק, ״עדות היא הראיה היותר מוכיחה לפי דיננו״.[2] אמנם, כבר הצביעו חוקרים על כך כי אין לראות את הכלל של [רק] ״על פי שנים עדים יקום דבר״ ככלל גורף ונוקשה, וכי הלכה למעשה בתי הדין מסתמכים דבר יום ביומו על פחות משני עדים, כמו גם על ראיות נסיבתיות,[3] אולם אין הדבר מפחית כהוא זה ממשקלם המכריע של שני העדים ובחשיבותם העצומה בקביעת התשתית העובדתית שעליה עומד פסק הדין.[4]

ומהו תפקיד העדים על פי המשפט העברי? כמה מן המלומדים מבקשים לאפיין את מוסד העדות כדרך מיוחדת המוסמכת להוכחת דבר ולהכרעת הדין.[5]

* מרצה בכיר וראש המרכז ליישומי משפט עברי (ישמ״ע), המכללה האקדמית נתניה.

1 דברים יט טו.

2 ראו א׳ גולאק, *יסודי המשפט העברי*, ספר רביעי (תל אביב: תשכ״ז), עמ׳ 113. ביטוי קולע ואופייני לתפיסה זו ניתן להביא מדברי המבוא ל״הצעת חוק הראיות הישראלי, תשי״ג–1953״: ״דיני הראיות במשפט העברי (ובמשפטים קדומים אחרים) עשו סייג לשקר ע״י אמצעי פשוט בתכלית: כל מי שיש לחשוד בו שאינו מקפיד על האמת, פסול לעדות... עוד סייגים עשה המשפט העברי בהצריכו לכל דבר שני עדים כשרים... והחמירו עוד כהנה וכהנה בדיני נפשות. התוצאה היתה, כי אמנם לא באו בפני בתי הדין אלא עדים מוחזקים לדוברי אמת, ושום דבר לא נחתך אלא על פי עדות שני עדים כאלה, אך כל דבר שאי אפשר היה להוכיח בדרך זו, אי אפשר היה להוכיחו בכלל.״

3 ראו למשל ח״ש חפץ, ״על פי שני עדים יקום דבר–האמנם? ראיות נסיבתיות בבית הדין–הלכה למעשה,״ *תקדים* ב (תשמ״ט), עמ׳ 84–59. במחקרו הנרחב של חפץ, ראיות נסיבתיות במשפט העברי, עבודת דוקטור, האוניברסיטה העברית בירושלים, תשל״ד, הוכח כי בניגוד לתפיסה המקובלת שאין המשפט העברי מכיר הכרה פורמלית בקבילותן של ראיות נסיבתיות, באופן מעשי מתחשב המשפט העברי בראיות הנסיבתיות במסגרת דיני האומדנא המתייחסים לשיקול דעתו ולהתרשמותו של הדיין. וראו על כך גם במאמרים הנזכרים להלן בהע׳ 8.

4 לסקירת הנושא ראו:
"Witness," Encyclopedia Judaica (2nd edition, 2007), vol. 21, 115–25.

5 מאפיין זה הודגש לראשונה במחקרו החלוצי של ח״ש חפץ, ״מקומה של עדות במשפט העברי,״ *דיני ישראל* ט (תשל״ח/תש״מ), עמ׳ נא–פד. לניתוח רחב של הדברים ראו:
Shimshon Ettinger, "The role of witnesses in Jewish law," 22 *Dine Israel* (2003), 7–37.

חיים חפץ דימה את מוסד העדות לחבר המושבעים של שיטת המשפט האנגלו-האמריקאית,[6] שהם כבית משפט של הדיוטות לקביעת עובדות, היושב בדין בצד השופט המומחה, ומשיתוף הפעולה ביניהם נחתך ומוכרע הדין. שמשון אטינגר הציג לאחרונה תפיסה שונה במקצת, ולדידו שני העדים הינם גוף עצמאי מעין-שיפוטי המוסמך לקבוע את עובדות המקרה, ואילו השופטים אינם קובעים את העובדות אלא הם מאמצים את עדותם של העדים ופוסקים על פיה.[7]

מעמד הבכורה המיוחד של העדים במסגרת קביעת התשתית העובדתית שעל יסודה ניתן פסק הדין אכן עולה מסוגיות תלמודיות מרכזיות, כמו גם מדבריהם של פוסקים לא מעטים. ואונם, במאמר זה אבקש להראות כי הרמב״ם נקט בסוגיה זו עמדה ייחודית שונה בתכלית, אשר חותרת תחת מעמדם הראייתי-האובייקטיבי של שני העדים ומצמצמת עד מאוד את תפקידם בקביעת העובדות, ומסיטה את מרכז הכובד לאומד דעתו הסובייקטיבית של הדיין, שעל פי דעתו ולבו יקום דבר ולא על פי העדים. כפי שנראה להלן הרמב״ם היה ער לסתירה לכאורה בין תפיסתו העקרונית והנועזת לבין האתוס המקובל של דיני הראיות ״על פי שנים עדים יקום דבר״, אלא שבמאמר זה אציע כי יש להבין את עמדתו של הרמב״ם-המפקפקת בדרך ההסתמכות על העדים כדרך אמינה לגילוי האמת (בהשוואה לדרכים אחרות)-על רקע תפיסתו המטה-הלכתית, הפילוסופית-הדתית והמדעית הייחודית, שעליה נעמוד בהרחבה.

## א. אומד דעת הדיין

### 1. אומדנא-כללי

האומדנא, כלי עזר המסור בידי הדיין כדי להכריע את הדין, משמשת בשני תחומים:[8] העיקרי, כדי לעמוד על כוונת האדם במעשהו או בדיבורו על ידי הערכת

6 ראו חפץ, שם, עמ׳ סז-סח, עח-פ.

7 בהקשר זה ביקש אטינגר (לעיל, הע׳ 5) לעמוד על הייחוד שבעמדת המשפט העברי בהשוואה לשיטות משפט אחרות. וכך הוא כותב (עמ׳ 15):

> The conceptual definition of witnessing in Jewish law is different from what is familiar to us from other legal systems. Witnesses usually are regarded as an instrument for revealing and ascertaining facts. This is not the case in Jewish law, which regards witnesses as an independent body with the authority to determine the facts of the case. The court accepts and recognizes these facts and rules on the basis of witnesses' testimony. In other words, in Jewish law, there is an official body that, in its role and status, matches the court itself.

8 להרחבה ראו: אנציקלופדיה תלמודית, תשל״ג, עמ׳ רצה-שב, ערך אומדנא; י׳ סיני, *יישום המשפט העברי בבתי המשפט בישראל* (תל-אביב: תשס״ט), עמ׳ 220-210; הרב א״ד כץ, ״האומדן בדיני הראיות,״ *משפטי ארץ*-טענות וראיות ב (עפרה: תשס״ה), עמ׳ 165-107; הרב א׳ רותם, ״הכרעת דין ללא עדות-על השימוש באומדן ובראיות המודרניות בבית הדין הרבני,״

מניעיו;[9] והמשני בשימושו בספרות ההלכה, כדי לקבוע קביעה עובדתית של פרטי אירוע על ידי הערכת נסיבותיו, המוכרת בשפה המשפטית בשם ״ראיה נסיבתית״,[10] שהיא ראיה הדורשת הסקת מסקנה מהראיה לצורך ההוכחה. דיוננו להלן יתמקד בתחום המשני, ובעיקר בניתוח תפיסתו המשפטית של הרמב״ם בסוגיה זו. נקדים ונאמר כי מלבד הדרישה הראייתית היסודית במשפט העברי–הצורך בשני עדים שיעידו על הדבר[11] לשם הוצאת ממון בתביעה אזרחית–יש דרכים נוספות לבירור התביעה בבית הדין.[12] ואולם בשאלת קבילותה של ראיה נסיבתית נחלקו חכמים, ואלו הדברים:

> שור שהיה רועה ונמצא שור הרוג בצדו, אע״פ שזה מנוגח וזה מועד ליגח, זה מנושך וזה מועד לישוך–אין אומרים בידוע שזה נגחו וזה נשכו. רבי אחא אומר: גמל האוחר בין הגמלים ונמצא גמל הרוג בצדו–בידוע שזה הרגו.[13]

רוב הפוסקים[14] פסקו כדעת חכמים (הדעה הראשונה במשנה), שאין לקבל ראיה מעין זו אף על פי שהנסיבות מובילות למסקנה ברורה למדי כיצד אירע הדבר. האם פסיקה זו משמעותה דחייה למעשה של האפשרות להוכחה על סמך אומדנא וידיעת בית הדין, ומעתה הדרך היחידה להוכחה היא על פי שניים עדים? לאו דווקא.

ואלה דברי הרמב״ם בריש פרק כ״ד מהלכות סנהדרין:

> יש לדיין לדון בדיני ממונות על פי הדברים שדעתו נוטה להן שהן אמת, והדבר חזק בלבו שהוא כן, אף על פי שאין שם ראיה ברורה. ואין צריך לומר אם היה יודע בודאי שהדבר כן הוא, שהוא דן כפי מה שיודע.[15]

---

שם, עמ׳ 106–96; חיים חפץ, ״גדרי אומדנא וחזקה בדיני נפשות במשפט העברי,״ *דיני ישראל* ח (תשל״ז), עמ׳ מה–סג; הרב ב׳ ליפקין, ״בגדרי אומדנא ורוב בדיני ממונות ובדיני נפשות,״ *התורה והמדינה* יא–יג (תש״ך–תשכ״ב), עמ׳ תקמו–תקסז. כן ראו המאמרים הנזכרים להלן בהע׳ 10.

9 נציין כאן שתי דוגמאות: רמב״ם, הלכות זכייה ומתנה פ״ח הי״ד; *שולחן ערוך* חושן משפט, סי׳ רנ סעיף ב, על פי סוגיית התלמוד בבבא בתרא קמו ע״ב. כן ראו לשון הרמב״ם, שם פ״ו הי״ב; *שולחן ערוך* אבן העזר, סי׳ פה סעיף ז, על פי סוגיית התלמוד בכתובות עט ע״א. לדוגמאות נוספות, ראו אנציקלופדיה תלמודית, שם.

10 ראו: אנציקלופדיה תלמודית, שם ; סיני (לעיל, הע׳ 8), עמ׳ 214–212; י׳ בן מאיר, ״ראיה נסיבתית במשפט העברי,״ *דיני ישראל* יח (תשנ״ה–תשנ״ו), עמ׳ פז–קמג; חפץ (לעיל, הע׳ 3); הנ״ל, ״מקומן של ראיות נסיבתיות במשפט העברי,״ *משפטים* א (תשכ״ח), עמ׳ 85–67; הרב ב׳ ליפקין, ״אומד הדיינים,״סיני כ (תש״ז), עמ׳ קעח–קצח. כן ראו המאמרים הנזכרים לעיל בהע׳ 8.

11 דברים יט טו.

12 כגון הטלת חיוב שבועה חמורה מן התורה על הנתבע, אם הוא מודה בחלק מן התביעה או כשיש לתובע רק עד אחד–ראו *שולחן ערוך* חושן משפט, סי׳ פז סעיף א.

13 בבא בתרא צג ע״א; סנהדרין לז ע״ב; שבועות לד ע״א.

14 רמב״ם, הלכות נזקי ממון פ״ח הי״ד; *מהרי״ק*, שורש קכט; שולחן ערוך חושן משפט, סי׳ תח סעיף ב.

15 רמב״ם, הלכות סנהדרין פכ״ד ה״א, וכן הוא בשולחן ערוך חושן משפט, סי׳ טו סעיף ה.

הרמב״ם העניק משקל מכריע ביותר לאומד דעתו של השופט במסגרת דיני הראיות. לדעתו, קביעת התשתית הראייתית בדיני הממונות מסורה ״ללבו של דיין לפי מה שיראה לו שהוא דין האמת״, ובסמכותו להסתייע באומדן דעתו האישי כדי לקבוע את האמת העובדתית. בהמשך ההלכה מביא הרמב״ם שלוש דוגמאות לעיקרון זה, המיוסדות על סוגיות תלמודיות. הראשונה היא בעניין נתבע שנתחייב שבועה דאורייתא, שאם הדיין שמע ממקור מהימן (אף כזה שפסול לעדות) שהנתבע חשוד על השבועה אל לו לפסוק כדין הרגיל ולהשביעו אלא יש לו להפוך השבועה על התובע בהסתמך על אותו המקור המהימן (״קים לי בגווה״). השניה היא בעניין המוציא שטר שהדיין שמע מאיש אמין (עד אחד בלבד) שיש פגם בשטר, אל לו להגבות על פי שטר זה על פי הכלל ששטר מקוים גובים בו אלא לא יגבה על פי השטר. הדוגמא השלישית היא שאחד טוען שהיה לו פיקדון אצל פלוני שמת ונתן סימנים מובהקים, וידוע שהטוען לא היה רגיל להיכנס לבית המת כדי שנוכל לתלות שראה אצלו חפץ זה בסימניו, והמת לא היה אמוד שיהיה אצלו חפץ כזה, והדיין משוכנע שחפץ זה לא היה של המת, אזי הוא נותן את החפץ לתובע.

לאחר שהציג הרמב״ם את הדוגמאות הללו הוא מסכם באומרו זאת:

> וכן כל כיוצא בזה, שאין הדבר מסור אלא ללבו של דיין לפי מה שיראה לו שהוא דין האמת. אם כן, למה הצריכה תורה שני עדים? שבזמן שיבואו לפני הדיין שני עדים ידון על פי עדותן, אע״פ שאינו יודע אם באמת העידו או בשקר.

ואמנם, הלכה למעשה הרמב״ם פוסק בהלכה ב׳ שאין לנהוג בימינו בדרך זו (של אומדן דעתו האישית של הדיין) ויש לדון אך ורק על פי ראיות ברורות; אך גם הוא משאיר פתח רחב דיו לדיין לחתור לפסיקה המשקפת את מה שעיניו רואות ולבו משוכנע בדבר.[16]

במוקד חלקו הראשון של המאמר יבוא ניתוח דברי הרמב״ם בתחילת פרק כ״ד מהלכות סנהדרין. ניתוח מפורט ויסודי של שיטת הרמב״ם נעשה לאחרונה במחקרו המעניין של יעקב בלידשטיין,[17] וקדם לו מחקרו המעמיק של חיים חפץ,[18] וכן

16 וכך כותב הרמב״ם בהלכה ב׳: ״כל אלו הדברים הן עיקר הדין אבל משרבו בתי דינין שאינן הגונים ואפילו היו הגונים במעשיהם אינן חכמים כראוי ובעלי בינה הסכימו רוב בתי דיני ישראל שלא יהפכו שבועה אלא בראיה ברורה, ולא יפגמו שטר ויפסידו חזקתו בעדות אשה או פסול וכן בשאר כל הדינין ולא ידון הדיין בסמיכת דעתו ולא בידיעתו כדי שלא יאמר כל הדיוט לבי מאמין לדברי זה ודעתי סומכת על זה, וכן אין מוציאין מן היתומים אלא בראיה ברורה לא בדעת הדיין ולא באומדן המת או הטוען. ואעפ״כ אם העיד אדם נאמן בדבר מכל הדברים ונטתה דעת הדיין שאמת הוא אומר ממתין הוא בדין ואינו דוחה עדותו ונושא ונותן עם בעלי דינין עד שיודו לדברי העד או יעשו פשרה או יסתלק מן הדין.״

17 ראו יעקב בלידשטיין, ״ה׳אמת׳ ככלי פסיקה במשנת הרמב״ם–להלכות סנהדרין כד, א–ג,״ דיני ישראל כד (תשס״ז), עמ׳ 160–119.

18 חפץ (לעיל, הע׳ 10) , עמ׳ 64–50.

מחקריהם של הרבנים מיכאל בריס,[19] בנימין ליפקין[20] וחיים דוד הלוי.[21] במאמר זה אני מבקש לעמוד על כמה היבטים מרכזיים בשיטת הרמב״ם, שלא הודגשו עד כה במחקר.

היבט ראשון, שבו נעסוק בדברינו שלהלן, נוגע לטיבו המשפטי של אומד הדיינים לשיטת הרמב״ם. אחדים מן החוקרים שעסקו בניתוח שיטת הרמב״ם שייכו את הלכת הרמב״ם בעניין אומד הדיינים לדיני הראיות בכלל, ולדיני הראיות הנסיבתיות בפרט.[22] לפי גישה זו, אין הבדל עקרוני, כפי שצוין בידי כמה מהחוקרים, בין תורת האומדנא של הרמב״ם לבין תורת האומדנא של הרא״ש,[23] אשר סבר שאומדנא ברמת סבירות גבוהה (״אומדנא דמוכח״) קבילה בדיני ממונות.[24] ואולם להלן נבקש להציג עמדה שונה, ולפיה דברי הרמב״ם אינם

19 ראו הרב מ׳ בריס, ״מבוא להלכות עדות: כללים נוקשים ושכנוע הלב–עיון בשיטת הרמב״ם,״ *משפטי ארץ* (לעיל, הע׳ 8), עמ׳ 67–43.

20 ליפקין (לעיל, הע׳ 10).

21 הרב ח״ד הלוי, ״סמכות הדיינים לדון על פי אומד הדעת,״ *התורה והמדינה* יא–יג (תש״כ–תשכ״ב), עמ׳ נד–סה [= הנ״ל, *דבר המשפט*, א (תל–אביב: תשכ״ג), עמ׳ 150 ואילך].

22 נראה כי רבים הלכו בעקבות מחקרו של חיים חפץ (לעיל, הע׳ 3). מטרתו של חפץ במחקרו היא ״לברר את מקומן של ראיות נסיבתיות במסגרת דיני הראיות של שיטת המשפט העברי״ (שם, עמ׳ 265), ובמסגרת זו הוא מדגיש כי ״מצאנו, מונח עברי שהוא לגמרי אקוויבילנטי למונח ׳ראיה נסיבתית׳, והוא המונח: אומדנה.״ במסגרת זו של דיני הראיות הנסיבתיות הוא דן ״בשלש תורות אומדנה כלליות,״ ובכלל זה בשיטת הרמב״ם (עמ׳ 266–267. תפיסה דומה, הרואה בדברי הרמב״ם כעוסקים בדיני הראיות הנסיבתיות, עולה ממחקרו של בן מאיר (לעיל, הע׳ 10), עמ׳ צא–צג. אף מיכאל בריס (לעיל, הע׳ 19) משייך באופן ברור את שיטת הרמב״ם לדיני הראיות, כפי שהדבר מתבטא כבר בכותרת מאמרו: ״מבוא להלכות עדות: כללים נוקשים ושכנוע הלב–עיון בשיטת הרמב״ם.״ כיוצא בזה מדגיש בלידשטיין (לעיל, הע׳ 17), עמ׳ 121–122, ש״החופש שהוא מנת חלקו של הדיין מקומו בתחום הראיות ואפילו בתחום הפרוצדורה; הוא אינו נוגע לקביעת הדין . . . ההוראה המימונית נוגעת לשאלה על מה מסתמך הדיין בבואו לפסוק את הדין, כלומר, על דיני הראיות.״ כן ראו א׳ אדרעי, ״בית הדין כאביהם של יתומים,״ דיני ישראל יט (תשנ״ז–תשנ״ח), עמ׳ כב הע׳ 56.

23 *שו״ת הרא״ש*, כלל סח סי׳ כג; כלל עח סי׳ ג; כלל קז סי׳ ו.

24 מעיון בספרות הפוסקים ובספרות המחקר המודרני עולה הנטייה הברורה לטשטש את ההבדל בין שיטות הרמב״ם והרא״ש ולהציגן כשיטה אחת. במחקר המודרני הדגיש חפץ (לעיל, הע׳ 3), עמ׳ 96, ש״כפי שהערנו והראינו בעת הרצאת תורות האומדנה הכלליות של הרמב״ם והרא״ש וניתוחן, אין ביניהן מבחינה מעשית כמעט ולא כלום. בבוא דיין להעמיד המשפט על תלו ולהוציא דין אמת לאמתו, והדרך היחידה להשגתם היא להשתמש באומדנות, יכול הוא להסתמך על פסקי הרמב״ם או על פסקי הרא״ש במדה שווה, בהבדלי סגנון. גם לפי הרמב״ם גם לפי הרא״ש, על הדיין להשתמש בהן לפי הבנתו ומומחיותו לשם שמיים לעשיית דין אמת וצדק.״ עוד הוא מדגיש: ״ואילו באשר להבדל היסודי שהבחנו בין התורות, דהיינו שביסוס עקרון האומדנה לפי תורת הרמב״ם נמצא אך ורק בתודעתו הסוביקטיבית של הדיין, ולפי תורת הרא״ש עיקר הדגש הוא בהערכה האובייקטיבית של כחן המשכנע של העובדות – ההשלכה המעשית של הבדל עיוני מופשט זה מועטה ביותר.״ ובסיומה של הערכת היחס בין דברי הרמב״ם והרא״ש מדגיש חפץ זאת (עמ׳ 97): ״יוצא, איפוא, שההבדל המעשי בין תורת הרמב״ם לתורת הרא״ש בקשר לעקרון האומדנה הוא כחוט השערה, אם לא דק מזה. אי לכך, מכיוון שעקרון השמוש באומדנה משותף לשתיהן, ומכיוון שניסוח תורת הרמב״ם נוטה יותר לצד ההכללה והמופשט, וניסוח תורת הרא״ש נוטה יותר לצד הפירוש והמעשי, אך טבעי הוא, לדעתי, שמיזוג התורות יתבסס על נוסח הרמב״ם, תוך עיצוב תורתו העיונית, מדעת או שלא

מכוונים לדיני הראיות, וכי רב המרחק בין שיטתו לבין שיטת הרא״ש. לאחר מכן נעסוק בהיבט שני: תפיסתו המטה-הלכתית הייחודית של הרמב״ם אשר עומדת ברקע תפיסתו המשפטית.

## 2. שתי קריאות של הלכת הרמב״ם בפרק כ״ד מהלכות סנהדרין

את דברי הרמב״ם המצוטטים לעיל ניתן לקרוא בשתי קריאות שונות: קריאה שמרנית וקריאה רדיקלית. על פי הקריאה השמרנית, העולה מדברי פוסקים וחוקרים אחדים, הרמב״ם איננו מתנגד לאתוס המקובל של ״על פי שנים עדים יקום דבר״. כלומר, הרמב״ם איננו קובע כלל מחודש שעל פיו על הדיין לפסוק עקרונית על פי אומד דעתו הסובייקטיבית ולא על פי העדים,[25] והוא מעולם לא ביקש לחתור תחת מוסד העדות, שהוא–ולא הדיין–הגוף המוסמך לקביעת ראיות. אף הרמב״ם סבר לשיטה זו כי על השופט לפסוק את הדין על פי עדותם של העדים, ואין ביכולתו לדחות עדותם רק על סמך שיקול דעתו האישי.[26] על פי הקריאה השמרנית יש לפרש בצמצום רב את אפשרותו של השופט לפסוק על פי אומד דעתו בלבד, שהרי ״בדבר שהוא רק ידוע להדיין פסלו רחמנא בגזירת הכתוב״.[27] ומכל מקום אין ביכולתו של הדיין לפסוק על פי אומדן דעתו אלא רק בשלוש הדוגמאות שנזכרו

---

מדעת, לכיוון הזדהות מלאה עם תורתו המעשית של הרא״ש.״ ואכן, העמדת דברי הרמב״ם ודברי הרא״ש כמציגים תפיסה משפטית דומה עולה בבירור, כפי שהראה חפץ, מדברי גדולי הפוסקים, מחברי *הטור והשולחן ערוך*, שבפסיקתם כרכו את דברי הרמב״ם והרא״ש בחדא מחתא–ראו *טור ושולחן ערוך* חושן משפט, סי׳ טו סעיפים ג–ד. העמדה המטשטשת למעשה את ההבדל בין שיטת הרמב״ם לשיטת הרא״ש אומצה אף במחקר אחר העוסק הנושא הראיות הנסיבתיות, שבו הוצגה הדעה שלפיה הואיל וגם לשיטת הרא״ש ״רמת הסבירות של האומדנה נמדדת כמובן בדעתו של הדיין, הרי ש״על כן, אין בעצם הבדל משפטי מהותי בין שיטת הרא״ש לשיטת הרמב״ם״–ראו בן מאיר (לעיל, הע׳ 10), עמ׳ צב.

25 ראו ש׳ אלבק, *הראיות בדיני התלמוד* (רמת גן: תשמ״ז), עמ׳ 66: ״אבל לאמיתו של דבר פירוש דברי הרמב״ם הוא, שבין דיין שאינו בעל בינה ובין דיין מבעלי הבינה שדן לפי אומדן דעתו, אין אומדן זה אלא אומדן אובייקטיבי ולא סובייקטיבי, שכן, גם דין לפי אומדן דעתו של הדיין ולא לפי הדין אינו אלא ׳אומדנא לכל העולם׳, ׳דכשם שידוע לו כך ידוע לכל העולם׳, ׳אבל בדבר שהוא רק ידוע לדיין׳ אין לו לדון,״ ודבריו מיוסדים על דברי בעל *נתיבות המשפט* הנזכרים להלן בהע׳ 27. לבסוף מסכם אלבק וקובע זאת: ״נמצא, שלעולם דן הדיין לפי אומדן דעתו, כזה אומדן לפי דעת כל העולם, אומדן אובייקטיבי.״ אין ספק שפרשנות זו איננה עולה בשום אופן מדבריו הברורים של הרמב״ם, שעולה מהם מנגינה סובייקטיבית עזה, אלא שאלבק נאלץ לפרש כן כדי שדברי הרמב״ם לא יעמדו בסתירה לתיזה העקרונית שאותה מבקש אלבק להציג בספרו בדבר ״האובייקטיביות שבדיני הראיות.״ אולם ברור כי הרמב״ם לא קיבל תיזה זו; ודוק.

26 ראו אטינגר (לעיל, הע׳ 5), בעמ׳ 22.

27 כדברי בעל *נתיבות המשפט*, סי׳ טו סעיף ב, שביקש לצמצם את הלכת הרמב״ם מכח הדין של ״אין עד נעשה דיין,״ שלכאורה שולל את האפשרות שמי שראה בעיניו יוכל לשפוט באותו מקרה.

בדברי הרמב״ם, אך אין הוא יכול להוציא ממון על סמך אומדן דעתו,[28] ואין צריך לומר שאין הוא יכול לפסוק כנגד עדותם המפורשת של עדים.

ואולם, עיון מדוקדק יותר בדברי הרמב״ם מורה על האפשרות לקריאה רדיקלית יותר, שאני סבור שהיא משקפת יותר את פשטות לשונו של הרמב״ם והיא אף עולה בקנה אחד עם תפיסתו המטה-הלכתית-הפילוסופית (שעליה נעמוד בנפרד בפרק ב׳). לפי קריאה זו חובתו של הדיין לדון בדיני ממונות ״על פי הדברים שדעתו נוטה להן שהן אמת והדבר חזק בלבו שהוא כן״–וזהו הכלל המנחה העקרוני של הפסיקה בדיני הממונות-״שאין הדבר מסור אלא ללבו של דיין לפי מה שיראה לו שהוא דין האמת״. החובה לדון על פי אומד דעת הדיין איננה חלה רק בשלוש הדוגמאות שציין הרמב״ם בהלכה א׳-ובצדק העיר יעקב בלידשטיין, ש״דומה כי הרמב״ם לא רק הכליל על בסיס דוגמאותיו אלא גם הוסיף על הנאמר בהן״[29]-ועל כן בהגיעו לדוגמא השלישית מוסיף הרמב״ם ״וכן כל כיוצא בזה״ ובסיום דבריו בהלכה ג׳ הוא חותם ״וכן בשאר כל הדינים״.

אני סבור, וכאן הנקודה המרכזית, שלדעת הרמב״ם חובתו של הדיין לדון על פי אומד הדעת והלב אינה חלק מדיני הראיות, כפי שהבינו חוקרים ורבנים, אלא מדובר בהלכה עקרונית הנוגעת לדרכי הפסיקה של הדיינים ולא לדיני הראיות. על כן ברור מדוע לא כלל הרמב״ם דין זה בהלכות עדות, כפי שהיה מתבקש לפי התפיסה המקובלת שלפיה הלכת הרמב״ם נוגעת לדיני הראיות, אלא הרמב״ם כללה בהלכות סנהדרין, ובמסגרת פרק כ״ד דווקא, שעוסק כולו ביכולתו של הדיין לפסוק על פי שיקול דעתו בדיני ממונות (הלכות א–ג) ובדיני העונשין (הלכות ד-י). אין ספק שמיקומה של ההלכה בעניין אומד דעת הדיינים בידי הרמב״ם בפרק כ״ד מהלכות סנהדרין נעשה בכוונת מכוון וממנו יש ללמוד על טיבה המשפטי של הלכת אומד הדיינים, בבחינת דבר הלמד מעניינו.[30] על כן מדגיש הרמב״ם בתחילת דבריו בפרק כ״ד שפסיקת הדיין ״על פי הדברים שדעתו נוטה

28 ראו *נתיבות המשפט* שם, שמסביר כי היכולת לפסוק על פי אומדן דעת הדיין מוגבלת רק להרעת כוחו של שטר או להיפוך שבועה אך לא להוצאת ממון (שתי הדוגמאות הראשונות שמזכיר הרמב״ם). אמנם, הדוגמא השלישית שמביא הרמב״ם נוגעת להוצאת ממון מיתומים, אך בעל *התיבות* נדחק להסבירה בקובעו שמדובר במקרה ״שהוא אומדנא לכל העולם . . . דכשם שידוע לו כך ידוע לכל העולם, ובדבר שהוא אומד של כל העולם אין זה בגדר עדות.״ אחרונים נוספים הלכו בעקבות בעל הנתיבות וסברו שאומד הדיין לא מועיל להוציא ממון–ראו *חמדת שלמה*, אבן העזר, סי׳ לב ס״ק ט–י; *קובץ שיעורים*, חלק ב סי׳ לח, בד״ה ומ״ש; *אבן האזל*, הלכות סנהדרין כד א (וראו גם מה שכתב בהלכות שאלה ופקדון ו ד, ובהלכות נזקי ממון ח יד).

29 בלידשטיין (לעיל, הע׳ 17), עמ׳ 129. אף הרב בריס (ראו להלן הע׳ 50) דייק מדברי הרמב״ם ״אם כן למה הצריכה תורה שני עדים״ כי הוא לא הגביל דין זה למקרים של שינוי בנטל הראיה גרידא.

30 על שיטת המיון של הרמב״ם ראו יצחק טברסקי, *מבוא למשנה תורה לרמב״ם* (ירושלים: תשס״א), עמ׳ 182–240.

להן שהן אמת והדבר חזק בלבו שהוא כן, אף על פי שאין שם ראיה ברורה״– ללמדך שאין מדובר כאן בדיני הראיות, שהרי אין כאן ראיה ברורה (שני עדים כשרים) הנצרכת לקביעה עובדתית בהתאם לדיני הראיות, אלא מדובר כאן בכוח מיוחד המסור לדיין במסגרת דיני פסיקת הדין. חובתם של הדיינים לפסוק הדין לאור אומד דעתם ולבם נזכרה בדברי הרמב״ם בהלכות סנהדרין, פכ״א ה״ט: ״ומצדיק את הדין בלבו ואחר כך יחתכהו״.[31] ויושם אל לב השינוי המשמעותי בלשונו הזהב של הרמב״ם לעומת המקור התלמודי: בתלמוד מובאים דברי ריש לקיש ״צדק את הדין ואחר כך חתכהו״,[32] ואילו הרמב״ם הוסיף ״ומצדק את הדין בלבו ואחר כך יחתכהו״–שמשמעו שתנאי מוקדם לפסיקה (״יחתכהו״) הוא שהדיין יהיה משוכנע בנכונות פסק דינו ולבו אינו נוקפו. ללמדך, שהדיין חייב להישמע לרחשי לבו לאומד דעתו בבואו לפסוק, וכידוע הלב מסמל, לדברי הרמב״ם במורה נבוכים, את המחשבה, השכל והרצון באדם וביקום.[33] אין ספק לדעתי שכלפי החובה האמורה בפרק כ״א (=״ומצדיק את הדין בלבו ואחר כך יחתכהו״) של הדיין מכוונים דברי הרמב״ם בראשית פרק כ״ד מהלכות סנהדרין, ש״יש לדיין לדון בדיני ממונות על פי הדברים שדעתו נוטה להן שהן אמת והדבר חזק בלבו״, שהוא כאמור כלל בהלכות הפסיקה של הדיינים ולא כלל בדיני הראיות.

נראה כי בתפיסתו האמורה של הרמב״ם, שלפיה בכוחו של הדיין לקבוע את התשתית העובדתית על פי ראות עיניו ושלא בהסתמך על ראיות קבילות, מתבטאת התופעה שעליה עמד חנינה בן-מנחם, שלפיה גישתו העקרונית של המשפט העברי שונה מזו של המשפט המערבי. וכך הוא כותב:

> גורלו של בעל הדין נמסר בידיהם של אנשים, לא בידי הכלל והחוק היבש, אף שגם במשפט העברי קיימים כללים וחוקים כמובן. תפיסתו העקרונית של המשפט העברי היא, שלדיין יש חופש פעולה נרחב, ולעיתים, הוא רשאי לסטות ממערכת הכללים הקבועה של המשפט העברי. אמנם, בדרך כלל יכריע הדיין על פי כללים וחוקים קבועים, אך עדיין, באופן עקרוני, הוא משוחרר מעולו של הכלל המשפטי. אין הדיין מחויב לדין, אלא לצדק, אף שברוב המקרים, לא יסטה השופט מן הכלל... משום כך, נתפס השופט המערבי כטכנוקרט בעיני המשפט העברי. שופט זה יודע אמנם היטב את החוק, אך אין הוא מחנך, קובע נורמות חברתיות, ואחראי לתיקון העולם.

31 על הזיקה בין דברי הרמב״ם בפרק כ״ד לבין דבריו בפרק כ״א הצביע הרב בריס (לעיל, הע׳ 19), עמ׳ 49.

32 סנהדרין ז ע״ב.

33 ראו *מורה נבוכים*, חלק א, פרקים לט, מו. וראו י׳ אבן שמואל (מהדיר), *ספר מורה נבוכים*, א, (ירושלים: תש״ט), עמ׳ 183–180.

לעומתו, הדיין נתפס כמחנך, קובע נורמות, ומכאן גם נובעת הדרישה לסגולות אישיות[34] מתאימות של הדיין.[35]

ואכן, בפרק כ״ד מהלכות סנהדרין הרמב״ם מעלה על נס את כוחו של הדיין לפסוק את הדין על פי שיקול דעתו, הן בדיני ממונות והן בדיני נפשות, הן במישור המהותי והן במישור של קביעת האמת העובדתית על פי דעתו של הדיין.[36] לפי גישה זו, המעניקה משקל רב כל כך לאומד דעתו של הדיין, אף מובן ביותר הצורך בסגולות אישיות נעלות של הדיין, ולא ייפלא אפוא שבהלכה ב׳ מסייג הרמב״ם את כוחו של הדיין לדון על פי אומד דעתו: ״כל אלו הדברים הן עיקר הדין אבל משרבו בתי דינין שאינן הגונים ואפילו היו הגונים במעשיהם אינן חכמים כראוי ובעלי בינה הסכימו רוב בתי דיני ישראל שלא... ידון הדיין בסמיכת דעתו ולא בידיעתו כדי שלא יאמר כל הדיוט לבי מאמין לדברי זה ודעתי סומכת על זה״.

תפיסתו העקרונית של הרמב״ם בעניין כוחו של דיין לקבוע עובדות לפי אומד דעתו ולבו עשויה אף להנהיר את עמדתו של הרמב״ם ביחס לאופן התמודדותו של דיין עם דין מרומה,[37] המוצגת בהלכה הבאה בפרק כ״ד (ה״ג):

> ומנין לדיין שהוא יודע בדין שהוא מרומה שלא יאמר אחתכנו ויהיה הקולר תלוי בצואר העדים, תלמוד לומר מדבר שקר תרחק. כיצד יעשה בו? ידרוש ויחקור הרבה בדרישה ובחקירה של דיני נפשות, אם נראה לו לפי דעתו שאין בו רמיות חותך הדין על-פי העדות. אבל אם היה לבו נוקפו שיש בדין רמיות, או שאין דעתו סומכת על דברי העדים אף על פי שאינו יכול לפוסלן, או שנוטה דעתו שבעל דין זה רמאי ובעל ערמה והשיא את העדים אף על פי שהן כשרים ולפי תומם הטעם, או שנראה לו מכלל הדברים שיש שם דברים אחרים מסותרין ואינן רוצים לגלותם, כל אלו הדברים וכיוצא בהן אם באו לדיין בדין אסור לו לחתוך אותו הדין, אלא יסלק עצמו מדין זה, וידוננו מי שלבו

34 על סגולות אלה ראו י׳ בזק, *השופט במשפט העברי* (ירושלים: תשמ״ה), עמ׳ 21–17.

35 ח׳ בן-מנחם, ״ענישה שלא מן הדין,״ *משפטי ארץ-דין דיין ודיון* (עפרה: תשס״ב), עמ׳ 153–152. להרחבה ראו:

H. Ben-Menahem, *Judicial Deviation in Talmudic Law: Governed by Men, Not by Rules* (Chur, Switzerland: 1991).

36 ויפה כתב חפץ (לעיל, הע׳ 3), עמ׳ 52 ואילך, שתפיסתו של הרמב״ם בראש פרק כ״ד מהלכות סנהדרין ״הופכת מן הקצה אל הקצה את המושגים היסודיים השוררים אצלנו על ׳יחסי הכוחות׳ בין דיין ועדים במסגרת דיני הראיות של המשפט התלמודי. הדיין, לפי תפיסת הרמב״ם הוא הוא העמוד העיקרי, כמעט הבלעדי, שכל בנין המשפטים שבין אדם לחברו עומד עליו. הוא ולא אחר קובע את האמת העובדתית. ואף אם נגד אמת זו יעמדו עדים רבים, אין הוא רשאי לדון אלא על-פי האמת הידועה לו, כי ׳אין הדבר מסור אלא ללבו של דיין, לפי מה שיראה שהוא דין אמת׳. שכנועו האישי וידיעתו הם העיקר, ולא שום גורם חוץ ממנו.״ תמונה דומה מציג אף רח״ד הלוי *בדבר המשפט* (לעיל, הע׳ 21), עמ׳ 151–150.

37 עליה הרחבתי ב-*השופט וההליך השיפוטי במשפט העברי* (ירושלים: תש״ע), עמ׳ 465–385.

שלם בדבר, והרי הדברים מסורים ללב והכתוב אומר "כי המשפט לאלהים הוא" (דברים א יז).

לדעת הרמב"ם, כשהדיין "יודע בדין שהוא מרומה" עליו להשתמש בכוחו ו"ידרוש בו ויחקור הרבה בדרישה וחקירה של דיני נפשות". אך מה קורה, לדעת הרמב"ם, כשהדרישות והחקירות לא הועילו ולא התבררה הרמאות, ואף על פי כן "לבו של הדיין נוקפו שיש בו רמאות"? במצב זה הוא דן בסיפא, שם הוא קבע שאסור לדיין "לחתוך אותו הדין, אלא יסלק עצמו מדין זה, וידוננו מי שלבו שלם בדבר". הרמב"ם סבר כי דיין שליבו נוקפו שיש בדין רמאות "יסלק עצמו מדין זה", אך יעבירנו לדיין אחר שלבו שלם בדבר, והלה יפסוק את הדין בהתאם לראות עיניו. ומדוע יעבירנו לדיין אחר, והרי אם הדיין הראשון הסיק שמדובר בדין מרומה הרי שמדובר בקביעה ראייתית וכיצד יכול דיין אחר להתעלם מקביעה זו ולפסוק את הדין בניגוד לקביעת הדיין הראשון? יותר הגיונית לכאורה עמדתם של הרא"ש והטור, שסברו שבמקרה שדיין קבע שמדובר בדין מרומה אסור גם לדיין אחר לדון בדבר[38] אלא הדיין הראשון "יסלק עצמו מדין זה וידוננו מלכו של עולם".[39] ואולם לדעתי יש להבין את דברי הרמב"ם לאור שיטתו הייחודית, השונה משיטת הרא"ש והטור, ולפיה כוחו של הדיין לפסוק על פי דעתו ולבו אינה כלולה במסגרת דיני הראיות אלא מדובר בסמכות ייחודית הקשורה לדרכי הפסיקה של הדיינים.[40] אם כך הדבר, מובן שקביעתו של דיין ראשון שמדובר בדין מרומה אינה קביעה ראייתית רגילה הכובלת דיינים אחרים, שהרי אין הדיין מסתמך על "ראיה ברורה" אלא על תחושתו הסובייקטיבית שהעדים העומדים בפניו אינם דוברי אמת. אמנם, אסור לדיין עצמו להתכחש לתחושותיו ואין לו לדיין אלא מה שעיניו רואות, אך הדבר נובע כאמור מדיני פסיקת הדין המורים לדיין לצדק הדין בליבו ואחר כך לחתוך אותו. ויש להדגיש: אין כאן כל קביעה ראייתית המחייבת דיינים אחרים, אלא כהדגשתו של הרמב"ם "הרי הדברים מסורים ללב", דהיינו ללבו של הדיין שעליו לצדק הדין לפני שחותכהו, ועל כן אם לבו של דיין אחד נוקפו שיש בדבר רמאות אין כל מניעה–ואדרבה הדבר רצוי[41]-שדיין אחר ידון בדבר ובלבד ש"ידוננו מי שלבו שלם בדבר".

38 כדברי הרא"ש בתשובתו, כלל סח, סימן כ, שבדין מרומה פסק "אני אומר שאין לשום דיין מישראל להשתדל בדין זה, וזה אני כותב וחותם ונותן ביד הנתבע." לדיון נרחב בשיטת הרא"ש בדין מרומה ראו חיבורי הנזכר בהערה הקודמת, עמ' 460–449.

39 *טור*, חושן משפט סי' טו.

40 מדברי הרא"ש המקשר במקומות שונים בין דין מרומה ובין אומדנא דמוכח נראה כי הוא ראה בשני אלו חלק מדיני הראיות (ראו *שו"ת הרא"ש*, כלל סח סי' כ; כלל קז סי' ו, ועוד). ואין כאן המקום להאריך בביאור ההבדל בין הרמב"ם לבין הרא"ש בסוגיה זו.

41 כפי שהראיתי בחיבורי (לעיל, הע' 37), בעמ' 425–423.

נמצא אפוא ש״בדינים שבלב״ עסקינן ולא בדיני הראיות שמעצם טבעם אובייקטיביים הם.

## 3. בין אומדנא דמוכח לבין אומדן דעת הדיין

על פי הפרשנות המוצעת בדברי הרמב״ם, שלפיה סמכותו של הדיין לדון על פי אומד דעתו נובעת מהלכות פסיקת הדיינים ולא מדיני הראיות, אפשר אף ליישב את אחד הקשיים המרכזיים שהעלו פרשני הרמב״ם וגדולי הפוסקים על שיטתו. דברי הרמב״ם בראש פרק כ״ד מהלכות סנהדרין, שניתן לדיין לפסוק על פי אומדן דעתו עומדים לכאורה בסתירה לדבריו במקומות אחרים, שעולה מהם כי עדות נסיבתית או אומדנא אינן קבילות הן בדיני נפשות[42] הן בדיני ממונות.[43] בתירוץ קושיא זו נדחקו הפרשנים רבות,[44] ברם לפי דרכנו אין כל סתירה בדברי הרמב״ם. שהרי אמנם על פי דיני הראיות אין לסמוך לשיטתו על עדות נסיבתית או על אומדנא אף בדיני הממונות, אך כל זה אמור כשאין לבו של הדיין משוכנע בדבר, שאז צריך הדיין להתבסס על הראיות, ובמקרה כזה אומרת לו ההלכה שאין הוא יכול להסתמך על פחות משני עדים. עם זאת, כאשר הדיין משוכנע בדעתו ובלבו שדבר

42 כדבריו בהלכות סנהדרין פ״כ ה״א: ״אין בית דין עונשין באומדן הדעת אלא על פי עדים בראיה ברורה.״ כן ראו דבריו הידועים *בספר המצוות*, לא תעשה רצ.

43 הרמב״ם פסק כשיטת חכמים האוסרים להסתמך על אומדנא, במחלוקתם עם ר׳ אחא בגמל האוחר בין הגמלים, שהוצגה לעיל ליד ציון 13; ואלו הם דבריו בהלכות נזקי ממון פ״ח הי״ד: ״שור שהיה רועה על גב הנהר ונמצא שור הרוג בצדו. אף על פי שזה מנוגח וזה מועד ליגח זה מנושך וזה מועד לישך אין אומרין בידוע שזה נשכו וזה נגחו אפילו גמל האחור בין הגמלים ונמצא גמל הרוג בצדו אין אומרין בידוע שזה הרגו עד שיראוהו עדים כשרים.״

44 ביישוב קושיא זו כתבו רבים כי אף הרמב״ם מודה שאומדנא ברמה גבוהה ביותר קבילה אף בדיני ממונות–ראו למשל: *אחיעזר*, חלק א סי׳ כה אות ד; *אבני נזר*, אבן העזר, חלק א סי׳ ל ס״ק ג, סי׳ קיט ס״ק קד; *תומים*, סי׳ צ ס״ק יד; *מהר״ם מינץ*, סי׳ כג; *קובץ שיעורים*, חלק ב סי׳ לח. אולם הסבר זה אינו עולה בקנה אחד עם לשונו הברורה של הרמב״ם בהלכות נזקי ממון פ״ח הי״ד, שלא הבחין בין רמות שונות של אומדנא. ואמנם אחדים מהפרשנים ביקשו להביא ראיה לשיטתם מדברי הרמב״ם בהלכות חובל ומזיק פ״ה ה״ד, שפסק כי הנחבל נוטל פיצויים גם על נזק שההוכחה שנגרם מבוססת על אומדנא דמוכח ש״היו שני עדים מעידין אותו שנכנס לתוך ידו שלם ויצא חבול ולא ראוהו בעת שחבל בו.״ אלא שאף מדברי הרמב״ם בהלכות חובל ומזיק אין כל ראיה שהוא סבר שניתן להסתמך בדיני ממונות על אומדנא דמוכח, שהרי שם מדובר על תקנה מיוחד של חכמים, כהדגשתו בתחילת ההלכה שם: ״קנס קנסו חכמים לאלו השוטים בעלי זרוע״ וכו׳. פרשנים אחרים ביקשו ליישב את הסתירה בדברי הרמב״ם בהבחינם בין הוצאת ממון על פי אומדנא, שאינה אפשרית לשיטת הרמב״ם, לבין פסיקה שאינה מוציאה ממון שבה יכול הדיין לפסוק על פי אומדנא (ראו ההפניות הנזכרות בהע׳ 28). אך כפי שכתבתי לעיל בסעיף 2 אין פרשנות זו עולה בקנה אחד עם לשון הרמב״ם. פרשנות אחרת שהועלתה בידי בעל *ישועות ישראל* (סי׳ טו ס״ק ד), שלפיה בשיטת הרמב״ם אמנם לא קבילה אומדנא בדיני ממונות, ואילו בפרק כ״ד מהלכות סנהדרין מדובר בגדול הדור שיכול לדון מכח הפקר בית דין הפקר. ואולם נראה שאף פרשנות זו אינה עולה בקנה אחד עם דברי הרמב״ם, שלא הגביל דבריו בגדול הדור דווקא, דבריו (בפשטות) נוגעים לכל דיין. ואדרבה, מהמשך דבריו בהלכה ב׳ על הדיינים שאינם חכמים ואינם הגונים משמע שאף דבריו בהלכה א׳ אמורים בדיינים אלו.

מסוים אירע, הרי שמכח הלכות פסיקת הדיינים אין לו לדיין אלא מה שעיניו רואות, והרי הוא מחויב לפסוק על פי מה שמורה לו לבו ובהתעלם מדיני הראיות. ההבחנה הברורה בין דיני הראיות–ובתוכם האיסור הקיים לדעת הרמב״ם להסתמך על אומדנא דמוכח–ובין סמכותו של הדיין לפסוק על פי מה שלבו ודעתו מורים, ואף בהעדרם של עדים קבילים, עולה מפורשות מדברי הרמב״ם בפרק ו׳ מהלכות שאלה ופקדון (ה״ד):

> מי שבא ואמר כך וכך הפקדתי אצל אביכם ונתן סימנים מובהקין ונמצא הפקדון כמו שאמר והיה הדיין יודע שלא היה המת אמוד שזה הפקדון שלו יש לדיין הזה ליתן הפקדון לזה שנתן סימניו. והוא שלא יהיה המפקיד רגיל להכנס לזה שמת אבל אם היה רגיל אצלו שמא של אחר הוא והכיר הסימנין שלו. באו עדים והעידו לדיין שאין זה אמוד אין מוציאין מן היתומים בעדותן, שאין זו ראייה ברורה ואומדן דעתן אינו אומד דעתו ואין לדיין אלא מה שדעתו סומכת עליו כמו שיתבאר בהלכות סנהדרין.

עינינו הרואות אפוא, כי הרמב״ם מבחין באופן ברור בין עדות הראיה הישירה של שני עדים (שרשאים להעיד על מה שראו בלבד), שהיא–ורק היא–״רְאָיה ברורה״, לבין כוחו של הדיין לפסוק על פי מה שדעתו סומכת עליו,[45] שאינו מדיני הראיות אלא מדיני פסיקת הדיינים כפי שהוסבר בהלכות סנהדרין.[46]

הנה כי כן, לשיטת הרמב״ם הדיין חייב לפסוק על פי האמת כפי שהוא מבין אותה, אף אם היא נובעת ממסקנות שהוא מסיק מתוך נסיבות המקרה ולא על פי ״ראיה ברורה״, אולם כאשר לא ברור לדיין מהי האמת הוא יכול להכריע רק על פי שני עדים שהם ״ראיה ברורה״. לפיכך הערכות שאין הדיין משוכנע בהן אישית מנסיבות המקרה, ונובעות רק מהערכת העדות הנסיבתית, דוגמת אומדנא דר׳ אחא

45 והשוו לדברי הרמב״ם בהלכות נחלות פי״א ה״א: ״אם ידע הדיין שאין זה אמוד.״

46 לפי דרכנו מובן היטב ההבדל בין שיטת הרמב״ם ובין שיטת הרא״ש הנזכרת לעיל ליד ציון 23, ואין לקבל את המגמה (הנזכרת לעיל בהע׳ 24) המבקשת לטשטש את ההבדל בין שתי השיטות. לדעתי, אין ההבדל בין שיטת הרמב״ם לשיטת הרא״ש נוגע רק לשאלה אם האומדנא שיש לסמוך עליה היא אובייקטיבית או סובייקטיבית, כהסברו של חפץ (כמובא בהע׳ 24), אלא מדובר בהבדל משמעותי הרבה יותר הנוגעת להבחנה בין דיני ראיות לבין דיני פסיקת הדיינים. הרא״ש, שלא כרמב״ם, סבר כי אפשר לדון בדיני ממונות על פי אומדנא דמוכח וכשיטת ר׳ אחא (ראו *שו״ת הרא״ש*, כלל סח סי׳ כג), ולדידו מדובר בחלק מדיני הראיות, כעולה מתשובותיו הנזכרות לעיל בהע׳ 38. הרמב״ם לעומת זאת סבר כי אמנם לפי דיני הראיות אין לקבל אומדנא בדיני הממונות, אלא שמדיני פסיקת הדיינים על הדיין לפסוק על פי מה שעיניו רואות, גם אם הדבר אינו מבוסס על ראיה ברורה הנצרכת על פי דיני הראיות. להבחנה עקרונית זו בין שיטת הרמב״ם לבין שיטת הרא״ש יש גם נפקויות הלכה למעשה (לדוגמא ראו מה שכתבנו להלן בהע׳ 55). דיון נרחב בניתוח ההבדלים שבין שיטת הרא״ש לבין שיטת הרמב״ם חורג ממסגרת מחקרנו ועוד חזון למועד, אי״ה.

הנזכרת למעלה, אינן קבילות לשיטת הרמב״ם. אמנם, גם לפי דעה זו אם ישתכנע הדיין שבנסיבות המקרה באמת יש קשר סיבתי בין מותו של הגמל לבין פעולתו של הגמל האוחר, אומדנא זו של הדיין תהיה קבילה.[47]

## 4. עדיפות אומד הדעת הסובייקטיבי של הדיינים על פני עדותם של שני עדים

מובן שהדגשת חובתו של הדיין לפסוק על פי שכנוע הלב, לפי שיטת הרמב״ם, עומדת לכאורה בסתירה לציווי התורה לפסוק על פי שני עדים. המתח האמור כבר הודגש בתלמוד בהקשר לביקורת שנאמרה, לפי אחת מהדעות, על דרך פסיקתו של שלמה: ״בקש קהלת לדון דינין שבלב, שלא בעדים ושלא בהתראה, יצתה בת קול ואמרה לו ׳וכתוב ישֶר דברי אמת׳ (קהלת יב י)– ׳על פי שנים עדים׳ (דברים יז ו) וגו׳״.[48] נראה כי עיקר הביקורת על משפט שלמה נסובה על שרצה לדון על פי אומד דעתו ולבו,[49] ללא הסתמכות על עדים וללא קיום הליכים משפטיים מקובלים. אף הרמב״ם חש במתח שבין חובת הדיין לפסוק ״דינים שבלב״ לבין דיני הראיות המורים ״על פי שנים עדים יקום דבר״, אך הוא הסיק מסקנה אחרת מזו הנזכרת בתלמוד.

ואכן, אף דברי הרמב״ם בסוף הלכה א–״אם כן למה הצריכה תורה שני עדים? שבזמן שיבואו לפני הדיין שני עדים ידון על פי עדותן אף על פי שאינו יודע אם באמת העידו או בשקר״–יש לקרוא על פי הקריאה הרדיקלית של הרדב״ז:[50] ״ומכאן יש

47 כפי שהעיר אל נכון חפץ (לעיל, הע׳ 3), תחילת עמ׳ 55. על דברי הרמב״ם (על פי ביאורו של חפץ) הקשה בן מאיר (לעיל, הע׳ 10), עמ׳ צא, וזה לשונו: ״יש מקום לביקורת על ההבחנה בין ׳אומדנה סובייקטיבית של הדיין׳, שהיא קבילה, לבין ׳אומדנה אובייקטיבית של העדות׳, שהיא לא קבילה–שהרי גם היא קבילה, באם הדיין מקבל אותה (בנסיבות המקרה) כאמיתית, שהרי אז היא אומדנה של הדיין. ובאם אין הדיין חושב שהיא נכונה בנסיבות המקרה–הרי בודאי שאיננה אומדנה מכרעת במקרה זה. בכל מקרה הרמב״ם היה צריך להזכיר שגם אומדנה של רב אחא היא קבילה, ובתנאי שהדיין חושב שהיא נכונה בנסיבות המקרה״. ואולם, לפי דברנו למעלה אין כל קושי בדבר. הרמב״ם הדגיש באופן ברור בהלכות שאלה ופקדון את ההבחנה בין ״ראיה ברורה״ לבין אומד דעתו של הדיין (ואין הדבר תלוי בסובייקטיביות מול אובייקטיביות, אלא בהבדל היסודי בין דיני הראיות לדיני פסיקת הדיינים), ושם אף הפנה להלכות סנהדרין (הואיל ואף שם דן בדוגמא שנזכרת בהלכות שאלה), ועל כן לא היה צריך לחזור על הדבר גם ביחס לאומדנא דרב אחא (בהלכות נזקי ממון), ובפרט ששם עסק אך ורק בהיבטים הראייתיים בלבד ולא בהיבטים הקשורים לפסיקת הדיין, שבהם הוא דן בהלכות סנהדרין. ודוק.

48 ראש השנה כא ע״ב. ביקורת נוקבת על דרך פסיקתו של שלמה עולה גם בקהלת רבה י טז (במהדורת וגשל פיסקא יח). להרחבה ראו כ״ץ (לעיל, הע׳ 8), עמ׳ 111–108.

49 ראו *תורה תמימה*, דברים יז י, אות יח, שמפרש שפסיקת שלמה היתה ״על פי אומדנא דמוכח שזה הרג את זה.״

50 בפירושו לדברי הרמב״ם שם, סוף ה״א. ושמא יש לדמות זאת למה שנאמר בתלמוד ביחס למשיח ש״מורח ודאין״ (סנהדרין צג ע״ב).

ללמוד שאם יודע שהעידו שקר לא יאמר יהיה הקולר תלוי בצואר העדים אלא ידון לפי מה שהוא יודע[51] ולא יחוש לעדים". ובלשון אחר: על הדיין לפסוק בהתאם "לדינים שבלב" ולאומד דעתו גם כאשר הדבר מנוגד למה שהעדים קובעים.

על רקע זה מובנת ביתר שאת שאלתו של הרמב"ם "אם כן למה הצריכה תורה שני עדים?"; בקשר לשאלה זו של הרמב"ם העיר יעקב בלידשטיין: "אני מתרשם (אם כי הנושא טעון בדיקה מקיפה) ששאלותיו המפורשות של הרמב"ם (במשנה תורה, לכל הפחות) מציגות בדרך כלל ערעורים רציניים למדי על תורותיו שלו".[52] ואמנם, יש בדיני הראיות הקבועים בתורה ואשר קובעים כי "על פי שנים עדים או על פי שלשה עדים יקום דבר" משום ערעור רציני של תפיסתו מרחיקת הלכת של הרמב"ם שלפיה האמת העובדתית נקבעת על פי דעתו של הדיין. אך למעשה נראה שאף תשובתו של הרמב"ם נותנת מענה חלקי בלבד לשאלתו "אם כן למה הצריכה תורה שני עדים", שהרי גם לפי תשובתו מקבל מוסד העדות חשיבות משנית בלבד, שהרי שני העדים משמשים רק כלי נוסף שאפשר לקבוע באמצעותו את התשתית הראייתית רק במקום שהדיין אינו מסוגל לקבוע את האמת העובדתית מדעתו ומלבו; ויפה הדגיש בלידשטיין, ש"הפסיקה על פי דברי העד אינה משקפת את הכרת הדיין כי העד דיבר אמת, אלא את הנורמה התורנית של פסיקה על פי עדים כשרים כל עוד לא הוכחו כמשקרים".[53] אך כאמור דרך המלך לדעת הרמב"ם היא שיש לקבוע עובדות על פי דעתו ולבו של הדיין – ולא על פי שני עדים[54] – וכאשר הדיין מסוגל לקבוע מדעתו ומלבו מהי האמת העובדתית, עליו לפסוק על פי האמת גם אם היא מתנגשת בשני עדים.[55]

51 ואמנם, כאמור בהלכה ב׳, הסמכות לדון על פי אומד הדעת צומצמה הלכה למעשה, ואם כן דברי הרדב"ז "אלא ידון לפי מה שהוא יודע" משקפים את "עיקר הדין" בלבד. ומכל מקום, יכול הדיין לדון בדין מרומה בהתאם למה שקבע הרמב"ם בהלכה ג׳.

52 בלידשטיין (לעיל, הע׳ 17), עמ׳ 125 הע׳ 17. המחבר מציין לדוגמא לדברי הרמב"ם בהלכות תשובה פ"ה ה"ה; הלכות ממרים פ"ב ה"ט; הלכות מלכים פ"א ה"ב.

53 בלידשטיין, שם, עמ׳ 126. וראה ראיותיו מדברי הרמב"ם במקומות אחרים ב*משנה תורה*.

54 ויפה כתב בריס (לעיל, הע׳ 19), עמ׳ 52: "פשוטם של דברי הרמב"ם מורה, אפוא, שהוא ראה באומדן הדיינים תחליף לדיני הראיות אשר אף עדיף על פניהם, ולא הגביל דין זה למקרים של שינוי בנטל הראיה גרידא."

55 אין צריך לומר שתפיסה זו אינה מקובלת על הרא"ש, שהרי הוא הדגיש בתשובתו (כלל קז סי׳ ו), שיש "רשות לדיין לפסוק לפי ראות עיניו, במקום שאין הדבר יכול להתברר בראיות ובעדיות, פעמים באומד הדעת." כלומר, הותר לדיין לפסוק על פי ראות עיניו רק כאשר אין אפשרות אחרת, שהרי "אין הדבר יכול להתברר בראיות ובעדיות." על פי שיטת הרא"ש ברור שאין הדיין יכול לפסוק לפי ראות עיניו בניגוד לעדותם המפורשת של שני עדים. בנקודה זו יש אפוא נפקות מעשית בין שיטת הרמב"ם לבין שיטת הרא"ש; ודוק. וראה דברינו לעיל בהע׳ 46.

## ב. היסודות המטה-הלכתיים

הרמב״ם היה ער, כפי שראינו בפרק הקודם, לכך שתפיסתו העקרונית והנועזת עומדת לכאורה בסתירה לאתוס המקובל של דיני הראיות ש״על פי שנים עדים או שלושה עדים יקום דבר״. בפרק זה אבקש להראות כי יש להבין את עמדתו של הרמב״ם, המפקפקת בדרך ההסתמכות על העדים כדרך אמינה לגילוי האמת-בהשוואה לדרכים אחרות-על רקע תפיסתו המטה-הלכתית, הפילוסופית-הדתית והמדעית הייחודית, שעליה נעמוד בהרחבה.

### 1. מקורות הידע האנושי

בשלושה מקומות בכתביו הרמב״ם הדגיש שאין לראות בעדותם של שני עדים מקור מידע ודאי, אלא שניתן להסתמך עליו אך ורק בגלל שהתורה חידשה זאת-הלא דבר הוא! הבה נעיין במקצת מהמקומות ונעמוד על פשר עמדה זו של הרמב״ם.

בהלכות יסודי תורה (פ״ז ה״ז) כתב הרמב״ם שיש לשמוע לנביא אם ״היה מהלך בדרכי הנבואה בקדושתה ובפרישותה, ואחר כך בא ועשה אות ומופת ואמר שהאל שלחו-מצוה לשמע ממנו, שנאמר ׳אליו תשמעון׳ (דברים יח טו)״; ואמנם, מוסיף הרמב״ם: ״ואפשר שיעשה אות ומופת ואינו נביא-וזה האות יש לו דברים בגו-ואף על פי כן מצוה לשמוע לו, הואיל ואדם גדול חכם וראוי לנבואה הוא, מעמידים אותו על חזקתו. שבכך נצטוינו, כמו שנצטוינו לחתך את הדין על פי שנים עדים כשרים-ואף על פי שאפשר שהעידו בשקר-הואיל וכשרים הם אצלנו מעמידים אותם על כשרותם. ובדברים האלו וכיוצא בהם נאמר ״הנסתרת לה׳ אלקינו והנגלת לנו ולבנינו״ (שם כט כח). ונאמר ״כי האדם יראה לעינים וה׳ יראה ללבב״ (שמואל א טז ז). הרמב״ם מבאר כי אמנם אנו צריכים להאמין שה׳ נגלה לכל נביא (מלבד משה), אך אין לנו דרך לדעת זאת אלא בצורה עקיפה, בקיום אותות המספקים לנו רמז והסתברות שהאדם שטוען שהאל התגלה לו הוא אכן שליח ה׳. כלומר, הציווי להישמע לנביא מבוסס על שיקול מסתבר מעדות החושים-ולא על בסיס טענה המוכחת באופן שכלי-דהיינו אם פלוני הראה אות ומופת, הרי הוא נביא אמת. על הסתברות כזו אכן מצווה אותנו התורה לסמוך, ולהחזיק לנביא את הטוען לנבואה אם מתקיימות בנבואתו כל שאר הדרישות ההלכתיות, כשם שהיא מצווה אותנו לסמוך על שני עדים שנחקרה עדותם ולחתוך על פיהם את הדין אם נתקיימו בהם כל הדרישות ההלכתיות.

כיוצא בזה כתב בהלכות יסודי תורה (פ״ח ה״ב) ביחס לעצם הציווי לשמוע בקולו של הנביא: ״כמו שצונו לחתך הדבר על פי שני עדים-ואף על פי שאין אנו

יודעים אם העידו אמת אם שקר–כך מצוה לשמע מזה הנביא, אף על פי שאין אנו יודעים אם האות אמת או בכשוף ולאט". וכן כתב באיגרת *תימן*.[56]

עינינו הרואות אפוא כי הרמב"ם ראה בעצם ההסתמכות על שני עדים חידוש של התורה, אשר אינו מחויב מן השכל. וכבר דייק מדברים אלו של הרמב"ם אחד מהאחרונים שעצם קבלת העדות של שני עדים היא "מצד חק התורה וגזירה דאורייתא... אבל אין לומר שכן הוא האמת דיש לומר גם שנים יש לומר דמשקרים רק התורה צוותה לנו לדון ולקיים דבריהם".[57]

וכאן המקום לשאול: מדוע הוצרך הרמב"ם להדגיש כל כך שאין לראות בעדותם של שני עדים מקור מידע ודאי לגילוי האמת? פשרו של דבר יתבהר לנו לכשנעיין במשנתו הפילוסופית-המדעית של הרמב"ם.

כבר לימדנו הרמב"ם באיגרתו אל חכמי מונטפשליר על גזירת הכוכבים (עמ' תעט במהדורת ר"י שילת) על שלושת מקורות הידע האנושי, שבאמצעותם ניתן לאמת דברים שונים, ואלו דבריו:

> דעו רבותי, שאין לנו להאמין[58] אלא באחד משלושה דברים: הראשון–דבר שתהיה עליו ראיה ברורה מדעתו של אדם, כגון חכמת החשבון וגיאמטריאות (=גיאומטריה) והתקופות (=אסטרונומיה). והשני–דבר שישיגו האדם באחד מחמשת ההרגשות (=החושים), כגון שידע בודאי שזה אדום וזה שחור וכיוצא בזה בריות עינו, או שיטעם שזה מר וזה מתוק, או שימשש שזה חם וזה קר, או שישמע שזה קול צרור וזה קול הברה, או שיריח שזה ריח ערב וזה ריח באוש, וכיוצא באלו. והשלישי-דבר שיקבל אותו האדם מן הנביאים ומן הצדיקים. וצריך לבעל דעה לחלק בדעתו ובמחשבתו כל הדברים שהוא מאמין בהם, ויאמר: זה האמנתי בו מפני הקבלה, וזה האמנתי בו מפני ההרגשה, וזה האמנתי בו מפני הדעה. וכל מי שיאמין בדבר אחר, שאינו משלשת המינים האלו, עליו נאמר 'פתי יאמין לכל דבר' (משלי יד טו).

56 עמ' קלט–קמ במהדורת ר"י שילת (ירושלים: תשמ"ז).

57 *אמרי בינה* (לר' מאיר אוירבך), חלק שני–חידושים לחושן משפט, הלכות עדות סי' א. והשוו לדברי בלידשטיין (לעיל, הע' 17), עמ' 127: "הרמב"ם מבהיר, אפוא, כי אין לתאר דברי עדים כ'אמת', הגם שהתורה מחייבת להתנהג כאילו זה המצב." ובהמשך דבריו כתב: "אם למדנו שעדות אינה ערובה לאמת, ניתן לראות גם את הצד השני של אותו מטבע: גילוי האמת אפשרי גם ללא תיווכה של עדות כשרה"; כך הוא למד מדברי הרמב"ם ב*פירוש המשנה* לסנהדרין פרק ט' משנה ה'. למקור נוסף המחזק את מסקנתו של בלידשטיין ראו דברינו להלן, פרק ג סעיף 2.

58 ומבאר שם ר"י שילת: "'להאמין' פירוש לאמת, לחשוב לאמיתי: 'ההאמנה אינה הענין הנאמר בפה, אבל הענין המצויר בנפש, כשיאמינו בו שהוא כן כמו שצויר' (מורה נבוכים, חלק א, פרק נ). ואחת היא–לענין המונח 'האמנה'–אם 'ההאמנה שהוא כן' מקורה בראיה שכלית, או בעדות החושים, או בקבלה."

מקורות הידע האנושי הם אפוא שלושה: הראיה, שהיא ההוכחה השכלית על פי ראיות, הראיה החושית, והקבלה מן הנביאים.[59] ויושם לב שלא זו בלבד שאין הרמב״ם מונה את שני העדים כאחד ממקורות הידע האמינים, אלא שבסוף דבריו הוא אף מדגיש: ״וכל מי שיאמין בדבר אחר, שאינו משלשת המינים האלו (ובכלל זה על העדות), עליו נאמר ׳פתי יאמין לכל דבר׳״. הלא דבר הוא, ואין הדבר מקרי כפי שנראה בהמשך הדברים.

נחיתותה של העדות בהשוואה למקורות ידע אנושי אמינים יותר עולה לא רק מהעדרה מרשימת שלושת מקורות הדעת, אלא שהדברים כתובים מפורשות ב*פירוש המשנה*, סנהדרין (פ״ז מ״ג):

> וכבר ידעת שהעדים הם שהורגים בידיהם איזה מיתה שתהיה, לפי שאותו הדבר אצלם ברור כיון שראוהו בחושיהם, ואצלינו אינו אלא ספור, לפי שאין לנו ידיעה אלא במה ששמענו מהם, ולפיכך צוה ה׳ שיהיו העדים עצמם ממונים על הדבר. וזה דבר נפלא.

מדברי הרמב״ם המאלפים הללו עולה שההסתמכות על העדות פחותה מבחינת רמת מהימנותה מההסתמכות על החושים, והיא אף אינה מקנה לשומע העדות גדר של ״ידיעה״ אלא רק גדר של ״סיפור״. ואמנם יש לשאול שאלה זו: האם הרמב״ם יוצר סולם דרגות בין שלושת מקורות הדעת הנזכרים באיגרת בעניין גזירת הכוכבים? שאלה זו חורגת אמנם מענייננו,[60] אולם לצרכינו נציין כי מדבריו בהקדמתו לפירוש המשנה הוכיח הרב יצחק שילת כי לדידו של הרמב״ם ישנה עדיפות לעדות השכל על עדות העין, ״דהיינו שהוכחה שכלית חותכת תקיפה לדעתו יותר מעדות החושים, כי החושים עלולים לסטיה ולטעות, ל׳אחיזת עיניים׳, ואילו השכל הבריא המשתמש בכללי ההיגיון בלבד, ׳יותר רחוק שתימצא בו

59 ויפה הסביר ר״י שילת, ״ראיה וראיה–על שיטות הכוזרי והרמב״ם בדרכים לאמונה,״ *מעליות* כה (תשס״ה), עמ׳ 96–97, ש״יש להבין שהקבלה ׳מן הנביאים ומן הצדיקים׳ [=לשון הרמב״ם] פירושה קבלה שמסרו הנביאים לצדיקים (לחז״ל ומהם לחכמי הדורות), ודרכם היא הגיעה אלינו. כלומר: מקור הידיעה השלישי הוא הנבואה, שבאמצעותה אפשר להשיג דברים שהשכל והחושים אינם יכולים להשיג. [עניין ׳הצדיקים׳, כאן הוא, שהואיל וצדיקים הם, אפשר לבטוח בהם שהם מוסרים דברים כהוייתם, והריהם צינור נאמן להעברת הידיעות הנבואיות אלינו. תדע, שהרי הרמב״ם אינו אומר ״מן הנביאים ומן החכמים,״ וצדקות כשלעצמה ודאי איינה מקור של ידיעה].״

60 וראו שילת, שם, עמ׳ 96–100, שמוכיח מדברי הרמב״ם במקומות שונים כי יש לדרג את מקורות הידע לפי מידת אמינותם, מן הקטן אל הגדול: חושים, שכל, נבואה.

טעות״.[61] ואכן, הרמב״ם קבע בכמה מקומות ב*מורה* כי הדיבוק אשר בינינו לבין הבורא הוא השכל.[62]

וכאן המקום לעמוד על היסודות המטה-הלכתיים העומדים בבסיס תפיסתו הפילוסופית-הדתית של הרמב״ם, שנתן מעמד בכורה לשכל האנושי. השתייכותו של הרמב״ם למרחב התרבותי של אריסטו ומפרשיו הערביים הובילה אותו להציע קריאה מחודשת לא רק ביחס למושגי היסוד התאולוגיים של היהדות, אלא אף ביחס למשמעותם של החיים האנושיים ולאופן שבו מתממש הפוטנציאל האנושי.[63] תפיסת האדם האריסטוטלית גורסת שהאדם מתייחד ביכולתו להבחין בין אמת לשקר, ומימוש הפוטנציאל האנושי שלו הוא השגת האמת על אודות העולם והאל ככל שמשיגה דעתו. לפי התפיסה האריסטוטלית המעלה האנושית על שאר היצורים היא היסוד השכלי שבנפשנו, והאדם מתאפיין ביכולתו לפעול מתוך שיקול שכלי או בניגוד לו. וכבר עמדו על כך שהרמב״ם קיבל עמדה זו על מובנם של החיים האנושיים,[64] ומפורסמים דברי הרמב״ם ב*מורה נבוכים* ביחס לצלם אלוקים שבאדם: ״כי השכל שאותו השפיע האלוקים על האדם-והיא שלמותו האחרונה . . . ובגללו נאמר שהוא בצלם אלוקים ובדמותו״.[65] על המימד האלוהי שבשכלו של האדם כתב הרמב״ם דברים אלה (שם): ״ומכיוון שהאדם נתייחד בעניין מופלא מאוד שבו, אשר איננו באף אחד מן הנמצאים שמתחת לגלגל הירח, והוא ההשגה השכלית, ששום חוש, איבר או צלע אינם מפעילים אותה, דימה אותה להשגת האלוה אשר איננה נזקקת לכלי. . . . בגלל השכל האלוהי הדבק בו, נאמר על האדם, שהוא בצלם אלהים ובדמותו״.[66] ברוח תפיסתו הפילוסופית של הרמב״ם יש להבין את המקום החשוב שהוא נתן במשנתו לשכל האנושי-האלוקי[67]

61 כך הוכיח שילת, שם, עמ׳ 98–97, מדברי הרמב״ם ב*הקדמת המשנה* (עמ׳ ל במהדורתו) בעניין הנביא המצווה בשם ה׳ לעבוד עבודה זרה, ומביא אותות לקיים טענתו; וזה לשון הרמב״ם שם: ״כי עדות השכל המכזיב טענתו חזקה מעדות העין הרואה מופתו, הואיל וכבר נתברר בראיה ברורה אצל אנשי השכל שאין ראוי לעבוד ולגדל אלא האחד אשר המציא הנמצאות והתייחד במכלל השלמויות.״

62 ראו למשל מורה נבוכים, חלק א, פרק א; חלק ג, פרק נא, והחתימה לספר.

63 לסיכום ממצה של הנושא ראו מ׳ הלברטל, *הרמב״ם*, ירושלים תשס״ט, עמ׳ 123–122. תיאור תפיסת האדם האריסטוטלית המובאת להלן בדברים שלמעלה לקוחה מתוך דברי הלברטל שם.

64 שם, עמ׳ 122.

65 *מורה נבוכים*, חלק א, פרק ב, עמ׳ 33 במהדורת שורץ (תל-אביב: תשס״ג). לפיכך מימוש החיים האנושיים מתבטא בידיעה דווקא, כדברי הרמב״ם שם, חלק ג, פרק כז, עמ׳ 517: ״ושלמותו האחרונה היא שיהיה מדבר בפועל, הינו שיהיה לו שכל בפועל וזאת בכך שיידע את מה שביכולת האדם לדעת מכל הנמצאים כולם, בהתאם לשלמותו האחרונה.״

66 *מורה נבוכים*, חלק א, פרק א, עמ׳ 31.

67 על מקום השכל וסמכותו במשנת הרמב״ם ראו יוסף פאור הלוי, *עיונים במשנת הרמב״ם* (ירושלים: תשל״ח), עמ׳ 151–144.

וכן את הדגשתו במורה נבוכים ובמקומות אחרים כי בשכל יבדיל האדם בין האמת והשקר.[68] הרמב״ם הביע אפוא את אמונו ביכולתו של השכל האנושי להשיג את האמת.[69]

הנה כי כן, לאור האמון שהביע הרמב״ם ביכולתו של השכל האנושי להשיג את האמת, המבוסס על תפיסתו הפילוסופית והדתית, ניתן כמדומה להבין טוב יותר את קביעתו בפרק כ״ד מהלכות סנהדרין, שלפיה על הדיין לפסוק בהתאם למה שדעתו ולבו מורים. ושמא יש לדמות זאת במידת מה לתפיסה המצויה בספרות המשפטית המודרנית, אשר ראתה בעקרון הכשירות הקוגנטיבית האוניברסלית טעם המצדיק את אידיאל חופש ההוכחה בדיני הראיות המודרניים.[70]

### 2. ״כי המשפט לאלהים הוא״

דומה כי אף הדגשתו של הרמב״ם בחתימת דבריו על אומד דעת הדיינים (סוף הלכה ג׳) ״כי המשפט לאלוהים הוא״ באה לבטא את השותפות בין האל לבין הדיין בשר ודם במעשה המשפט-וממילא גם לסיעתא דשמיא בפסיקת הדין לאמיתו[71]- המתבטאת לדידו של הרמב״ם, כאמור, בשכל האנושי, שהוא ״השכל האלוהי הדבק בו . . . שהוא בצלם אלהים ובדמותו״.

הרעיון של ״והמשפט לאלהים הוא״ כביטוי של שותפות האל במעשה המשפט מפורש במדרש תהלים, מזמור פב א, מהד׳ בובר עמ׳ 368:

68 *מורה נבוכים*, חלק א, פרק ב, עמ׳ 33. והשוו לדבריו בהקדמות *לפירוש המשנה*, עמ׳ נז במהדורת שילת: ״ומצאו [החכמים] כי תכליתו [של האדם] פעל אחד בלבד . . . והוא ציור המשכלות וידיעת האמתות כמות שהן.״ למקורות נוספים ראו פאור, שם, עמ׳ 145 הע׳ 5.

69 דוגמא יפה לכך יש להביא מתיאורו של הרמב״ם את מסעו של אברהם לגילוי האמת, בהלכות עבודה זרה פ״א ה״ג: ״ולבו משוטט ומבין עד שהשיג דרך האמת והבין קו הצדק מדעתו הנכונה וידע שיש שם אלוה אחד . . . ובן ארבעים שנה הכיר אברהם את בוראו.״ ויפה הדגיש הלברטל (לעיל, הע׳ 63), עמ׳ 185, שמדברי הרמב״ם עולה כי ״אמונת אברהם היא תוצר של תהליך פילוסופי ארוך שהגיע להבשלתו בגיל ארבעים, והיא לא החלה בהארה ובהתגלות פתאומית״ (בניגוד לראב״ד שם).

70 ראו: ד׳ מנשה, *הלוגיקה של קבילות ראיות* (חיפה וירושלים: 2008), עמ׳ 288–278.

71 ואמנם, אפשר לפרש כדברי *הסמ״ע* (חושן משפט סי׳ טו ס״ק יא), שכוונת הרמב״ם היא שאל יתנצל הדיין לומר איני רואה בטענות שום צד של רמאות, כי דברים אלה מסורים ללב, והקב״ה יודע מה שבלבו, ועל כגון זה נאמר ״ויראת מאלהיך״ (ויקרא כה יז), ודרשו חכמים בבבא מציעא נח ע״ב ״כל דבר המסור ללב נאמר בו ויראת מאלהיך.״ ואולם, כבר הטעים בעל *קרית ספר* (על אתר), כי דברי הרמב״ם בתחילת פרק כ״ד מהלכות סנהדרין מיוסדים על דברי חז״ל ״׳ועמכם בדבר משפט׳ (דברי הימים ב יט ו)-אין לך אלא מה שעיניך רואות״ (תוספ׳ סנהדרין, פ״א ה״ט, מהד׳ צוקרמנדל עמ׳ 416). ומעתה אפשר לפרש כי כלפי רעיון זה של השתתפותו של האל בהליך המשפטי מכוונים גם דברי הרמב״ם כאן ״והמשפט לאלהים הוא,״ וכמוסבר למעלה. על השפעת המימד הדתי על השפיטה ראו ב׳ ליפשיץ, ״פשרה,״ *משפטי ארץ-דין, דיין ודיון*,(לעיל, הע׳ 35) עמ׳ 151–137. כן ראו Y. Sinai, "The religious perspective of the judge's role in talmudic law," 25 *Journal of Law and Religion* (2009/2010), 357–77.

"מזמור לאסף אלהים נצב בעדת אל בקרב אלהים ישפוט". זהו שאמר הכתוב "לא תכירו פנים במשפט" (דברים א יז), וכן יהושפט "ויאמר אל השופטים ראו מה אתם עושים כי לא לאדם תשפטו כי לה' ועמכם בדבר משפט" (דברי הימים ב יט ו), וכתיב "כי המשפט לאלהים הוא" (דברים א יז). שלא יאמרו הדיינין אנו יושבים לעצמנו בדין, אלא אמר הקב"ה לדיינין הוו יודעין כי עמכם אני יושב, שנאמר "אני ה' אוהב משפט" (ישעיה סא ח), ואם הטיתם את הדין אותי אתם מטים, שנאמר "וקרבתי אליכם למשפט" (מלאכי ג ה). הוי "בקרב אלהים ישפוט"–באמצע הדיינין, ישפוט. ומאן אלהים? דיינא, שנאמר "עד האלהים יבא דבר שניהם" (שמות כב ח).

יסוד הדברים כבר נזכר בדברי תנאים בתוספתא סנהדרין פ"א ה"ט, מהד' צוקרמנדל עמ' 416 (ובבלי, שם ו ע"ב):

יהו הדיינין יודעין את מי הם דנין ולפני מי הן דנין ומי הוא דן עמהם . . . ואומר "אלהים נצב בעדת אל בקרב אלהים ישפוט" וכן הוא אומר ביהושפט "ויאמר אל השפטים ראו מה אתם עושים כי לא לאדם תשפוטו כי אם לה'". ושמא יאמר הדיין מה לי בצער הזה? והלא כבר נאמר "ועמכם בדבר המשפט"–אין לך אלא מה שעיניך רואות.

הנה כי כן, האל מצוי עם הדיינים בדבר המשפט, וכאשר הדיין פוסק על פי שכלו (האלוהי כהדגשת הרמב"ם) ועל פי מה שעיניו רואות, הרי האל מסייע לו מלמעלה; וכעין דבריו הידועים של הרמב"ן, שהאל מסייע לדיינים בבית הדין הגדול לכוון לאמת, "כי רוח ה' על משרתי מקדשו ולא יעזוב את חסידיו, לעולם נשמרו מן הטעות ומן המכשול".[72]

וכבר העמידנו ברכיהו ליפשיץ במאמרו המאלף על "פשרה" על תפקידו רב הפנים של האל במשפט לאור מקורות חז"ל, ואלו דבריו:

נוכחותו של הא–ל בתהליך השיפוט היא זו שמכרעת. הא–ל הוא השופט: "לפני ה'–ולא לפני עקיבה בן יוסף". לכן נקראים הדיינים "אלוהים", והם שותפים עמו במעשה בראשית מתמשך (שבת י ע"א). הא–ל הוא הנשפט: "כי לא לאדם תשפטו כי לה'", "ואמר הקב"ה לדיינין היו נוהגים באימה בעצמכם כאילו אותי אתם דנין" (תנחומא, שופטים ז). הא–ל מסייע לדיין בפסיקתו: "עמכם בדבר המשפט". ותוצאותיו של דין מוטעה מחייבות את הא–ל: "כי המשפט לאלוהים הוא . . . אמר הקב"ה: לא דיין לרשעים שנוטלין מזה ממון ונותנים לזה שלא

72 *פירוש הרמב"ן על התורה*, דברים יז יא (על הפסוק "לא תסור מן הדבר אשר יגידו לך ימין ושמאל").

כדין, אלא שמטריחין אותי להחזיר ממון לבעליו" (סנהדרין ח, א), "הוו יודעים כי עמכם אני יושב ואם הטיתם את הדין, אותי אתם מטין" (מדרש תהלים, פ״ב), ו"אם לא נעשה הדין למטה, נעשה הדין למעלה" (דב״ר, פ״ה). "הוא אל, הוא היוצר . . . הוא המבין, הוא הדיין, הוא עד, הא בעל דין והוא עתיד לדון" (אבות ד, ב).[73]

ואמנם נוכחותו של האל בשפיטה הודגשה בידי הרמב״ם עצמו בפרק שלפני פרקנו (פכ״ג ה״ח–ה״ט):

לעולם יראה דיין עצמו כאילו חרב מונחת לו על צוארו וגיהנם פתוחה לו מתחתיו, וידע את מי הוא דן ולפני מי הוא דן ומי עתיד להפרע ממנו אם נטה מקו האמת, שנאמר "אלהים נצב בעדת אל", ואומר "ראו מה אתם עושים כי לא לאדם תשפטו כי לה׳". כל דיין שאינו דן דין אמת לאמתו גורם לשכינה שתסתלק מישראל, וכל דיין שנוטל מזה ונותן לזה שלא כדין הקב״ה גובה ממנו נפשות שנאמר "וְקָבַע אֶת קֹבְעֵיהֶם נָפֶשׁ" (משלי כב כג), וכל דיין שדן דין אמת לאמתו אפילו שעה אחת כאילו תקן את כל העולם כולו וגורם לשכינה שתשרה בישראל שנאמר "אלהים נצב בעדת אל". ושמא יאמר הדיין מה לי ולצרה הזאת תלמוד לומר "ועמכם בדבר משפט", אין לדיין אלא מה שעיניו רואות.

ומעתה נראה כי הדברים הללו המדגישים את מקומו המכריע של האל במשפט הם שעומדים אף ביסוד דברי הרמב״ם בתחילת פרק כ״ד, והוא שהדגיש בסוף הלכה ג׳ "כי המשפט לאלוהים הוא".

## ג. ביטויים לתפיסה החותרת תחת מעמדם של שני העדים כמוסד מעין–שיפוטי

הרמב״ם לא קיבל את העמדה העולה ממקורות הלכתיים שונים, ואשר נזכרת בפתיחת המאמר, שלפיה מעמדם הראייתי–אובייקטיבי של שני העדים כמוסד מעין–שיפוטי מהימן מעניק להם את הסמכות הבלעדית לקביעת ממצאים עובדתיים, ואילו השופטים אינם קובעים את העובדות אלא הם מתפקדים כ"שחקני משנה" בלבד המאמצים את עדותם של העדים ופוסקים על פיה. אדרבה: כפי שראינו, הרמב״ם רואה את מקומם של העדים כמשני בהשוואה ל"שחקנים הראשיים", שהם הדיינים המופקדים על קביעת האמת העובדתית–ולא העדים או המושבעים. ואמנם, קביעת האמת העובדתית על פי דעתו ולבו של הדיין הרבה

73 ליפשיץ (לעיל, הע׳ 71), עמ׳ 146.

פעמים אינה מבוססת על היסק לוגי טהור של הדיין אלא על התרשמותו ממהימנותם של העדים המעידים בפניו. אף כאן פעמים רבות הדבר ״מסור ללבו של דיין לפי מה שיראה לו שהוא דין האמת״, במידה שדברי העדים נבדקו היטב שאין הם משקרים ולבו של הדיין שלם בדבר (כגון במקרה של ״קים לי בגווה״ הנזכר בראש פרק כ״ד מהלכות סנהדרין). ויודגש: לשיטת הרמב״ם תפקידו של הדיין במלאכת קביעת העובדות מרכזי ביותר, ואין הוא שונה באופן מהותי מהתפיסה המקובלת בדיני הראיות המודרניים,[74] שבמסגרתם ניתן משקל רב להתרשמותו של השופט ממהימנותם של העדים ועל פיו נקבעת טיבה של הראיה. כך גם נקבע במשפט הישראלי, בסעיף 53 *לפקודת הראיות [נוסח חדש], תשל״א-1971*: ״ערכה של עדות שבעל-פה ומהימנותם של עדים הם ענין של בית המשפט להחליט בו על פי התנהגותם של העדים, נסיבות הענין ואותות האמת המתגלים במשך המשפט״. נראה כי ניסוח זה עשוי להתקבל גם על דעתו של הרמב״ם, ובדומה למשפט הישראלי שבו אין שיטת המושבעים נוהגת, כך גם לשיטת הרמב״ם אין כל מוסד מעין-שיפוטי של עדים מושבעים.

עמדה זו עשויה להנהיר ביטויים שונים במשנתו ההלכתית של הרמב״ם, שנראים כמבקשים לחתור תחת מעמדם שני העדים הן כמקור מהימן הן כמוסד מעין-שיפוטי סמכותי שעל פיו יש לקבוע את האמת העובדתית, ולהלן אעיר עליהם.

### 1. עדות שאי אתה יכול להזימה אינה עדות

בביאורו של הרמב״ם לכלל ״עדות שאי שאתה יכול להזימה אינה עדות״ מתבטאת מגמתו הכללית לפקפק במהימנותם של שני העדים ותחת זאת להשתמש בכלי משפטי נוסף-הכלל האמור-שמטרתו לספק לבית הדין מקור מהימן יותר, המסייע בקביעת האמת העובדתית. במשנת סנהדרין (פ״ה מ״א) נאמר כי אם אחד מהעדים משיב ״איני יודע״ במענה לחקירות ששואלים אותו בית הדין (שאלות הנוגעות לנסיבות הזמן והמקום של האירוע), עדותו בטלה. ובתלמוד ביארו כי הבסיס להלכה האמורה הוא הכלל ״עדות שאי אתה יכול להזימה אינה עדות״.[75]

בטעמו של דבר כתב הרמב״ם *בפירוש המשנה* שם (פ״ה מ״ב):

> והטעם שבגללו אם אמר אחד משני העדים בחקירות איני יודע עדותן בטלה, ואם אמרו כולם בבדיקות אין אנו יודעין עדותן קיימת, הוא מה שאני מסביר לך, והוא שמן הכללים אצלינו כל עדות שאין אתה יכול להזימה אינה עדות,

74 שיטת הרמב״ם אינה עולה בקנה אחד עם הטענה הנזכרת לעיל בהע׳ 7, שלפיה יש הבדל לעניין זה בין המשפט העברי לבין המשפט המודרני. ודוק.

75 סנהדרין מא ע״ב.

ולא תתקיים ההזמה אלא אחר כוון הזמן והמקום שהיה בהם אותו המעשה, אומר להם המזים והלא עמנו הייתם באותה שעה במקום פלוני כמו שיתבאר לקמן, ושבע חקירות אינן אלא כוון הזמן והמקום. ואם אמר בחקירות איני יודע לא תהיה ההזמה אפשרית בה כלל, ולפיכך עדותו בטלה, לפי שאנו אומרים עדות שקר היא וזה אמר בחקירות איני יודע כדי שלא תתכן נגדם הזמה.

בדומה למקורות בהלכות יסודי התורה שנזכרו בפרק הקודם, אף מדברים אלו של הרמב״ם עולה החשש שהעדים משקרים,[76] שכפי שראינו הוא פועל יוצא של תפיסה עקרונית רחבה של הרמב״ם. הרמב״ם מבאר שיש מקום לחשוש לעדות שקר בעדותם של עדים שאינם מצביעים על נסיבות הזמן והמקום של האירוע שעליו הם מעידים, ״לפי שאנו אומרים עדות שקר היא וזה אמר בחקירות איני יודע כדי שלא תתכן נגדם הזמה״. ובלשון אחר: תכלית הכלל ״עדות שאי אתה יכול להזימה אינה עדות״ לפי דברי הרמב״ם היא לסייע בחיזוק מהימנותם של העדים, שבחושפם את נסיבות הזמן והמקום של האירוע הם מסתכנים שיבואו עדים אחרים ויזימו אותם ויתקיים בהם ״וַעֲשִׂיתֶם לוֹ כַּאֲשֶׁר זָמַם לַעֲשׂוֹת לְאָחִיו״ (דברים יט יט), ועל כן עדותם נחשבת מהימנה.

מאלפת ביותר ההשוואה בין דברי הרמב״ם הללו לבין אחד מכללי מהימנות הראיות במשפט המודרני המבוסס על תורת המשחקים, שהצביע עליהם אלכס שטיין:

> Credibility rules often involve a game–theoretic technique: costly signaling. By making his or her signaling costly, to himself or herself, a person may separate it from cheap talk and make the prospect that fact–finders will find his or her signaling credible [and] more probable.[77]

שטיין כותב כי לפי התאוריה הכלכלית של דיני הראיות ולאור התפיסה של costly signaling על החוק לעודד עדים להשתמש ב-credible signaling באמצעות יצירת תמריצים משפטיים שיעודדו עדים להעיד עדות שרמת מהימנותה גבוהה, מצד אחד, ומצד שני יגרמו שלא יהיה משתלם להם להעיד עדות שרמת מהימנותה נמוכה.[78] נראה כי אף הכלל של ״עדות שאי אתה יכול להזימה אינה עדות״ עשוי להיות על פי הסברו האמור של הרמב״ם דוגמא מצוינת לכלל משפטי היוצר תמריץ חיובי לעדים להעיד עדות שרמת מהימנותה גבוהה, שהרי כלל זה גורם

76 וכבר העיר על כך בעל *אמרי בינה* (לעיל, הע׳ 57).
77 ראו: *A. Stein*, Foundations of Evidence (Oxford: 2005), 165.
78 שם, עמ׳ 167.

שהעדים יהיו חייבים למסור פרטים מדויקים על נסיבות הזמן והמקום של האירוע כדי שעדותם תחשב כראיה. החוק מקבל רק עדות הכוללת את פרטי הזמן והמקום, שהרי לעדות זו רמת מהימנות גבוהה יותר משיש לעדות שאינה כוללת פרטים אלו, שכן היא חושפת את העדים לסיכון של הזמה, ועצם זאת שהעדים לא חוששים לסיכון זה מחזקת את מהימנותם. ואמנם, לאחר שנחקרו העדים ונבדקו בידי בית הדין ונמצאו מהימנים אפשר לסמוך עליהם. ברור שייתכן עדיין שהם משקרים, אבל אם אין אפשרות טובה יותר להוכחה יכול בית הדין להסתמך על עדותם במידה שהוא מתרשם ממהימנותם של העדים.

## 2. העדר הצורך בעדות שני עדים

הדגשת מקומם המשני של שני העדים עולה מפורשות מביאורו של הרמב״ם למגמת הסטייה הגדולה מהסטנדרט הרגיל של דיני הראיות שיש למצוא בהתרת עגונות.[79] וכך הוא כתב בהלכה החותמת את הלכות גירושין:

> אל יקשה בעיניך שהתירו חכמים הערוה החמורה בעדות אשה או עבד או שפחה או גוי המשיח לפי תומו ועד מפי עד ומפי הכתב ובלא דרישה וחקירה כמו שבארנו, שלא הקפידה תורה על העדת שני עדים ושאר משפטי העדות אלא בדבר שאין אתה יכול לעמוד על בריו אלא מפי העדים ובעדותן כגון שהעידו שזה הרג את זה או הלוה את זה. אבל דבר שאפשר לעמוד על בריו שלא מפי העד הזה ואין העד יכול להשמט אם אין הדבר אמת כגון זה שהעיד שמת פלוני, לא הקפידה תורה עליו, שדבר רחוק הוא שיעיד בו העד בשקר, לפיכך הקלו חכמים בדבר זה והאמינו בו עד אחד מפי שפחה ומן הכתב ובלא דרישה וחקירה כדי שלא ישארו בנות ישראל עגונות.

עינינו הרואות, שהרמב״ם מדגיש שלא בכל התחומים יש צורך להסתמך על שני עדים וניתן לקבוע ממצא עובדתי אף בהיעדרם של שני עדים, ״שלא הקפידה תורה על העדת שני עדים ושאר משפטי העדות אלא בדבר שאין אתה יכול לעמוד על בריו אלא מפי העדים ובעדותם״–רק אז יכולים בית הדין לעמוד על בוריו של דבר בהסתמך על עדותם של העדים, שהרי אין ברירה אחרת–אולם, במקום שניתן לעמוד על בוריו של דבר ללא עדים אין נזקקים לעדותם.

הרמב״ם סבור שיסוד מגמת ההקלה בדיני הראיות שבעדות אישה עגונה קשור לאופיה הייחודי של עדות זו. בעוד שישנם תחומים, כגון דיני נפשות ודיני ממונות,

79 לדיון נרחב בסוגיה (ובכלל זה בשיטת הרמב״ם) ראו מאמרי ״חקירת עדי עגונה–להתהוותן של תפיסות משפטיות,״ *שנתון המשפט העברי* כב (תשס״א–תשס״ג), עמ׳ 368–329 [=נדפס מחדש בחיבורי הנזכר לעיל בהע׳ 37, עמ׳ 339–311].

שבהם ״אין אתה יכול לעמוד על בוריו אלא מפי העדים ובעדותם״, הרי עדות אישה שמת בעלה הוא דבר ״שאפשר לעמוד על בוריו שלא מפי העד הזה ואין העד יכול להשמט אם אין הדבר אמת״. הרמב״ם מכוון ליסוד המכונה בתלמוד ״מילתא דעבידא לגילויי [=דבר העשוי להתגלות]״,[80] ואשר בכמה סוגיות הוא מוזכר כטעם אפשרי למגמת ההקלה בעדות עגונה.[81] לפי טעמו של הרמב״ם, מגמת ההקלה בדיני ראיות קשורה לטיבה של הראיה–כזו העשויה להתברר ואין לחשוש לכך שהעד ישקר.[82] אף כאן, בדומה למה שראינו בסעיף הקודם ביחס לכלל ״עדות שאי אתה יכול להזימה אינה עדות,״ נראה שהכלל המשפטי האמור מכוון לאפשר קבלת עדות שרמת מהימנותה גבוהה, שהרי בדבר העשוי להתגלות ״דבר רחוק הוא שיעיד בו העד בשקר״.

### 3. מרכזיות הדרישה והחקירה

ביטוי נוסף לתפיסה אשר חותרת תחת מעמדם הראייתי–האובייקטיבי של שני העדים כמוסד בעל מעמד מעין–שיפוטי לקביעת ממצאים עובדתיים, ותחת זאת מעניקה תפקיד מכריע לדיינים, המשתמשים בכלי פיקוח משפטיים בבואם לקבוע את האמת העובדתית, עולה מהמשקל הרב שנתן הרמב״ם להליך הדרישה והחקירה במסגרת הדיון המשפטי.[83] הרמב״ם עוסק בדרישה ובחקירה ובפרטיהן ברוב ההלכות שבשלושת הפרקים הראשונים של הלכות עדות! עובדה זו מלמדת, שהרמב״ם ראה בהליך הדרישה והחקירה כלי שיפוטי חשוב–אם לא החשוב ביותר–שהשופט משתמש בו במלאכת בירור הראיות; הרמב״ם ראה חשיבות רבה במעורבותו של השופט בחקירת העדים ככלי המשפטי העיקרי לצורך חשיפת האמת. השופטים חוקרים חקירה מאומצת המלווה בריבוי שאלות לגבי יסודות העבירה ונסיבותיה (=״חקירות״ ו״דרישות״) וכן בנוגע לעניינים צדדיים (=״בדיקות״).[84] ותכליתה המשפטית של הדרישה והחקירה לדעת הרמב״ם קשורה קשר הדוק לאופן התנהלותו של השופט בהליך חקירת הדין: לא לפסוק את הדין בחופזה ובלא התבוננות, אלא לחקור ולדקדק בחקירת העדים, וכפי שכתב בספר המצוות (עשין קעט): ״הצווי שנצטוינו לחקור עדות העדים ולדרוש אותה היטב, ואז

80 ראו למשל ראש השנה כב ע״ב: ״כל מילתא דעבידא לאגלויי, לא משקרי בה אינשי.״

81 ראו יבמות צג ע״ב, קטו ע״א, קטז ע״ב. בסוגיות אלו העמידו שני טעמים: ״מילתא דעבידא לאיגלויי״ ו״אשה דייקא ומינסבא.״ דיון בדעת הרמב״ם באשר ליחס שבין שני טעמים אלו מצריך דיון נרחב בפני עצמו, החורג מענייננו.

82 ליתר בהירות השוו ללשון הרמב״ם, הלכות גירושין פי״ב הט״ו: ״בדבר העשוי להגלות לכל ואי אפשר להכחיש ולא לטעון טענה, שאם הוא חי סופו לבוא או יודע שהוא חי.״

83 לניתוח רחב של שיטת הרמב״ם בעניין תכלית מערכת הדרישות וחקירות ראו חיבורי הנזכר לעיל בהע׳ 37, עמ׳ 267–264, 274; להלן מוצגים רק עיקרי הדברים.

84 להרחבה ראו יובל סיני, ״׳דרישות׳ ׳חקירות׳ ו׳בדיקות׳–פרק בגיבוש הלכות הרמב״ם,״ סידרא כא (תשס״ו), עמ׳ 50–35.

נעניש ונפסוק הדין. ולדקדק בכך ככל האפשר, כדי שלא נוציא פסק בדיבור ראשון ובמהירות, ונרע לזכאים".[85] בתכלית דומה עוסק הרמב"ם בפרק א' מהלכות עדות בזה הלשון: "מצוות עשה לדרוש העדים ולחקור אותן ולהרבות בשאלתן ומדקדקין עליהן ומסיעין אותן מענין לענין בעת השאלה כדי שישתוקו או יחזרו בהן אם יש בעדותן דופי". וכך מבאר הרמב"ם בפירושו למשנה את הטעם שלעולם שואלים את העדים את כל שבע ה"חקירות": "וכל זה לפי שאמרו מסיעין את העדים ממקום למקום כדי שתתטרף דעתן עליהן ויחזרו בהן, כלומר שגם מאריכין עליהם ויוצאין עמהן מענין לענין ומכבידים בשאלות כדי שיקוצו ואם היה בעדותם מרמה יחזרו בהם מלהעיד".[86] כיוצא בזה כותב הרמב"ם ביחס לתכלית המשפטית של ה"בדיקות" שהדיינים שואלים את העדים שאלות אלו שמכבידות על הנחקר ומבלבלות אותו ומסייעות לגילוי האמת, כפי שכתב הרמב"ם בפירושו למשנה: "ומדקדקין עליהן [=על העדים] ומסיעין אותן מעניין לעניין בעת השאלה כדי שישתוקו או יחזרו בהן אם יש בעדותן דופי".[87]

הנה כי כן, אין להתייחס לדברי העדים כאל "אמת" הכרחית, ואין לראות בהם מוסד מעין-שיפוטי המוסמך לקבוע העובדות. הדיינים הם אלו שמוסמכים לקבוע העובדות, ובמסגרת תפקידם מוטלת עליהם החובה לברר האמת העובדתית, ואת זאת הם עושים באמצעות החשד במהימנות העדים ובאמצעות הליך דרישה וחקירה המכוון לבירור האמת.

### 4. עדות שבשטר אינה קבילה מדין תורה

ביטוי נוסף למגמתו של הרמב"ם שלא להסתמך על עדותם של שני עדים שעדותם לא נחקרה כראוי בידי בית הדין מתבטא בעמדתו הייחודית של הרמב"ם בעניין תוקפם המשפטי של שטרות החתומים בידי עדים כראיה קבילה בבית הדין לגבי העובדות הנזכרות בהם.[88] כלל מרכזי בהקשר זה מבוסס על מימרתו הידועה של ריש לקיש "עדים החתומים על השטר נעשו כמי שנחקרה עדותן בבית דין".[89] הפרשנות המקובלת של מימרת ריש לקיש היא, שישנה הבחנה מהותית בין עדות בשטר ובין שאר סוגי העדויות. ברוב העדויות אין לוותר בדרך כלל על הליך

85 והשוו לדברי הרמב"ם בהלכות סנהדרין פ"כ ה"ז. הזיקה בין חקירת העדים לציווי "הוו מתונים בדין" מתבטאת אף בהקדמתו לפירוש המשנה (עמ' מח במהדורת שילת), אגב דונו במסכת אבות: "צריך, איפוא, השופט להתחנך בכל מה שכוללת אותו מסכת אבות, מן המתינות בדינים, ומעוט חריצתם מהר, לפי שאם ימהר לחרץ – אפשר שיהיה באותו הדין דבר נסתר... וירבה לחקר העדים, ויזהר בעת החקירה פן ילמדו מדבריו מה שינחם אל מטרתם."

86 *פירוש המשנה* סנהדרין פ"ה מ"א.

87 שם שם מ"ב.

88 לנושא זה ראו בהרחבה במאמרי "תוקפה של עדות בשטר במשנתם של הגאונים והרמב"ם," *דיני ישראל* כב (תשס"ג), עמ' 149–111; להלן הבאתי רק את עיקרי הדברים בלבד.

89 כתובות יח ע"ב; גיטין ג ע"א.

כלשהו של חקירת העדים בידי השופט ואילו שטר אפשר לקבל כראיה בלי שהשופט יקיים חקירה כלשהי של העדים החתומים, והשטר קביל אף במקום שבו לא הייתה לשופט אפשרות להתרשם מהעדים, והם אינם מצויים לפניו. מכיוון שבנוגע לעדי השטר קיימת פיקציה משפטית שעדותם נחשבת ״כמי שנחקרה בבית דין״. אך למעשה בית הדין אינו מעורב כמעט בהליך קבלתו של השטר, ותפקידו מתמצה בבדיקה טכנית של השטר ושל חתימות העדים.

גדולי הראשונים והאחרונים עסקו בסוגיית תוקפה של עדות בשטר. התפיסה המקובלת על רובם היא, שמעיקר דין תורה עדות בשטר תקפה[90] ונחשבת ״כמי שנחקרה״ ורק בשלב מאוחר יותר תיקנו חכמים את תקנת קיום השטרות, שלפיה על התובע על פי השטר מוטלת החובה להוכיח את אמיתות חתימות העדים. אך גם לאחר שנתקנה תקנת קיום שטרות אין צורך לחקור את עדי השטר על תוכן עדותם, ודי בהוכחה שהחתימות אינן מזויפות.

לעומתם פסק הרמב״ם בהלכות עדות פ״ג ה״ד, שרק ״מדברי סופרים [=מדרבנן][91] חותכין דיני ממונות בעדות שבשטר״, אך מדין תורה עדות בשטר אינה קבילה. שיטת הרמב״ם לגבי תוקפה של עדות בשטר עוררה עניין רב בקרב ראשונים ואחרונים[92] והם הקיפוהו בקושיות חמורות ביותר, עד כדי כך שהרמב״ן כתב על שיטתו ״וכבר השיבו עליו חכמי הדורות בזה תשובות גמורות אינן נעלמות מכל מבין עם תלמיד״.[93]

במקום אחר הראיתי שיש להבין את הלכת הרמב״ם על רקע המשקל הרב שנתן הרמב״ם, כאמור, להליך הדרישה והחקירה במסגרת הדיון המשפטי.[94] הלכת תוקפה של עדות בשטר ממוקמת בכוונת מכוון במסגרת דיונו הרחב בדרישה וחקירה בפרק ג׳, ודבר הלמד מעניינו: משום חשיבותה וחיוניותה של חקירת העדים לא יעלה על הדעת–כך סבר הרמב״ם–לקבל עדות בכתב/שטר בלי שהשופט יחקור את העדים. נמצא אפוא כי שיטת הרמב״ם מסתברת מבחינה משפטית–עניינית; ואדרבה: מבחינה זו קשה להצדיק דווקא את ההבחנה המקובלת בראשונים בין עדות בכתב ובין עדות בשטר. הראשונים הציעו הבחנה שאופיה

90 ראו ש״ך, חושן משפט סי׳ כח סקי״ד (לפירוט השיטות ראו *הלכה פסוקה* על חושן משפט, ירושלים תשמ״ז–תשנ״ט, עדות כח יב, עמ׳ קצד–ריא). כן ראו:
Abraham M. Fuss, "*Shetar*," Encyclopedia Judaica, 14, 1385–90.

91 על גדרו של המונח ״דברי סופרים״ במשנת הרמב״ם נשתברו כידוע קולמוסים רבים. ברם, הואיל וכאן קבע הרמב״ם שטעם הפסיקה על פי עדות בשטר הוא ״כדי שלא תנעול דלת בפני לווין,״ הרי שהכול מודים כי דברי סופרים כאן הם במשמעם הרווח: דרבנן (שלא כמשמעות שיוחסה למונח זה באי–אלה מקומות קשים, כגון בהלכות אישות פ״א ה״ב).

92 לשם המחשה, ראו הספרות העצומה הנזכרת בספר המפתח של מהדורת פרנקל, על אתר.

93 ברי הרמב״ן בסוף השגתו המפורסמת על השורש השני שבספר המצוות. ועיינו שם גם בהמשך הדברים.

94 ראו סיני (לעיל, הע׳ 88), עמ׳ 120–119.

פורמלי–טכני, אך לא מצאתי בדבריהם הסבר מניח את הדעת לעצם הוויתור על קיום הליך של דרישה וחקירה בעדות בשטר והשימוש בפיקציה של "כמי שנחקרה". יתירה מזו: ההסתמכות על עדות בשטר בלא דרישה וחקירה עשויה לשמש פתח לרמאויות, שכן "כל אדם שירצה יזייף ויכתוב ויחתום מה שירצה ויגבה ממנו".[95] [96]

95 *תוספות* כתובות כח ע"א, ד"ה "קיום שטרות." וראו באיזו מידה הם נדחקו שם. ואמנם רוב הפוסקים הניחו כי מדין תורה ""לא חציף איניש לזיופי"–אך זאת מנין?

96 אני מבקש להודות לפרופ' ברכיהו ליפשיץ על הערותיו המועילות. כל הציטוטים *ממשנה תורה*, הם ממהדורת פרנקל (בני ברק: תשל"ה–תשס"א). כל הציטוטים *מפירוש המשנה*, הם ממהדורת ר"י קאפח (ירושלים: תשכ"ג–תשכ"ז), מלבד הציטוטים מההקדמה לפירוש המשנה הלקוחים ממהדורתו של ר"י שילת, *הקדמות הרמב"ם למשנה* (ירושלים: תשנ"ב).

# בית הדין הרשמי בירושלים בשנים 1921–1841: הרכבו החברתי ומעמדו בקרב קהילות יהודיות

אלימלך וסטרייך*

## פרק א. מבוא

מחקר זה ידון בבית הדין הרבני הרשמי, שפעל בירושלים בשלהי התקופה העות׳מאנית החל משנת תר״ב (1842/1841), עת ״הראשון לציון״ זכה בתואר העות׳מאני הרשמי ״חכם באשי״ עד לשקיעתו המהירה סמוך למלחמת העולם הראשונה. אתמקד בבחינת ההרכב החברתי והתרבותי של הדיינים ורמתם המקצועית וכן במעמדו של בית הדין כלפי קהילות יהודיות אחרות בירושלים ומחוצה לה.

בית הדין היה חלק מן הרבנות הרשמית, שהייתה חלק מן הארגון הקהילתי היהודי ובראשם עמד ״הראשון לציון״, החכם באשי. בתחילת התקופה הייתה העדה הספרדית העדה העיקרית והשלטת ביישוב היהודי בירושלים כך ש״הראשון לציון״ וחברי בית הדין נמנו עם עדה זו, שאף שלטה במוסדות הבוחרים והממנים השונים. בשל שינויים במערך הפוליטי הבין-מדינתי וכן בשל תהליכים שהתרחשו בעולם היהודי חלו שינויים מפליגים בהרכבה של הקהילה היהודית בירושלים. האשכנזים, יהודי אירופה המזרחית והמרכזית, החלו לזרום לעיר בראשית התקופה שבה אנו עוסקים ובשנות השבעים של המאה הי״ט היו לעדה היהודית הגדולה ביותר. גם בני עדות שונות מן המזרח המוסלמי, מן המגרב ומרכז אסיה, עלו לירושלים והקימו בה מרכזים חדשים שערערו על ההגמוניה הספרדית. עולים אלה יצרו בסביבה הירושלמית מפגש תרבותי ובין-עדתי מסיבי ואינטנסיבי ביותר בממדים שלא נודעו בעבר, אף לא בקהילות היהודיות במזרח התיכון. בסופה של התקופה החל להופיע לראשונה באזורנו ״היהודי החדש״, שהתעצב באירופה המודרנית וספג ממנה את עולם ערכיה. טיפוס זה לא היה מחויב יותר למסורת ההלכתית בת אלפי השנים אלא ראה את מרכז זהותו בלאומיות היהודית, שאותה קיווה לממש במולדת הלאומית ההיסטורית–ארץ ישראל.

* פרופ׳ חבר הפקולטה למשפטים, אוניברסיטת תל-אביב.

תופעות אלה של שינויים במוסדות היהודיים וכן נוכחות הולכת וגדלה של קהילות יהודיות ממוצא עדתי שונה ריתקו את תשומת לבם של חוקרים בשנים האחרונות ונזכיר את מחקריהם להלן, אולם בשל הזיקה ההדוקה בין המוסדות השונים ובייחוד בשל היות בית הדין חלק ממוסד הרבנות שהממונה עליו היה החכם באשי, לא יוחד מחקר של ממש לבית הדין היהודי הרשמי כשלעצמו. מחקרים אלה עסקו בעיקר בקהילה היהודית, במעמדו של החכם באשי ומוסד הרבנות והזכירו את בית הדין כנספח למוסדות אלה. מחקרנו בא להשלים חסר זה. יתר על כן, עניין מיוחד יש במחקר של בית הדין בירושלים מכיוון שבשעה היסטורית זו חדלו זה מכבר להתקיים בסביבה האשכנזית באירופה מוסדות שיפוטיים יהודיים אוטונומיים. אמנם, במרחב הספרדי והמזרחי, שרובו היה באימפריה העות׳מאנית, התקיימו מוסדות שיפוט רשמיים אולם החל כבר תהליך שקיעתם והתדלדלותם. רק לבית הדין בירושלים היה פוטנציאל של פריחה והתעצמות, שנבע מכמה גורמים מצטברים: המעמד הרשמי שהוא זכה לו, הגידול הדמוגרפי העצום של האוכלוסייה היהודית, שהיה קרוב לפי עשרה בתקופת מחקרנו, הנהירה של גדולי תורה מן המרחב הספרדי והמזרחי, בואם של רבנים חשובים מן הסביבה האשכנזית וחידוש הקשר עם המרכז האשכנזי העצום שבמזרח אירופה ומרכזה.

במחקרנו נראה כי בית הדין הרשמי בירושלים הצטיין באיכות גבוהה של דיינים ובתוצרים משפטיים מעולים שהתבטאו בספרות משפטית שנכתבה; כמו כן זכה בית הדין במעמד גבוה בקרב מעגלים שונים של קהילות שלא היו כפופות לו באופן רשמי: בירושלים, בארץ ישראל במרחב הספרדי והמזרחי ובארצות האשכנזים. לקראת סיום מחקרנו נפגוש את בית הדין מתמודד בפרשת השמיטה באופן מבטיח עם האתגר שבהופעת ״היהודי החדש״ המבקש להעדיף ערכים מודרניים, וזכייתו בהערכתם העמוקה של גדולי הפוסקים האשכנזים. לעומת זאת, לא מצאנו את בית הדין מתמודד התמודדות של ממש עם האתגר האחר, הוא המפגש הבין-עדתי האינטנסיבי.

נפתח את מחקרנו בהצגת רמתם המקצועית של הדיינים, שהיה בה כדי להבטיח מעמד ויוקרה למוסד ובד בבד נצביע על האחידות העדתית של הדיינים, שתרמה מן הסתם ליעילות השיפוט אך מנעה אפשרות של התמודדות עם המפגש הבין-עדתי.

## פרק ב. רמתם המקצועית של הדיינים וסביבתם התרבותית והחברתית

בית הדין הרשמי בירושלים היה חלק בלתי נפרד של מוסד הרבנות, והיה זה טבעי שבראשו עמד הרב הראשי אשר תוארו היהודי הפנימי היה ״הראשון לציון״

והחיצוני "החכם באשי";[1] ברור שמעמדו המקצועי של החכם באשי כשופט ואיש הלכה וכן יוקרתו האישית תרמו במישרין למעמדו של בית הדין עצמו וליוקרת המוסד. בפרק זה אציג פרטים ביוגרפיים מרכזיים על אודות החכמים השונים שכיהנו בתפקיד חכם באשי או בתור ממלא מקומו וכן דיינים בולטים אחרים שכיהנו בתור אבות בתי דין וכדיינים מן השורה,[2] ואפרט את חיבוריהם המשפטיים, שהם המעידים המובהקים על רמת מחבריהם וקובעים את מעמדם בקרב קהיליית החכמים ובקרב הציבור הרחב; כמו כן נודעת לחיבורים השפעה של ממש על עיצוב תוכני בית הדין והתנהלותו, בייחוד אם הם מתפרסמים בחיי מחבריהם. אציין גם לסביבה התרבותית שבה נתעצבה תורתם ודמותם ההלכתית משפטית של החכמים שהייתה גורם נכבד שהשפיע על תפקודו של בית הדין ומעמדו בקרב קהילות אחרות.

קבוצת החכמים שכיהנו בתפקיד החכם באשי או ממלא מקומו ניתנת לחלוקה לשלוש קבוצות משנה בהתאם לשלוש תקופות המשנה של התפקיד: תקופת המעבר משנת תר"ב ועד שנת תרכ"ט (1842–1869), תקופת הזוהר משנת תרכ"ט ועד שנת תרס"ו (1869–1906) ותקופת השקיעה משנת תרס"ו ועד שנת תרפ"א (1906–1921). בקבוצה הראשונה יש למנות את ארבעת הרבנים הראשיים שכיהנו תקופה קצרה, כל אחד מהם קרוב לשבע שנים בממוצע. הללו נבחרו לתפקידם לאחר יצירת המוסד ה"חכם באשי" אך בטרם נחקק בשנת 1864 החוק העות'מאני המכונה "ח'אח'אם ח'אנה" ("Haham haneh"), שהסדיר את המבנה המוסדי של המילת היהודי וקבע את הרבנים כחוליה המקשרת בין השלטונות לבין הקהילה.[3] הקבוצה השנייה מורכבת משלושה רבנים שכל אחד מהם כיהן כשתים עשרה שנים בממוצע וביחד שלושים ושבע שנים, ופעילותם משקפת את תקופת השיא של התפקיד. בקבוצה השלישית נמנים שישה רבנים, שכיהנו בתפקיד במשך תקופה קצרה בת חמש עשרה שנים–שנתיים ומחצה בממוצע לכל רב–מבלי להותיר חותם של ממש על העשייה המשפטית.

ראשון החכמים שכיהן בתפקיד חכם באשי היה ר' אברהם גאגין (אג"ן), שנולד בשנת תקמ"ז (1787) באיסתנבול, עלה לירושלים בהיותו ילד קטן והתחנך

1 ראו מאמרו החשוב והבסיסי של י' ברנאי, "מעמדה של הרבנות הכוללת בירושלים בתקופה העות'מאנית," *קתדרה* 13 (תש"ם), עמ' 69–47.

2 ראו צ' זוהר, *האירו פני המזרח,* (תל אביב: תשס"א), עמ' 222–195, "על החכמים בארץ ישראל ותפיסתם העצמית."

3 ראו אבנר לוי, "התמורות במנהיגות הקהילות הספרדיות המרכזיות באימפריה העות'מאנית במאה התשע-עשרה," *ימי הסהר –פרקים בתולדות היהודים באימפריה העות'מאנית בעריכת מינה* רוזן (תל אביב: תשנ"ו), 265; ברנאי, לעיל,הערה 1, עמ' 57. תרגום לעברית של דבר חקיקה זה שכותרתו בעברית "חקי בית ועד החכמים" ראו אצל א"מ לונץ, ירושלים שנה רביעית (תרנ"ב) עמ' 202–188.

בישיבותיה שרובן ככולן היו ספרדיות.[4] קדמו לו בתפקיד ה״ראשון לציון״ חכמים מפורסמים ביותר בכל המרחב הספרדי דוגמת רפאל יוסף חזן, שכיהן משנת תקפ״ד ועד שנת תקצ״ו (1818–1821) ומהר״ם סוזין שכיהן משנת (1824–1836), ושהעניקו לתפקיד יוקרה רבה. הרב אג״ן מייצג את שלב המעבר מן התקופה שבה רב ראשי ובית הדין היו עניין פנים יהודי אל העידן המודרני, שבו בית הדין הפועל בחסות החכם באשי ובפיקוחו היו למוסדות מוכרים באימפריה. חיבורו המרכזי של הרב אג״ן הוא שו״ת חוקי חיים, שנדפס על ידו בירושלים בשנת תר״ג (1843); רוב התשובות עוסקות בנושאים משפטיים ואלה ניתנו על ידו בטרם היכנסו לתפקיד חכם באשי. ראוי לציין כי הרב אג״ן ובית דינו זכו להערכה רבה מצדו של ר׳ חיים פאלאג׳י, מגדולי חכמי תורכיה והבולט בחכמי ארץ זו במאה הי״ט. בסכסוך על אודות ירושת השר חיים פרחי, שנידון על ידי כמה בתי דין ברחבי האימפריה העות׳מאנית ובכלל זה בית הדין בירושלים בראשות הרב אג״ן, הוא מכנה את הרב אג״ן שוב ושוב הרב הגדול ואת בית הדין הוא מכנה ״בית הדין הגדול בירושלים״.[5]

אחריו כיהן בתפקיד ר׳ יצחק קובו. נולד בשנת תק״ל (1769/1770) בשלוניקי, שבה התחנך וחי רוב ימיו ורק בסוף ימיו עלה לירושלים והתמנה ל״ראשון לציון״ משנת תר״ח ועד שנת תרי״ד (1848–1854) בלי לקבל מינוי שלטוני רשמי מטעם הסולטאן. הרב קובו לא הותיר אחריו חיבורי הלכה שנדפסו והטביע חותם מועט בתפקיד ראש מערכת המשפט. אחריו כיהן בתפקיד ר׳ חיים נסים אבולעפיא (חנ״א) משנת תרט״ז ועד שנת תרכ״א (1854–1861) וגם הוא לא זכה בתואר הרשמי חכם באשי.[6] הרב חנ״א נולד בשנת תקנ״ה (1794/1795) בטבריה למשפחת אבולעפיא הספרדית המפורסמת, ובעיר זו למד תורה וכיהן בתפקיד אב בית דין עד שבגיל חמישים עבר לירושלים. הרב חנ״א התקשר בקשרי נישואין עם משפחת הרב אג״ן. גם הוא לא הותיר אחריו חיבור שו״ת ובו פסקי דין שפסק. עם זאת, הוא ישב קודם לכן בהרכבים שונים של בית הדין בירושלים ובכלל זה בהרכב החשוב של הרב בנימין נבון, ופסקי הדין שנתן מפוזרים בחיבורים שונים של חכמי התקופה.

4 א״ל פרומקין, *תולדות חכמי ירושלים* (מהדורת א׳ רבלין), (ירושלים: תרפ״ח-תר״צ), כרך ג עמ׳ 276–278. הפרטים אודות רפאל יוסף חזן, שם, עמ׳ 191–193; אודות מהר״ם סוזין, שם, עמ׳ 194–195.

5 ראו *שו״ת חוקות החיים* (איזמיר: תרל״ג), סי׳ א-ב. במקרה היו מעורבים בתי הדין של ירושלים, צפת, טבריה, דמשק, שלוניקי ואיזמיר ורק בית הדין בירושלים בראשות הרב אג״ן זוכה בתואר ״בית הדין הגדול״.

6 אודות הרב קובו ראו מ״ד גאון, *יהודי המזרח בארץ-ישראל*, חלק ב (ירושלים: 1937), עמ׳ 615; אודות הרב אבולעפיא ראו שם, עמ׳ 7.

אחרון בקבוצה זו היה הרב חיים דוד חזן (ח״ד חזן), בנו של הראשון לציון ר׳ רפאל יוסף חזן, שנימנה עם המשפחה הספרדית המפורסמת משפחת חזן. הוא נולד באיזמיר בשנת תקנ״א (1790) ובמרכז היהודי הגדול שבעיר זו הוא גדל והתחנך, וכיהן בה כרב העיר שנים רבות וזכה לפרסום רב.[7] לעת זקנתו בשנת תרט״ו (1855) עלה לירושלים וכיהן בתפקיד החכם באשי משנת תרכ״א ועד לפטירתו בשנת תרכ״ט (1861–1869). חוקרים סברו שאף הוא לא זכה במינוי רשמי מאת הסולטאן ואולם מכתביו מתקבל הרושם שאכן היה לו מינוי רשמי. הרב ח״ד חזן הותיר אחריו כמה חיבורים שיצאו לאור עוד בחייו, למשל שו״ת נדיב לב, שנדפס בסלוניקי בשנים תרכ״ב-תרכ״ו (1862–1866); רובם המכריע של פסקי הדין שנתפרסמו בחיבור זה הם מן התקופה שקדמה לכהונתו בירושלים.

בקבוצה השנייה אנו מוצאים את שני הרבנים הבולטים ביותר בכל התקופה, שהביאו את בית הדין לפסגתו, ר׳ אברהם אשכנזי (ר״א אשכנזי), שכיהן בתחילת התקופה משנת תרכ״ט ועד שנת תר״ם (1869–1880) ור׳ יעקב שאול אלישר (יש״א), שכיהן משנת תרנ״ג ועד שנת תרס״ו (1893–1906) וסיים את תקופת הזוהר.[8] הרב אברהם אשכנזי נולד בשנת תקע״א (1810/1811) בתורכיה והגיע בשנת תק״פ (1820/1819) לירושלים כילד קטן וכאן התחנך בישיבות הספרדיות שבעיר.[9] כבר בשלב מוקדם נקלט בתוך המערכת המשפטית והרבנית וניתן לומר כי הוא עבר תהליך מקיף של חניכה תוך מפגש בלתי אמצעי עם ראשיה. כך למשל, לפי בקשת החכם באשי הרב אג״ן הוא ערך ביחד עם חכם נוסף את קובץ תקנות ירושלים, שהיה למסמך משפטי בעל חשיבות רבה. ר״א אשכנזי עבר את כל שלבי התפקידים במערכת המשפט, החל מחבר בהרכב של הרב בנימין נבון, עבור לתפקיד ראש אב בית דין ועד הפסגה של חכם באשי. הוא נחשב אישיות רבנית מן השורה הראשונה ופסקיו מפוזרים בחיבורי בני דורו.[10] חשובה ביותר עדותו ״כי רוב ככל העולם מריצים שאלתם וספיקם אלינו״[11]-לאמור, בית הדין בירושלים היה למוסד שיפוט מרכזי שהכול פונים אליו. תשובותיו, שנתפרסמו בחיבורים שונים,

7 שם עמ׳ 249. אביגדור לוי (לעיל ,הע׳ 3), עמ׳ 250 הע׳ 44, מטיל ספק בכך שהרב ח״ד חזן היה רבה של איזמיר ומציין שגאון אינו מביא מקור לדבריו. אך ראה *שו״ת חוקות חיים* (סי׳ שם) שהרב ח״ד חזן מכונה ״רב הכולל״ שהיה התואר שניתן לרבה של עיר בקהילות הספרדיות באימפריה העות׳מאנית. ראו אביגדור לוי, ״הקמת מוסד החכם באשי באימפריה העות׳מאנית והתפתחותו בשנים 1835–1865,״ *פעמים* 55 (תשנ״ג), עמ׳ 39, 45, 46.

8 הרב אלישר כונה בפי כל בשם ״יש״א ברכה״ וכך נודע בספרות הרבנית המאוחרת. על תפיסת עולמו של היש״א ברכה ראו זוהר (לעיל, הע׳ 2), עמ׳ 236–223.

9 גאון (לעיל, הע׳ 6), עמ׳ 122–121.

10 ראו פרומקין (לעיל, הע׳ 4), עמ׳ ,282 המביע דברי ההערכה המופלגים כלפיו: ״האדם הגדול בענקים בתורה וביראת חטא״.

11 ראו יעקב משה הלל, *תולדות הגאון המחבר רבנו אברהם אשכנזי זלה״ה, שו״ת מהר״א אשכנזי* (ירושלים: תשנ״א), עמ׳ 31. כך גם העידו עליו חכמים בירושלים: ״ומכל קצווי ארץ וים רחוקים מריצים אליו שאלתם״ (שם, עמ׳ 32).

עם כמה פסקי דין שהיו עדיין בכתב יד, התפרסמו רק בשנים האחרונות וכונסו בשם ״שו״ת מהר״א אשכנזי״.[12] הרב אשכנזי היה מעורב בכמה פרשות משפטיות שהסעירו את חכמי ספרד והמזרח ביניהן פרשת השר נסים שאמאמא, שהיה עשיר מופלג והותיר רכוש עצום לעדה הספרדית בירושלים באמצעות צוואה שערך לפי הדין הצרפתי.[13] הרב אשכנזי היה מעורב ככל הנראה גם בפרשת תביעת הפיצויים של החכם באשי רפאל קצין לאחר שהודח ממשרתו בבגדאד והוחזר אליה.[14] כמו כן היה מעורב גם בפרשת הירושה של השר חיים פרחי[15] בהיותו עדיין צעיר לימים ובראשית דרכו.

נוכחות לא בולטת הייתה לר׳ מאיר רפאל פניז׳יל (מרפ״א), שנבחר לתפקיד בהיותו זקן וחולה אף על פי שכיהן בתפקיד שלוש עשרה שנים (1880–1893). הוא נולד בשנת 1804 בעיר טאטר פזארדג׳יק (Tatar Pazarcık), בבולגריה של היום ועלה לארץ ישראל בהיותו בגיל שלוש. בגיל שבעים ושש התמנה לחכם באשי ולסגנו נבחר מחותנו הרב יש״א ברכה, שהיה יד ימינו, ובשל תשישותו של המרפ״א היה המוציא והמביא שהכול פונים אליו ומחכים למוצא פיו. היה זה אך טבעי שלאחר פטירת המרפ״א בשנת תרנ״ג (1893) נבחר היש״א ברכה לתפקיד החכם באשי, והיה ככל הנראה הגדול והמפורסם מכל החכמים שכיהנו בתפקיד זה.[16] הרב אלישר נולד בשנת תקע״ז (1817) בצפת ולאחר פטירת אביו נישאה אמו בשנית לרב בנימין נבון, שהיו אב״ד בבית הדין הספרדי בירושלים ומחשובי הרבנים בה. רב זה גידלו כבן וגם היה מורו ורבו בתורה ובהתנהלות הרבנית בכלל. את מלאכת השיפוט החל בשנת תרי״ג (1853) בהיותו בן שלושים ושש והתמיד בה למעלה מחמישים שנה. הרב אלישר התמנה ככל הנראה לתפקיד אב בית דין בעת שהרב אשכנזי נתמנה לחכם באשי, ושיתוף הפעולה ביניהם בתחום השיפוט היה הדוק מאוד. הרב אשכנזי נהג להעביר לעיונו של הרב אלישר שאלות ומקרים וביקש את חוות דעתו, בד בבד כתב הרב אלישר פסקי דין מקיפים והמתין לקבלת הסכמה עליהם מאת הרב אשכנזי. לפסגת פעילותו הגיע משנתמנה לחכם באשי ובתפקיד זה כיהן עד לפטירתו בשנת תרס״ו (1906).

12 על מקורות התשובות שכונסו בחיבור זה, ראו שם, עמ׳ 13–9.

13 פסק הדין פורסם בספר *ישמח משה* (ירושלים: תרל״ד), והוא נדפס מחדש *בשו״ת מהר״א אשכנזי*, סי׳ לג.

14 *שו״ת מהר״א אשכנזי*, סימן ג. ר״א אשכנזי פסק מבלי לדעת כי מדובר בחכם הנזכר.

15 המקורות שדנו בפרשה פרחי נזכרו לעיל, הע׳ 5.

16 היש״א ברכה כתב אוטוביוגרפיה מקיפה שנתפרסמה בידי א״מ לונץ ב*לוח ארץ ישראל* לשנת תרס״א, עמ׳ 39, ובה מפורטים ציוני הדרך של חייו. דברינו להלן מבוססים על הדברים שכתב שהובאו אצל גאון (לעיל, הע׳ 6), עמ׳ 68–62, והועתקו במלואם על ידי משה הלל זרי, הקדמה ל*שו״ת יש״א איש* (ירושלים: תשנ״ז), עמ׳ 25–18. וראו גם נ׳ אפרתי, *משפחת אלישר בתוככי ירושלים* (ירושלים: תשל״ה), עמ׳ 226 ואילך.

משך פעילותו הארוכה של הרב אלישר במערכת המשפט הולידה גם יצירה משפטית ענפה שהרב עצמו דאג להוציאה לאור בימיו רובה במהלך תפקודו במערכת המשפט. חיבור הביכורים שפרסם היה שו״ת ״בני בנימין וקרב אי״ש״ (ירושלים תרל״ו), שכלל פסקי דין של מורו ורבו ואביו חורגו, ר׳ בנימין נבון וכן כלל פסקים שלו עצמו. הפסקים שהתפרסמו בחיבור זה משקפים את התקופה המוקדמת שלו כדיין. בשנת תרמ״ח (1887/1888) פרסם את ספר השו״ת השני שמחה לאי״ש, וארבע שנים לאחר מכן פרסם את שו״ת ״מעשה אי״ש״. בהיותו כבר חכם באשי פרסם שני ספרי שו״ת נוספים, ״ישא אי״ש״ (ירושלים תרנ״ו) ועולת אי״ש (ירושלים תרנ״ט). לאחר פטירתו הדפיס בנו הרב חיים משה אלישר (חמ״א), תשובות נוספות שלו בחיבור שו״ת ״שאל האי״ש ופני חמ״א״ (ירושלים תרס״ט). הישׂ״א ברכה זכה גם ליוקרה רבה מחוץ לתחום השיפוט של ירושלים וחכמים ספרדים ואשכנזים פנו אליו לקבלת חוות דעת הלכתיות, וכדברי לונץ: ״וכל רבני קצות ארץ תוגרמה, מערב, איטליה ואשכנז יריצו אליו את שאלותיהם בענייני דת והלכה״.[17] להלן נציג את פרשת היתר המכירה בשנת השמיטה שתבליט את המעמד המיוחד שהיה לחכם ספרדי גדול זה בקרב גדולי חכמי רוסיה בתקופה. שפע היצירה ומעמדו הרם בעולם היהודי של הישׂ״א ברכה הקרינו גם על המעמד שהיה לבית הדין בתקופת פעילותו במהלך של למעלה מחצי מאה שנים.[18]

עם פטירתו של הישׂ״א ברכה הסתיימה תקופת הזוהר של מוסד החכם באשי בירושלים ומתחילה התקופה השלישית, שהתאפיימה בהתדרדרות מואצת של בית הדין כחלק ממוסד הרבנות בכללותו; להשלמת התמונה נציג בקצרה את האישים השונים שכיהנו בתפקיד מבלי שהותירו חותם של ממש. אחרי הישׂ״א ברכה נבחר בשנת תרס״ו (1906) לתפקיד החכם באשי ר׳ יעקב מאיר, שנולד בשנת תרט״ז (1856) בירושלים למשפחה שמוצאה מרודוס והתחנך בה. כמה מפסקיו המוקדמים פורסמו כבר בחיבורי הישׂ״א ברכה ובחיבורים אחרים בני הזמן, אך הוא לא הותיר אחריו ספר שו״ת. כעבור זמן קצר נאלץ הרב מאיר לעזוב את תפקידו בעקבות מלחמת חורמה שניהלו נגדו קבוצות שונות בעדה הספרדית. המאבקים הפנימיים המשיכו והאיצו את ההתדרדרות של המוסד הרבני והשיפוטי. אחרי הרב מאיר התמנה ר׳ אליהו פאניז׳יל, שנולד בשנת תר״י (1850) בירושלים וכיהן בתפקיד משנת תרס״ז עד שנת תרס״ט (1907–1909) בתואר ממלא מקום חכם באשי. החליף אותו בתפקיד הרב נחמן בטיטו, שנולד בשנת תר״ו (1846)

17 ראו *נתיבות ציון וירושלים–מבחר מאמרי אברהם משה לונץ* (ג׳ קרסל, עורך), (ירושלים: תשל״א), עמ׳ 196.

18 קשה להבין את דבריו של ברנאי (לעיל, הע׳ 1), עמ׳ 66, כי הישׂ״א ברכה ינק את כוחו מהסמכות שהייתה בידו כעסקן. אין ספק שעיקר סמכותו נבע מגדולתו בתורה ומסגולותיו כשופט ופוסק.

במרקש שבמרוקו ועלה לירושלים כנער ובה התחנך ובישיבותיה למד. הוא כיהן כאן כרבה של עדת "המערבים" בירושלים ומשנת תרס"ט ועד שנת תרע"א (1909–1911) כיהן בתפקיד ממלא מקום החכם באשי. אחריו כיהן ר' משה פראנקו, שנולד בשנת תקצ"ז (1837) ברודוס ובה כיהן כרבה של הקהילה משנת תרס"ו עד שנת תרע"א (1906–1911). לאחר שעלה לירושלים בשנת תרע"א התמנה לממלא מקום החכם באשי במקומו של הרב בטיטו, תפקיד שמילא משנת תרע"ב עד שנת תרע"ה (1912–1915). אחריו התמנה לתפקיד הרב נסים יהודה דאנון, שנולד בשנת תרל"ד (1873/1874) בירושלים וכיהן בתפקיד בתוך מלחמת העולם הראשונה משנת תרע"ו עד שנת תרע"ח (1916–1918). חתם את התקופה, והיה אחרון בתפקיד, הרב חיים משה אלישר, שנולד בשנת תר"ה (1845) בירושלים לאביו היש"א ברכה וכיהן בתפקיד משנת תרע"ט עד שנת תרפ"א (1919–1921), עד לביטול המוסד בידי השלטון הבריטי. אחד מגילויי הירידה הוא שהרבנים הראשיים בתקופה, למעט הרב חמ"א, כמעט שלא הותירו רישום בתחום היצירה המשפטית ולא פרסמו חיבור שו"ת המשקף את פסיקתם.[19]

לצידו של החכם באשי שימשו בתפקידים שיפוטיים חכמים נוספים, שכיהנו כאבות בתי דין או כדיינים מן השורה, וכמה מהם הצטיינו בתפקידם ופרסמו עוד בחייהם חיבורים שכללו פסקי דין נבחרים שנתנו: אזכיר את הבולטים שבהם ושמות חיבוריהם ואת מוצאם החברתי וסביבתם התרבותית. הרב שלום משה חי גאגין (שמ"ח), (נפטר בשנת תרמ"ג [1883]) היה בנו של החכם באשי הראשון הרב אנ"ן, וחתנו של החכם באשי השלישי הרב חנ"א.[20] הוא פרסם שו"ת "ישמח לב", שנדפס בירושלים בשנת תרל"ח, ובו פסקי דין רבים שפסקו הוא ועמיתים שלו בבית הדין ובכלל זה רבנים ראשיים. הרב מיכאל יעקב ישראל נולד בשנת תק"נ (1790) ברודוס וכיהן בה כרב ולאחר מכן התיישב בירושלים בשנת תר"ג (1843), בהיותו בן חמישים ושלוש. בשל גדולתו בתורה התמנה לראב"ד בשנת תרי"ד (1854) על ידי הרב חנ"א, וחשובי הדיינים בירושלים כיהנו בהרכב שלו, ביניהם החכם באשי לעתיד ר"א אשכנזי. חיבורו המשפטי הוא שו"ת יד ימין שנדפס לאחר מותו באיזמיר תרי"ט. אחד מחברי ההרכב של הרב מיכאל ישראל היה ר' אהרון עזריאל, שהיה יליד ירושלים וחניך ישיבותיה, וחיבר את שו"ת "כפי אהרון", שנדפס בשנת תרל"ד. חתנו היה ר' יעקב מאיר, שכיהן לימים בתור חכם באשי ולאחר הכיבוש הבריטי כיהן בתור הרב הראשי הספרדי הראשון לארץ ישראל. חבר נוסף בהרכב היה ר' משה פארדו שנולד כנראה בירושלים והתחנך בה, וכיהן בתפקיד דיין וראב"ד במשך שנים רבות. בשנת תרל"א (1871) עבר לכהן כרב

19 פרטים ביוגרפיים על חכמים אלה ראו אצל גאון (לעיל, הע' 6), בערכיהם.
20 שם, עמ' 7.

ודיין באלכסנדריה שבמצרים וכאן פרסם בחייו את שו״ת ״שמו משה״, שנדפס באיזמיר בשנת תרל״ה, ובו פסקי דין שלו ושל עמיתיו לדיינות בירושלים.[21] חכם אחר שנולד ברודוס היה ר׳ רחמים פראנקו (תקצ״ה-תרס״א [1835–1901]) שעלה לירושלים בהיותו כבן שלושים. כאן הצטרף לבית הדין של היש״א ברכה ושל הרב אשכנזי ובשלב מסוים נשלח על ידי החכם באשי של ירושלים לכהן כרבה של העיר חברון. חיבורו שו״ת ״שערי רחמים״, יצא לאור בירושלים בשנת תרס״ב (1902), לאחר פטירתו. נזכיר גם את ר׳ יוסף נסים בורלא (תקפ״ח-תרס״ג [1828–1903]), שנולד בירושלים והתחנך בה ונימנה עם גדולי רבניה. כאן כיהן כדיין וראב״ד לקראת סוף המאה הי״ט[22] ופרסם את חיבורו ״לקט יוסף״ (ירושלים תרס) הכולל פסקי דין שפסק בשבתו כדיין בירושלים.

ראשי המערכת השיפוטית, אבות בתי הדין ודיינים מן השורה בבית הדין הרשמי בירושלים היו אפוא בעלי רקע תרבותי וחברתי משותף, היא המסורת הספרדית. אחידות זו הובילה לכך שיצירתם המשפטית נשאה אופי דומה מאוד, שהוא חיבור השאלות והתשובות (שו״ת), האופייני לחכמים ספרדים בדורות האחרונים. כך נוצר קורפוס רחב היקף של ספרי שו״ת, שחלקם הגדול הוא פסקי דין שנפסקו בבתי הדין בירושלים או חוות דעת על שאלות משפטיות שהופנו אל הדיינים מחוץ לתחום שיפוטם. חשיבות מיוחדת נודעת לעריכת ספרי שו״ת אלו בידי כותביהם ולהבאתם על ידם לבית הדפוס בעודם בחיים ולא בידי מלקט מן העיזבון, שמידת האקראיות שולטת בבחירותיו. כך יכולים אנו להניח שהחכמים הנזכרים פרסמו את פסקי הדין שהיו חשובים בעיניהם וכאלה שיש בהם משום חידוש.[23] אחידות חברתית ותרבותית זו אפשרה גם לבית הדין בירושלים לתפקד ביעילות למרות ריבוי העמדות והגישות והיעדר מנגנון הכרעה בהלכה היהודית, שהיא אחת המכשלות הכבדות הרובצת לפתחו של בית דין הדן לפי דין תורה. דייני בית הדין יכלו אפוא לפלס דרך מאוחדת למדי של קביעות משפטיות העולות לכדי מסורת משפטית מגובשת, המדברת אל הציבור בקול מאוחד וברור. בד בבד סייעה היצירה המשפטית הענפה שנתפרסמה ויצאה לאור לגיבושה של דרך משפטית מאוחדת שכל הדיינים צועדים בנתיבותיה.

הסוגה הספרותית של שו״ת שפרסמו דיינים העושים במלאכת השיפוט מזכירה את סדרות פסקי הדין, שרווחות בארצות ששלטת בהם שיטת המשפט של הקומון לאו (Common Law) בראשן אנגליה וארצות הברית וכן במדינת ישראל, שמשמשים תשתית לכל עיון ומחקר משפטי. חיבורים אלה שימשו בידי חכמי הלכה

21 שם, עמ׳ 541–542.

22 שם, עמ׳ 137–138.

23 זאת, להבדיל מתקופות קודמות, שבמקרים רבים ארגון החומר והוצאתו לאור לא נעשו בידי מחברי התשובות, אלא בידי גורם אחר והוא פרסם חומרים שהגיעו אליו, לעתים באקראי.

ומשפט אחרים כמקור וכאסמכתא וכן שימשו בתור אמצעי חניכה וגיבוש של קהיליית משפטנים בירושלים. בהיעדר ארכיון משפטי מן התקופה העות׳מאנית[24] ממלאים חסר זה חיבורי השו״ת של גדולי הדיינים ונותנים בידי חוקרי משפט והיסטוריונים אפשרות לחקור את העשייה המשפטית של התקופה. כמותם המצטברת של פסקי הדין ורמת פסקי הדין שנתפרסמו מלמדים על מערכת משפטית באיכות גבוהה, דינמית ואפקטיבית. היא נותנת בידינו פריסה טובה וחשובה של חומר משפטי, מהטובים ביותר שיש להלכה לאורך ההיסטוריה שלה עד הקמת המדינה; היקף היצירה ומגוון הפונים אל רבני ירושלים ודייניה מלמדים גם על מעמדו הרם של בית הדין בירושלים מחוץ לגבולות השיפוט הרשמיים שלו. נפנה עתה לבחון את מעמדו של בית הדין כלפי חוץ, ונתחיל ביחסם של בני העדות המזרחיות בירושלים.

## פרק ג. עדות מזרחיות בירושלים

בתקופה שאנו דנים בה החלו להתכנס בירושלים עדות לא-אשכנזיות ממזרח וממערב שחתרו להגיע לעצמאות מסוימת מול העדה הספרדית השלטת. נושא זה נידון בהרחבה בהקשריו החברתיים, הארגוניים והרבניים בידי חוקרים שונים, ואתייחס כאן רק להיבט הנוגע לבית הדין כמוסד השיפוטי. העדה הראשונה שחתרה לעצמאות הייתה העדה ״המערבית״, שרוב מניינה היו יהודים בני מרוקו.[25] הללו החלו לגלות סממני עצמאות כבר במחצית הראשונה של המאה הי״ט אך עברו לפסים של ממש בהנהגתו של הרב דוד בן שמעון שעלה ארצה בשנת תרי״ד (1854).[26]

היו שהניחו שמעמדו של החכם באשי נפגע בעקבות צעדים מעין אלה של עדת המערביים, ובכלל זה נפגע גם מעמדו של בית הדין הספרדי כמוסד שיפוטי בשל ייסוד בית דין מערבי עצמאי,[27] אך נראה שיש להסתייג מהנחה זו. אין ספק שהעדה המערבית החלה לנוע לכיוון של עצמאות, אולם היא יצרה לעצמה מוסדות

24 היו רבנים ראשיים שיצרו וטיפחו ארכיון פרטי, כמו ר׳ חיים אברהם גאגין והרב יש״א ברכה, אלא שהארכיונים הללו לא נשמרו ורק חלקים מהם שרדו והגיעו לידינו. על ארכיונו האבוד של הרב גאגין ראה ב״צ דינבורג, *מאסף ציון*, 1 (ירושלים: תרפ״ו), עמ׳ 87; על גורלו של הארכיון של היש״א ברכה ראה גאון (לעיל, הע׳ 6), עמ׳ 67.

25 לסקירה מקיפה על נושא זה ראו י׳ ברנאי, ״העדה המוגרבית בירושלים במאה התשע עשרה״ בתוך י׳ בן פורת ואחרים (עורכים), *פרקים בתולדות היישוב היהודי בירושלים*, כרך א (ירושלים: תשל״ג), עמ׳ 140–129. על הדמוגרפיה של המערביים בירושלים וארגונם החברתי והמוסדי, ראו מיכל בן יעקב, עלייתם והתיישבותם של היהודים המערביים (יהודי צפון-אפריקה) בארץ ישראל במאה הי״ט, עבודת דוקטור, האוניברסיטה העברית, תשס״א, עמ׳ 215–191.

26 ראו י״מ טולידאנו, *נר המערבי–תולדות ישראל במרוקו* (ירושלים: תרע״א), עמ׳ 210.

27 ראו ברנאי (לעיל, הע׳ 1) עמ׳ 65.

אוטונומיים חלקיים בתוך המסגרת של העדה הספרדית השלטת ולא מחוצה לה. היא לא נפרדה לגמרי מן העדה הספרדית והמשיכה לחלוק עם הספרדים מוסדות משותפים, לאחר שהגיעו לפשרות בעניינים שונים, בעיקר כלכליים.

השאלה הנוגעת לנו היא אם כוננה העדה המערבית בית דין עצמאי לכל דבר. בעניין זה לא מצאתי ראיות של ממש אצל החוקרים ואני סבור שעצם הקמת רבנות וגוף מנהל עדיין אינה מחייבת שנוסד גם מוסד שיפוטי עצמאי לגמרי. הרי כל רב פוסק הלכות בענייני הלכה ולעתים הוא אינו מסתפק בפסיקה בתחומים ריטואליים (אורח חיים ויורה דעה) אלא אף גולש לתחומים משפטיים כמו דיני משפחה (אבן העזר) ואף חושן משפט, ואין בפסיקות מעין אלה משום יצירת מוסד שיפוטי מובהק. דומה שנוכל לתמוך השערה זו אם נבחן את היצירה ההלכתית והמשפטית של הדמות הרבנית המרכזית של העדה המערבית, הרב דוד בן שמעון (דב״ש).

עד כה לא הגיע לידינו שום חיבור של שו״ת משל הרב דב״ש, שיש בו כדי להעיד על פסקי דין עצמאיים שפסק במסגרת בית דינו העצמאי,[28] ויש לשער שספר כזה לא התחבר. כך ניתן ללמוד מתוך דברים שכתב בנו החכם המפורסם הרב רפאל בן שמעון בהקדמה לחיבור שפרסם, שו״ת ״ומצור דב״ש״: המחבר כותב שהחליט לפרסם בתוך חיבורו פסקי דין משל אביו משום שהוא לא פרסם בחייו חיבור מעין זה, ומספרם של הפסקים שנתפרסמו מועט ביותר. חלקם של הפסקים נשלחו כחוות דעת לחו״ל לקהילות מערביות (=מוגרביות) וכן נתנו כמה פסקים בארץ, לאו דווקא משפטיים. בתשובותיו המשפטיות האחרות הוא ביקש את אישורו של החכם באשי ר״א אשכנזי או של בתי הדין הספרדיים הקיימים.[29] רק פסק דין אחד בנושא משפטי פסק הרב דב״ש מבלי לבקש את הסכמתם או אישורם של גורמי שיפוט ספרדים. מדובר בפרשה שהופנתה אליו מחיפה, שלא הייתה כפופה לירושלים, בעניין בעל ממוצא מוגרבי שנהג באלימות כלפי אשתו והאישה תבעה גט בעקבות זאת. יש בפסקים שהתפרסמו ללמד לכאורה כי הרב דב״ש לא הוציא עצמו לעצמאות מתחום השיפוט של בית הדין הספרדי בירושלים, וכשפעל בתחום המשפט ביקש את ההסכמה של חכמי הדין הספרדים.

מידה זו של עצמאות של העדה המערבית הלכה ופחתה לאחר פטירתו של הרב דב״ש, בשנת תר״ם (1880)–מריבות בין פלגים שונים החלישו את העדה וככל שנחלשה הלכה זיקתה לספרדים וגברה. בשנות השמונים התערב הישׁ״א ברכה בסכסוך ולתפקיד רב העדה המוגרבית נבחר הרב נחמן בטיטו; לימים נבחר רב

28 טולידאנו (לעיל, הע׳ 26) מביא רשימה של ספרים שחיבר הרב דב״ש, ואין ביניהם ספר שו״ת.

29 שם, חלק יו״ד, סי׳ כז; שם, חלק אע״ז, סי׳ ז׳ שאלה מטנג׳יר בעניין קנס שידוכין; שם, סימן ט׳ בעניין גביית כתובה לפי תקנת ירושלים, מציין הרב דב״ש כי הוא ניהל וויכוח על כך עם הרב אהרון עזריאל וכן עם החכם באשי הרב ח״ד חזן (המכונה על ידו ״המלך דוד״).

זה לעמוד בראש העדה הספרדית וכיהן בתור ממלא מקום חכם באשי משנת תרס״ט עד שנת תרע״א (1909–1911). אלא שאיחוד מחודש זה התרחש בעת שהעדה הספרדית ומוסד החכם באשי היו נתונים בתהליך של שקיעה.[30]

עדה מזרחית מובהקת שחתרה לעצמאות בעקשנות הייתה העדה התימנית, וגם התנהלותה משמשת ראיה בידי ברנאי לפיחות מוסד הרבנות בירושלים.[31] אלא שהתימנים החלו להגיע לירושלים רק בשנת תרמ״ב (1882), סממני התארגנות ראשונים הופיעו כעבור כעשר שנים, ואילו הפירוד בפועל מן העדה הספרדית התרחש בשנת תרס״ח (1908), שנתיים לאחר פטירתו של הרב יש״א ברכה.[32] כך שבמהלך תקופה של כשישים שנה של קיום מוסד שיפוט רשמי לא התעורר איום על מעמדו של בית הדין של ירושלים מצדם של התימנים, והצלחתם להגיע לעצמאות התרחשה רק בתקופת הירידה של העדה הספרדית ומוסדותיה. נראה שניתן לומר שבית הדין הספרדי בירושלים היה בית דינן של העדות הלא אשכנזיות–ספרדים, מזרחיים ומערביים–עד סמוך לפרוץ מלחמת העולם הראשונה בעת שהחלה תקופת הירידה המהירה.

## פרק ד. המרחב הספרדי והמזרחי מחוץ לירושלים

התעצמותו של בית הדין הרבני הספרדי התבטאה גם במעמד ובחשיבות שנודעו לו מחוץ לתחומי סמכותו האישית והטריטוריאלית הישירה. סמכותו הישירה של בית הדין מכח הפירמאן שקיבלו כל חכם באשי חלה על מחוז ירושלים ולגבי אזרחים עות׳מאניים בלבד,[33] אבל אין ספק שסמכותו הדתית והמוסרית של בית הדין הספרדי בירושלים חרגה הרבה מעבר לגבולות המחוז. בשל כך רבו הפניות אליו מכל רחבי הפזורה הספרדית והמזרחית ושאלות לרוב הגיעו אל בית הדין בנושאים רבים וגם בנושאים משפטיים מובהקים;[34] למשל, בענייני ייבום היו כמחצית מן השאלות שהופנו לבית הדין הספרדי בירושלים מחוץ לתחומי שיפוטו. הפניות אל בית הדין בירושלים הגיעו מכל המרכזים של קהילות ספרדיות ומזרחיות שהיו קיימים במעגל הקרוב ובמעגל הרחוק.

30 ראו לעיל, טקסט ליד הע׳ 19.
31 ראו ברנאי (לעיל, הע׳ 1) עמ׳ 65.
32 ניצה דרויאן, ״עולי תימן בירושלים: קווים לתולדות בני העדה בשנים תרמ״ב-תרע״ד״, בתוך אלי שאלתיאל (עורך), *פרקים בתולדות ירושלים בזמן החדש–ספר זיכרון ליעקב הרצוג* (ירושלים: תשמ״א), עמ׳ 223.
33 ראו ברנאי (לעיל, הע׳ 1), עמ׳ 63.
34 רשימה חלקית ניתן למצוא בהקדמה ל*שו״ת יש״א איש* (לעיל, הע׳ 16), שבו מיין המהדיר את רשימת הפונים לרב אלישר. קל לראות שמדובר במספרים גדולים ומקומות שונים ברחבי העולם, ועדיין לא מנינו פניות שהגיעו לרבנים ראשיים אחרים או שנתפרסמו בחיבורים אחרים.

במעגל הקרוב אנו מוצאים קהילות בארץ ישראל שלא היו בתחום הסמכות של בית הדין הירושלמי, דוגמת קהילת טבריה וקהילת צפת, שהרבו להפנות שאלות לירושלים.[35] נוכל להצביע גם על מקרה אחד שבו פסק בית הדין הספרדי בטבריה בעניין חלוקת עיזבון בין אלמנה ליורשים ולאחר מחאותיה של האלמנה הפנה בית הדין את הנושא להכרעת היש״א ברכה בירושלים.[36] מקרה אחר מטבריה נזכר בשו״ת שמחה לאיש, אע״ז אבן העזר סי׳ ד. השאלה הופנתה לראש״ל ר״א אשכנזי וכותב התשובה הוא היש״א ברכה ועמו חתם גם הרב שמ״ח גאגין. גם מבית הדין הספרדי בצפת הגיעו פניות רבות ונצביע כאן על כמה מקרים הנזכרים בקובץ התשובות של הרב שאקי, שהיה אב״ד בבית הדין הספרדי בצפת.[37] כמו כן פנו חכמים אשכנזים מצפת ונזכיר זאת בפרק הבא, על היחסים עם האשכנזים.

מעגל שני היו קהילות ספרדיות בסביבה הסמוכה לארץ ישראל, בעיקר במצרים ובסוריה– מקהילת אלכסנדריה וקהיר הגיע מספר ניכר של שאלות וכן הגיע מספר לא מבוטל של שאלות מקהילות חלב ודמשק. לא מן הנמנע שערוץ זה התרחב משהגיעו חכמים ירושלמים לכהן בקהילות הללו, כפי שנראה להלן, והם הרבו לפנות לצור מחצבתם שראו בו גם מקור של סמכות. כך למשל, הרבה רבה של דמשק הרב יצחק אבולעפיא לפנות לחכמי ירושלים בשאלות מגוונות בנושאים משפטיים. גם בעת הסכסוך הגדול שפרץ סביב כהונתו בתפקיד החכם באשי של דמשק הוא ניסה לערב את חכמי ירושלים ובאותה מידה ניסו גם יריביו לעשות כן. ניסיונם של שני הצדדים לרכוש את לבם של רבני ירושלים במאבקם הפנימי נובע מן המעמד הגבוה שהיה לבית הדין הרבני של ירושלים בעיניהם.[38]

קהילות מרוחקות יותר בארצות המזרח דוגמת בבל ותימן הפנו אף הן שאלות לבית דינו של החכם באשי, והן ביטאו יחס של הערכה וכבוד למוסד השיפוטי שבראשותו בירושלים.[39] נראה שככל שהתרבו העולים מארצות אלה נוצרו ערוצי תקשורת בין חכמי הקהילות בארץ המוצא לבין בית הדין בירושלים. על רקע זה יש לראות גם את המספר הניכר של פניות שהגיעו גם ממרכז אסיה ממקומות כמו בוכרה וגיאורגיה (גרוזיה). גם הנוכחות הקבועה של בני המגרב בירושלים הביאה לריבוי פניות מצד חכמים מארצות צפון אפריקה לבית הדין בירושלים–אחד הנושאים הבולטים שהופנה לירושלים היה תקנה להפקעת קידושין שנועדה

35 בעניין סכסוך בין כוללים אשכנזים בעיר צפת, ראה *שו״ת שמחה לאי״ש*, חושן משפט, סי׳ יד, תשובת המרפ״א והיש״א ברכה.

36 הנושא התפרסם בעיתונות דווקא; פרטיו המלאים פורסמו למשל ב-*חבצלת*, 14 ביוני 1880.

37 ראו *שו״ת רוח קדים*, סי׳ ה, ו, יד, טו.

38 י׳ הראל, *בין תככים למהפכה–מינוי רבנים ראשיים והדחתם בבגדאד, דמשק וחלב בשנים 1750–1914* (ירושלים: תשל״ז), עמ׳ 199–198.

39 ראו *שו״ת שמחה לאיש*, אע״ז, סי׳ כה, פנייה של ר׳ יוסף חיים מבבל.

להתמודד עם החוקים הצרפתיים בתחומי הנישואין והגירושין אשר הוחלו על יהודי אלג׳יריה.[40]

טבעי למדי שקהילות הבלקן ואסיה הקטנה ובראשן סלוניקי, איסתנבול ואיזמיר הרבו לנהל משא ומתן הלכתי עם בני ירושלים, שהרי שני המרכזים הללו היו למעשה בית מדרש אחד שהזרימה ההדדית ביניהם הייתה הדוקה ורציפה.[41] עם זאת, יש לציין כי לפחות בעידן של הרבנים אשכנזי והיש״א ברכה הרושם החזק הוא שכיוון הזרימה הוא כנראה יותר ויותר מתורכיה והבלקן אל ירושלים ולא מירושלים אליהן.[42] עם מותו של ר׳ חיים פאלאג׳י, רבה המפורסם של איזמיר בשנת תרכ״ח (1868)[43] ובנו ממשיכו ר׳ אברהם פאלאג׳י, לא הופיעה על הבמה הרבנית אישיות בעלת שיעור קומה דומה ועולם התורה בקהילות הבלקן ואסיה הקטנה החל לשקוע. ביטוי לכך ניתן למצוא בהזמנתו של ר׳ יעקב מאיר בשנת תרס״ט (1909) לכהן כרבה הראשי של סלוניקי מיד לאחר שהודח מתפקיד החכם באשי בירושלים. עם זאת, יש לזכור כי רבנות ירושלים הייתה כפופה מבחינה פוליטית לפחות לרבנות קושטא וכדי למנות בה חכם באשי נדרשה הסכמה של החכם באשי בקושטא.[44]

ערוץ נוסף של השפעה היה ביצוא של רבנים בולטים בשדה המשפט העברי לקהילות במעגלים השונים, ואזכיר רק כמה אישים בולטים. הראשון הוא ר׳ ישראל משה חזן שהתפרסם בספרות המחקר בשל דעותיו החדשניות בזכות המודרניות וקליטת ערכים מערביים.[45] רי״מ חזן התחנך בירושלים[46] והסתופף בצלו של סבו, הראשון לציון ר׳ יוסף רפאל חזן, וכיהן תקופה מסוימת בבית הדין בירושלים. לדברי פאור התנגש רי״מ חזן עם חוגים שמרניים של ירושלים ובשל כך יצא לקהילות ישראל באגן הים התיכון.[47] תחילה כיהן כרבה של רומי משנת תר״ז ועד שנת תרי״ב (1852–1847) וכאן פרסם את ספר השו״ת שלו ״כרך של רומי״, שבו אסף פסקי דין שלו בעת כהונתו בעיר; לאחר מכן עבר לאי קורפו וכיהן כרב הקהילה משנת תרי״ג ועד שנת תרט״ז (1855–1853). הוא הוזמן לכהן באלכסנדריה בשנת תר״ז (1857) ולאחר תקופה קצרה בתפקיד זה נפטר לבית עולמו בשנת תרכ״ג (1863).

40 ראו שם, סימן כ, פניית חכמי אלג׳יריה בעניין זה.
41 ראו למשל שם, סי׳ ו. טז, וכן תשובות רבות נוספות.
42 קביעה זו היא מתבססת על רושם מצטבר מעיון במספר רב של ספרי שו״ת, אך היא איננה מוחלטת.
43 ראו גאון (לעיל, הע׳ 6), עמ׳ 561–560.
44 בעימות סביב מינויו של ר׳ יעקב מאיר מילא תפקיד מרכזי הרב משה לוי, רבה של קושטא הבירה; ראו גאון שם, עמ׳ 365–364.
45 ראו י׳ פאור, *רבי ישראל משה חזן-האיש ועבודותיו* (חיפה: תשל״ח), עמ׳ 61–35.
46 ראו גאון (לעיל, הע׳ 6), עמ׳ 252–251.
47 פאור (לעיל, הע׳ 45), עמ׳ 18–15.

שני לו הוא קרובו ר׳ אליהו חזן, שנחשב לאחד הפוסקים החשובים בסביבה המזרחית והספרדית בשלהי המאה הי״ט.[48] הוא נולד באיזמיר בשנת 1845 וכילד עלה לירושלים בשנת 1855 והתחנך על ברכי סבו החכם באשי ר׳ ח״ד חזן; כיהן כדיין בבית הדין בירושלים בהרכב של החכם באשי ר״א אשכנזי. לאחר שנים נסע לטרבלסי, היא טריפולי שבלוב, ולאחר מכן בשנת תרמ״ח (1888) עבר לכהן כרבה של אלכסנדריה במצרים ושם נפטר בשנת תרס״ח (1908). חיבורו המפורסם שו״ת תעלומות לב כולל ארבעה כרכים של תשובות שהשיב לקהילתו ולקהילות ישראל במצרים ובאגן הים התיכון.[49] ר׳ אליהו חזן היה מעורב בחקיקת תקנות קהיר משנת תרס״א (1901) על סדרי הקידושין, שעיקרם הוא ביטול קידושין שלא נעשו בהתאם להוראות שבתקנות.[50] חקיקה זו חוללה שינוי עמוק בתחום הפרוץ של סדר הקידושין והיא מופת של יוזמה ועשייה בתחום דיני המשפחה בדורנו. הרב אליהו חזן תמך גם ביוזמת רבה האשכנזי של קהיר הרב מנדל כהן לכנס אסיפת רבנים בקרקוב לדון בבעיות השעה.[51]

בתקופה שר׳ אליהו חזן כיהן כרבה של אלכסנדריה כיהן ר׳ רפאל בן שמעון כרבה של קהיר, משנת תר״נ ועד שנת תרפ״א (1890–1921).[52] כאמור לעיל, חכם זה גדל בירושלים והתחנך אצל אביו הרב דב״ש, שניבש את קהילת המערביים בעיר והוליכה לאוטונומיה קהילתית אך לא משפטית. נראה שר׳ רפאל היה הדוחף הגדול מאחורי תקנות קהיר בעניין קידושין שנזכר לעיל. נוסף לכך הוא יזם הוצאה לאור של חיבורים שונים של חכמי מרוקו, שהיו ספונים בכתב יד וביניהם חיבורו החשוב של ר׳ יעקב אבן צור ״משפט וצדקה ביעקב״. ר׳ רפאל כינס את תשובותיו בחיבורו שו״ת ומצור דב״ש שיצא לאור בירושלים בשנת תרע״ב וניתן למצוא בו פסקים חשובים מאוד שמקצתם עוסקים בהתמודדות עם אתגרי המודרניות.[53]

לסוריה, שכנתה של ארץ ישראל בצפון, הגיעו שני רבנים בולטים מירושלים. ר׳ יחזקיהו שבתאי נולד בשלוניקי בשנת תרכ״ב (1862) ומילדותו התחנך בירושלים ובה נפטר בשנת תשט״ו (1955).[54] תחילה נבחר לכהן כרבה של טרבולסי משנת תרס״ד עד שנת תרס״ח (1904–1908) ולאחר מכן עבר לכהן בקהילת חלב שבצפון סוריה ואף זכה בפירמאן מאת הסולטאן, שהעניק לו סמכויות נרחבות

48 ראו גאון (לעיל, הע׳ 6), עמ׳ 246–247.

49 חיבור בולט אחר שלו הוא ״נוה שלום״ על מנהגי אלכסנדריה וקהיר.

50 ראו צ׳ זהר, *מסורת ותמורה–התמודדות חכמי ישראל במצרים ובסוריה עם אתגרי המודרניזציה 1880–1920* (ירושלים: תשנ״ג), עמ׳ 116–133.

51 שם, עמ׳ 90–92.

52 שם, עמ׳ 116–133, 159–172.

53 ראו שם, במפתח בעמ׳ 313 בערך בן שמעון, רפאל אהרון.

54 ראו גאון (לעיל, הע׳ 6), עמ׳ 661–662.

בתחום המשפט.[55] (תקופת כהונתו בחלב ידעה מתחים ומאבקים רבים והיא מתוארת בהרחבה בחיבורו של ירון הראל.[56]) לאחר מלחמת העולם הראשונה שב לארץ ישראל וכיהן כאן כראש אב בית הדין הרבני הספרדי, ודיין בבית הדין הרבני הגדול.

לקהילת דמשק שבסוריה הגיע ר׳ יצחק אבולעפיא, שהיה נצר למשפחה מפוארת אשר רבים מבניה כיהנו בתפקידי רבנות.[57] הוא נולד בדמשק בשנת תק״ץ (1830) ומנעוריו התחנך אצל סבו הרב חנ״א תחילה בטבריה ולאחר מכן עבר עמו לירושלים, וחי בה עד שנפטר בשנת תרכ״א (1861).[58] לאחר שעבר לדמשק לכהן בה כרב ראשי נקלע ר׳ יצחק למאבקים מרים וקשים שהעיקו עליו עד מאוד.[59] ראוי לציין כי גם בעת שהותו בדמשק הוא נחשב עדיין על חכמי ירושלים וזכה במענקים מקופת העדה הציבורית בירושלים.[60] יצירתו המשפטית מקיפה מאוד והיא כוללת שישה כרכי שו״ת ״פני יצחק״ שנדפסו ובהם התכתבות ענפה עם חכמי ירושלים.

לקראת סוף התקופה שאנו דנים בה יצא מירושלים ר׳ יעקב מאיר לכהן בתור רב ראשי בקהילת סלוניקי. קהילה זו הייתה דורות רבים מן החשובות שבקהילות ישראל ובלטה בתור המרכז הספרדי הגדול בבלקן ובאסיה הקטנה, ומפורסמת הייתה בשיעור קומתם של חכמי ההלכה שלה. סלוניקי, יחד עם הקהילות הראשיות האחרות, איזמיר ואיסתנבול, היו המוקד והמרכז שממנו יצאו התורה והמשפט העברי למרחבי הקהילות הספרדיות, וירושלים בכלל זה. אין ספק שהיה במינוי זה ביטוי מובהק לחילופי התפקידים בין שני המרכזים הספרדיים הללו, ומכאן ואילך כיוון ההשפעה היה מירושלים ולא אליה. את מקומו של הרב יעקב מאיר בתפקיד רבה של קהילת סלוניקי החליף בשנת 1923 הרב ב״צ עוזיאל, אף הוא מילידי ירושלים הספרדית ומפירותיה המפוארים. אלא שכהונתו של הרב עוזיאל משקפת את דמדומי התפקיד של החכם באשי באימפריה העות׳מאנית, שבראשה ניצב סולטאן שהיה גם הח׳ליפה, ושעמדה על סף פרוק וחיסול. על פתחה של התקופה בירושלים ניצבה כבר הרבנות הראשית החדשה, שבמרכזה עמדה העדה האשכנזית שהייתה הקשורה באופן הדוק לתנועה הציונית ולסדר הבריטי החדש. אלא שאנו עדיין בעידן של השליטה הספרדית בתוך הסדר

55 כך למשל, נקבע שכל נישואין וגירושין בתחום שיפוטו שלא יקבלו את אישורו לא יהיה להם תוקף. כמו כן ניתנו לו סמכויות אכיפה מרחיקות לכת כמו גירוש בני קהילה מן העיר מבלי שיהיה פיקוח שיפוטי על מעשהו.

56 ראו הראל (לעיל הע׳ 38).

57 שם, עמ׳ 149.

58 שם, עמ׳ 149–150.

59 שם, עמ׳ 171–200.

60 שם, עמ׳ 198 הע׳ 102.

העות׳מאני הישן, ונבחן אפוא את מערכת היחסים בין בית הדין בירושלים לבין העדה האשכנזית, שנמנתה עם היישוב הישן.

## פרק ה. היישוב האשכנזי הישן בירושלים

היחסים בין בית הדין הרבני הספרדי לבין העדה האשכנזית בירושלים היו כרוכים במכלול היחסים בין העדה האשכנזית לבין העדה הספרדית ומוסדותיה, והתאפיינו בדינמיות מתמדת.[61] במהלך המאה השמונה עשרה חוסלה הקהילה האשכנזית בירושלים ובעשורים הראשונים של המאה התשע עשרה חיו בעיר רק משפחות בודדות שהסוו עצמן כספרדים. בשנות השלושים, תחת שלטונו של מוחמד עלי, נפתחה הדרך להתיישבות אשכנזית בירושלים, שהתבססה בתחילה על תלמידי הגר״א שישבו זה מכבר בארץ ישראל במקומות אחרים.[62] בראשית התקופה שבה עוסק מחקרנו, בשנת 1841 מנתה הקהילה האשכנזית בירושלים כאלף וחמש מאות נפש לעומת כשלושת אלפים ספרדים,[63] ומליטא הגיע ר׳ שמואל מסאלנט (רש״ס), שהקים כאן עד מהרה את בית דין של העדה האשכנזית הפרושית. בשנת 1859 הגיע לירושלים ר׳ מאיר אויערבך מן העיר קליש שבפולין, שהיה גדול בתורה, והוא הועמד בראש בית הדין למשך עשרים שנים בקירוב.[64] עם בואם של חסידים במספרים ניכרים התפצלו האשכנזים, והחסידים יסדו אף הם בית דין משל עצמם שהתחרה בבית הדין הפרושי.[65] עלייתו של רש״ס, שהנהיג את היישוב האשכנזי הישן במשך כשבעים שנים, מסמלת את תחילתו של זרם עולים אשכנזים שהלך וגבר. כבר בשנת 1870, בעת שהתחילה תקופת המשנה השנייה של בית הדין הספרדי הרשמי, השתווה מספרם של האשכנזים למספרם של הספרדים ומכאן ואילך הם יהיו לעדה היהודית הגדולה בירושלים.[66] למותר לציין כי כל האשכנזים בשעה זו נימנו עם הציבור המסורתי, וחלק מן הבאים עזב את מרכז אירופה ומערבה כדי להתרחק ממגמות החילון שהלכו והתעצמו שם.

61 על מערכת היחסים בין שתי העדות ראו י׳ קניאל, ״שיתוף פעולה בתחום התרבות והרוח בין הספרדים והאשכנזים בירושלים במאה התשע עשרה״ (לעיל, הע׳ 25), עמ׳ 300–289.

62 על ההתיישבות האשכנזית בירושלים בראשית המאה התשע עשרה ראו מ׳ אליאב, ״היישוב היהודי בירושלים בשלהי התקופה העות׳מאנית (1914–1815)״ (לעיל, הע׳ 32), עמ׳ 141–132.

63 ראו י׳ בן אריה, ״גידול הקהילה היהודית בירושלים במאה הי״ט״. בתוך י׳ בן פורת ואחרים (לעיל, הע׳ 25), עמ׳ 108, בטבלה המסכמת.

64 ראו מ׳ אליאב, *ארץ ישראל ויישובה במאה הי״ט* (ירושלים: 1978), עמ׳ 154.

65 שם, עמ׳ 155. רק בשנת 1892 הגיע לירושלים מנהיג חסידי מפורסם, ר׳ שניאור זלמן ליאדר שהיה רבה הראשי של לובלין, והוא שימש בתור אב בית הדין החסידי.

66 ראו בן אריה (לעיל, הע׳ 63), וראו גם:
U. Schmelz, "Some demographic peculiarities of the Jews of Jerusalem in the nineteenth century," in M. Maoz (ed.), *Studies on Palestine during the Ottoman Period* (Jerusalem: 1975), 120.

ציבור זה של אשכנזים פגש כאן מוסד שיפוטי יהודי מסורתי הדן לפי דין תורה, שהייתה לו סמכות רשמית אשר דוגמתה כבר לא נמצאה בארצות מוצאם:[67] העדה הספרדית של ירושלים שלטה בכל מוסדות הקהילה הרשמיים ובכלל זה בבית הדין הרבני, וניהלה אותם ברוח המסורת היהודית ובכפיפות הציבור למרות הרבנים מייצגי ההלכה. אך האשכנזים חתרו לשמור על עצמאותם ובקשו לנהל את ענייניהם הציבוריים במוסדות שלהם, ובכלל זה בית דין משלהם, בהתאם למסורת האשכנזית; ייתכן שגישה זו התאימה למורשת האשכנזית הקדומה שהחשיבה יותר את המסורת שלהם על פני המסורת של הספרדים. ביטוי חזק לכך נתן כבר הרא״ש בספרד במאה הארבע עשרה, שהיה מעורב במישרין בעימותים בין שתי המסורות.[68] תחושת העדיפות הובילה בעבר את האשכנזים לגישות שתלטניות כלפי מסורות אחרות, בייחוד בתחום דיני המשפחה. וודאי שהיא הניעה את האשכנזים לחתור לעצמאות שיפוטית ולא להיות כפופים למוסדות שיפוט ספרדיים.

החתירה לעצמאות לאורך כל תקופת מחקרנו הלמה גם את תחושת הביטחון והעוצמה של העדה האשכנזית, שנשענה על עורף חברתי וכלכלי שהלך ונתעצם בממדיו בהשוואה ליהדות הספרדית והמזרחית. לקראת סוף המאה הי״ט ישבו במזרח אירופה ובמרכזה כעשרה מיליון יהודים בקירוב, כשמאות אלפים אשכנזים הולכים ומציפים את אמריקה הצפונית והדרומית. בשני המרכזים הגדולים, רוסיה הצארית והקיסרות ההבסבורגית, התקיימו מרכזי התורה והחסידות הגדולים והחלה עלייתן של הישיבות החדשות בליטא. לא ניתן היה לצפות ממי שתפשו עצמו כנציגים של הציבור הגדול והמפותח הזה להסכים לכפיפות מוסדית לעדה הספרדית הקטנה.

מרכיב חשוב בעצמאות השיפוטית של האשכנזים כמו גם בעוצמתם כקבוצה היה שרבים מביניהם היו נתינים של הקונסולים הזרים.[69] בית הדין הספרדי היה מוסד שיפוט עות׳מאני, ובהתאם למשטר הקפיטולציות היו אזרחי מדינת הקונסול כפופים לסמכות שיפוטו של הקונסול ולא לסמכות השיפוט של בית המשפט העות׳מאני.[70]

67 על אובדן האוטונומיה השיפוטית של האשכנזים בארצותיהם, ראו מנחם אלון, *המשפט העברי–תולדותיו, מקורותיו, עקרונותיו* (ירושלים: תשנ״ב), עמ׳ 1320–1319, והמקורות הנזכרים שם בהע׳ 1.

68 ראו א׳ וסטרייך, "הכרעות שיפוטיות של הרא״ש בספרד," בתוך מ׳ בר (עורך), *גבורות–לרב פרופ׳ עמנואל רקמן* (רמת גן: תשנ״ד), עמ׳ 182–157.

69 אליאב (לעיל, הע׳ 64), עמ׳ 109–104.

70 ראו: F.M. Goadby, *International and Inter-Religious Private Law in Palestine* (Jerusalem: 1926), 58.

כפיפות האשכנזים לקונסולים נתנה להם מרחב פעולה שיפוטי עצמאי בענייני נישואין וגירושין בהתאם למשפט מדינת האם ולמדיניות הקונסול. הקונסול האוסטרי למשל, שרבים מן האשכנזים היו אזרחיו, הותיר בידי בית הדין סמכות שיפוט בענייני נישואין וגירושין; בעניינים אחרים נאות הוא לכל היותר להכיר בבית הדין רק בתור בורר.[71]

ראוי לציין שגם לפני שהחלה הנוכחות הקונסולרית הגדולה בירושלים לא שמענו על מאבק ספרדי שנועד להכפיף את האשכנזים לסמכות השיפוט של בית הדין הרבני שלהם. זאת, למרות המאבקים החריפים שהתנהלו בין האשכנזים לבין הקהילה הספרדית המאורגנת בשל רצונם של הראשונים להקים לעצמם מוסדות עצמאיים ובלתי תלויים.[72] חריף במיוחד היה המאבק שהתנהל סביב דרישתם של האשכנזים להקים מערכת שחיטה עצמאית,[73] שגררה קולות צורמים מצדם של רבנים ספרדים חשובים, דוגמת הספק שהטיל אחד הרבנים הספרדים בנוגע להיותם של האשכנזים צאצאי אברהם אבינו.[74]

ייתכן שהיעדר המאבק בתחום הסמכות המשפטית נבע מן הגישה הפלורליסטית הבסיסית שקיימת במסורת הספרדית לגבי המסורת המשפטית של האשכנזים. ביטוי מוקדם לגישה אנו מוצאים כבר במאה השש עשרה בפסיקתו של ר׳ שמואל די מדינה, שהיה מחשובי הפוסקים באימפריה העות׳מאנית.[75] הוא סירב לדון בתביעתו של אשכנזי נגד אשתו שמרדה בו, וטען כי נושא זה מוסדר באופן מיוחד במסורת האשכנזית וצריך להידון בפני בית דין אשכנזי; רק לאחר שכל הדיינים האשכנזים בסלוניקי הלכו לעולמם הסכים להזדקק למקרה ושפט בו בהתאם למסורת האשכנזית. אכן, בדברים שכתב הרב עובדיה יוסף על אישיותו של היש״א ברכה הוא מציין בהבלטה רבה מסורת זו של פלורליזם ורואה בה אחד מקווי ההיכר המובהקים של שיטתו ההלכתית של היש״א ברכה.[76]

הניתוק בתחום השיפוט בין האשכנזים והספרדים הביא לכך שדייני בית הדין הספרדי היו רובם ככולם ממוצא ספרדי. בספרי השו״ת שמתקופת המחקר התפרסמו מאות רבות של פסקי הדין, ולא נתקלתי עד כה בדיין אשכנזי שכיהן באחד ההרכבים; מקורות אלה מלמדים גם שמעט מאוד אשכנזים הופיעו בתור

71 ראו מ׳ אליאב, *בחסות ממלכת אוסטריה–מבחר תעודות מארכיון הקונסוליה האוסטרית בירושלים 1849–1917* (ירושלים: תשמ״ו), עמ׳ 292, 391.

72 ראו י׳ קניאל, *במעבר–היהודים בארץ ישראל במאה הי״ט בין ישן וחדש ובין יישוב ארץ הקודש לבין ציונות* (ירושלים: תש״ס), עמ׳ 120–145.

73 שם, עמ׳ 139–145.

74 *הלבנון* 9, י״א אייר תרכ״ו, עמ׳ 132–133.

75 ראו א׳ וסטרייך, *תמורות במעמד האישה במשפט העברי–מסע בין מסורות* (ירושלים: תשס״א), עמ׳ 255–257.

76 ראו הרב עובדיה יוסף, ״משנתו של ישא ברכה״. *שבט ועם–במה לברור בעיות חברה ותרבות של יהדות ספרד והמזרח בארץ ובגולה*, סדרה שניה א (ו), תשל״א, עמ׳ 95–103.

מתדיינים בבית הדין הרבני הספרדי. נראה אפוא שבית הדין האשכנזי שירת את הציבור האשכנזי ושימש עבורו מוסד שיפוטי החל מתחילת התקופה שאנו דנים בה ואילך. הדבר ניכר גם בחיבורי השו״ת של הרב ישׁ״א ברכה שלא מצאתי בהם פנייה של צדדים אשכנזים בירושלים להתדיין בפני בית הדין הספרדי שבראשותו.[77]

עם זאת, לא הדירו אשכנזים את רגליהם לחלוטין מבית הדין הספרדי ונתקיימו קשרים של ממש בין חכמי ההלכה של שתי העדות. בעניין זה הרחיב את הדיבור י׳ קניאל, במחקריו על היחסים בין ספרדים ואשכנזים.[78] כך למשל, לפי עדותו של הרב פארדו, ששימש דיין בירושלים עד שנת תרל״א (1871), החסידים ״מתדיינים על פי הרוב מבית הדין שלנו״.[79] קניאל הצביע שם על מקרים של קשרים בתחום זה, הן בהזדקקות של אשכנזים לבית הדין הספרדי והן בהחלפת רעיונות וחוות דעת. בחלק מן המקרים מדובר היה בסכסוך בין שני מוסדות אשכנזים ובשל כך נאלצו לפנות למוסד שיפוטי נייטרלי ובחרו בבית הדין הספרדי.[80] היו מקרים של פניות אל בית הדין הספרדי מצדם של אשכנזים, ככל הנראה כשנדרש אישור רשמי על שטרי מכר ומסמכים אחרים. חלק אחר של המקרים היו פניות של חכמי הלכה אשכנזים לקבל חוות דעת מצד בית הדין הספרדי.[81] אך גם אלה לא היו רבים ועיון בתשובותיו ופסקיו של ר׳ שמואל סלאנט אכן מצביע על כך: בשלושת כרכי תשובותיו ופסקיו שפורסמו לאחרונה מתנהל רובו המכריע של המשא והמתן ההלכתי עם חכמים אשכנזים בארץ ובחו״ל ורק מיעוט קטן עם חכמים ספרדים, ובולט ביניהם הרב אברהם אשכנזי.[82]

חרף נתונים אלה לא הצליח ככל הנראה בית הדין האשכנזי לכבוש לעצמו מעמד גבוה. עובדה היא שדייני בית הדין האשכנזי לא הותירו אחריהם חותם ספרותי של ממש בצורת קבצים של פסקי דין. ביטוי מובהק לכך הוא פרסום כתביו של ר׳ שמואל מסלאנט כמאה שנים לאחר פטירתו אף על פי שהיה הדמות הרבנית המרכזית במשך שבעים שנים לאורך כל תקופת מחקרנו–זאת, בניגוד גמור לבית הדין הספרדי, שדייניו וראשיו הפגינו יצירתיות מרשימה בפרסום חיבורי פסיקה כבר במהלך כהונתם בתפקידם. ייתכן שהדבר קשור בפיצול הפנימי בין חסידים לבין ״מתנגדים״ וכן בפיצול בין המתנגדים עצמם והחסידים עצמם, כשכל קבוצה מקימה לעצמה אף בית דין. ייתכן גם שהכפיפות לקונסולים אפשרה לכל קבוצה אשכנזית לשמור על עצמאותה השיפוטית, שכן מבחינה חוקית לקונסולים

77 ראו עדותו של לודביג אוגוסט פרנקל שביקר בירושלים בשנות החמישים, שאשכנזים וספרדים אינם פונים אלה לבית דין של אלה, ב-קניאל (לעיל, הע׳ 61), עמ׳ 296.

78 שם, עמ׳ 298–295.

79 *שו״ת שמו משה*, איזמיר, תרל״ד, אבן העזר סי׳ ג.

80 קניאל (לעיל, הע׳ 61), עמ׳ 296.

81 קניאל, שם. וראו גם *שו״ת שמו משה*, אבן העזר, סי׳ י, יא.

82 ראו נ׳ טיקוצ׳ינסקי (עורך), *תורת רבנו שמואל סלאנט זצ״ל* (ירושלים: תשנ״ח).

הייתה סמכות השיפוט לגביהם. ואולי שחיקת האוטונומיה השיפוטית באירופה ואובדנה המלא באזורים מסוימים גרמו להיעדר תשתית אינטלקטואלית נאותה להמשך פיתוח המוסדות המשפטיים. אין לך ביטוי מובהק יותר לחולשתו של בית הדין האשכנזי מאשר דבריו המפורשים של ר׳ שמואל מסלאנט שנתפרסמו בשנת פטירתו: ״את בתי הדין יסדתי אנוכי ... ואין לבתי הדין שום כח אלא להיות מפשרים״.[83]

בית הדין הספרדי לעומת זאת תפש מקום מרכזי וחשוב והדבר הקרין על מעמד מוסד הרבנות הראשית בתקופת השיא משנת 1869 ועד שנת 1906. עיון בספרות השו״ת של דייני ירושלים יוצר רושם ברור שמספר הפניות מצדם של חכמים אשכנזים לחכם באשי בירושלים אכן גבר ואלה הגיעו גם ממרכזי התורה הגדולים במזרח אירופה; הדבר מבטא שינוי במגמת ההתעלמות מן היצירה הספרדית של הדורות האחרונים, שרווחה אצל חכמי הלכה אשכנזים קודם לכן.[84] כך למשל פנה ר׳ שמעון סופר, נכדו של החתם סופר, שכיהן כרבה של ערלוי, וביקש חוות דעת בעניין יום טוב שני של גלויות במושבות החדשות.[85] (תשובה בעניין זה ופניות נוספות מן הסביבה האשכנזית ימצא הקורא בחיבור שו״ת שאל האי״ש.[86]) אלא שאף במקרים אלה הפניות היו בדרך כלל בתחומי הלכה שאינם משפטיים מובהקים. לשיא הגיע תהליך זה בפנייתם של גדולי חכמי רוסיה לחכמי הספרדים ובית דינם בעניין השמיטה שנדון בו להלן.

המפגש בין בית הדין הספרדי לבין האשכנזים התנהל אפוא בתוך החברה המסורתית; האשכנזים הסדירו את ענייניהם המשפטיים בתחום המשפחה בבתי הדין שלהם, של החסידים או של המתנגדים, ולא הרבו לפנות לבית הדין הספרדי. מורכב יותר היה המפגש בין מוסדות המשפט והרבנות הספרדיים לבין העולים

83 ראו מ׳ פרידמן, ״על מבנה הנהגת הציבור והרבנות בישוב הישן האשכנזי בשלהי השלטון העות׳מאני״ (לעיל, הע׳ 25, עמ׳ 287).

84 ראו *שו״ת רב פעלים*, ירושלים, תרס״א, א, או״ח בפתיחה מותח המחבר, ר׳ יוסף חיים מבגדאד, ביקורת על התנהגותם של גאוני אשכנז ״שאין דרכם לתור ולחפש בספרי האחרונים, אלא פונים דוקא לספרי הראשונים וכותבים מה שנראה להם לפי הכרעת דעתם וסברתם כאשר תשיג ידם״. עמדה זו זכתה לברכתו החמה של הרב עובדיה יוסף שאותה אפיין: ״שפתים ישק משיב דברים נכוחים״ (*שו״ת יביע אומר*, א, או״ח בפתיחה). הרב עובדיה יוסף מנגיד את ההתנהגות האשכנזית עם ההתנהגות הספרדית: ״ובדרך זו נוהגים חכמי הספרדים בפסקים ותשובות שלהם, לתור ולדרוש מכל הספרים ראשונים ואחרונים ואחרוני האחרונים ככל אשר תשיג ידם כדי לברר ההלכה בתשובותיהם״ (שם. משפט זה מופיע כציטוט מתוך דברי ר׳ יוסף חיים, אולם לא הצלחתי למצוא אותו במהדורה שבידי. א״ו). ברור לגמרי, שגישה המתעלמת מחיבורי החכמים בדורות האחרונים תבוא לידי ביטוי חריף יותר לגבי חכמים הנמצאים במקומות מרוחקים ופחות לגבי חכמים המצויים בסביבה הקרובה, ומשום כך ההתעלמות מן היצירה הספרדית הייתה קיצונית יותר.

85 *שו״ת שאל האי״ש*, או״ח סי׳ ח.

86 דומה שבחיבור זה נמצא את מספר הפניות הרב ביותר מסביבה אשכנזית. הפניות הן מסוף ימיו של היש״א ברכה בעת שהיה חולה ובנו הרב חמ״א השיב על חלקן הגדול.

הציוניים, והוא היה אתגר לדייני בית הדין הספרדי וגם לעולים הציוניים. קבוצה זו של עולים ציונים נפתחה להשכלה המערבית והחלה עוברת תהליך של חילון והתרחקות מעולם ההלכה והמסורת, שעמדו ביסוד המשפט שהחיל בית הדין הרבני. מקרה בולט של מפגש כזה היה פולמוס השמיטה שהסעיר את הרוחות ביישוב היהודי בארץ ובמרכזיו הגדולים, במזרח אירופה ומרכזה.

## פרק ו. מול הישוב החדש בארץ ישראל

מעמדה הגבוה של מערכת המשפט והרבנות הספרדית משתקף במפגש מיוחד שהיה בינה לבין זרמים שונים בעדה האשכנזית לקראת השמיטה של שנת תרמ״ט (1889/1888). מצוות השמיטה בעיקרה מטילה חובה על בעלי הקרקע להימנע מעבודות בסיסיות בשדות וכן מצווה אליהם להניח את היבולים הפקר לכל המעוניין. התורה מייחסת חשיבות רבה למצווה זו והיא מזהירה בתוקף שביטולה יגרום לחורבן ולגלות מארץ ישראל; חשיבות המצווה אינה נגרעת אף אם סבורים רוב הפוסקים שהמצווה בימינו היא רק גזירת חכמים. עד כה לא הייתה משמעות מעשית למצוות השמיטה ושאלת קיומה לא טרדה כלל את תודעתם של חכמי האשכנזים באירופה ובארץ ישראל ומעט מאוד העסיקה את חכמי הספרדים, שכן היהודים הספרדים לא עסקו בחקלאות ולא היו עובדי אדמה, וכמותם גם האשכנזים בני היישוב הישן. רק יישוב בודד אחד פתח תקווה נוסד בשנת תקל״ח (1878) על ידי אשכנזים יוצאי היישוב הישן והשמיטה לא עוררה בפועל קשיים מיוחדים או סערת רוחות.

בשנת תרמ״ב (1882) החלה העלייה של ״חובבי ציון״ הנחשבת לעלייה הציונית הראשונה, ואשר ראתה עצמה כמתחילה את הישוב החדש בארץ ישראל.[87] תכליתה המרכזית של העלייה הייתה התיישבות חקלאית יהודית בארץ ישראל ותוך שנים ספורות נוסדו כמה וכמה יישובים חקלאיים. בעלייה זו חברו יחדיו שני זרמים בקרב יהודי רוסיה: זרם חרדי-לאומי, שרוב העולים השתייכו אליו, וזרם חילוני-לאומי, שהיה מיעוט בתנועה אך בעל היוזמה וכושר העשייה. ההנהגה הרבנית בקרב ״חובבי ציון״ ואנשי הזרם החרדי-הלאומי ראו בעלייתם ארצה חלק מן החזון המשיחי עתיק היומין של שיבת עם ישראל לארץ ישראל בהתאם להבטחת הנביאים, וההתיישבות החקלאית הייתה הדרך הראויה להגשים את החזון ובד בבד גם לפתור מצוקות כלכליות קשות שהיו ״בתחום המושב״. הזרם החילוני-הלאומי כלל יהודים מודרניים שראו בהתיישבות החקלאית תחילתו של

87 על היישוב הישן והיישוב החדש ראו: י׳ ברטל, *גלות בארץ–יישוב ארץ-ישראל בטרם ציונות, קובץ מחקרים ומסות* (ירושלים: תשנ״ה), עמ׳ 89–74; י׳ קניאל, *המשך ותמורה, היישוב הישן והיישוב החדש בתקופת העלייה הראשונה והשנייה* (ירושלים: תשמ״ב), עמ׳ 34–21; קניאל (לעיל, הע׳ 72), עמ׳ 73–34.

תהליך שיביא למודרניזציה ופרודוקטיביזציה של העם היהודי; קבוצה רדיקלית יותר ביניהם אף ראתה בהתיישבות החקלאית ביטוי להעתקת מרכז הכובד של זהותם העצמית של היהודים מן העולם הדתי והמסורתי אל ערכים לאומיים ומודרניים.

העימות בין הזרמים לא אחר לבוא והוא התרחש כבר לקראת השמיטה הראשונה שהייתה כאמור בשנת תרמ״ט. ברור היה כי קיום מצוות השמיטה כהלכתה יגרום נזק כלכלי כבד לחקלאים ולבני משפחותיהם, על כל הנובע מכך ועלול גם לסכן את עצם ההתיישבות החקלאית הצעירה. אנשי היישוב הישן ורבניהם לא ראו חשיבות מיוחדת בהתיישבות החקלאית ודרשו במפגיע לקיים את מצוות השמיטה כהלכתה, יהיה מחירה הכלכלי וההתיישבותי אשר יהיה– מנגד, דרשו הלאומיים החילונים שלא לסכן כמלוא הנימה את ההתיישבות, שהיא היא שתוביל אל גאולת הכלל והפרט. בתווך ניצבו כמה מחכמי רוסיה שתמכו בתנועת ״חיבת ציון״ וראו חשיבות מיוחדת בהתיישבות החקלאית בארץ ישראל אך בד בבד ייחסו כמובן משמעות רבה למצוות התורה בעניין השמיטה. הפתרון שבחנו האחרונים, ובראשם גדול הפוסקים ברוסיה ר׳ יצחק אלחנן ספקטור מקובנא, היה להסתמך על פיקציה משפטית שעיקרה מכירת השדות לגויים עד לאחר שנת השמיטה (להלן: היתר מכירה).

רבני העדה האשכנזית של היישוב הישן התנגדו בתוקף רב להיתר המכירה והתערבו באופן אקטיבי ביותר כדי להנחיל את עמדתם, אך בית הדין הספרדי בראשותם של החכם באשי הרב מרפ״א וסגנו היש״א ברכה, התרחק בתחילה מן העימות בנימוק שמדובר בעניין אשכנזי פנימי, שכן אין בנמצא חקלאים ספרדים. אין ספק שבכך באה לידי ביטוי הגישה הפלורליסטית של חכמי הספרדים המניחים לאשכנזים לכלכל את ענייניהם בעצמם. אלא שעד מהרה פנו רבני רוסיה שתמכו בהיתר המכירה אל חכמי הספרדים וביקשו מהם לחוות את דעתם בעניין. הרב יש״א ברכה הוא זה שהשיב תשובה מפורטת ומנומקת שהובילה אותו למסקנה חד-משמעית כי יש להסתמך על היתר המכירה.[88]

עמדת היש״א ברכה, שייצג את רבני הספרדים, הייתה אסמכתא איתנה עבור הרב יצחק אלחנן ספקטור מקובנא וחבריו לאמץ את הפתרון של היתר המכירה.

88 ראו *שו״ת שמחה לא י״ש*, בסוף החיבור. בתשובתו הסתמך היש״א ברכה על תשובת רבה של חברון במאה הי״ח, הרב מרדכי רובייו, *שו״ת שמן המר*, ליוורנו, תקנ״ג, יו״ד סי׳ ד, וכן על *שו״ת המבי״ט*, ב, סד מן המאה הט״ז. אולם, פסקי הדין הללו ועוד אחרים שנזכרו בהם, מתייחסים למקרים פרטיים חד פעמיים ולא להסדר מקיף וכולל של יישובים שלמים. על עמדה זו שב היש״א ברכה לקראת השמיטה שלאחר מכן. בשנת תרנ״ה (1895/1894) פרסם שוב את הוראת היתר המכירה והיא נזכרת במכתבם של מתיישבי ראשון לציון בכ״ט אב בתרנ״ה; ראו מ׳ אליאב (עורך), *ספר העלייה הראשונה*, ב, (ירושלים: תשמ״ב), עמ׳ 273–274; התעודה נמצאת בארכיון יודילביץ, A192/201.

דברי הערצה מופלגים כלפי חכמי הספרדים הארץישראליים השמיע ר׳ יהושע מקוטנא, מגדולי רבני רוסיה בתקופה זו שאף הוא צידד בהיתר המכירה; וכך כתב: ״בפרט כי גדולי רבני ספרד אשר צפרנם עבה מכריסם של חכמי אשכנז הם מתירים שיעבדו הנכרים בשביעית על ידי מכירה״.[89] גם הרב יצחק אלחנן ספקטור אימץ את עמדתם,[90] וצעד צעד נוסף לכיוון בית הדין הספרדי: הוא ציווה על המבקשים להשתמש בהיתר המכירה להכין את המסמכים המתאימים ולבצע את הפעולות המשפטיות הנדרשות או בבית הדין האשכנזי או בבית הדין הספרדי בירושלים. יהיה מי שיאמר כי דבר זה מלמד על מעמדה הנחות של הרבנות הספרדית ובית הדין הרבני שלה[91] ולא היא: הרב יצחק אלחנן ספקטור ידע היטב כי בית הדין האשכנזי מתנגד להיתר המכירה בחריפות וכי הוא לא ייתן את ידו לחתימה על שטרי מכר לגויים, וההיתר לעולים האשכנזים להזדקק גם לבית הדין הספרדי, פרושו היה עקיפה למעשה של בית הדין האשכנזי והעברת ניהול העניין לידי בית הדין הספרדי. דומני שעמדה זו של גדול הפוסקים ברוסיה כלפי בית הדין הרבני הספרדי בירושלים יש בה לשקף יותר מכל את מעמדו הגבוה של בית הדין הספרדי בעולם היהודי כולו.

היו שטענו כי הרב יצחק אלחנן ספקטור הוטעה בידי גורמים שונים מחוגי ״חיבת ציון״ ובשל כך סמך ידו על היתר המכירה והפנה לבית הדין הספרדי, אולם הרב יצחק אלחנן ספקטור חזר על עמדתו גם בשמיטה שלאחר מכן, בשנת תרנ״ו (6)/1895. בתעודה מכתב ידו של ר׳ יצחק אלחנן ספקטור שפרסם יהושע קניאל לפני מספר שנים, הוא חוזר ומאמץ את תמיכתו בהיתר המכירה ושוב מפנה את הצדדים לבית הדין הספרדי;[92] בראש בית הדין הספרדי באותה שעה עמד היש״א ברכה שגם פסק את פסק הדין המקורי שבע שנים קודם לכן. בשעה היסטורית זו נראה היה כי לבית הדין הספרדי בראשות החכם באשי שמור תפקיד נכבד בניתוב היישוב היהודי ההולך ומתחדש מן המאגרים האנושיים הגדולים, בכמות ובאיכות, שבמזרח אירופה.[93]

אלא שכעבור עשור שנים בלבד החלו להופיע גורמים מחוללי שינוי משמעותיים ביותר. בשנת תרס״ו (1906) הלך יש״א לעולמו ומוסד החכם באשי

89 ראו שו״ת *ישועות מלכו*, סי׳ נג.
90 שם, סי׳ נה.
91 ראו ברנאי (לעיל, הע׳ 1), עמ׳ 68–67.
92 ראו י׳ קניאל, ״היישוב הישן וההתיישבות החדשה״ (לעיל, הע׳ 88) א, עמ׳ 278, (בארכיון יודילביץ A192/201).
93 על ניסיונותיו של היש״א ברכה להביא לאיחוד בין האורתודוקסים והניאולוגים בהונגריה והפולמוס שניהלו נגדו רבני הארץ ראו בהרחבה אצל יצחק הרשקוביץ, חזון הגאולה של הרב יששכר שלמה טיכטל הי״ד–תמורות בתפיסתו המשיחית במהלך השואה, עבודת דוקטור, אוניברסיטת בר-אילן, תשס״ט, עמ׳ 43–29.

ומוסדות ספרדיים אחרים החלו להתדרדר במהירות רבה. בד בבד בשנת 1905 החלה להגיע לארץ "העלייה השנייה", שהביאה ארצה עולים סוציאליסטים רדיקליים ואף אנטי-דתיים; אלה עתידים להיות, לאחר הכיבוש הבריטי, לקבוצה העיקרית ביישוב היהודי בארץ ישראל. עמם הגיע גם הרב א"י הכהן קוק, שהיה אחראי יותר מכל לעיצובה החדש של הרבנות בירושלים ובארץ ישראל כולה, ומערכת השיפוט שבמסגרתה. הרבנות ובית הדין ימשיכו במובנים רבים את המוסדות הספרדיים המקבילים שפעלו בשלהי התקופה העות'מאנית, אולם יהיה בהם גם שוני לא מבוטל לעומת קודמיהם. בית הדין ירכז במסגרתו דיינים מכל העדות וכן תחול סמכות שיפוטו על בני כל העדות ביישוב הארץ ישראלי, תחת השליטה הספרדית המוחלטת תבוא עתה שליטה אשכנזית ונוכחות ספרדית של ממש ותחת הסדר העות'מאני הישן, שבמסגרתו הוקם ופעל בית הדין הספרדי יבוא עתה הסדר הבריטי שבמסגרתו יפעל בית הדין של הרבנות הראשית.

## פרק ז. לקראת סיום

בית הדין הרבני בירושלים התאפיין באחידות גבוהה ביותר של הדיינים, שהייתה בו בזמן מקור כוח אך גם מקור חולשה. כל הדיינים, החל מן החכם באשי שעמד בראש בית הדין, עבור באבות בתי הדין וכלה בדיינים מן השורה, היו ממוצא ספרדי והם התחנכו במוסדות התורניים של עדה זו בירושלים או בבלקן ובאסיה הקטנה. אחידות זו של קהיליית הדיינים סייעה ביותר לתפקד באופן יעיל ותקין של המערכת המשפטית, שבהיותה מבוססת על ההלכה חסרה מנגנון הכרעה וחילוקי דעות הלכו והצטברו במשך דורות רבים. להשתייכותם של הדיינים למסורת משפטית מסוימת, המסורת הספרדית, הקלה עליהם לנקוט עמדות מוסכמות במקרים רבים ולהכריע. אך לעומת זאת, אחידות של קהיליית הדיינים עשויה לגרום לניכור של קבוצות אחרות שלא נימנו עם העדה הספרדית דוגמת האשכנזים, התימנים והמוגרבים. קבוצות אלה אכן ניסו לרכוש עצמאות מבית הדין הספרדי במידה כזו או אחרת, הן במישור של מוסד הרבנות בכלל והן במישור של מוסד בית הדין.

אמנם, האחידות הנזכרת לא פגעה במעמד בית הדין כלפי קהילות אחרות והוא היה לבית הדין החשוב ביותר במרחב הספרדי, המוגרבי והמזרחי שאליו הרבו לפנות מן המרכזים השונים באגן הים התיכון והגלויות האחרות. קשרים אלה עם הקהילות השונות התהדקו בשל עלייתם לירושלים של חכמים בולטים מן המרכזים השונים והצטרפותם לקהיליית הדיינים בה, ובד בבד הוציאה ירושלים מתוכה דיינים מעולים שכיהנו כרבנים בקהילות הפזורה הספרדית. גם עלייתם של רבנים גדולי תורה מן התפוצה היהודית, שהצטרפו למערכת הקיימת–אך לא

הוזמנו כדי לעמוד בראשה–וכן ההתעצמות של היישוב היהודי בירושלים במישור הדמוגרפי, הכלכלי והפוליטי תרמו לחיזוק מעמדו של בית הדין הרבני הספרדי, שהיה המוסד השיפוטי היחיד המוכר באופן רשמי. כמובן, היה בגורמים אלה, ובייחוד בבואם של אשכנזים רבים וכן בני עדות אחרות כדי לערער ולסכן את מעמד בית הדין, אולם במשך כשבעים שנים שמר בית הדין על מעמדו הגבוה ונראה כי תרמו לכך תבונתם של הרבנים הראשיים ר״א אשכנזי והרב ישׂ״א ברכה וגדולתם ויוקרתם ההלכתית. ביטוי חזק לתבונתם השיפוטית ולמעמד הגבוה של בית הדין לקראת סוף תקופת הזוהר שלו היה בהפנייתם של גדולי הפוסקים האשכנזים במזרח אירופה את הסכסוך בשאלת היתר המכירה בשמיטה, לבית הדין הספרדי.

פטירתו של הרב ישׂ״א ברכה בשנת תרנ״ו (1905/1906) סיימה את התקופה הגדולה של בית הדין הרבני הרשמי בירושלים, שהיה ספרדי במהותו, ומיד לאחר מכן החל מוסד החכם באשי להזדעזע בזעזועים קשים ביותר, שנבעו ממאבקים חריפים בתוך העדה הספרדית. פריצתה של מלחמת העולם הראשונה בסמוך לכך, שמוטטה את האימפריה העות׳מאנית ואת הסדר הפוליטי והמשפטי שלה, הורידה את המסך על בית הדין בירושלים שנידון במחקר זה. שאלה מרתקת היא עד כמה המשיך בית הדין הזה להיות נוכח בסדר הבריטי והציוני החדש, אלא שהדבר חורג ממסגרת מחקר זה.[94]

94 תודתי למרכז-על ע״ש צגלה למחקר בינתחומי של המשפט על התמיכה במחקר זה.

STYLE SHEET

## STYLE SHEET

In preparing your manuscript, please conform to the following guidelines. Manuscripts not so prepared will be edited by JLA staff or returned for revision.

1 Please provide a line or two of information about yourself, such as an institutional affiliation, before the first footnote.
2 Manuscripts should be submitted both as hard copy and electronically, in WORD 2007 or less. Papers should be double-spaced (text and footnotes).
3 Neither the file nor the hard copy should contain tracked changes, comments, highlighting, underlining, different font colors, or other markings. 12 pt. font, preferably Times New Roman, should be used throughout, including the notes.
4 The paper should not contain electronically linked cross-references.
5 All references must conform to the *Jewish Law Annual* house style specified below.
6 All references containing titles originally in Hebrew should provide both the original title of the work in transliteration, and the official title in English if it is given in the book or appears in an English table of contents (often found at the end of the volume). If no English title is given, please suggest a translation, indicating that it is your own.
7 Authorized Version abbreviations for books of the Bible, listed in dictionaries and style guides such as *The Chicago Manual of Style*, should be used. In referring to the Talmud, tractate names should not be abbreviated. m, b, j, or t should be prefixed to the tractate name to indicate whether the Mishnah, the Babylonian Talmud, Jerusalem Talmud or Tosefta is being referred to.

## CITATION STYLE

### Halakhic literature

*Beit Yosef*, OH 156, YD 147.
Maimonides, *Code*, Laws concerning Robbery and Lost Property 11:1.
R. Joshua Falk Katz, *Perisha*, HM 201:1 (at the end).
Rashi, bBaba Kama 27a s.v. *lemikah umimkar*.
*Responsa Beit Shlomo*, OH #57.

*Responsa Mabit*, #37.
*Responsa Maharam Mintz*, #5 (Jerusalem: 1991, 16).

**Books**

W.C. Kaiser, *Toward Old Testament Ethics* (Grand Rapids MI: 1978), 99.
E. Urbach, *The Sages: Their Concepts and Beliefs*, trans. I. Abrahams (Jerusalem: 1987), 1:343.

**Journal articles**

R. Kleinman, "Early interpretations of the Bible and Talmud as a reflection of medieval legal realia," 16 *Jewish Law Annual* (2006), 25–50.
Joseph Raz, "Legal principles and the limits of law," 81 *Yale L.J.* 823, 830 (1972).
A. Shaffer, "Cuneiform tablets from Palestine I: the letter from Shechem" (Hebrew), *Beer-Sheva* 3 (1988), 163–69.

**Articles in edited volumes**

B.S. Jackson, "Legalism and spirituality," in E.B. Firmage, B.G. Weiss and J.W. Welch (eds.), *Religion and Laws: Biblical, Judaic and Islamic Perspectives* (Winona Lake IN: 1990), 243–61.
D. Sinclair, "Defending the lives of the mortally ill, the embryo, and the non-Jew" (Hebrew), in G. Frishtick (ed.), *Human Rights in Judaism* (Hebrew), (Jerusalem: 1992), 37 n. 19.

**Cross-references in notes**

23 D. Sperber, *Material Culture in Eretz-Israel during the Talmudic Period* (Hebrew), vol. 1 (Jerusalem: 1993), vol. 2 (Jerusalem: 2006).
24 See Englard 1991, n. 11 above, 67.
25 Ibid., 121.
26 Sperber, n. 23 above, 2:126–33.

## TRANSLITERATION

Wherever possible, essential Hebrew is to be transliterated into English rather than word-processed in Hebrew characters, as follows:

| | | | |
|---|---|---|---|
| alef | a | lamed | l |
| bet | b | mem | m |
| vet | v | nun | n |
| gimel | g | samekh | s |
| dalet | d | ayin | a |
| hei (pronounced) | h | pei | p |
| vav | v | fei | f |
| zayin | z | tzadi | tz |
| het | h | kuf | k |
| tet | t | reish | r |
| yod | y | shin | sh |
| kaf | k | sin | s |
| khaf | kh | tav | t |

| | |
|---|---|
| patah; kamatz | a |
| hirik | i |
| shva (pronounced) | e |
| segol | e |
| shuruk; kubutz | u |
| holam | o |
| tzeire | ei |

No diacriticals, apostrophes, hyphens, doubling of consonants or capitalization should be used as elements of the transliteration or to indicate prefixes and the definite article.

These transliteration guidelines are not intended to apply to papers addressing linguistic or philological issues.

For Product Safety Concerns and Information please contact our EU
representative GPSR@taylorandfrancis.com
Taylor & Francis Verlag GmbH, Kaufingerstraße 24, 80331 München, Germany

www.ingramcontent.com/pod-product-compliance
Ingram Content Group UK Ltd.
Pitfield, Milton Keynes, MK11 3LW, UK
UKHW020013200926
475702UK00014B/1860
*9780367602093*